FROM EULOGY TO JOY

A Heartfelt Collection Dealing With

The Grieving Process

Cynthia Kuhn Beischel
in collaboration with
Kristina Chase Strom

Library of Congress Number: 00-192186
ISBN #:   Hardcover   0-7388-3798-9
               Softcover   0-7388-3799-7

This is a work of nonfiction and fiction which is autobiographical in nature, based on real events. Some names and locations have been changed for reason of privacy.

This book was printed in the United States of America.

To order additional copies of this book, contact:
Xlibris Corporation
1-888-7-XLIBRIS
www.Xlibris.com
Orders@Xlibris.com

FROM EULOGY

TO JOY

compiled by
Cynthia Kuhn Beischel
in collaboration with
Kristina Chase Strom

968-BEIS

CONTENTS

CHAPTER 1
THE FUNERAL AND THE EULOGY

Actual eulogies and personal accounts of funerals are presented.

CHAPTER 2
CHILDREN'S DEATHS: INFANTS
THROUGH ADULTHOOD
Parents share their heartache and the experiences they faced
while dealing with the loss of their children.

CHAPTER 3
THE DEATH OF PARENTS
Adults discuss what it means to lose a parent by offering their
journeys, their feelings of loss of connection, and the value of
holding onto memories.

CHAPTER 4
SPOUSES, MATES, AND EX'S

People address the impact of losing their significant partners.

CHAPTER 5
THE LOSS OF FRIENDS

*Men and women describe the importance of friendship
as they discuss their losses.*

CHAPTER 6
WHEN SOMEONE YOU "HATE" OR
ARE ANGRY WITH DIES

*Brave women tackle the taboo subject of how one deals with the
death of a person they were very angry with or who had caused
them great pain.*

CHAPTER 7
DEALING WITH "UNNATURAL" DEATHS
Deaths of children and adults by murder, suicide, and accidents are reflected upon by those who were close to them.

CHAPTER 8
CHILDREN'S PERSPECTIVES
The feelings and impressions of death are revealed through the eyes of children.

CHAPTER 9
THE "KNOWN" FEELINGS

The raw emotions are expressed that appear in the various stages of grief: shock, denial, depression, anger, guilt, and forgiveness.

CHAPTER 10
THE IMPORTANCE OF RITUAL AND FAMILY TRADITION

The deaths of children, parents, mates, and friends are the basis for poignant stories which reveal the importance of rituals and traditions for the living who remain.

CHAPTER 11
GRANTING TIME TO GRIEVE

These contributors explore the significance of allowing time to mourn, both in pre-death and post-death situations, and show how in some cases, many, many years are required to work through all the stages to reach acceptance over the death of a loved one.

CHAPTER 12
REACHING OUT TO GOD
AND SPIRITUALITY

The role of faith is shown to be helpful and sustaining during the grieving process.

CHAPTER 13
JOURNALING

Journaling proves to be a useful tool for coping with the stress and difficult emotions that follow the death of loved ones.

CHAPTER 14
THE GIFT OF SUPPORT

The comfort received from support of family, friends, and groups plays a significant role in the healing process of the bereaved.

CHAPTER 15
THE ROLE OF CAREGIVERS

Professionals discuss the impact of helping others who are dying or who have lost a loved one.

CHAPTER 16
ALTERNATIVE ORIENTATIONS
TOWARD DEATH

The benefit of metaphysical approaches to healing when the death of a beloved one is presented.

CHAPTER 17
MEMORIALS

Touching stories explain how donor gifts helped soothe the pain from loss.

CHAPTER 18
TRANSITION TO JOY

With time and humor, things do get better.

CHAPTER 19
JOY

And, finally, an upbeat note allowing those in the early stages of grieving to see that, in fact, there can be good times ahead.

In memory of Jerome Keith Beischel,
my husband, friend, and work mate

Dedicated to my mother, Mildred Edna Lang Kuhn,
and my father, Howard Frank Kuhn, MD,
who taught me to strive for my best in life
and that death is a natural part of the cycle

And to my daughters,
Merritt Ann and Lindsay Piper,
who have added such joy to my life

Cynthia

In memory of my mother,
Lois Moulton Chase Strom

Dedicated to my father, Raymond Olaf Strom,
and my spiritual mother, Polly Green Strom,
whose lives are now filled with joy

And to my daughters,
Kia Strom Kuresman,
Kamala Strom Kuresman,
Kimberly Strom Kuresman,
and Kara Strom Kuresman,
for their unwavering support.

Kristina

THE BIRTHING OF FROM EULOGY TO JOY

There are only a handful of events in life that without exception touch every single living human being—death is one of them.

Based on statistics from the National Center for Health and the National Funeral Directors Association, over 2,365,000 people will die this year in the United States. With increases in the population, the numbers will rise in the future. The deaths will leave millions of loved ones who remain with the challenge of coping with their losses.

***

On June 7, 1992, standing on a beautiful beach in South Carolina, I helplessly witnessed a series of events happening out in the ocean that I had difficulty understanding. I could not mentally grasp that my husband, after successfully helping to save our younger daughter's life, had just been dragged down into the depths by an undertow and drowned. I was numb with disbelief; devastation and despair would come later.

Now, after eight years, I have reached a calm place of being ready for new beginnings. One of my new adventures is wanting to offer support, helpful information, and hope to grieving individuals. I have my own story and know that in many ways I can relate to others who are grieving, but I also know there are many other situations concerning loss that I cannot personally address.

My past interests and accomplishments in writing led me to the idea of compiling a collection of written works, all shared from the heart and first-hand experiences, which would deal with the stages and events that are part of the grieving process. I wanted people to be able to have a book which would comfort and reassure them that what they were feeling was normal and appropriate, that their attitudes and behavior were typical for persons in their situation. I knew that my story alone could not reassure all individuals, so I gathered the words and personal accounts of people who are "experts" by having experienced grief directly in a myriad of situations: loss of children, mates, parents, friends; loss through accidents, illness, suicide, murder.

068-BEIS

I looked for all the scenarios that have helped people through the process, allowing them to finally reach inner peace and renewed joy.

I believe people place worth on reliable, true, factual information. For that reason, *From Eulogy To Joy* is not a "How To" book, but rather a "How It Is" book, filled with genuine heartfelt expressions and useful knowledge concerning the hard work of grieving and the peaceful acceptance that finally follows. The contributions are graphic. The authors aren't just telling about what they lived and grew through; they show it with the specific details of their personal experiences. As a result, they offer support, helpful information, and courageous ideas for others going through very difficult times in their lives.

The message derived from the hundreds of submissions was that bereaved people needed to share their feelings with others whom they felt could understand or listen with an empathic ear. In reading *From Eulogy To Joy*, you will not only know that you are not alone, but will see that the many different reactions, stages, time frames, and individual ways of coping are all okay. If you are dealing with the death of someone close to you, you will recognize yourself in the writings, which in turn will allow you to feel comfortable with whatever stage of the grieving process you are presently in. The writers have created a support system for all who read it.

While assembling the articles, I struggled with the categorization of the pieces. While each essay is individual and unique, all of them contain and explore myriad elements of the grieving process. I hope that over time you will read chapters that do not at first attract your attention, because every chapter has elements that touch upon the subject matter of others.

My wish for all of you is that you understand the strengths, faith, and rewards that can be gained through the self-work of openly and honestly addressing all the issues of death, even those that involve emotions and feelings we aren't "supposed" to have. I hope that this book will become a powerful communication tool and inspirational guide during your survival.

Cynthia

HOW TO USE THIS "HOW IT IS" BOOK

Whether your perspective is personal or professional, *From Eulogy To Joy* is not a book meant to be read from cover to cover, but rather to be used as a reference tool and resource guide throughout the entire grieving process. The table of contents is annotated so that you can turn to the chapters which will help you the most in the moment and, eventually, gain an overview of the vast range of experiences, responses, and orientations that are possible following the death of someone close to you.

On a personal level, *From Eulogy To Joy* is a source of support and inspiration: a "how it really is" book as opposed to yet another quick-fix, redemptive "how-to" manual that makes you feel deficit because you haven't gotten over a significant person's death in a proscribed amount of time, or you are still wearing black, or you are still crying after all these years, or any variation of this theme. The hard core and revolutionary fact revealed in these pages is that the death of someone close is something you never "get over" and actually never should. Rather, death is something to "get through" and learn and grow and evolve from. Deaths permanently mark our lives, changing us forever. When all is said and done, death is for the living.

Like birth, death is a part of a magnificent cycle that is unavoidable in the physical world. Experiencing the death of family members, friends, and people important to us is something we all eventually share. Paradoxically, how each of us deals with this inevitability is ultimately unique and intensely private. In today's climate of self-improvement, replete with prescriptions for optimal living, you are expected to "get over it" in a specified amount of time and navigate the stages of mourning in a precise order. If you don't, if you get "stuck" in a specified externally imposed "phase" or, even worse, if you don't experience any of these stages, you feel that something is wrong with you which compounds your feelings of despair and intensifies your sense of being abjectly alone and misunderstood.

The essays in *From Eulogy To Joy* provide validating comfort during these unavoidable times and offer support that you might not find anywhere else— the message is loud and clear that wherever you are and however you feel and whatever you are doing right now to cope is absolutely all right in the long run, no matter what anyone else thinks. In addition, over time, these heartfelt

968-BEIS

sharings provide the necessary inspiration or jump-start to carry on when the time is right for you.

This is not a book to glance at once and then stow away forgotten on a shelf somewhere. Rather, as time goes on, you will find yourself picking it up again and again and reading sections that you did not read before, as well as reading parts you have read before but now experience in a different way. Most significantly, *know that this book is yours* to make use of in whatever way that serves you. Mark it up, break the binding. Tear out pages you don't like and burn them if that's what you need to do in the course of this long difficult journey. Tear out pages that resonate to you, that speak to your innermost soul, and take them with you to read over and over as you go about the required motions of daily living.

From a professional point of view, the material in *From Eulogy To Joy* represents nothing less than a quantum leap in the literature to date regarding this universal aspect of life, in that it provides a wealth of data as to how people individually respond to the spectacle of death. Though this information was not gathered nor processed in a scientifically kosher manner, so to speak, it does represent the honing of more than 500 people's diverse responses and methods of coping with mourning from a grass-roots perspective which I think is something to pay close attention to for several reasons.

First, this compilation serves as a meaningful springboard for the further research clearly needed in these times as the majority of the population (aka the "Baby Boomers") comes face to face with the aftermath of natural and expected death, to say nothing about the growing numbers of suicides and senseless homicides rampant in our tumultuous society.

Secondly, the need for empathic and informed counseling regarding this facet of life is increasing. However, no one in this field can be expected to be able to relate to each client's unique presentation around response to death in a way that speaks to him or her in a meaningful way. *From Eulogy To Joy* bridges that gap by providing firsthand accounts that broaden a mental health practitioner's understanding of the plethora and complexity of responses to this universal experience, as well as being a good book to recommend to colleagues and clients.

Finally, from both a clinical and research orientation, the documentation is significant not only by revelation, but also by quantity and omission. Some of the chapters are lengthy; others are short. Openly exploring human reaction to death and the ramifications thereof has only recently surfaced in this life arena that was formerly not "talked about".

The shorter chapters provide a clue as to the aspects of deathing that most people are somewhat reticent to share with others, or even look at themselves. For example, people seem to be most hesitant to share their feelings after someone they hated or were intensely angry with died. Kudos to those who were courageous enough to do so, for they have broken through a barrier most people are not yet willing or perhaps permitted to confront. More glaring are the aspects that not *one* person among the hundreds of submissions wrote about, the foremost being money and wills and the result-ant struggles and emotional upheavals which ensue following death. Clearly, talking about the psychological ramifications of inheritance is but one deeply held residual taboo that demands attention during the future course of deathing work.

From Eulogy To Joy, from its inception, has been a cooperative venture. Your participation, personal or professional, is now an intrinsic part of a process that can only enhance all of our lives. To further engage in this process, you may wish to visit our website: www.celestialperspectives.com/fromeulogytojoy

Kristina

ACKNOWLEDGEMENTS

On several occassions I joked that writing the acknowledgement section might be the hardest part of the book for fear of forgetting someone I need to thank. Added to that was the problem of choosing an order to the list.

I'm going to start by acknowledging my collaborator, Kristina Strom, for offering ongoing effort and encouragement from the moment of the book's conception. From the beginning, she underscored the importance of the project and the belief that we were going to be offering a worthwhile gift to the many grieving individuals who would read it.

I am equally grateful for the support I received from my daughters. Lindsay and Merritt took over many of my duties, and worked side by side with me on a great deal more jobs, so that I could continue to plow through the various stages that brought this book to completion. Most of all, I want to thank them for believing in me.

More deep appreciation goes to my parents, Howard and Mildred Kuhn, for being my literary angels by helping this project fly during difficult financial times. Even though there were moments they questioned my sanity in pursuing this goal, they stood behind me.

I want to also thank my husband's parents, Jack and Rose Beischel, for assuming some of Jerry's roles during the time following his death; his brother, Jim, and sisters, Vickie and Jill, their families, TJ, and the rest of the clan for continuing to include us in family events; and to Sister Lucy, who has, without fail, acknowledged the yearly anniversary of Jerry's passing with lovely, kind notes.

Thanks goes to the people who helped type the manuscript after it was obvious that my pecking method would prolong the project by years: Mary Goodlander, Kim Hogel, Beverly Konicov, and Kia Kuresman. I am also very appreciative of the editing work done by my experienced friends who believed in the project: Tom Ford, Mary Goodlander, Kristina Strom, Su Ready, and Bob Wolff. Not only did all of these people do a great job, they did it for bargain prices to help the cause.

Many thanks and laughs go to Alex Johnson who on several occassions made me "his first priority" and drove the distance between Indianapolis and Cincinnati so that he could help me figure out my computer problems, reformat the manuscript, and execute an assortment of other jobs.

A multitude of thanks goes to Larry Ward, our webmaster. He jumped on board and took us to places we'd only dreamed of before.

To Tom and Jean Smith, I send thanks for letting me enter their home at all hours of the day and night to use the fax machine.

I also thank Jean, as well as my dad, my sister and brother-in-law, Carolyn and Wilson Taylor, and long time friend, Kathi Winterrowd, for all contributing to the effort of finding the right publishing company for this project.

Thanks goes to Bet Lankes Stephens for letting her printer "live and work" at my house for several months.

Thanks to Mike Del Favero for tolerating a plethora of continuous phone conversations between Kristina and me at all hours, as well as providing construction advice for one of my diverse projects.

More thanks go to Tim Lanham for not only providing a photograph of myself that I am happy with and translating my Microsoft emails into Mac language, but for also donating his time, spending hours and hours on the phone contacting contributors.

Kristina and I are very grateful for the generosity of Dr. Christiane Northrup, Judy Goodman, Linda Stein-Luthke and Cindy Bullens who voluntarily offered to endorse the book in their various publications and programs.

Thanks to Robin Lewis-Wild for graciously allowing us to use her monumental work, "Enchanted Garden", for the cover. The photograph originally appeared on the back cover of *Threads* magazine. (c1993 The Taunton Press Inc. Reprinted with permission from issue 46 of *Threads* magazine, Box 5506, Newtown, CT 06470-5506. To order a copy, call 1-800-888-8286.) "Enchanted Garden" is part of the Quinlan Visual Arts Center's permanent collection. For information about the Center which is located at 514 Green Street N.E., Gainesville, GA 30501, you can contact them by e-mail at qvac@bellsouth.net or by calling 770-536-2575.

I wish to express appreciation to Linda Ewing for introducing us to Richard Carlson.

Thanks also goes to Todd Bacon, Ed Brueggeman, and Bill Wyler for legal lessons.

I want to express gratitude for the work that was done by the Find People Fast company. Claud Turner, the Director of Operations at Infomax,

Inc., had Find People Fast help us locate two of the contributors we "lost" during the three year span of searching for an agent and publisher. They can be contacted at their website: www/fpf.com or by calling 1-800-829-1807.

Many thanks to the staff at Xlibris, particularly Lisa Adams, Donald Evanoff, Damali Kenya and Lisa Modica, for their cooperation and expertise during the publication process.

And last, but obviously not least, are the over 130 contributors who offered their stories and experiences to help others through the painful days following the death of people close to them. I truly appreciate that you did not give up on the project during the six years it took for the anthology to materialize.

Thank you, everyone.

Cynthia

CHAPTER 1

THE FUNERAL AND THE EULOGY

Actual eulogies and personal accounts of funerals are presented.

At A Memorial — June 1, 1989
by Alan Zweibel

This piece is an excerpt from Bunny Bunny: Gilda Radner—A Sort of Love Story *which was published by Villard Books in 1994 and then received critical acclaim as an off-Broadway play.* Bunny Bunny *will be released as a feature film for Warner Brothers.*

About fourteen years ago I was hiding behind a potted plant and this girl asked if I could help her be a parakeet, and I've been smitten with Gilda ever since. When we met, we were just these two kids in a big city and, because we made each other laugh, people invited us places we never got to go before. And now? Well, I haven't mourned, and I haven't cried yet, because even though she's dead, I just don't want her to die. I don't know why God makes people and then takes them back while they're still having fun with the life he gave them in the first place. Just like I don't know if I'm supposed to celebrate the fact that Gilda was in my life, or feel cheated that she's not here anymore. But even though her body grew to betray her, spirits just don't die. And that's what Gilda was. Even as an adult, she was still a little girl who believed in fairy tales and that if she said "Bunny Bunny" on the first day of every month, it would bring her love, laughter, and peace. Well, Gilda, this is June 1st and if you're in a place where you can't say it, I'll say it for you— "Bunny Bunny" and I hope you're okay. I'm gonna miss you, Gilbert.

Angel's Trumpet
In Celebration Of Raymond Lokken's
Life 1948—1997
by Kristina Chase Strom

As most everyone knows, Raymond and I were very closely connected throughout our lives. From the time we were wee children, we would see each other every summer and reestablish our bond at Lake Millicent, that place which has so much meaning for all of us no matter how we are intertwined in the vast matrix called the Strom clan.

Oh, the memories we all share of those smorgasbords out at the cottages, memories from the mundane to the magnificent, which now flood through my heart and soul. I remember Eleanor and Jesse setting up two picnic tables to play a lightening speed game of Double Solitaire, and how they gently allowed Raymond and me to participate.

As we grew older, Raymond and I would always find time, usually in the middle of the night, to sit on the dock and dangle our feet in the water and talk about the Order of the Universe, or rather what life is all about. He always told me that my arrival each year broadened his world view; I countered him by saying being with him centered mine.

Over the years, this bond that we had, and will have forever no matter what, never faltered. He and I were known as the "zany" ones: there was something different about us, each in our own way. Grandma Mary recognized this and even suggested one night after a dance down on Second Street that we get married! Simultaneously Raymond said "But Aunt Mary!" and I said "But Grandma," "We are cousins!" She did not seem to care, but we knew otherwise. We both felt the love and support she extended to us.

There is so much I could share about the depth and breadth of Raymond's and my relationship that continued throughout the years, no matter what were our individual life circumstances. The beauty is that each of us knew, realized, and honored this, even when we disagreed.

Three years ago, Raymond sent me a cutting from his garden via overnight express. Among the things he and I shared, perhaps the deepest bond was our reverence for Mother Earth. We believed we had a responsibility to sustain and maintain the glory of this planet in a co-creative way.

When the package arrived, my four daughters were enthralled: "Oh Mom, what is it?" Imagine their crestfallen faces when I opened the parcel: it was a stick carefully wrapped in sodden newspaper. They could not understand why I was so excited, but found out the following fall when "Mom's and Raymond's Stick" blossomed into a glorious plant that was not supposed to grow, let alone thrive, in this climate.

The generic name of this plant is "Angel's Trumpet", which is common throughout the south. The variety Raymond sent me is quite rare. I took photos of this plant as it grew and mailed them off to Raymond. We both celebrated in a way few people could comprehend when the plant bloomed. The blossoms of this plant descended gracefully from a precarious perch on towering branches, pale yellow trumpet-like blossoms at once so fragile, yet strong. In the middle of the night, when the windows were open, a scent unlike any other wafted through the windows. I sensed that this delicate plant felt comfortable in the night, in the safety of moon glow. I believe it represented what a challenge life could be in the context of being different, of being able to face the darkness each of us have in our lives and still be able to carry on in the spirit of giving love and light to all.

Last week, on May 2, this plant died inexplicably. I could not figure out why and felt that I had somehow neglected it. I thought Raymond would be so angry when he found out. I now know otherwise . . . that was the day Raymond went to the Light.

Somewhere out there, Raymond, like Gabriel, is playing sweet music on the trumpet that was once a part of the garden we shared. As I listen to, and yes, even smell this celestial music, I know that he will be with all of us forever.

Sunstruck
by Debra Ayers Brown

The sky thundered as I glanced in the rear view mirror at Atlanta's disappearing skyline. The 1996 Olympic signs flickered past, one by one. However, all I could see was the fiery car crash that left two victims a mere three weeks ago. "One, a married man who left behind a wife and three little girls. A devoted family man," the television reporter had said. "The other, a 38 year-old single man."

I was stunned. My cousin, Doug, though never married, was also a devoted family man. He was committed to his relatives, to his work, and to his friends. As a Captain in the Department of Transportation, Doug had dedicated the past year to the Olympic venue at Lake Lanier in Gainesville, fifty miles from Atlanta.

My clean-cut younger cousin, who had a passion for eclectic antiques and fine clothes, wore a law enforcement uniform and carried a shotgun during the week prior to July fourth. His team patrolled the waters of Lake Lanier and rehearsed the twelve hour workdays of the upcoming rowing events. By all accounts, he was as excited about this once-in-a-lifetime event as the well trained, hopeful Olympic athletes.

That was nothing new for Doug.

He liked challenges and fourth of July fireworks. "My Independence Day spectacular will be better than ever!" he promised. Each year family members joined him at his contemporary Lake Hartwell home to watch clusters of red, white, and blue rain down on the lake, transforming it into a pool of incandescent glitter as rockets whistled and burst, trailing white smoke across the night sky.

No one expected this year's July third explosion as Doug drove home from an all-night shift. News of the early morning head-on collision with the delivery truck seared my heart and sent shockwaves throughout the rural community as his already purchased fireworks lay silent.

The hundreds of mourners at the funeral home stood in line like fans waiting to see the Dream Team play basketball at the Georgia Dome. Amazed, Mom and I squeezed through the door into a gathering that would have overwhelmed and amused Doug, even if it had not been a holiday weekend.

Local dignitaries and the Governor's aide mingled with Peanut from Shoney's and Doug's high school classmate who had just won the five million dollar Georgia lottery.

"Naturally, Doug was the first to call and congratulate me," the lottery winner said. I smiled, not surprised. "He was so excited about my good luck that we all planned to take a cruise," she said, pulling Doug's close friend, Karen, over to join us.

"We were saving our money for a trip this fall," Karen said, beginning to sob as we stood alone, unbelieving, by the closed casket.

An earlier photo of Doug was our only physical reminder of him. A neat mustache, wire-rimmed glasses, dark-fringed sapphire eyes, and a genuine smile stared back at us. I could almost hear his words: "Perk up. Life is too short for that many tears!"

I concentrated on his salt and pepper hair in the photo. Over time, Doug's hair had become completely gray. Again, I could hear him say in his Southern drawl, "Better to turn gray than to turn loose." I held Karen close and wondered how a cruise with Doug would have been. Memorable, to say the least. Our last trip together to Mexico was just that. *Hadn't I threatened to wring his neck like the plucked chickens we had seen in old Cancun?* I giggled.

Karen stared at me, curious.

Happy to recount my trip, I said to her, "The two of us went to Cancun with my mom and some other friends a couple of years ago. Of course, Doug got into the Mexican mode as soon as we arrived."

"You mean more laid back than normal?" she asked, raising her eyebrows. "I can't imagine."

"You can't!" I agreed as I envisioned Doug strolling through the straw markets, raising his dark glasses as he asked, "Is *this* the price?" At once, an easy grin passed between him and the vendor as they negotiated, item by item, both oblivious to "La Cucaracha, La Cucaracha" forever blaring in the background.

"We took a pirate boat over to Isle Mujeres, commonly called the Island of Women, to tour and shop," I told Karen. "And somehow, we got separated from Doug." Panic filled me anew as I remembered our frantic search for him. "We looked *everywhere*, but NO DOUG. Finally, exasperated, we went back to the boat and prepared to leave."

"You left him?"

"Not exactly," I explained. "Two seconds before the boat departed, Doug appeared in the middle of the crowd on shore. At first, all we could see was this enormous straw hat dancing through the last of the peddlers and panhandlers." Doug was like a hummingbird sampling the exotic hibiscus, flitting from one treasure to the next, as the unrelenting Yucatan sun beat down on us. "He was a sight to behold. You had to see him to believe it. A carved wooden sculpture jutted out from under one arm as he balanced pastel-striped wool blankets on the other."

Karen laughed.

"To top it all," I said, returning her laugh, "he was holding a frozen margarita way up high in the air like the Olympic torch." Immediately, the reality that Doug would not be part of the Olympics hit me. "Anyway," I continued, "we were terrified that the boat was going to sail without him, but just in time he sashayed up the gangway, pausing long enough to toast every person in his path."

"I can picture him now."

"Me too," I said, shaking my head. "We were furious until we got a good look at him—a walking six-foot tall tourist ad. He looked so ridiculous that we couldn't stop laughing, nor could anyone else on the boat. Of course, they liked him on the spot."

Karen smiled. "Well, he never met a stranger, and he had a knack of making everything a special occasion," she said, her voice cracking. "In fact, yesterday was my birthday and Doug would have called. He always remembered mine; somehow I never remembered his."

"He never forgot mine, either," I admitted. "He always sent a card," I whispered, ashamed that I had taken this gesture for granted. All my special occasions flashed before my eyes. Doug was always present, at least in spirit.

"And he's the way I kept up with you," she said, grinning. "He was always happy to give us the scoop on your family and the big city of Hinesville." She paused, touching Doug's photo. "He hated that he didn't see much of you."

"Me too," I said, sorry that life's hectic pace and a four hour drive had kept me away too often. Still, I was able to keep up with everyone because of Doug. He loved to chit-chat. Since he never met a stranger, he always had a wealth of information to share. I loved it! Everyone did.

"You know that he loved you, Debbie," Karen said, startling me, as she leaned over to smell the sugary-sweet carnations that always reminded me of funerals.

"I loved him, too," I whispered, saying the words out loud for the first time as I blinked back the unshed tears. *Why had I never told him? Somehow, he had to know.*

"The widows at the lake are devastated, too," Karen said, handing me a tissue. "They couldn't even talk about the accident."

I knew that Doug had gotten to know his neighbors at the lake. He had shared with me some of the gourmet recipes they had used for their elaborate neighborhood dinner parties, recipes I never had time to try.

"It won't be the same without his famous sourdough bread," Karen said.

How could I forget the sourdough bread? "He gave me a starter jar that sat in my refrigerator for months until I finally trashed it, not sure of what I was actually growing."

Little by little, I realized that Doug had shared a piece of himself with everyone around him. The risk of rejection was as foreign to him as the notion that I wouldn't know what to do with his gift and would discard the starter jar altogether. Doug knew that with the right nurturing, the sourdough would be passed on to another person to enjoy. In essence, it would never die.

"His dough would always rise to perfection," I said. "Unfortunately, mine was a different story."

She nodded. "Mine too, but Doug could make anything grow," she muttered, turning her attention to a long-stemmed red rose. "He took all my half-dead plants home with him, and in a couple of months, they were flourishing again."

Karen was right. Doug would tend the soil so that the vulnerable seeds would germinate and be fruitful. From season to season, his efforts would crop up and bloom.

"He definitely had a green thumb," I said, reluctant to leave Karen's side as the family shifted from the funeral home to the waiting cars.

Outside, dark clouds slid across the afternoon sun as more than a dozen official vehicles with honor guards led the procession through the winding country roads as a soundless why? why? why? seemed to echo through the grassy hillsides. Nameless bystanders poured from their homes to watch the endless stream of flashing blue lights climb the steep hills. I thought I heard

Doug chuckle, "This is perfect! It's more like a chase scene in *Smokey and The Bandit* than a funeral."

At the cemetery, the plain-spoken D.O.T. Chaplain said, "Doug worked extra hard on his last assignment, the upcoming Olympics. His planning skills have left us in good shape for the venue, but he will be missed more for the way he cared about everyone around him. Their problems were his problems."

The rise and fall of his words soothed my spirit as I watched the stone-faced honor guards, many older than Doug, who had told me earlier in passing, "Doug trained me last year," or "I made Captain a few years after Doug." It was apparent that my cousin, who had gone straight to the D.O.T. from the University of Georgia, had skyrocketed through the ranks to make Captain.

Earlier, his dad had told me, "Doug is being buried in his uniform." I was surprised. However, this fact was comforting to Uncle Nelson, and to me.

"We meant to get a picture of him in uniform," Aunt Polly said of her only son, their firstborn. "He had promised me one for Mother's Day but he was too busy . . . "

Uncle Nelson only nodded as he whispered, "We were so proud of him," proud of a son who had embraced their family values and work ethics.

My thoughts returned to the present as the Chaplain coughed, then continued. "More important than doing a job that would make his family proud, Doug taught us to look for the beauty in things that most of us never notice. I'll never forget the day he found an unexpected sparkle of mica in a clump of North Georgia red clay during a company picnic. It was something I'd stepped on all day, but Doug saw it as a gem from his childhood, from days playing with his sisters, Melinda and Leanne, and his cousins on the family farm."

He paused as the family members inhaled his words, and I remembered summer days of chickens and cows, Black Angus bulls and fields of cotton, and the hard farm work that builds integrity. Scratchy dust tickled my nose as boisterous baby chicks scurried through the suffocating heat. Again, I followed Doug and Uncle Nelson as they kept the "doodies" churning. "Keep moving," Doug cooed to them, fanning his arms, "and you'll be cooler."

An unseasonal cool breeze brushed the crowd as the Chaplain said, "We teased him about calling his mother every morning, but he'd just smile. He knew what was important."

At once, the brilliant July sun burst through the threatening storm clouds.

White specks flickered in front of my bleary eyes like doves ascending to the heavens.

And then it was clear: Doug had lived in the now. He savored the moment, rather than living between now and later or dwelling on the past. He nurtured those around him, thus the important things of life. Doug had realized that life is a precious gift that can end at any moment. Like the sourdough and the tiny seeds, he had flourished in the warmth of the sunshine, embracing all around him.

I was suddenly struck by how Doug had enhanced my life with bright spots of kindness, humor, and caring, even when I had been blind to such precious moments. By remembering him and how he lived, he would never die, and by following his example, I would live. Instantly, I realized that my life would forever be touched by the unfailing light of Doug's radiance, which was like sunlight. An inner peace filled me as the Chaplain said, "Best of all, Doug was a devoted family man."

In Memory Of My Cousin, Ray Lokken
by Martha Strom

> clouds low
>> over Lake Millicent
>>> we drifted into the bay
>>>> among the steamy cattails
> the oarlocks creaking
>> as if they
>>> would never stop
> you bent over
>> toward me
>>> and whispered this:
> when i am gone
>> think of me
>>> as the water lily
> forever floating
>> beautiful as sunlight
>>> and casting no shadow

The Spiritual Side Of Grief
by Adele DelSavio

This piece was originally published in the Oswego, NY Palladium-Times.

As a Roman Catholic, I have a deep faith in God and in life after death. Observation and experience have also led me to believe in "the big picture" which we, experiencing just a small segment, may never fully comprehend in this life.

I feel lucky that my faith—my feeling that there's more to life than we can see or understand—didn't fail me when I needed it most when our oldest son Mike died at seventeen years of age.

A low point shortly after he died brought an insight that is still important to me. I was sitting in a front pew with my family at Mike's funeral, letting my eyes wander around the front of the church. Memories were crowding in: his Confirmation there the previous year; the Sunday Masses; the time he'd found a good spot for taking pictures of his youngest sister after her First Communion seven months earlier.

Now here we were at the church again, attending his funeral. *What was the use?* I kept asking myself. *All those years of raising him, of teaching him our morals and values, taking him to church on Sunday and to religious education classes during the week, and preparing him to receive his sacraments and celebrating when he did. Why did we bother? Why did we work so hard, putting together a life that would only last for seventeen years?* It seemed like wasted effort, as if it had all been done for nothing because now Mike was dead.

Suddenly the realization hit me. Our efforts hadn't all been for nothing. Of course, the care we had taken of his body was in vain. The immunizations, the food and clothes, the fluoride treatments at the dentist's office, the conditioning exercises he put himself through for football were all of no use to him now. He no longer needed the skills, like driving, that he had learned, or the many facts and skills that had been taught to him at school.

However, the care we had taken of him spiritually and the things he'd done for himself spiritually were the things that would last. I realized that because of these things his soul was in the best shape possible to assist him in the life that awaited him. What we had done for him actually *did* have a purpose.

In that moment, right then, at Mike's funeral, I incorporated into my way of dealing with this death the realization to which my faith had led me. Although Mike's life here was cut short—terribly, achingly short—the love, care, and spiritual guidance we gave him will endure forever with his spirit.

The Star-Spangled Receipt
by Grant Hasty

It was only 11:00 AM, but the humid Charleston, South Carolina heat was already past the broiling point, so I was grateful that the church service had come to a merciful end. Surrounded by the cool crisp air of the air-conditioned limo provided by the funeral home, I watched quietly as the pall bearers carried my father's flag draped coffin out of the front door of St. John's Lutheran Church to the back of the hearse. After carefully placing it inside the vehicle, the pall bearers shook hands and chatted briefly. I didn't know any of the men very well, though over the last couple of years I had met all of them at one time or another.

My mother, in her black veil, said she thought it was especially kind that these gentlemen had volunteered their services. My brother was not so appreciative. He said, "Oh they just want to look important in front of a bunch of other people." Aunt Rose scolded him for his lack of graciousness. Uncle Don, Dad's younger brother, and I watched silently as the back door of the hearse was shut for the long ride to the military cemetery located down in Beaufort, South Carolina, which was seventy miles away.

The ride was a green and gray blur as we rolled past the miles of live oaks and hanging Spanish moss on Coastal Highway 17. I felt distant and detached from the world as if I were in a trance. Only during the burial ceremony when the soldiers of the honor guard fired their rifle volleys in memory of my father's thirty years of service in the Army did I become aware again. A titanic thunderbolt parted the sky as black inky clouds swirled overhead, hiding the sun. The rain then came down in withering sheets, pounding the small canopy that sheltered us.

Uncle Don turned to me and said, "Your father is not going quietly."

No, I thought, *he's not going quietly. He's leaving as if he were giving his final orders to his troops in his last parade.* I recalled the times he told me of his early days with the 37th division when MacArthur's forces fought a horrific month long battle with the Japanese to recapture the Philippines' Capital of Manila. Later he described for me the terrors of Vietnam, a war of booby traps and snipers. Even now we still keep a dud Chinese mortar shell that could have killed him at the tiny hamlet of An Khe. He had earned his Colonel's rank the hard way and without the benefit of going to West Point. I looked down at the folded blue triangle of stars the squad leader had given to my mother on behalf of a grateful nation, which was all we had left: a star-spangled receipt. Another lightning bolt streaked overhead, and the thunderclaps exploded like incoming artillery shells. All my mother could do was clutch her flag to her breast while the young soldiers marched slowly away in the sad, sad, rain.

The Funeral
by Florence Clowes

My year had begun badly. I was sent home from the Peace Corps to recover from surgery, and Mom was in the hospital two hours away. Within a month my brother phoned asking if I could stay with her when she was discharged from the hospital. Fortunately, I was free to do so though I had been warned to be careful because of my recent back surgery.

My heart sank when I saw her. She had taken a nap on the glider in the sun porch and couldn't get up. For eighty-seven years this woman had been a lively, cheerful person, taking care of the family, operating a beauty shop, and active in several organizations. She was a staunch Polish-American and supported all things Polish. Now she was weak and ill, and I could see that her illness was serious.

During the next two months Mom and I spent many hours at the doctor's office, in the emergency room, or in the hospital. I felt frustrated and helpless as Mom grew weaker. When the doctor became reluctant to do anything, my brothers and I complained to Mom's HMO headquarters. We were assured that outside consultants would be called in. Before we knew it, there were several specialists examining her, an intervention that turned out to be too late: early in April Mom was diagnosed with inoperable cancer.

Mom took the news better than my brothers and I did. I thought of her life, how she had graduated from hairdressing school without a high school diploma, raised four children with a husband out of work during the Depression, and the many heartaches and few proud moments we had given her. When our father had died twenty years before, all of us were married and out of state. My brothers followed in her footsteps and became beauticians. Nevertheless, she had kept up her home, painting windows, planting a garden, mowing the lawn, and operating her beauty shop. She planned great get-togethers on holidays and urged the family to remain close. She was active in her church and the community, so we often had to call before visiting her to learn if she was free.

All Mom wanted was to go home, so when arrangements had been made with a hospice, we took her home. Mom's own bed had been dismantled and carried out to the garage to make room for a hospital bed. A wheelchair and bedside table were also provided, but we managed to bring in her favorite rocking chair for the few times she was able to get out of bed.

Despite all the agony, grief, and sorrow of knowing Mom would not recover, I listened to well-meaning visitors say, "Sophie, you'll get better; we'll go picking mushrooms soon," or "Will your mother be running for president of the Rosary Society again?" or "I'd like to make an appointment to shampoo and set my hair." I wanted to scream, "Don't you see she's dying? She'll never do those things!"

The following weeks were hectic, and when I asked the nurse whether I should travel to Connecticut for my doctor's appointment over the weekend she strongly advised me not to go. I went out into my mother's flower garden, absentmindedly picking flowers, and cried. I cried for her suffering. I cried for my helplessness and loss, dreading what was to come. Finally I returned to the house. I called my brothers and urged them to come home. I sat by her side while she died quietly early Saturday morning, in her own bed, in the home she and my father built sixty years earlier. Now it was over. Dad gone, Mom gone. Our lives were changed forever.

My brothers and I needed to make arrangements for the funeral, and we called the funeral home used by most Polish-Americans in the city. Terry, the Polish-Ukranian funeral director, had grown up in our neighborhood, and he and I knew each other well. Now he would be the one to direct us. Numb with the finality of death, two of my brothers and I went to the home to make the arrangements and choose a casket. Respecting Mom's frugality, we chose a wooden casket that looked very nice.

"Bring her clothes down," Terry said. "The Rosary Society usually provides a rosary spray of flowers. I'll order family flowers. What would you like to have on the ribbons? 'Grandma,' 'Babcia,' 'Mom?' Would you like the newspaper announcement in other city papers? Sit down with your brothers and write up her obituary, or I can help you do it. I'll call the priest and make arrangements for the Mass. What day do you want to hold the funeral?"

I was overwhelmed. So much needed to be done. There seemed little time to grieve, but I had grieved continually while Mom was still alive and suffering. Children, grandchildren, relatives, and employers had to be notified. Friends and neighbors had already learned of her death. Mom had been an active leader in the Holy Family Church, and president of the Rosary Society for fifty years. She had belonged to many organizations in the city, was proud of her Polish heritage, and willingly shared with all who were interested. Everyone seemed to have known her.

My brothers and I decided we would extend the usual three day waiting period for the funeral. Because there were so many grandchildren scattered through the country, we needed another day for them all to come home.

When my brother John arrived he was shocked to see Mom's white hair because she had always been diligent in coloring and styling her own hair. She had styled the hair of hundreds of her friends, living and dead, and now her son would return the favor. I picked out a favorite dress of hers. The four of us began writing her obituary. Fortunately, after my father died, Mom had drawn up a short history of her life. When we found the paper, we felt like she was there, telling us her life's story.

"Sophie Ann Gramkowska was born in Mendzehowa, Poland, in 1906 while her mother was there visiting her family. They returned to the States and her father when she was one and a half years old. She always had trouble legalizing her birth certificate. At age fourteen, she had to quit school to help with family finances and went to work. There were seven other children in the family, and the years following World War I were difficult. But by the time she was eighteen, she had earned enough money to put herself through hairdressing school, and began working as a beautician, an occupation she held for seventy-five years."

In 1927 she married Charles Waskelewicz. Dad also came from Poland and worked on the Boston & Albany Railroad as a conductor. He and Grandpa built our home in two years. Four children arrived, myself (Florence) in 1928, Edwin in 1932, John in 1936, and Joe in 1940. After Dad died in 1970, Mom lived in and took care of her home alone. Before her death, Mom had been honored by the city in a "This Is Your Life" presentation in which the Mayor and many politicians, business people, and friends were present. Sophie's life ended on April 16, 1994. What I dreaded was the funeral.

My daughter, Sue, and brother, Ed, offered to visit the priest at the old Polish church. Father Tom had already agreed to conduct the Mass at ten o'clock on Wednesday, but they wanted to take part in the liturgical readings. Another grandchild, Todd, said he would like to offer a eulogy.

Father Tom resisted their requests. The priest didn't like losing his authority to these strangers. "Absolutely not. You are not members of this church!" After many protests, however, he relented. "One of you can read, but from *this* passage only," he commanded as he pointed out a section in the Missal. Since Sue was a reader in her Arizona parish, she knew there were a variety of passages that could be used. When she told the priest this, he became furious.

"This is my church, and you will read what I say! And the vice-president of the Rosary Society has already requested she be allowed to give the eulogy."

Edwin wanted to take part in the Mass also.

"Where do you live?" the priest asked. "Do you go to church?" When he found out Ed wasn't registered at any church, Father Tom refused to let him take part in the service.

Sue and Ed returned home boiling with indignation. "No wonder the Catholic Church is losing its people. The nerve of that fat old goat! You wouldn't believe what he said!"

We all felt as if we were out of control. Things around us were just happening. The house began to fill with family, while friends brought food, flowers, fruit baskets, sympathy cards, and made phone calls. Someone is flying in to Albany, can he get picked up? Where should we send flowers? Who else has bedrooms to spare? Come and eat something. Have you got something to wear to the wake and funeral? Who will take care of the children? Has anyone talked about a reception?

I wanted to have a coffee-and-cake reception, but was voted down. My high school friend put her arm around me and said, "No, the Rosary Society will provide the reception in the church hall, following the burial at the cemetery. Your mother was president of the Society for fifty years, and this is the least we can do! It's all taken care of. We will do everything. Don't worry about a thing."

Sue and Ed returned to the church the following day, armed with the passage she wanted to read. Ed had also found a verse. Boldly, they gave their selections to the priest. They reminded him of the support the family had provided for almost a century and the faithful service Mom and had given during her lifetime. He grumbled and mumbled, and finally agreed. "But you must paste your passages in this book, and no other changes, you understand?"

From Arizona, Sue had brought a blue coffin shroud that she and her husband had draped on their young son's coffin a few years earlier. She told the priest the family wanted it draped over Mom's coffin instead of the usual black one. The pale blue would match the Rosary women's blue neck ribbons. The priest threw up his hands in resignation.

Perhaps the money realized from the many Mass cards that poured into the church office softened his stubbornness. Or had word from the Parish Council changed his mind? We will never know. Meeting once again with the funeral director, we set dates for the wake and time for the family to say goodbye to Mom for the last time. We set a time for two evenings, knowing the huge crowd that would want to offer their condolences. Terry suggested an afternoon as well. We sighed as we visualized the many tearful expressions of sympathy.

Then we thought Mom would like our walking to the church from the funeral home. In Poland, the family and mourners followed the priest and casket from the church to the cemetery. Here we could at least walk from the funeral home to the church. Getting into cars and driving the two blocks to arrive at the church made little sense.

"I don't know if Father will like that," Terry hesitated.

"We won't tell him! He won't have to know! He'll be here to say prayers in the morning and then leave to prepare the Mass, which is when we'll form a procession and walk to church."

"All right," agreed Terry, "but I must insist the casket go in the hearse—we aren't carrying the casket that distance."

"Fine, we'll walk behind the hearse."

On the morning of the funeral, the home was overflowing with people paying their last respects to Mom. The Society ladies recited the rosary, walked out and went to the church. They stationed themselves down the aisle as honor guards, fifty of them standing at attention on both sides of the aisle, their blue Sodality ribbons with the Blessed Mother medallions draped around their necks, holding candles ready to light.

At the funeral home, Father prayed once more and blessed Mom before leaving for the church. Then Terry announced that we were walking to the church and anyone who wanted to join us could follow. The family drew close to Mom's casket for the last time and went outside to form a line. When everyone was outside, the casket was closed and placed in the hearse. The procession began.

Dozens of people silently lined the sidewalk in the cool April morning air. Traffic had been rerouted while we slowly made our way down the street. At the door of the church the pale blue fabric gently encompassed the coffin and the priest led the way into the church. The Rosary Society women stood on guard, their candles lit, tears streaming down their cheeks.

I wept at the thought of the many, many lives Mom had touched and influenced. Here were her friends standing together one last time and the church was filled with people who had known and respected her. The choir, without her, sang favorite Polish hymns.

The priest offered the Mass graciously, never knowing that Ed and Sue who gave the readings had been divorced and remarried. Grandchildren offered up the communion and wine to the priest, and the entire congregation received communion. Finally the Society vice-president gave her eulogy and the Mass was over. We went on to the cemetery, this time by car.

Todd gave his eulogy, reminding us our loss was less when we remembered her full life and the many people she had touched. Sophie's spirit will live on through her four children, thirteen grandchildren, and seventeen great-grandchildren. He concluded with an invitation to return to the church hall for a meal. Knowing the Rosary Society women, I knew there would be a large assortment of salads, golumki, pirogi, kielbasa, and kapusta, along with polish breads, pastries, and drinks. The get-together was great, and I am sure Mom was pleased.

The Wake
by Vera Koppler

Once they said that
when the soul left the body
it entered the candle flame
above the bier.

And there were those who said
that when the candle had burned out
they saw the flame still burning

but they were superstitious
and given to imaginations.

The Irish and the Scots danced
and sang wild songs around the casket;
they ate and quaffed whiskey
to show their respect.

The waning of the moon,
old women said,
and the ebb-tide
these were the times to expect death.

They were pagans all
and looked for strange signs.

The people at this wake
are intruders (though they wish us no ill).

They are holding family reunions
where only death issues the invitations.

"How sad that we only see you when there's
a funeral," they will say . . .
"Aren't the flowers beautiful?"

But I am alone and there is no candle,
and no songs,
I am not given to dreams . . .
But sitting here I felt
your soul leave your body
and enter mine.

Commencement
A Eulogy For Warren Charles Bonner 1916-2000
by Linda Bonner Ewing

After high school, Warren C. Bonner earned degrees in education (Bachelor of Science) and business administration (Master of Arts). During World War II he served in Naval Intelligence. He then taught high school history for 32 years. Upon retirement, he devoted his days to art, creating over 100 exquisite pen and ink drawings of local landmarks and sites. He and his wife were happily married for 57 years.

***

I have something from my dad I wish to share with you. He was the valedictorian of his high school class in 1934. The words he wrote at that time, to commence his new life, are timeless. I want to share his speech with you because I see Dad's passing as yet another commencement, both in his life and ours.

Dad *was* a teacher, and one of my very best. While dying, in the spirit of commencement, Dad gave me a profound experience and a personal teaching in life-after-life. He modeled by example to the very end, showing me that death is actually a new beginning. What a wonderful dad! What a great teacher!

As you listen to his courageous words, written at age eighteen, reflect upon his life and *feel* his integrity. This is a new beginning for him, as it is for us all. Together, we are now standing on that same, brave threshold. How would Dad want us to proceed from here?

I wish to dedicate this reading to my mom, his wife, Elaine Kolb Bonner, so that she will feel this new beginning for herself.

***

Reverend Fathers, Members of the Faculty, Classmates, Ladies, and Gentlemen:

This evening marks the close of four years' work. Now just how well was this work done? This is the query which confronts us. To answer it truthfully, we must examine carefully both the past and the future. It is true we have gained much knowledge. But what is the good of this knowledge if it is not put into practical use? The great question after all is not so much what we possess, but just how we determine to use to the best advantage that which we have.

We are old enough, I believe, to realize that there is something radically wrong with the world of today. What is it? That is the question which we must face and essay to answer.

Wherever we turn, we are confronted with an indefinable current of restlessness, suspicion, and deception. There exists a perfect willingness to take advantage. Things once regarded as dead wrong, things which in their character have not changed, are now looked upon as permissible, and even laudable. Men have scoffed at the simple teaching of Jesus of Nazareth, who said, "Love your enemies." That doctrine, they say, is too idealistic, too impractical. Their doctrine, the doctrine of practical men: "In a competitive world, we must be armed to fight our enemy. That is the safe way, the inexpensive way." Thus they speak. They have determined to set aside all scruples, all moral responsibility in order to serve their own inclinations. This is the world we must face. These are the conditions we must encounter. How shall we meet them?

We realize more and more the responsibility which must be shouldered when we are no longer "just schoolboys". Some of us will be failures in life, and some of us will be successes, but still the majority will lead normal, useful lives and die unknown outside of their limited circle of friends. So, after a preparation of four years in High School, we are about to strike out for ourselves and to adjust ourselves, each according to his own individual likes and dislikes, to our vocation in life.

Doubtless, our individual programs will differ. But whatever be the methods of each of us, all of us must lay sufficient stress and emphasis on our moral duties. A character in which purity and self-sacrifice dominate is the greatest possession attainable by mortal man. God's idea for the working basis of our lives is moral perfection. Emerson admonishes us to hitch our wagon to a star. He wishes to impress upon us the necessity of making perfection in all our endeavors our highest aim.

Members of the Faculty! If this evening we leave this auditorium realizing our duty in life and that we must strive towards high ideals, the credit belongs much to you. You have taught us the proper attitude towards life and you have encouraged us by your bright example, which we shall never forget. Wherever our lots may fall, whatever our work may be, we shall be mindful of your vast influence on our lives. With the most profound reverence and gratitude, we bid you, our teachers, our friends, farewell!

Classmates! The time for our parting has arrived. This is undoubtedly the last time we shall ever be together. During the days to come, let us often recall these High School years and face our duties with courage and hope.

To you all, our beloved friends, the Class of 1934 bids a last farewell!

***

Now let me repeat this last paragraph with a slight update:

Family and Friends: The time for our *parting* has arrived. *This* is undoubtedly the *last* time we shall ever be together. During the days to come, often recall these years and face your life with love, courage, and hope.

To you all, my beloved family and friends, I bid a final farewell.

CHAPTER 2

CHILDREN'S DEATHS: INFANTS THROUGH ADULTHOOD

Parents share their heartache and the experiences they faced while dealing with the loss of their children.

Saying Goodbye To Our Baby
by Holly Lentz

My husband took Monday afternoon off work so he could witness my ultrasound. We had been through this before with our first baby, who was now fifteen months old, and I remembered how fascinating it was to see her wiggling around on the screen. Somehow, seeing our baby had made her more real.

After the ultrasound, we returned to the doctor's office. With a solemn look on his face, he recommended I schedule an appointment for a Level II ultrasound. When he asked us if I had had blood drawn for a Alpha-fetoprotein test, I knew the situation was critical. AFP tests are for birth defects like Down's syndrome and spina bifida. My husband and I had refused the test, feeling we could not abort our pregnancy under any circumstances.

My doctor explained that there were dilated ventricles on our baby's head, signaling the possibility of water on the brain. He said the problems could be caused by a variety of defects, some of which could benefit from surgery in utero and others that could not. I will always remember him saying, "I can't tell you not to worry, but don't worry yet."

His words kept echoing in my mind; I told myself to be optimistic. I hoped the ultrasound was just a precautionary measure.

Even so, I slept restlessly the next two nights, worrying about what the ultrasound might reveal. On Wednesday morning my husband and I headed to the hospital. The ultrasound technician told us she doubted they would be able to see dilated ventricles this early in my pregnancy. Her comment bolstered my hope that this was all a mistake.

The technician spread warm soothing jelly over my belly and started the ultrasound. The doctor looked closely at our baby, especially the head and spine. My heart ached as he showed us the water on the brain. He pointed out the head was tilting back, not forward in the normal fetal position. My voice cracked as I muttered, "Our poor baby, it's in such bad shape."

When we asked the doctor if we could do anything to help our baby, he referred us to the Genetic Counseling Center at Children's Hospital. This center had researched how babies with this condition manage outside of the womb.

He also urged that I undergo amniocentesis. Even though the test would not necessarily pick up our baby's problem, it would be beneficial to see if other defects were present. As I signed the consent form, I suddenly hoped the procedure would cause us to lose the baby. It seemed like a sinful wish, but then the decision would be made for us. Still, I felt guilty.

That night we called family and close friends to share our devastating news. It was the worst night. As I felt the baby kicking in my belly, I felt sick that it was in such bad shape. The most difficult part was not knowing where the prognosis would lead us, what decision we would make.

At this point, we had two alternatives. If the doctors could give us any hope, we would carry full term, praying for the best. In spite of our earlier conviction, we decided we would terminate our pregnancy if the prognosis was hopeless.

At "best", I imagined a baby whose surgically implanted shunt had to be pumped to remove excess fluid and whose future would be in question. At "worst", the baby could die shortly after birth. I dreaded the thought of watching our baby suffer as much as I dreaded the thought of terminating.

I secretly wanted the baby to be in such bad shape that there would be no question about what we had to do. I was not prepared to watch my child suffer.

On Thursday morning, we visited Children's Hospital, where our wait seemed like a lifetime. Every time someone opened the door to the counseling office anxiety gnawed at my belly because I thought it was time to learn our baby's fate. I looked over at my husband and said, "I have a big knot in my stomach."

To my surprise, he said, "So do I." Only then did I realize he was as upset as I.

The counselor finally summoned us, seating us in a private room. After taking a family history, she determined that our problem was probably not hereditary and informed us we would have to wait for the physician's diagnosis.

When the doctor arrived, she explained that our baby had been diagnosed with iniencephaly, a rare neural tube defect. She said our baby would almost surely die soon after birth, or worse yet, if our baby survived it would be in a vegetative state. The water on the brain was so severe that the brain was unable to develop. As proof, the doctor told us our baby's face, a mirror of the brain's development, was misshapen.

Every time the counselor looked at me to say, "I am so sorry. I know it must be hard," I wept uncontrollably. In contrast my husband remained in control, showing little emotion. I had mixed emotions, feeling alternately upset about our baby's condition and relieved that our decision was clear cut. We knew we'd terminate our pregnancy. Now it was just a matter of how and when.

The counselor directed us to the phone where we consulted with my OB/GYN. We agreed with his recommendation to undergo Dilation and Evacuation (D&E), a more-palatable term for late-term abortion, instead of inducing labor. Although the D&E would not allow for an autopsy, it was preferable to staying two or three days in the hospital while they induced labor. The thought of giving birth to a dead or dying baby was unbearable. I wanted to spare myself the emotional pain of seeing my deformed baby.

To my dismay, my doctor told me I would have to make the appointment with the abortion clinic because he could not be involved, presumably for fear of pro-life reaction. I was disappointed when the clinic informed us the three-day Dilation and Evacuation procedure would not start until Tuesday, meaning we had to wait an entire week before this ordeal would be over. It was a sick feeling carrying a baby we knew we were going to abort.

We decided not to go to my husband's extended-family Memorial Day celebration. I wasn't ready to cry in front of a large group of people or try to explain our situation to small children. Instead, we spent the weekend with close friends and family, finding comfort in the warmth of their support.

One morning during the painful days of waiting, I was standing naked in the bathroom when my husband slipped his arms around me, his hands wrapping my enlarged belly. I said, "Give our poor baby a big hug," to which he replied, "We have to say good-bye to our baby." As I was telling him it was all right to cry, I turned around to see my husband shed his first tear since learning of our bad news.

Tuesday morning finally came, the beginning of the end of this horrible nightmare. I have never felt so loved as when my husband wrapped one arm around me tightly as we walked up to the clinic.

The wait at the clinic seemed endless, since we were anxious to put this behind us. Before the procedure could begin they gave me yet another ultrasound, determining they would be able to complete the procedure in two days, not three. What a relief—the quicker the better.

We were finally ready to begin the procedure. The doctor inserted laminaria to dilate my cervix. My belief that the procedure involved little pain soon faded as I rode home with the worst cramps of my life. All night I tried to rest but was interrupted by excruciating physical and emotional pain. The baby's kicks were amplified by my anxiety about terminating our pregnancy.

On Wednesday the evacuation procedure began. When the doctor started performing the evacuation, I sobbed heavily. In response, the doctor asked me to calm down, warning any movement could be dangerous for me. The nurse attempted to distract me by starting a conversation. As I told her I was lucky to have a wonderful baby girl at home who was fifteen months old, I couldn't ignore the sucking sounds and the tugging caused by the evacuation procedure.

When they released me to my private recovery room, where my husband was waiting, I felt hollow inside. My baby was gone. The tears would not stop flowing. My husband held me tight in a futile attempt to comfort me.

That night, although I felt better physically, I still had trouble sleeping. I was haunted by doubt. What if the doctors were wrong and our baby was actually healthy?

Our counselor called the next day, referring me to another woman who had terminated her pregnancy. She conceived two children with severe genetic defects. Her first was born and died at two years of age and her second she aborted. The reality of her situation helped me to finally believe that if we had not terminated our pregnancy we would have watched our baby die. That night, for the first time in over a week, I slept peacefully.

Even though we miss our baby terribly, we are grateful for the legacy our child has left behind. We now have the confidence that comes from knowing our marriage can withstand any problem we encounter. And we share the peace that follows the revelation that day-to-day problems are trivial in comparison to losing a child. My relationship with my husband is much stronger. We cherish each other, as well as our daughter, because we now know the pain of losing a piece of our family.

As for the future, we are working on expanding our family. With every glance and flash of a smile, our first baby, Jackie, reminds us that parenthood, with all its risks, is still the most rewarding job we'll ever know.

Roma Was Here
by Violeta Balhas

"When a child is born, it is already nine months old," the Chinese say. Add to that a lifetime's amalgam of wishes, plans, hopes, and fears, I say.

My subconscious was aware that I was pregnant before I consciously knew. One night, I had a vivid dream about Persian meringues—little meringue balls with fruits inside.

"If that's not a pregnancy dream, I don't know what is," I said. Not being fluent in the symbolic language of dreams, however, I neglected to fully notice that the fruits in my dream were dried.

An ultrasound scan revealed that I was three months pregnant. Life had grown within me without my suspecting a thing as I continued to raise our two other children, study, and work . . . and religiously take the Pill.

I had trouble coming to terms with the fact that I had not really decided to become pregnant. "We didn't plan it this way," I told my doctor. He laughed, and said, "We didn't plan it this way, either." My doctor and his wife had five children. After saying "no more", she had gotten pregnant again—with triplets.

Once I let myself be happy about expecting another child, my entire family became excited. My five-year-old daughter Sarah was forever hugging me, saying, "I love you so much Ma, because you're going to have a baby!" We started unpacking baby clothes. My mother started crocheting a baby shawl. For my family, preparing for the new baby was "all systems go".

We decided to take Sarah and our three-year-old son Jeremy to the next ultrasound. The procedure took longer than usual, but I thought nothing of it. Finally, the radiologist said that he wasn't happy with the baby's head: it was too round and slightly smaller than average. My husband Stephen looked concerned and perplexed. My heart leaped into my mouth. A doctor came in, took a look at the screen, and diagnosed hydrocephalus. His ultrasound machine was fairly limited, so he told us to go to the Fetal Diagnostic Unit in the capital for confirmation.

As the doctor left me to get changed and gather my wits, he said, "See, this is why ultrasounds are so important. It's so much better finding out now rather than later." I thought, *Why? Why is it better?* His comment was the first example of an attitude that I was to confront again and again: if a baby is to die, it will hurt less if it happens earlier.

When we experience grief, things hurt as much as they can, and it is useless to compare our hurt to anyone else's. Each circumstance compounds grief in its own way. How wrong to think I had not attached and bonded to this baby, and that she wasn't as real as a born child. In time, memories of a dead loved one can become a comfort. The cruelty was that I would have so few of them.

That night, Stephen and I talked and wept in each other's arms. We had considered what it would mean to have a handicapped child and had decided we could handle it. Our doctor had also reassured us and offered us signs of hope.

In the F.D.U. at the Monash Medical Center in Melbourne, my mind and my insides were in turmoil. I was nauseated. I could feel my heart pounding inside my chest. Finally, we were called in to speak to the doctor who was to perform the ultrasound scan. She took all sorts of detailed notes, looking for clues. She warned us that if she found something wrong, she wouldn't beat around the bush. We nodded in relief.

In the darkness of the ultrasound room, with Stephen chattering nervously, the doctor gave us the news within a minute.

"I must tell you right now, it looks really bad."

"How bad? In what way?"

"Baby's brain has not developed properly."

"Is there any chance of life?"

"No."

I felt as if everything rushed to my head. The walls closed in and the ceiling was about to crash down on me. The baby did not have fluid on the brain, but fluid instead of brain. The possibility of us having a baby, even a severely handicapped one, disappeared. The doctor confirmed that the baby was a girl, as we had suspected, and an amnio was performed.

Outside while waiting to see the head of the Unit and a counselor, we wept again. Our world had been pivoted upside-down and, white-knuckled, we were trying to hang on.

"What about us? What will happen to us?" I asked Stephen. My husband is a grief counselor, and I knew the statistics: the majority of couples who lose children end up divorced. My relationship with Stephen is my rock, and even that now seemed under siege.

"Let's make a promise now," Stephen said, taking my face in his hands. "We'll never stop talking."

The head of the Unit told us what we needed to know. Our baby had an extremely rare condition: hydro-holoprocencephali. Then he gave us something that meant the world to me, and I clung to it: choice. We were free to induce the baby now, or to wait until full term. There was no right nor wrong decision, but it was a decision only we could make. He suggested we take a few days to talk about it between ourselves, and to put it to thought, and if we needed, to prayer.

On the way home, we gave our emotions some focus. We named the baby Roma. We made plans for her birth and funeral. We planned to gather as many memories as possible. We talked about the best way to tell the children. Despite my nerves, Stephen insisted there was only one way—with honesty.

At home, we sat the children down in front of us. I wrung my hands and let Stephen do the job.

The next three weeks were tough. I was familiar with sadness, but at that time I discovered depression. For me, depression was a pit. I could see no light, nor any way out. I sat and cried for two weeks. I began to talk to

Roma, to tell her what I wanted to show her about the world. I would hold my swollen belly, feeling frustrated that this was as close as I could get to her. Coming out of the shower, I would look at my naked self in the full-length mirror. Roma was growing and I was growing with her, and my breasts had a new, ignorant fullness, awaiting the birth. Inside me, she was safe. She was a part of me, and I, a part of her. She grew, kicked and moved, and was living the life I was sharing with her. I knew that being born would kill her and could not decide whether it should be now, or whether it should be later.

The decision to start labor was ours (I refused to say "terminate" the pregnancy, and would always say "induce labor"), but Stephen told me that ultimately he could not force me either way. I began to resent his decision. I wished it would be taken from me, that nature would take its course, or that Stephen would lay down the law either way. The head of the F.D.U. had told me that I would know our decision within a short time, but I didn't. All sorts of people who had no right to have an opinion shared it with us.

After many setbacks, I realized that my indecision was my decision. As soon as I decided to carry Roma to term, it was as if a great weight had been taken from me. My grief was constant, but the depression lifted. I was able to concentrate on the all important task of gathering memories. I began a diary and planned the birth. We wanted Sarah and Jeremy involved every step of the way and had to explain ourselves to concerned family members.

"Don't you realize that Sarah will never forget it?" my sister asked me when I told her that Sarah and Jeremy would come in to see Roma after she was born.

"That's the point," I said. Babies do not belong in coffins. Sarah and Jeremy deserved to know their sister and to say goodbye.

I had to laugh at a friend of mine who kept telling me how brave I was to carry Roma until full term. I kept saying that I wasn't, and he thought I was being modest. I was only doing this because I was so afraid: I didn't want her to die, and I was keeping her with me as long as I could.

I began to do a lot of reading. One of the books said that people would tell me things designed to comfort me, which actually downplayed the enormity of the loss. I read how these clichés often made the bereaved angry and resentful. I have never been one for resentment, so I took to saying, "Yes, but . . . ". It was important for me to tell people why I hurt and that the hurt was real and enormous, bigger than my belly.

"Don't forget, you are blessed to have another two children," someone would say.

"Yes, but I hurt for Roma," I would reply.

I also needed to tell my friends that I couldn't cling merely to the spiritual for comfort. The eternal nature of the human soul and of families is fundamental in my beliefs, but these beliefs don't ease the pain. I have always considered bearing children as perfect soul work: that is, the body combined with the spirit. Bearing children puts you in the position of creator, and harnesses the two together. Thinking about Roma's spirit and my spiritual bond to her at this time was only part of the equation. I needed to hold her, nurture her, breast feed her, smell her, and watch her grow. Being denied these things, I hurt with all of my being.

A week before Roma was due, I went to the bathroom and found I had a blood stained show. My heart pounding, I called Stephen. I cried, then was angry. I asked myself, *What did I expect? How much longer did I think I could go on?* I had to face the fact that I wasn't ready and never fully could have been.

Doctors examined me and found it was indeed time. One of my worst fears had to be realized. Fluid had swollen Roma's head so that she couldn't fit through the birth canal and had to be drained away. Everyone was concerned about me, and I was all but shouting that I didn't give a damn about myself, or whether I lived or died.

Details of the birth became hazy. The events blended into each other. Even in a case like this, the experience of the labor became routine. I was a little nervous during the birth, but surprised at my calm. But I could not escape the feeling that I was in a nightmare from which I could not escape. Roma kicked during labor, and whenever she did, I would touch my belly and smile. She was communicating. Our time together was fast running out.

I had an experience when I was dozing, which wasn't a dream. I had been thinking about Sarah and Jeremy when I suddenly felt a lovely warmth and heaviness on my chest, belly, and arms. It was just like Jeremy when he lies on top of my husband and me when we are on our backs. The heaviness actually took shape and felt substantial. The feeling had dimensions: I was being hugged. The hug was enormously comforting and very real. I just lay with my eyes closed and enjoyed it, smiling. Then I felt it ease, and as I opened my eyes, it was gone. After that, I didn't feel Roma kick again.

Soon, I felt pressure on my perineum and knew it was time to push. By now nerves and tears were no longer possible, just a grim determination. The labor was so quiet, but Stephen couldn't keep a note of excitement from his voice: his little girl was being born. But no lusty cries, no hustle and bustle. I told Stephen to take her, and I cried.

"Oh, my. My baby's gone, and I didn't even get to say goodbye!"

The medical staff was doing all sorts of things to me, and all I wanted to do was devote myself to Roma. I said to Stephen, "You hold her, darling. I've had her for nine months, now it's your turn."

He sat with her in his arms, weeping over her, kissing her. Such love and acceptance. Such hurt. Then he handed her to me, and I saw that he was right, she did look like my mother. I sang to her. I kissed her cheeks. Her hands were perfect: long fingered, delicate and elegant. Long feet! She would have been a tall girl.

Sarah and Jeremy came in and said, "Hi, Roma." Sarah asked if she could hold her, and sat and did so. "She's beautiful," she said. Jeremy didn't want to hold Roma, so we didn't make him. They were so sweetly innocent, so matter-of-fact, so loving in their simplicity. I treasure the memory of that time with them.

I let a nurse dress Roma for me, and as I watched, I noticed with quiet panic my growing numbness. It stole over me like a blanket, protecting me, but also isolating me from this child.

We buried Roma one week later, on a grey humid day, at a simple grave side service. We were surrounded by the people we loved best. When Stephen and his father lowered the coffin into the grave, a white butterfly flew out of the crevice and flitted away from sight.

After the funeral, Stephen and I felt an overwhelming need to be to-gether again: we craved the physical and emotional closeness. When we made love, it was as if I was being tapped into the core of my being. Every-thing came pouring out and wouldn't stop. It was so big, and came from so deep, and hurt so bad. Strangely, I felt thankful. Thankful that my heart was broken. Somehow I knew that only then could healing begin.

Healing was hard work. Every day without Roma seemed an eternity, yet the weeks flew by. I worried about people breaking into the house, not for stealing the television or stereo, but scattering our little box of cards, pressed flowers, and Roma's photographs, hand and foot prints, tufts of hair.

Certainly I have thought of Roma every day since becoming aware of her existence, and it's not scary or weird. I think of my living children also, three of them now, since Julian was born two years after her, as they are all a part of me. Sometimes the thought is fleeting, sometimes it lingers, and sometimes tears come.

What does a life mean? I don't know, but if one can measure it by the impact it's had rather than how long it was, then I know Roma's coming to us had a purpose. We have learned and grown. We are strong. Both of us, but Stephen in particular, has been blessed to be put in a position to be of help to others who have also lost babies. The quality of care we have given is only because of Roma. We have learned to look beyond the immediate concerns of everyday life. She left us with a great sense of grace and beauty, of sorrow and joy.

Roma was here.

Jeremy
by Ron Orendi

We were a young married couple, barely into our twenties. We had a four-year-old son and my wife was half way through her second pregnancy.

After dinner, one cold February night, we'd planned a night of watching television and playing with our son. Suddenly my wife began to experience gut wrenching pain. Something was definitely happening that was not right.

We called the hospital and threw together items she might need. She was in severe pain and bleeding. Our drive to the hospital seemed to take forever.

My parents met us at the Emergency Room. I watched as nurses and hospital staff placed her gently in a wheel chair. Within a few minutes a gurney was brought to my wife's side. The hospital employees huddled around her and hoisted her onto the clean white sheet.

At this point my hands were tied. My wife and baby's life were left in the care of both God and an experienced medical team. I paced the floor, trying to remain upbeat, but fearing the worst.

The staff gave me their viewpoint on her status. I was told that they felt my wife's "problem" was more mental than physical. However, upon further examination, the doctors determined my wife was in premature labor. I went into the room and saw my twenty-three year old wife laying there wracked in pain.

My wife sobbed knowing in her heart what such an early birth meant. I tried to be strong. I didn't want her to know how worried and scared I really was. She looked up at me and said, "The baby's coming. It's too soon!" I held her as gently as I could, trying not to bump the bed or put any of my weight on her.

The doctor came into the room and sat on the edge of the bed. In a very matter of fact voice, he told us, "The baby is coming. We're very busy tonight. You know this baby will only weigh about a pound? There's not much hope since its lungs aren't developed well enough to survive." Then looking into my face he said, "I need you to stay here with her. Call me when the labor pains get real close together." Then slowly he got up and left the room.

We were all alone. Just the two of us standing in the doorway between life and death. Looking around, I couldn't understand why a big city hospital known for its maternity care had no equipment in the room to prepare for my new baby's arrival. Although I am not a medical expert, I couldn't figure out why there was no respirator, no life support systems, no oxygen in the room. I thought hospitals and doctors were supposed to keep people alive no matter what. Yet there we were, just the two of us, a bed, a sink, and some basic labor room necessities.

Time seemed to pass very slowly. Looking back on the situation it seemed impossible that only ninety minutes had passed.

Suddenly, my wife's contractions came close together. Everything started to happen very quickly! My wife lay screaming in labor pain; I yelled for help. I yelled a second time for help. Still no response from the staff.

Looking down on the bed, I could see the baby's head crowning. At that point, I really didn't care if it was a boy or a girl, I just wanted everything to be all right. I yelled again. A nurse walking past the room heard me. She yelled in the room to us, "I'll get the doctor!" Her voice echoed in the hall, "Come quick, she's in delivery!"

Within seconds there were doctors, nurses, and medical staff all around my wife's bed. Remembering the routine from my first child's birth, I asked if we were going to the delivery room. In a rushed voice the doctor said,

"We can't tie up the delivery room for this case. The survival rate is low. Besides she's in delivery, it's too late."

I stood there, knowing that the lives of my wife and newborn were in their hands, hands that seemed to be more clinical than caring. Suddenly, I heard a baby cry. It was my newborn son! There he was wiggling and squirming. "My God," I whispered. "He's alive. He survived!"

I reached down to touch him. I wanted to feel the softness of his skin. One by one, medical personnel left the room until there was just the doctor, my son, my wife and I.

"He's alive," I said with a beaming grin. The doctor doused my joy instantly when he said, "Only until I cut the cord. He's living off his mother right now. By law, I have to cut the cord. All the kicking and moving will stop."

I held my newborn son, basking in his earthly arrival, as the doctor continued about his work. I faintly heard a cutting sound. I didn't want to look, to see what the doctor was doing. I didn't want the reality of what was happening to take over. Subconsciously, I knew what was about to happen.

Instantly, our son stopped moving. Tears began to flow from my eyes. I lost all control of my emotions. I sobbed as I looked down at my newborn son, now lifeless in my arms. My mind raced with questions. *Isn't there something that could be done? Isn't there some medical technique that could save my son?*

From across the room, I saw the doctor scrubbing his hands and arms at the sink. He turned and looked back toward me. We made eye contact. "Oh, I almost forgot," he said, "did you want the baby baptized?" My wife, in her exhausted state said, "Yes."

From about six or eight feet away, the doctor splashed some water in the baby's direction. "There, he's baptized," he said in a sarcastic voice. My mouth fell to the floor. There we were still holding on to our newly deceased baby, and this man made a mockery of our religion.

A nurse entered the room and took the baby from my arms. She informed me that I would need to make the proper arrangements with a funeral director. I kissed my wife telling her that I loved her. Then, I slowly walked out of the room. When I reached the reception area, I wept uncontrollably. I was filled with anger. I was angry at the doctors. Angry at the nurses. Angry at myself. And even angry at God! *How could he let this happen to a little child?*

I pounded the wall in the hallway in frustration. I didn't know what to do. My mom and dad came over to me. At no time in my life while growing up can I ever remember needing them more than I did then.

Thankfully they were there, offering their support, their love. Although we really didn't speak that much, it felt good to have them there. They didn't need to say a word.

We had a small private burial, just the funeral director, my wife and I. There was no viewing. It was just the three of us and the small box.

Mentally, I don't think there is anything that can prepare one for that experience. Death is tough to deal with in the first place. However, the death of a child takes that difficulty to the nth degree.

On that cold February night back in 1981, I didn't have answers to why things happened the way they did. But now, after looking at the whole picture, I've found some benefits. Losing Jeremy not only brought us closer together, but my wife and I have been able to share our experience and comfort many other people who have had to deal with the loss of a loved one.

Am I still angry? I'd be lying if I said no. But there are times I use the loss of Jeremy to help myself to carry on. There is always someone that needs me to be there for them.

Will I ever get over the sadness that rests in my heart? I don't know. I do know that along with those few moments of his life, Jeremy made me beam with joy. He made me a proud father, just like my other two children have. Even though he's gone on to heaven, I can still love him!

I Never Heard Him Cry
by Wanda Denson

The familiar scents I'd come to associate with healing surrounded me—green soap, rubbing alcohol, and disinfectant. As the hospital staff transferred me to a stretcher, I was vaguely aware of my husband's frantic voice answering the clerk's questions. The staff rushed me through the emergency entrance doors. I'd been through those doors many times as a member of the nursing staff but never entered as a patient.

Each pregnancy had gone smoothly until now. This baby, not due for another month, was to be our third.

The day had started like any other. Our two little boys were playing in the yard as I did the daily chores around the house. But by early afternoon I began to feel weak. My hands were clammy. Blaming this on the sultry August weather, I stopped for a glass of iced tea.

When my abdomen began to ache, I still wasn't concerned. But when I stood to go check on the boys, I became lightheaded and severe abdominal pain gripped me. Suddenly I realized the baby who had been so active recently had not moved in the past hour. Something was wrong.

My husband reached home minutes after receiving my phone call. He called my obstetrician, then he called a friend to come get our boys. Soon we were at the clinic. After examining me, Doctor Bill called the hospital and arranged for a surgeon to perform an emergency Caesarean section. Moments later we were speeding toward the hospital.

As I lay in the emergency room, I went over the implications of his diagnosis in my mind. Soon Doctor Bill came in to explain what had happened and what course the medical team would take. I tried to follow what he was saying but was engulfed by pain and thirst. The nurse gave me an ice chip; I couldn't have water before going into surgery.

They were waiting for blood to arrive for my transfusions. Doctor Bill said, "If they don't get here soon, I'll give blood; my type is the same as hers." I was deeply touched by his concern. I knew my life was at risk as time lapsed. The wait seemed endless as my abdomen grew more rigid and the pain increased. I longed to be in surgery and rid of the pain. Finally I was taken to surgery and I prayed our baby would survive. I felt relief and peace. The anesthesiologist told me to begin counting backward from one hundred. I began, "One hundred, ninety-nine, ninety-eight, ninety-seven . . . "

I woke in a private room with my husband and parents beside my bed. My husband's stricken expression filled me with dread. I closed my eyes, hoping to delay what I knew he was about to tell me.

"I'm sorry," he said, "we lost the baby, a little boy." Trying desperately not to feel, not to think, I didn't move or speak.

Then Doctor Bill came in and explained that the placenta had separated from the uterine wall, cutting off the baby's oxygen supply. "It's a rare occurrence, happening in only one in a thousand births, and it couldn't have been prevented." After he left, I welcomed the oblivion of sleep.

During the night I woke with tears streaming down my face. My first thought was, *I never heard him cry!* I felt imprisoned by the IV tubes in both arms and by my weakened body. These circumstances would prevent me from attending my own baby's funeral. I wouldn't get to choose the clothes baby Tad would be buried in. Then my thoughts turned to our other two sons. *How confused and frightened they must be.*

In the morning, a nurse came in carrying the basket that held our baby. Anxiety washed over me. Would I go to pieces when I saw Tad for the first and last time? Bracing myself, I peered into the basket. He lay as though asleep, his plump little body forever still. He looked so healthy; how could he be dead? I strained to focus on every detail of Tad's face and body. Knowing this would be the last time I'd see him, I had to make the memory indelible.

The next morning, I watched the clock move toward 10:30, the time set for the service. I was filled with overwhelming guilt. My baby was about to be buried, and I, his mother, would not be there. My own mother sat quietly by my bed, permitting me to mourn in silence.

Later the same day a friend gave me a poem about the death of a child and his being sheltered by God until some future reunion. After reading it, I felt peace and absolute assurance that Tad was in the fields of God and someday there would be a reunion.

For now, I had to get well and go home to my two precious sons. The healing had begun.

Resolving Grief On The Road To Happiness: Subsequent Pregnancy After The Death Of A Baby by Mary E. Kuenzig

At first, I could not even believe I might be pregnant again. Before I became pregnant with our first son Carl, my husband Mark and I had tried for several years to have a baby. We went through many medical procedures to help my infertility condition, procedures that were both expensive and very painful. Thinking I might be pregnant so soon after Carl's premature birth and death twenty-one hours later felt like an obscene curse. After all, we were still grieving.

Even taking the pregnancy test was difficult for me. I couldn't bear to take it alone. I brought the test kit home and insisted that Mark actually do it. We were together when we read the positive results. Strangely enough, this happened exactly one year to the day after the test I'd done by myself. The coincidence made me very uneasy.

The blood test that was taken at my doctor's office was also exactly a year to the day after the one done earlier at the hospital—another coincidence. I couldn't help but wonder whether this entire pregnancy would mirror the first one or if these similarities were signs from God that things would be okay.

The heightened concern Mark and I had about this pregnancy put stress on our marriage, especially when sexual activity was not permitted.

Another stress was the weekly doctor visits, not only because of the physical risk, but because the nursing staff at my doctor's office wasn't accustomed to giving such special treatment. I became my own "case manager", taking a more active role in my care. I imagine some of the nurses thought I was being a pushy patient, but after the loss of Carl it didn't matter to me what other people thought.

The doctors decided that more frequent ultrasounds should be performed during this pregnancy which they looked at more closely. Every time we were able to see the heart still beating, we were comforted. We even insisted on a videotape of the ultrasound exams. I found myself clinging to these videotapes as the only proof of my baby's health and existence. How I wished I had a videotape from Carl's ultrasounds.

The months passed and I allowed myself to "be pregnant" at home where I felt safe, but not pregnant while we were out in public or at work. Sometimes I felt guilty about acting this way, like I was denying the existence of this second child. I don't understand this guilt except to say that I did what I had to do to cope with the pressures.

For the same reason, Mark and I did not tell our families about our second pregnancy. Neither of our families were as supportive as I hoped or wanted them to be after the death of Carl. They seemed to get over his death very quickly, too quickly as far as I was concerned.

I felt that it was my responsibility, in honor of our first son, to keep this second pregnancy a secret at least until the one year anniversary of Carl's death had passed. That seemed the very least we could do to honor his memory.

After the anniversary passed, we began to tell our families about this current pregnancy. No one understood why we weren't jumping up and down with excitement, nor why we weren't decorating the nursery.

We didn't set up a nursery until the last two weeks. If the baby had come early, we figured he could sleep in a padded dresser drawer and borrow clothes if necessary. To do otherwise would have been too painful if this baby did not survive either.

Our doctors were concerned that in the last few ultrasound exams only two blood vessels seemed to be present in the umbilical cord. Of course, this just gave Mark and me another reason to worry more.

Our families' excitement did not even mellow when they heard this piece of news, but Mark and I were terrified, to put it mildly. We had met many couples through the infant loss support group we were attending who experienced subsequent losses, and we kept reminding ourselves that the same thing could happen to us. Even though another loss was almost unspeakable, we had to be realistic.

My mother-in-law sent us a video for expectant mothers, which depicted how you should begin to nurture the unborn infant during the nine months of pregnancy. The mother should talk, play with, and sing to her baby as if it was already in her arms. She should keep a positive attitude and have happy emotions throughout the term. The video proclaimed that when a person is feeling happy emotions their body releases positive endorphins which impact the well-being of the fetus in utero and that both positive and negative emotions on the part of the mother pass through to the fetus via these endorphins. Watching the video made me feel terrible. I had been pretending to the outside world that I was not pregnant. I had been terrified for months. There was no way I could sing to and joyfully poke around my abdomen to play with my baby.

What was meant as a very thoughtful gift had me in hysterical tears. I only watched this video once. The thought of my paranoia and emotional fears actually doing possible harm to my second child was more than I could bear. Frankly, I just couldn't wait to get it out of my house. I have a fairly good relationship with my in-laws, but I never told them how hurt I felt about this incident because I didn't think they would understand.

Although we wouldn't have had it any other way, all the extra precautions and secrecy took their toll. I found myself actually jealous of other pregnant women who were openly telling everyone of their news. I was not willing to make myself vulnerable to those feelings again.

A Caesarean birth was scheduled two weeks prior to my calculated due date as a result of the previous vertical uterine incision. Because of this there was a slightly decreased risk of cord strangulation or related accident in utero and during delivery. We liked the decreased risk because during the last few months we had heard many sad stories of perfect pregnancies going to term only to have the baby strangled at the last minute or before labor even got started.

About a month before the delivery was scheduled, an ultrasound confirmed that this child was a boy. My heart sank. When I was pregnant for the first time, I secretly wished for a boy while my husband thought he would prefer a girl. After our first son was born and died, I blamed myself for his death. It was as if I had wished for a boy so hard that God gave him to me and then quickly whisked him away again as a lesson to me. I was afraid that I would mentally use this second boy to replace Carl.

Selecting a name for our second son was very difficult. Part of me wanted to use our first child's name as our second child's middle name. I never would use it as a first name again—I just thought that reusing it for a middle name would be a nice tribute to Carl. When our second son grew up and asked why we selected his name, we could say his middle name was chosen in honor of his older brother who would always be watching over him from heaven. I wanted our second son to carry Carl's name with him so that he would never forget that he had a big brother because I was, and still am, determined not to let our families forget about our first son.

Mark would not hear of using any part of Carl's name for our second son. He would not even allow me to reuse the same initials or even to discuss the possibility, and so the matter ended. I still thought it would have made a nice tribute, but it just wasn't worth fighting about or causing hard feelings. We decided on the name Adam.

Two weeks before the scheduled Caesarean, we spoke with a pediatrician and told him about our prior loss experience and also about the possibility of only two vessels in the umbilical cord. At first I think he was surprised that Mark and I had prepared so many detailed questions for him, but after telling him about Carl's death he was very understanding and answered all of our questions.

I also told the pediatrician my fears about Sudden Infant Death Syndrome. We were paranoid that after a healthy pregnancy and delivery we might still lose our baby to SIDS. For that reason I wanted to put the new baby on a breathing monitor from the very beginning. We told the doctor that we didn't care if our insurance paid for this service or not because it was too important to us. The pediatrician told us to think about it some more because babies frequently have unsteady breathing patterns which are perfectly normal for them, differing from child to child. A monitor could go off more times than needed and make us even more paranoid, as if that could be possible. After thinking the matter over for a while, we finally opted not to use a breathing monitor. That decision did not stop Mark and me from checking in on the baby frequently while he was sleeping. Even though Adam is eleven months old now, we still frequently check on him when he is asleep.

There were many times when I was afraid to go into the baby's room by myself to check on him. I insisted that Mark do it or that he go with me. I think I was just afraid I would find that Adam had stopped breathing and I would blame myself. The feeling still crops up once in a while for me. It's a hard one for me to shake.

Keeping the date of the Caesarean delivery a secret was at my insistence. It was not because we wanted to have an element of surprise. I was already so nervous and fearful about the outcome that I didn't need anyone else around me in the same condition. Having my mother or my in-laws around would have made me even more nervous. Mark and I wanted to get through the delivery together as privately and calmly as possible.

Some people did not understand our decision not to tell family and friends the scheduled date, but as I've said before, we did what we felt we had to do to cope. Our pastor once said, "What other people think of you is really none of your business."

After the delivery, when Mark and I knew that Adam was healthy, we did telephone family and friends. They may have been perturbed that we had not told them ahead of time, but they quickly got over it with the excitement of a healthy new baby. We might use the same tactic if I am ever pregnant again because it worked well for our situation.

I had a very dear friend who was an OB nurse in our hospital at the time. She gave us the greatest favor that anyone could by thoroughly informing the staff members of our loss and our bad experiences. I never had to explain to any of the staff members what I felt and why. Everyone was completely sympathetic and understanding during our entire five day stay. I wish all other couples who have experienced a prior loss could be so fortunate in their subsequent hospital care experiences. It meant a great deal to my well-being. Her gift was the most wonderful anyone gave us!

During the first few days in the hospital when the nurses brought Adam to me, I was perfectly content to watch Mark or someone else hold the baby, but I was terrified to hold him myself. He looked exactly like Carl. That shouldn't have come as a surprise to me, but it did. I was really startled to see such a resemblance. I was afraid to hold Adam, afraid that I might contaminate him or jinx him. I tried to work through these feelings quietly, never verbalizing them, not even to Mark. I wanted Mark or a nurse to be there with me at all times when I held the baby. I was so afraid of doing something harmful. I realize now that such fear is common in subsequent pregnancies.

In the hospital during those first five days and then for weeks afterward, I found myself calling the new baby Carl by mistake. I would cry and cry every time this happened. We hadn't had much time with Carl in our lives so I didn't understand why his name kept coming to my lips.

Mark was very understanding about this idiosyncrasy which he thought was actually a good experience. He felt that it reinforced the fact that our first son had really existed, was real to us, and that we still remembered him clearly. However, the first time the tables were turned and Mark called our new baby Carl by mistake, his face became as white as a sheet. He was really shocked. He finally understood how I had been feeling.

When Adam was born I had to decide whether or not to return to work. If I quit work and then something happened to Adam, I was afraid I would regret my decision and would not be able to return to my workplace at the same salary and job level. On the other hand, we had gone through so much to have this healthy child. How on earth could I possibly rely on someone else to take care of him? In the end I decided to take the plunge and quit my job. Now that our healthy boy is here, it is very hard to leave him even for a short period of time with a babysitter. We are still working through this problem, slowly but surely.

Mark and I faced another dilemma when we would take Adam out with us. People would come up to us and ask if this was our first child. If we said no, they expected to hear how old the other children were. We discovered that they really didn't want to hear the true story. Some people thought it too morbid or depressing for them to hear with this new, cute little bundle of joy around to talk about. If we answered the question yes, we felt guilty for somehow denying the existence of Carl. If it was just a stranger asking, the true story probably didn't matter to them. In similar situations, I have trained myself to say that this baby is our first living child. Sometimes it has helped people who have also had a loss to open up and share a similar experience.

As I said, Adam is now eleven months old. When he and I have a bad or frustrating day together or I get angry or impatient with him, I chastise myself. I feel like maybe our first baby was really the lucky one to have died so that he wouldn't have to endure my impatience.

When Adam is sick, Mark and I get very fearful. We immediately think the worst, like a fever will cause him brain damage. My husband and I have been so uptight when Adam is sick that we have had the worst fights of our whole marriage, screaming at each other. It's scary when someone so precious to us becomes sick and we don't know how to help him.

Mark and I attended our monthly infant loss support group meeting throughout our second pregnancy. While I was pregnant, I concealed my physical size and didn't talk about the pregnancy to any of the other people there, for fear it would make them feel worse. Attending the group while I was pregnant was a strange feeling, reminding us of how fragile this pregnancy was and that no matter how closely we guarded this pregnancy, the outcome was still out of our control.

Many times I wished there was a support group for people like us— parents who had lost a baby but were now pregnant again. We had so many mixed feelings throughout the pregnancy that some days I didn't know whether to smile or cry, and having a support system would have helped me.

Now that Adam is with us, I still attend the support group meetings as often as I can. Usually Mark stays home with Adam so that I can attend. Some people ask me why I still need or want to go to these meetings. I go because it really is the only place where I am allowed to talk about Carl, to wonder what life would be like now if we had both little boys with us. It is the one time each month when I can grieve for Carl as I need and want to.

I also continue to go to the support group because my past experiences might help someone else. Often I learn something from hearing other people relay their own heartbreaking stories. Sometimes it helps me to put things in perspective, forcing me to realize I'm on the road to resolving my grief. Most importantly, I am reminded that although our loss was devastating, others have had more tragic experiences than ours.

Cardboard Boxes
by Adele DelSavio

This piece was originally published in the Oswego, NY Palladium-Times.

A seventeen year old does not leave much behind in the way of possessions. After our son Mike died we packed his things away to sort out later: some stereo equipment, a few bags of clothes, and five cardboard boxes.

The cardboard boxes held what probably would be called his "personal effects". These were the flotsam and jetsam of his life that were valueless in themselves but priceless to those who cared about him.

The clothes and stereo equipment were easy enough to deal with. The stereo equipment stayed in the house, and the clothes either went to family members, were donated, or were packed away again to be saved.

But those boxes.

When we'd emptied Mike's desk and gathered the "stuff" that seemed to be all over the room, I was still in a haze of grief. Handling the things that he'd used just days before made his death seem impossible. Going through his desk felt like invading his privacy. The things in the boxes were too emotionally charged. Going through them would have to wait.

As the months passed I made tentative dips into the boxes, sometimes months apart. I tried sorting things by categories: school papers, mementos, knickknacks, football papers, newspaper clippings, notes, photographs, school supplies, junk, and so forth. But I couldn't sort without pausing over each item, reading notes, delving into the pictures, and savoring each item.

Had Mike lived, he probably would have eventually tossed half this stuff into the trash. Now, though, each broken pencil and each scrap of paper was precious, a connection to him. After a few half-hearted sorting attempts, Mike's things ended up back in the boxes.

Next I began to take things at random from the boxes, spent time with each item, and put them into another box. This was slow going too, but I was making progress. The past blended into the present.

Among all of Mike's things, most special were the folder he had tossed on the back seat of the car after school on Friday, which was still there the next morning when he died, and his wallet. Both provided a freeze-frame of Mike's life as it was at its end. They held his driver's license, school ID cards, and the assignments he wouldn't live to complete.

Twenty months after Mike's death, I have one more box to go. Like his clothes, some of his things are getting new life by being put into family use. We write with his pens and use his glue and paper clips. Each of us has chosen mementos as well, and the rest of his things are stored.

Was dealing with Mike's boxes emotionally draining? Yes. Was it necessary? Yes. When that last box is packed away, a little bit of the pain of losing Mike will go with it.

Fall Out
by Nancy Dubuc

Thursday, September 16, 1993, while at an evening work meeting, I received a phone call that is still changing my life. My husband said, "Come home, Michelle has been killed."

In my shock and disbelief, I responded, "You're kidding."

The hurt reply came to my ear, "I wouldn't kid about that."

Calmly I said, "I'll be there as soon as I can." Gently, I hung up the phone, took three steps, fell to my knees, and put my head in the lap of our program's infant teacher, my friend.

All I could say as I sobbed and gulped for air was, "My baby's dead. My baby's dead." I heard soft words of comfort near my ears, and in the background I heard many saying, "Oh my God." I am not at all sure how long this took place, but suddenly I had an immense urge to smash.

I said in a moderate tone, "I need to smash something."

"What did she say?"

Someone behind me said, "She needs to smash something."

Louder and firmer I said, "I need to smash something."

"I know," I heard, and a twenty-pound bag of clay was on the floor before me. I made a fist and pounded it with every bit of strength I had. The lines between my clenched fingers left line upon line in the clay. A strange voice which I began to realize was mine kept softly yelling, "No. No. No. Not my baby." As quickly as it began, it ended. I rose and said, "I must go home. They need me at home." Someone drove me.

When I arrived, I hugged and comforted my husband, my son-in-law's mother, and my grandchildren. A little later that evening, I held my son-in-law tightly and told him how much my daughter loved him and how happy he had made her. I felt a strength I had not felt since giving birth.

In the fog of the days that followed, I listened to the streams of people who came to comfort me. I wrote a poem for her eulogy and attended the funeral and memorial service holding my power pouch of polished stones in my hand to ground myself. At the memorial feast, I ate robustly after four days of scarcely eating. I told people of their importance in my daughter's life and how they influenced who she had become.

During the next two-and-a-half weeks, I made list after list and did each task in its order, top to bottom. Some small, and some taking guts and grit. I could not go to my daughter's home and remove her belongings, but I could see that they were packed into a room until they would be dispersed. The room took on the smell of her perfume.

Since my husband was unemployed and had no income, I returned to work. Days became months as I threw myself into work, and caring for my grandchildren before work, and sharing my grief with a wide circle of friends.

For close to a year and a half, sleep was not normal. I used the insomnia and disrupted sleep as opportunities to cry in private or to write and draw.

Attending church, which had been a weekly ritual, became more difficult. I frequently wept in silence, then went to hide briefly in the bathroom until I was composed. I wrestled with feeling as if the religious platitudes had become too sugary to have meaning in my painful place. I was angry with God and would mentally shout, *You got my first born. I have paid my dues. I owe you nothing else.* Little did I know at the time that I was just beginning to deal with payment.

The day after we buried Michelle, my husband disconnected. He busied himself with classes, church grief group meetings, gym workouts, frequent visits with cronies, and every other possible distraction. Within four months he was hospitalized for the first of three severe asthma attacks. He was emotionally unavailable to anyone. He spent less and less time helping with the household. When bills needed to be paid, he left them on the dining room table and told me they needed to go out that day. Any money he had was spent on himself and his personal desires.

By the time six months had past, my husband was working a short-term contract and began to talk about feeling the need to separate. He wanted to go away to decide if we would continue our marriage. He spent one week away at his aunt's home and every three months for the next year the subject of separation would resurface. Two years and two months after our daughter died, he found a job out of state five to six days a week. After one month of hearing him talk about how he could love another woman, how he could financially recover if he lost everything, and how he had no time for a personal life, I asked for a separation. Just six weeks later he countered by telling me he was getting a divorce. This was just four days before our thirty-second wedding anniversary.

Now seven months into the divorce litigation, I find myself repeating my process. I watch the three-month marks come and go. Now when I cry, I know the crying will get shorter in duration and less intense. There are days when I think I may not stop crying, but now I cry for Michelle on important days. I have begun to be comfortable with my son-in-law's new girlfriend, though it was very upsetting at first. Even though I hurt for my losses, I struggle to keep connected and loving towards that which I still have.

I am not finished, but I have an idea of what completion may look like. When it all looks like too much to deal with, I insist my mind concentrate on what is immediately before me. When I am asked, "Can you . . . ?", I say yes, unless I am not feeling like a yes. When I wrote my daughter's eulogy three years ago, I realized she had done more in twenty-five years and ten days than some do in twice the time. I will honor her lesson by fighting to live with passion even if that means being sad for a little while. I am becoming stronger wherever I am on the emotional continuum. Joy is fleeting but I can see it once again.

Released
by Lilamae Mueller

I lost my son at thirty-one years. I still can't believe that he is gone. He is never coming back. I prayed for him to be released from his pain and suffering, but I couldn't grasp that this meant forever.

At the moment of his death there was a profound grief and an overwhelming relief. I had been through so much trying to sustain his life, searching for hope, and helping him in every way humanly possible to comfort him on his journey.

It is not supposed to happen this way. It is out of the natural order of things. He was taken from us too soon. Was this as long as his life was to be? Who decides? It isn't fair. I feel cheated that I won't see his life unfold. There will be no carrying on of the family name.

As every mother feels at peace when she finds that her child is safe after a trip, or feels the warm relief when she hears the car returning after a late date night, I yearn to have some tangible assurance that Michael is all right after his journey. Just an "I'm OK, Mom!" would help so much to take away this terrible heartache.

Sometimes I wonder if it would be easier to live someplace where we had not shared so much of life together. Memories that are supposed to some day make me glad make everyday living difficult. My every turn reminds me of him; someplace we went, something we did, something he thought and talked about, something he loved.

I had often heard of people who had such a sense of regret when a loved person died. During Michael's three-year illness I was determined not to let that happen to me. I did everything I could to ease the suffering and to bring some joy to him. This time Mom couldn't fix it or make it better and that gives me great remorse, but not with a sense of guilt that I could have somehow done more.

I find myself experiencing such heartache when others tell of their son's lives. I hope that my responses somehow mask the pain I'm feeling. I do want to know of their children's progress, and I do not want to diminish their delight and joy. Life does go on, but will I ever be able to let go of the heaviness and sadness I feel?

The phone doesn't ring as much any more. Michael and I would talk two or three times daily. Even though the calls were often of discouragement and dreams of a better day, I loved talking to him and encouraging him. I have a tape that he had made a few years ago of a birthday message to his grandmother when she turned ninety. I can not bring myself to play it yet, even though I yearn to hear his voice.

I have always known that the main outlet of grief for me is through tears, but I never dreamed that it would be so effusive and triggered by so many things. It is often embarrassing. Once when I was in a grocery store a few days after Michael's death, every aisle reminded me of food he liked or some food I got to encourage him to eat near the end. I had to abandon the cart and rush from the store.

My gardens, all planned and developed by Michael, should serve as wonderful memories of him and his love of nature and flowers, but I can't visualize it that way yet. He loved the newness of spring. Maybe these gardens will bring me joy and solace someday, but not yet. They are just daily reminders of how very much I miss him. Maybe next year. The grief is all too new and the wounds too deep. Healing will come, I am told, along with my freedom and a return of joy.

CHAPTER 3

THE DEATH OF PARENTS

Adults discuss what it means to lose a parent by offering
their journeys, their feelings of loss of connection, and
the value of holding onto memories.

That Was My Job
by William L. Phelps

Cancer. What the insurance companies call a dread disease. Treatment
is expensive, painful, and not at all certain. *Oh God! Not my Dad. No.* Those
thoughts ran through my head like a juggernaut. I collected myself enough to
reassure my mother when she called me on February 7th.

My life was toast. I was just finishing a messy divorce. After taking the
red-eye into La Guardia Airport and a two hour layover, I was at T. F. Green
Airport. Welcome to Warwick, gateway to Rhode Island. So, I was home.
After twenty years in the Air Force, broke and divorced at forty I was going
back to my old room. A concept I just couldn't get behind. But my mom
needed help. There were hospital visits, doctor's appointments, general repairs and puttering around the property. That was my job.

Mom was busy putting the best face on things. My father knew he was
sinking. He was a gentle and practical soul, the product of his Pentecostal
mother, Helen, and Lee, his bootlegging father.

Born in 1930 and raised during the hard times that never really left rural
Kentucky, he learned to do what had to be done. Patch-up, fix-up and make-do

a while longer. Share abundance with those who have need. God will provide, never beg from want.

I was putting a patch on the mortar holding the field stones in the wall that bordered the driveway when my father came out of the house. It was early March, nippy and raw. The recent round of chemotherapy hadn't been kind to him. "Dad, you shouldn't be out here. That's all you need to do is catch cold."

"I want to talk."

"I can come inside in a few minutes."

"No, I need to talk now. What do you think my chances are? Really."

We had gone to the oncologist just that morning. The tumors were growing and spreading. The doctor had given him the last advice possible. The tumors weren't reacting to the chemo. He could try another couple of rounds, or discontinue; it was up to him. Don't worry about taking too many pills, just medicate for comfort. The death sentence pronounced in modern clinicalese. "Well, you have cancer and you're sixty-two years old. You know the chemo isn't working," I said. There was a look I had never seen in his eyes before. Resignation and a profound sadness that seemed to come from his soul.

"How long do you think I have?" he asked leaning back, soaking-up whatever warmth was offered by the sun.

"If you somehow get through this, and you stay clean for five years, you'll die of old age. How much do you want to live?"

"I don't know."

"Mom, Barbara?" I was going to be fine and he knew it. A southern man will go to extraordinary lengths to protect the womenfolk.

"Mom'll be fine. Your sister is married."

"Then for yourself, what you want to do. Find a reason, if you have to." I wanted him to live to retire after working most of his life. Retirement would mean that he could finally take the train trip he'd been putting off for over twenty years. We could hear the train horn. The old country boy's eyes were far away. To him, the sight and sound of that iron horse always meant freedom from the hills. I wanted him to be around.

Now I was angry, upset because I'd put off coming home. There was a void where we hadn't shared anything really. It had gone too far, and I was too late.

"Think it's just too late, boy."

A little over a month later he developed that last tumor. It was on his pancreas. He died of what was probably anaphylactic shock on May 3rd. The last intelligible thing he said was, "Hi baby . . . " when my sister visited him in his hospital room the day she arrived from Wyoming. I closed his eyes; that was my job: some things can't be left to strangers.

Shock and disbelief marked the funeral arrangements. We chose a coffin as if we were in a furniture store picking out a new couch for the living room. It had to be comfortable so Dad would nap while watching television. The funeral director smiled knowingly and did his best not to laugh. My mother chose the funeral home because it was right next to the factory where she and my father had worked for many years. Friends wouldn't have to go too far.

Contracts, assignment of social security burial benefit to the Veteran's Cemetery, and other goodies had to be taken care of. The fact of death isn't "official" until you see the notice in the newspaper. Death certificates have to be produced in the appropriate number of copies for insurance companies, VA Cemetery, banks, and the Navy.

Death is never untimely, no matter what anyone thinks. Man proposes and God disposes. He has written the fate of every man on his forehead. I mourned then. I mourn still.

My father wasn't a signed-up, card carrying member of any church. So we asked the hospital chaplain to do the honors. The eulogy was conducted at the funeral home and the rite of internment at the Veteran's Cemetery in Exeter. Afterwards the chaplain visited and listened to us as we reminisced about dandelions, lawn mowers, flower beds, and critters.

In this modern world, where a man is measured by the gold he leaves, he was a modest man. My father left little treasure that man might steal or corruption consume. He did leave a peaceable kingdom of sorts. The backyard was a place where many small animals lived and never came to harm. A man of simple wants and needs who never knowingly harmed another living creature had made it so.

While he is physically gone, what Leo M. Phelps wasn't in that box in the ground in Exeter, Rhode Island. His gentle legacy of love and respect live through my sister and myself. So long as his memory is alive, a man is never truly dead.

Deep Breaths
by Jacqueline M. Honoré

"Hold a finger over your right nostril and first breathe out. Next, take several short, slow breaths in for as long as you can. Then take even more short, slow breaths out. Switch nostrils and repeat. Remember . . . we must always thank Mother Earth for giving us air, the key to life, by giving back to Her more air than we take."

Well, sometimes we cannot give back more than we take, I recently reflected, while following a Hatha Yoga lesson on TV.

Sometimes we must gulp all the air we can, in spite of Mother Earth.

Like the time my first pet goldfish, Penelope, seemed to turn purple while slowly moving her mouth up and down for dear life, making small bubbles at the top of my little fish bowl. For months afterwards, I couldn't shake the image of Penelope's mouth moving up and down, frantically fighting for that one last deep breath.

Sometimes we must gasp all the air we can, in spite of Mother Earth.

Like the time I suffered my first asthma attack two years later, at age six. During this attack, breathing became a luxury, a struggle to shove a few wisps of air into lungs that behaved like collapsed balloons.

"Am I gonna die like Penelope?" I asked my mother between painful gasps.

"Hush, child, and continue to breathe deeply," Mommy exclaimed. "This discomfort you're feeling is merely temporary. In just a little while you'll be back to your normal self. I promise."

Still the fear that the next asthmatic episode might be my last persisted . . . until I finally outgrew my asthma in my early twenties. Then, like a doubting Thomas, I knew for sure Mommy had been right (as mothers usually are).

Sometimes we must heave all the air we can, in spite of Mother Earth.

Like after the time Mommy discovered some bad news that would change her life . . . and mine. Forever.

Mommy saw me sitting in an awkward, half-lotus position in front of the den TV, attempting classical breaths, like a good Hatha yogi.

"What on earth are you doing?" Mommy asked, taking a small whiff of the burning sage incense as she sat down next to me.

"Practicing my breathing," I said.

"Oh," she mumbled. "Well . . . I don't think I'll ever be able to breathe like that," she replied, with a grin that only accentuated her melancholy.

"Of course you can, Mommy. While I'm here for the holidays I'll show you how. Let's practice together right now."

Mommy stared at the TV for a few minutes, but made no attempt to follow along. "You don't understand. I should have told you earlier . . . and I hate to tell you now, but . . . "

"But what?" I interrupted, as I put both hands and feet on the Oriental rug and arched my back up and down like a cat.

"You remember when I was coughing up blood while we were visiting Mother in New Orleans this summer?"

"Yes," I replied. "But I thought you told me you saw Dr. Bautista a month ago and everything checked out."

"Well, at the time I called you Dr. Bautista was still conducting tests, so I didn't want to worry you. But now you really should know . . . " Mommy stopped talking and resumed staring at the Hatha yoga instructor.

"Would you stop beating around the bush and please tell me," I grumbled.

"Okay, okay." Mommy sighed, then announced, "I have an inoperable form of lung cancer. So there."

"Lung cancer?" I gasped and collapsed on my stomach, before sitting up to face her. "That can't be. You've never smoked in your life. In fact, you've rarely been sick in your life."

"Yes, well, that's what I told Dr. Bautista." Mommy stopped to catch her breath. "I'm afraid it means breathing's going to become more and more difficult."

"Like it was for me when I had my asthma?" I blurted.

"Well I'm afraid it'll probably get worse than that," Mommy muttered. "But I'm expecting a miracle, God willing."

Perhaps the real miracle was that Mommy lived almost a year after over a pint of fluid was found in each lung.

However, even during chronic, life-threatening situations old habits can be hard to break. And Mommy appeared to be doing just about everything wrong. WRONG. WRONG. WRONG. WRONG. WRONG.

"You must promise me you won't call Dr. Bautista up again and give her a hard time," Mommy insisted during a phone conversation.

"I hardly think questioning her about your treatment is giving her a hard time," I snapped. "How will I ever find out what's really going on, given that I live four hundred miles away?"

"Dr. Bautista's a good doctor and a good Christian. I trust her. She'll help me do what's best. Your sister can keep you informed. She lives right here, you know."

"She's never at home when I call. Besides, you know Patricia and I don't get along."

"Yes, well I think it's simply disgraceful my only children are always at each other's throats," Mommy groaned. "So it would be a bigger help to me if you tried to improve your relationship.

Mommy's treatments, such as they were, didn't seem to be working. Just a series of low-dose chemotherapy sessions that contributed to gradual weight and hair loss, but only negligible remission. Which explained why several bottles of the same painkiller prescribed by Dr. Bautista and two other specialists cluttered Mommy's medicine cabinet. (I mean, were these doctors trying to help her commit suicide, or what?)

"Why don't you try a macrobiotic diet and avoid all these meats, sweets, and salty snacks?" I pleaded, during one of my frequent visits.

"That's all right. Like I keep telling you, Dr. Bautista said that kind of diet will make me too weak and cause me to lose too much weight. She suggested I should eat whatever I have an appetite for. She did say, however, there wasn't any harm in taking the vitamins you suggested in moderate doses and drinking Red Clover tea. See, my dear, she isn't against all your suggestions."

No, just the ones she thinks won't do any good, I thought. "Well, don't you think you should at least ask Paul to stop smoking in your house when he comes to visit? That's not good for your condition."

"Why I'll suggest no such thing. Paul has been so supportive . . . and besides, he usually smokes in another room."

Mommy fought to catch her breath as she reclined in her leather rocking chair and propped up her feet. "Now, I know you mean well, but you can't expect me to adopt your vegetarian diet. The meals Patricia makes for me are working out quite well, thank you. Unlike you, I like to eat meat.

Mother raised us on Southern cooking and look how old she is now . . . nearly ninety. And Daddy lived to be ninety-two."

Neither of them had lung cancer, I wanted to say, but didn't. "I know Mommy, but the meats Paul keeps buying for you have cancer-causing nitrates in them . . . "

"Enough. Enough. Dr. Bautista doesn't seem to think they're harmful . . . and neither does Paul, or he wouldn't be bringing them to me. You are simply aggravating my condition." She grabbed her plastic tube and forced air through it as hard as she could, heaving her chest forward in the process. Then she blew air out, causing the inner, mini-ferris wheel to spin at a much slower pace than seemed possible for all the effort she was expending. Next she closed her eyes and sighed before putting the tube down and touching her sides, where incisions had been made to drain the fluid from her lungs.

"Why don't we try Hatha yoga breathing now," I whispered, a few hours later, after Mommy awakened from her nap, hoping to find her in a better mood. "Look how easy this is," I remarked.

"Oh, that's for normal people," she snapped. "Dr. Bautista insisted I shouldn't stray from her procedures." Then Mommy snatched her plastic tube from the end table and almost jabbed me with it while shaking it at me. "For Christ's sake, why don't you try to be more like Patricia."

"Now why on earth would I try to do that?" I groaned, shocked she'd even make such a ridiculous suggestion.

"Because instead of nagging me all the time, Patricia makes sure I follow Dr. Bautista's orders."

"Well . . . if that's how you really feel about it, I'll stop nagging you," I croaked, fighting back tears.

I was convinced Mommy's chronic condition had ruined her better judgment.

But from that day on, I held my breath.

And for the next several months, Mommy continued to struggle with hers, breathing in and out and taking deep gasps for air, eventually heaving more deeply than I'd ever done during my worst bouts of asthma. Until . . . my eyes confirmed what my heart refused to believe. Mommy would soon be out of breath. Forever.

Ten years later, I'm listening with more respect to the Hatha yoga instructor's tribute to the air. For Mommy's sad bout with lung cancer has caused me to cherish the same air I tended to take for granted after I out-grew my asthma.

Now, effortless breathing is all the more precious. After all, you can live for several days without food. Perhaps a few days without water. But most creatures couldn't live for more than a few minutes without air. Not even my pet goldfish, Penelope.

So just before my daily aerobics, I practice my classical breathing. And sometimes, during a vigorous run or a series of sprints, I think about Mommy's struggle for her last deep breaths. Afterwards, it doesn't seem to hurt so much, if I have to wheeze to catch my own breath.

In My Father's House
by Mary Goodlander

He appeared strong, chest and arm muscles
developed from years of hard factory work
but wouldn't say why his mother whipped him,
or why he spent that Christmas alone in St. Louis,
or how, during the Depression, he'd walked
from Fort Lauderdale to Hopkinsville looking for work.
He never spoke of being raped as a child
or how he felt when his best friends were killed
in the Second World War
and why he had bitter arguments with his sons.

George spent his middle years drunk,
entertaining others with stories about his hobo days.
At my eighth grade graduation, he called
the main speaker a fool.
Got drunk and missed my performance
in a high school play.
The night I married, though he hated fast food,
he brought home supper and stayed sober
until after we walked down the aisle.

Slammed near death by a heart attack,
he emerged sober and remorseful.
When I took a belated path through college,
once a week I ate lunch he fixed,
the sweets he bought from a bakery blocks away.
Living long enough to be forgiven,
he died sober,
released finally by his damaged heart;
his wife and five children present.

Dealing With Two Deaths:
The Death Of My Mother
And The Death Of Expectations
by Lois Truffa

Alzheimer's is a cruel disease. It kept my mother in its grip for ten long years—those ten years were my mourning period.

I am the only child in my immediate family. My parents had married when quite young, but I wasn't born until Mother was thirty-two. Two years later my father died. I had cousins galore, and I suppose that was my salvation. Had it not been for the rest of my family, I would have lived a very secluded life. My mother remarried when I was only four.

Mother was a cool and non-demonstrative person who lived her life very privately. I don't ever remember company coming to our house, with the exception of my grandmother from Boston who stayed with us each summer—I was also her only grandchild and much pampered and loved. But my own mother never hugged or kissed me. Our relationship was always guarded and without warmth. Although I had no doubt my mother loved me, showing affection was impossible for her. I recall my mother telling me that the best days of her life were those when her career was in full swing. When my stepfather died, I was married and living across the country, and she was independent and alone.

As years passed and my own children and grandchildren came along, I did my best to show them affection in every way possible. Our family grew into a strong and healthy unit which encompassed neighbors, friends, and some of their relatives. Mother visited briefly each year and just as quickly left. The children loved having their beautiful, youthful grandmother come, but between visits an occasional phone call was our only contact. Our relationship never improved even though I began to hug her and tell her I loved her.

Mother worked until she was eighty years old. She truly loved her job, and it offered her just what she wanted in life—an opportunity to be around people in superficial relationships while remaining aloof and independent. When Alzheimer's struck, she was a strong, vibrant woman, blessed with excellent health. The year she turned eighty she broke her arm while staying with us. It was the beginning of the end of her life and the start of the grieving for those of us who cared for her.

It took almost ten years for my mother to die—years of coming to the reality that I was now in charge and she was the child, years of doing my best to give out of love and not only out of duty. Someone told me it was important that I do that for my own peace of mind. I'm sure they were right. It was, however, the hardest thing I've ever had to do.

When Mother had to be put in a nursing home, I visited each week. I spent two days preparing myself for the visit and two days struggling to recover. There was something about her former strength that made the current situation even more touching. It was hard to let go and be able to truly see the parent as a child. On an Alzheimer's wing there are moans and cries—one poor soul begged constantly for someone to take her away. It was a heartbreaking place to have to put a loved one, especially your mother who had always been so strong, so beautiful, and so proud of her independence.

My mother seemed very happy at the home where she was always comfortable and given the best care. It was painful for me when visiting to see her this way—she, at least, didn't remember what she had once been. After visiting her, I would wake in the middle of the night in a cold panic wondering how I could do better. The answer was nothing. I was doing all I could, which was really not much but making sure she received loving care and paying the bills each month.

At some point she stopped recognizing me. As difficult as that was for me, it was much more difficult to know that now I had lost all hope of having that mother/daughter relationship I craved. By this time, Mother had required full care for a number of years, and that included diapering, hand feeding, and showering. The grandchildren visited less and less since she didn't know them. I didn't mind. I felt it was better they remember her as she had been—they at least had that choice. She now identified more closely with her care givers. Her old charm, as always, was seeing her through what seemed to be an intolerable situation, and she appeared to be doing just fine.

My mother would have been ninety years old had she lived another six months. After all the years I had prayed for God to take her and end the suffering, she was really gone. I'd felt guilty even thinking such thoughts, but they were only to end what she was going through. Although frail, she was very healthy until the end. No extraordinary life-saving devices were to be used, and at the last she simply drifted off as the result of a slight infection.

Her death was not a shock. It was the answer to my prayers—or was it? The conventional mourning period for me lasted only a few weeks. After all the years of seeing my mother lose first one capability and then the next, who could be sorry to see that end? My son sobbed as my mother passed—how hard it was for him to say goodbye. But in not seeing much of her in her final years of life, he simply didn't realize that she was no longer his grammie.

When my mother died, it was an anticlimax. Losing someone you love from a heart attack, or even a long-term debilitating disease, can't possibly be any more cruel than the ten-year struggle we had. Those who suffer through the death of a loved one from Alzheimer's disease are forced to grieve endlessly as long as that person is alive, as they slowly lose each physical and mental capability.

At the end, there is simply nothing left. It's not clean and it's not fair. It's hard to call up the "good old days" when the bad days have been with you for so long. It is the cruelest kind of grieving.

When people lose loved ones, they often feel that person returns to them in spiritual form. I felt none of that. All that is left is an aching void. Death is very final, and the time for trying is over. I hoped for a spiritual contact, but nothing happened.

I've read that those who believe in the return of the spirit to a new life feel that these spirits will try to stay near those they love. And so I continue to watch for my mother as babies are born around me. After all these years of grieving, I now know that death is not the end of life. My mother is still with me just as surely as she has always been, and perhaps at some time we will be together again, because I know now that we still have a way to go.

Letter To My Father
by Sylvie Malaborsa

Frequently, when I reminisce about the most painful and unexpected events that stirred my life, memories of your fatal illness immediately emerge in my mind. I recollect vividly the strong physical pain which had overwhelmed me when the family learned that a tumor had started to ravage your body and that the treatment could only reduce your suffering. We all assumed you would match your father's longevity and live to be an octogenarian. However, at sixty-five years old, instead of a well-deserved retirement, you had to get ready for the ultimate voyage. I could not fathom that you would shortly be forever erased from my life. I bargained with God to let you live but He had decided that your time had come.

For Mother's sake, I concealed my grief, but whenever I reached my room, I let go of my anguish. I wept for the father who would not give me away on my wedding day. I wept for the old man I would never know and who would not bounce my children on his knees while telling them stories only a grandfather could tell. I also wept for Mother who needed you so much, who would never be the same. Nevertheless, apart from selfishness, which played a major part in my sorrow, an acute awareness troubled me: I had loved you too little, too late.

Hidden behind an austere mask, you were such a complex individual. You were coincidentally soft and passionate, shy and aggressive, impulsive and hesitant—contrasts which were difficult for a child to understand. Only after a certain dose of maturity and self-analysis was I capable to diagnose these disparities which had amazingly emerged in my own personality.

Sometimes I try to imagine your life before you became my father. I feel you in my heart, the third child of poor Italian immigrants. I feel your humiliation and your shame, as a teenager, when you and your father searched through people's trash, hoping to discover decent wares for the family. I sense your misery at the announcement of the death of your mother who passed away during childbirth at forty-nine years of age. I see you cringe as your father's new wife abruptly takes control of the household. I picture you in your army uniform, serving proudly at a significant period in your life. I imagine how handsome you looked on your wedding day, when your destiny was linked to the daughter of other Italian immigrants. Throughout the following years, I share your joy at the birth of three sons, and sense your excitement when I arrived into this world.

During my childhood and adolescence, Mother seemed to be the only devoted parent, as you were too busy earning a living. We were properly educated, medicated, nourished, loved, and disciplined but your workaholic temperament left us begging for attention. In order to survive financially, in spite of meager resources, you followed the bank manager's advice and risked an investment in real estate while starting a new career as manager in a grocery outlet. This new adventure became your passion. The passing years had not obliterated memories of youth's privations, so for over a decade you labored more than twelve hours a day in your business. When your sons became your regular workers, they had to endure angry outbursts from a man who was an impatient teacher and a demanding employer. I am sure you did not mean to demolish their self-esteem when you tactlessly corrected their mistakes; your awkwardness with words and your temper are mostly to blame for these faux pas. Your ambition also prevented you from truly participating in our upbringing, which was essentially entrusted to Mother. Unfortunately, you found out too late that climbing the ladder of success did not bring the rewards you anticipated. The cost had been too high—fatigue, alienation from the family, and loneliness. If only your obsession at erasing a gloomy and humiliating past had been less intense, and if only we had been mature and perceptive enough to understand your dedication.

And so, as the years passed, a gulf widened between you and us. We cared for one another but seldom related on a meaningful level. A channel of mystery had appeared, only connected by the love that Mother had for all of us. I was eighteen years old when I realized you had become a stranger in your own house. For five years, my heart ached as your attempts to get closer to us failed. We were too uncharitable and selfish to recognize your efforts.

Oh, Dad! I know you were not prepared to die. You pretended to accept your fate, but your tears on several occasions betrayed you. Again, witnessing your resignation and your sorrow, my lips could not utter soothing words. Overcome by my own sadness and fear, I remained somewhat at a distance, as I observed Mother, priests, relatives, nurses, doctors, and social workers prepare you for death. I now wish to tell you that although I failed to reveal my love, I spent each moment at your side memorizing your smile and the sound of your voice.

It seems unfair that it took your illness to make me realize how much I love you. Although our relationship had evolved since your retirement, I never imagined that losing you would be so painful. This tragedy truly gave me a deeper awareness of myself.

Dad, what happened to you is heartbreaking, and yet some good has come of it. God takes whatever lies at hand and fashions it into something fresh and new. First of all, it emphasized the importance of living every day to the fullest. We never know when He will call us to Him. After your death, desperate for solace and wishing to fill a void, I made a journey to Christ. For several years, I walked a lonely path, spending lots of time reading the Gospels and thinking. I nourished my faith by returning to Mass, praying, reading, and exchanging with priests and sisters. At first, I found praying difficult, but I applied the formula of Ste-Therese de Lisieux, the candid Carmelite nun who often asserted that she spoke to God in a sincere and unadorned manner, and that he had always understood her. Through prayer, God grants us peace and makes us see what is necessary for our peace. I saw the importance of putting God first and letting Him guide my path. A few years ago, I felt that He showed me that in my writing I would be celebrating His presence. Tentative at the beginning, I eventually became a contributor to a religious magazine.

I pray that my spiritual life will constantly grow and that the Holy Spirit will continue to inspire me.

Dad, you have closed your eyes on a world of mundane things, of tiresome roads, of pain of the body and of the mind, of challenges and deceptions. You have opened them in a world of glory, beyond dreaming or imagining. Please accept this token of my admiration and understanding. Over the years, I have discovered that your ambition, mingled with an excessive zeal, practically shattered your influence in our lives. However, it is clear that your objective was not to accumulate a fortune, but to guarantee us superior expectations. I frequently recognize your fingerprints on my life, because whenever adversity is encountered in my career, your model of perseverance urges me to strive on. I consider myself blessed to have inherited your determination, your foremost characteristic, which constitutes the most valuable asset of your legacy. Should God ask me to be born again and invite me to choose a father, I would undoubtedly select you. Pray for me that I may live fully the time that I have. Amen, Dad. Rest in peace.

Sentimental Journey
by Bill Millhollon

The young doctor said, "This is the hardest thing I ever have to tell anyone."

My mother interrupted him, "I told you when you started that I had cancer."

The young doctor agreed, "Your situation could not be much worse; there is cancer of the pancreas and a malignant tumor on the liver. Considering the extent of the cancer, there is really nothing that can be done."

He did not know she was actually ninety-one; she had put seventy-five on her last application. He did not recommend radiation or chemotherapy and the surgery was not an option. "How much longer will I have doctor?"

He replied hesitantly, "Any time from two months to two years."

My mother was still very active, still driving her car and eating out at least once a week. She was living alone; my dad had died the previous November. In less then two months she had lost thirty pounds, began feeling weak and decided to get a physical. Fortunately my sister Jane lived next door to my mother's lake home and kept in touch, looking in on her each day. I hurried to her when I received the bad news.

The medical tests were so conclusive, Muddie (the name we always called her) did not care to get a second opinion. I told her, "Life is like staying at a motel, there is a check-out time for every guest."

She agreed she couldn't complain; she had enjoyed a good and long life and she was ready to die if that's what God wanted. I was glad to hear her say that; she had never won any awards for church attendance.

I told her all about Hospice. I explained she could die in dignity, that dying did not have to be a slow lingering process. She could spend her last days in her own home with her dog and family. I knew she feared suffering for months in a hospital.

I cannot say enough for those wonderful people in Hospice; each individual involved was thoroughly trained and filled with sincere caring compassion.

I told Muddie that I honestly believed death would be an interesting experience; so many people who have undergone near death experiences spoke of it as very peaceful, filled with joyful anticipation. I explained that many believe death is only a continuation of life on a much higher plane.

We talked about how the Hindu believe in reincarnation. I told her I liked that idea and, that ever since accepting Christ my life, here on earth was like heaven. I mentioned that in the Hindu belief one sometimes comes back as an insect or animal. Neither of us liked that idea too much.

Muddie said she hoped she'd get to see her loved ones that are already in heaven. She said it would really be nice to see her mother, dad, brothers, and sister again, and especially my little thirteen year old son who died years back. That one brought a lump to my throat for a minute.

Muddie said she thought she had lived an honorable life and accomplished some good in the world. "I raised you and Jane, and you both turned out respectable, and I enjoyed a lot of good living." Jane and I both were adopted as infants by Muddie. As children, I had tuberculosis and my sister had polio and suffered through many leg operations. This was during the Depression. We both owed our mom a lot.

I asked her if she adopted us because she really wanted kids or if she did it in hopes of saving her marriage. My first adopted dad was an alcoholic.

"I did it to try to save our marriage. I thought he might stop drinking."

We discussed getting her will and finances in order. I also suggested she quit driving, and she agreed she would sell her car. I tried to get her commitment to fly to Las Vegas with us soon, but she would only agree to think about it.

Muddie was feeling better, so we decided to drive over to her favorite lakeside restaurant and eat some catfish.

A younger couple joined us at the restaurant for a short while. They often hunted deer with my mom. She was eighty-nine when she shot her last buck.

We went home rather late. The next morning my mother got up, fixed breakfast, and laid down on the couch and covered up with a blanket. She decided she would not go to church. It scared me; I could tell she felt quite bad. I started asking where she hurt and how bad the pain was; I was afraid the worst was starting. She smiled and said, "Bill, it's not my insides that hurt. It's my head; I've just got a terrible hangover."

Anyway, it was a nice sentimental night out for two "lovers", our last fun time together. I thank the Lord for it. I was beginning to have a spiritual hangover; the finality of it all was beginning to touch me.

On my next trip I was surprised my mother was not sitting on her front porch with her dog Susie. She always had been there waiting before. I went in the house and found her lying on the couch with her dog sitting on her stomach. She did not even get up, and I noticed she was using a four-legged walking stick.

Hospice had already been out and made all the necessary arrangements to start taking care of her. She said they were so nice, so loving, and so thoughtful. They were even coming out several times a week to bathe her and shampoo her hair.

She insisted on fixing a big breakfast the next morning. I had brought her fresh cantaloupe and tomatoes; she loved them at breakfast. She fixed toast which she burned as usual. I noticed she was much weaker and ate very little; yet, she had my favorite lunch already waiting to be popped in the oven: pork ribs and sweet potatoes.

I took her to the attorney, and we managed to get all the papers signed. I suggested she keep a lifetime estate. It would stay under her control until her death and would save the expense and trouble of probate. She decided against it. She just hated to turn loose; it was the finality of it all.

My mom was now staying on the couch nearly full-time. I told her I was going to move the couch out and she nearly panicked. She wanted to know why. I told her, "To keep you from lying around so much, you need to stay up and keep active." Poor thing, I guess she felt a lot worse than I realized.

We only spent three days together on that trip; I had to return Sunday because of business. I promised to be back the very next weekend; it turned out I had to fly back the following Thursday. Mom was much worse.

My brother-in-law picked me up from the airport. I was shocked; my mom was so tired and drained looking. She was conscious, though, and was as glad to see me as I was to be there.

My sister and I took turns sitting beside her bed. There was not much we could do except talk to her, hold her hands, and love her. The first night she would barely respond. We would give her an antibiotic every few hours or a morphine pill if she seemed in pain or was restless.

The next morning I managed to get her to drink a little coffee and eat a little oatmeal. No one had been successful in getting her to eat anything the day before. That was the last time I managed to get her to eat.

I would talk to her about past fun times, and Thanksgiving day, which was not too far off. It disturbed me that she would not eat or drink, but Hospice said it was a normal part of the dying process, and that she would choke if I tried to force feed her.

The Hospice ladies came out once a day at first. Then more often after the third night. They were always available by phone for any kind of advice or any emergency.

I have never been associated with such caring, understanding people. They are truly dedicated to making a sad situation as pleasant and painless as possible for all concerned. The fourth night we were worried about my mom possibly getting bedsores. My sister and I would try to roll her over every few hours.

Around 2:00 that morning, my sister and I must have turned Mom the wrong way; she suddenly became very vocal and agitated waving her hands and moaning. It appeared that the catheter must be hurting her very badly. My poor, tired, little sister went to pieces emotionally. She kept saying, "Muddie deserves better than this!"

I was inclined to agree with her. I have never been in such a predicament in my life. In the first place, I never imagined having to fool with anything as personal as a catheter. In the second place, I had no idea how they worked. I could not get it out.

I couldn't seem to stop the pain, and my mom seemed to be suffering badly. I called Hospice. They answered immediately and assured me it was not as bad as it seemed; their confidence was reassuring.

The woman on the phone explained that the catheter was held inside the body by a small balloon which is filled with water; it is then capped. She told me to cut the cap off, let the water out, and remove the catheter. Fortunately, about that same time, my sister came back in crying and I told her to just be calm, to help me a few seconds, and everything would be fine.

I found the little cap, had my sister hold a plastic cup under it, and I cut the cap off. The water from the inflated balloon came out and the catheter slid right out. I don't know who felt more relieved, me or my poor mother.

My sister was still quite emotionally upset; she had even called the city hospital about admitting my mom. I told her I would not mind if they would agree to no life support machinery. I had promised my mother that would not happen.

I called Hospice back and told them I had been successful, my mom was resting again, and then asked, "Now what?"

The Hospice lady said she thought the catheter should be put back in so the drainage could continue; there was a danger of swelling if we waited. I was about to resign until she explained she was talking about someone else doing it. She said they would call me back very soon. In less than ten minutes a Hospice lady called I gave her directions to find us. It was over twenty miles of winding hill country road to my mother's home; the nurse was there in less than thirty minutes.

She was a true angel of mercy and compassion. She completely remade my mom's bed with my mom in it, put the new catheter in, calmed Muddie down and had her sleeping like a baby in less then twenty minutes. It took her a little longer to calm down my sister. The nurse was in no hurry to go anywhere until everyone was content.

She explained that our mother had been lying there peacefully and the sudden change startled her; that the pain was not nearly as bad as we imagined. She also explained to my sister that our mom was very close to death; she doubted our mother would live through a ride to the hospital.

She assured Jane that Muddie was much better off where she was than in a busy impersonal hospital ward, and that the close personal attention we were giving her, our very presence, was the best. She put a pillow on my mom's chest and wrapped her arms around it. She was like a kid with a teddy bear. I guess we all still need a security blanket once in a while.

I realized my poor sister was very tired; she had been going through a traumatic vigil days before I arrived. I talked her into getting some sleep in the adjoining room. I talked to my dying mother for hours, and I felt she heard what I was saying. I prayed that she would not suffer, that she might quit fighting and just take the hand of the Master who was calling her home. She hated to let go. I couldn't do much more than be there and express my love; she was very peaceful.

These are very touching moments; watching the one you love slowly die. I went through repeated emotional and spiritual peaks, and even deep canyons of depression; some times I felt I couldn't go through another.

It is not an easy or comfortable experience. It is a profound journey that modern civilization seems to have decided to let their loved ones walk alone.

About 9:00 the next morning my mom's slow and steady breathing was interrupted by a couple of short quick little gasps. I called out to my sister to come quickly and hold Mom's other hand, that I thought this was it.

Together, we held her hands. Her little chest never rose again, the life spring inside had finally run down . . . our mom's spirit had finally let go.

I called Hospice and told them Muddie had passed on; they sent someone right out. The Hospice lady checked my mother, made up a death certificate, and had us sign it. She had already called the funeral home to come and move my mother. The Hospice lady listed the drugs and had me sign an affidavit that confirmed the drugs she picked up and the morphine which we flushed down the commode. She picked up all the equipment, cleaned everything up, and said someone would pick up the hospital bed that afternoon.

I am so glad we were right there with my mom at that very time; it meant a lot to me, and I believe it meant a lot to her.

The Ninth Inning Ended
by M. Darlene Sandrey

Dad had been hooked up to life support for two weeks before the family decided to let the Eternal Manager take over the game plan. The next day his breathing became labored and the hospital staff gently informed us he was actively dying.

Saturday afternoon I sat vigil at his bedside. I turned on the radio to the Indians' game, held his hand, and remembered the cherished times we shared through the national pastime.

Dad and I traditionally went to every opener and then down to Jim's Steak House to continue the celebration of the new hopefully winning season. When I was a youngster, that day was a "religious" holiday in our neighborhood, the only legitimate excuse to skip school or work.

I sat by his bed, held his frail hand, and tried to follow the game.

Dad slipped into a coma the night before but I knew he was listening with me. In the eighth inning two men were on base. Cory Snyder came to bat. On the first pitch he slammed the ball over the bleacher fence. The fans went wild. I leaned over and told Dad the new score and felt him squeeze my hand weakly. The ninth inning ended, the Tribe victorious. Herb Score was giving the final stats as I felt Dad's hand grow cold. His breathing was no longer labored. He was finally at peace after months of suffering.

That was six years ago. The Tribe finished fourth in their division that year, eleven behind Boston. Last year's season was memorable. This one is equally as stressful for an addicted fan like myself. The past two years, however, have been emotionally hard on me. I miss sharing the excitement of a pennant winning year with my father. He never got to Jacobs Field or witnessed a whole town become instant fans.

Dad taught me many lessons through this game of baseball: the value of living this life to the best of my God-given abilities, practicing sportsmanship, and understanding that a win isn't as important as playing fair and having fun. Competitiveness is fine as long as you don't forfeit friends in the quest. He believed successful people accomplish their home runs by discipline, not luck. He taught me not to dwell on mistakes, but to look forward to the next challenge. I guess that's why he never kept losing score cards.

As a believer in an afterlife, I'm confident Dad is still cheering on the Tribe, proud that finally they are the best of both leagues, at least until the playoffs.

In the movie *League of their Own,* the manager, Jimmy Dugan, screams at a woman baseball player after she makes an error, telling her that crying is not allowed in the game of baseball. It isn't? Last year I saw grown men crying in frustration, other men crying victorious tears, and this daughter crying at the loss of her favorite fan.

Grieving For An Unknown Mother
by Tim Elliot

I've never known a mother. Mine died when I was born. A teacher of teachers, she was thirty-nine years old when she married my father one glorious day in April. The following January, in the gloom of a Philadelphia winter, she died in childbirth. My father never discussed her with me except on rare occasions to refer to her as "your sainted mother".

My father's mother who helped raise me through the years of infancy danced around the reason for her death. She had kidney problems was her quick answer to my questions. Actually, my mother bled to death. Years later I found her death certificate. Postpartum hemorrhages was what it said. Today a push dose of fibrin or some related chemical would have stopped the bleeding.

A child who's never known a mother cannot mourn for a specific person. His mourning must be for an absent relationship which is only learned about as a distant observer: that woman who escorts a classmate to school his first day, who presides over a tenth birthday party for a playmate, and who comforts with loving arms a youngster who's had a fall. It was that relationship I wondered about, and missed, and sometimes longed for. Mostly though, I just wondered about it. What must it be like?

Then one day I had an insight. My father's mother died when she was eighty-four years old and I was six. By family custom, the funeral was held at the home of my aunt May, and grandmother's body was laid out in the parlor for mourners to say their last goodbyes. My uncle Will, standing beside his mother, leaned down and kissed her on the forehead. I sensed that here was an ending to a mystic relationship I'd never known. Suddenly, I broke out in loud wails of anguish. I wasn't so much bewailing the loss of the person, as an awareness that some precious fabric had been torn asunder.

There were harsher consequences of not having a mother. One day a year or so later, I walked up the street to Hilda's house. Her mother answered the doorbell. "Timmy, I don't want you to come around anymore," she said. "You don't have a mother, and there's no one to teach you right from wrong. I just don't want you playing with Hilda. I'm sorry. If you had a mother things would be different." Then she slammed the door.

What was that all about? I asked myself as I walked back home. *What does having a mother have to do with anything? There must be something here I don't understand.*

Over the years I've tried to comprehend the best I can the relationship of mother and child. Neither my mother nor I ever knew this bond of nurture and dependency. I only know that she gave her life that I might have mine. And for this, I shall be eternally grateful. And forever mourn the relationship she and I have never known.

The Gerbil Funeral
by Christina Keenan

They stood silently watching. The only sound was the scraping of soft earth. The hole got bigger, and bigger. My daughter stood near the hole. Grief etched crystalline traces down her face, and my son tried to remember the words to the Hail Mary. We talked a little about the gerbil babies, and we decided that they never really had a chance to survive.

My children want to know why the mother wouldn't take care of her babies, why they had to die. We sit for awhile. The air is crisp, the leaves are beginning to change, and fall. The sun is warm, and we finish our prayers and decide to mark the tiny grave with small crab apples that have fallen from a tree overhead.

Five years ago today the call came. My mother, my beloved mother, lie dying. Now, my mind is filled with the memories of how my mother was laid to rest in the soft earth, on a day quite like this one. The trees were in full glory, and I remember thinking that the world shouldn't have this explosion of color when in my heart everything looked gray.

My son is concerned now that the garden we plan to dig in the spring will disturb the gerbil grave. I sit on the grass and watch my children console one another.

I remember my mother in her garden. How tenderly she would attend her delicate blooms. She would laugh as she showed me her latest crop. I would find her kneeling in her garden with dirt on her hands and a smile of pure delight on her face. She always had dirt under her fingernails in the summer and fall. Holding her hand in the hospital, on the day she died, I saw that she had dirt under her nails. I cried when I saw it, I cried then harder than ever before because I knew that my missing her would never be a simple thing.

When she was gone from my life, everything about her was gone with her: her gardens of flowers; the vegetables and the herbs; her puppies; her kitchen, her books, the embroidery, and the crocheted blankets; her favorite recipe at Christmas; her twist records, her laughter, her kind spirit; and most of all, her gentle soul.

The loss of my mother filtered down to me in layers. First I missed her presence, then over time I missed her essence, and that is when the real grief work began.

Now here I sit with my children; loss is not the lesson they are learning today. It is the feelings loss evokes that they are just starting to learn, and I will help them. The sun is warm in my hair, and there is a knot of emotion in my throat as I think of my mother.

In the spring I will also have a grand garden, and I will care for it very tenderly. I will offer it up to her as my gift. Life goes on. It will probably still hold some sharp edges, but as long as there is tenderness and bright sun shine, something beautiful will grow.

I learned this from my mother.

Together Forever
by Veronica Breen

On November 12, 1992, my father and stepmother were buried. My father had married Mary in 1977, after ten years of widowhood. Having lost my mother at age twelve, I became very attached to my stepmother. Our father's remarriage brought me into a large, wonderful family which included Mary and her five children. All of us were happy that our lonely parents had found each other.

From the beginning, neither my father nor my stepmother were in the best of health. Between his diabetes and infected ulcerations on his feet, and the heart condition that had plagued her since her childhood, these two lovebirds were in and out of hospitals for most of their marriage. Unfortunately, in the fall of 1992 things got very distressing. Dad's foot became terribly infected, and there was no alternative to a below the knee amputation.

On Halloween night, one week after Dad's amputation, Mom turned to my brother John, said "Oh, Johnny", clutched her chest, and collapsed. My younger sister Lorraine, a nurse, was called to help. She did CPR, and Mom was alive in the ambulance. By the time the rest of us arrived at the hospital, we were told there was little hope that she would survive.

Aside from our horror that we were going to lose our mother, how and when would we tell Dad? Since Dad had a slight heart condition, in addition to his diabetes, we requested that his cardiologist break the news to him. Dad's reaction was sadness and silence.

We were advised by a neurologist that Mom's EKG showed minimal brain function. After a grueling discussion, we agreed to suggest that Dad sign a DNR (do not resuscitate) order. The DNR would mean that the medical staff would not take any extraordinary measures to save Mom's life.

It was with great anxiety that two of my sisters, Liz and Nancy, told Dad the reality of his wife's condition. Dad was staunch and strong and agreed that Mom would never want to live that way; he signed the DNR. We then found ourselves in the strange position of praying for someone to die.

Mercifully, late on Friday, God took Mom. It was hard going into Dad's room, telling him it was over and watching him cry, but we were relieved that Mom was at peace. Little did we know that from that point on Dad's condition would deteriorate.

On Saturday when we visited with Dad, he complained of intense stomach pains. Tests revealed a severe intestinal infection. It was painful for all of us to watch him suffering, but we honestly believed that he would eventually improve. It was obvious that grief, as well as sickness, was taking a toll on Dad.

An urgent phone call early Sunday morning summoned us back to the hospital. Dad's condition was critical; he was being transferred to the ICU because surgery was necessary. My sister Liz asked the dreaded question, "Are we going to lose him too?" The answer was simply that it was possible.

We went to visit Dad before he was moved to the ICU. I remember we were begging him not to leave us. His response was "Leave me alone. I want to be with Mama." Within two hours of being summoned to the hospital, our father was dead. When the doctor first said that he was sorry, it didn't sink in. All over the room, you heard one person or another saying "What? Dad's gone." "What did he say? Daddy's dead?" We were all in shock; this could not really have happened. My sister Liz, who also has diabetes, became so ill she was admitted to the hospital and wasn't discharged until the morning of the funeral.

Most of the wake for my parents is a complete blur. I remember standing in the funeral parlor, looking at two caskets and remarking "How are we suppose to get through this?" Having lost other loved ones I knew how robotic one becomes during the funeral. You greet people and you accept condolences. You even occasionally smile and then, later, you barely remember a thing. We wrote a message to be read at the church and selected the music and scripture readings. Looking back I don't know how we did it.

Going back to a day-to-day life was hard. During the funeral I had something I absolutely had to do everyday, but later I was at loose ends. Because of the circumstances, my employer had been very understanding, and I was told to take as much bereavement time as I needed. My younger sister Lorraine and I clung to each other during the initial days after the funeral. Yet, we found that sitting together day in and day out wasn't helping at all. One afternoon I said to her, "This isn't working. I can't spend every day sitting here looking at your sad face. I feel like I'm looking in the mirror."

The idea of going back to work seemed impossible. I didn't really think I could function. But a week after the folks' burial I returned to work. Looking back I realize that was a very healthy decision. Unfortunately the first three months or so were very difficult, and luckily my employer and co-workers were very understanding.

The one area in which I found that my family and I were fortunate was when it came to selling our parents' house and dividing their belongings. I had heard horror stories of families that fought so vehemently over their parents' property that they never spoke again. We were very different. The closest thing to a conflict we had was when one family member would insist that another take something. I think we were all agreed that after everything that had happened to us, the last thing we were going to do was fight over money and property.

My family celebrated the holidays of 1992 tearfully and quietly. Looking back I can't remember whose house I spent Christmas at or whether I bought any gifts or sent Christmas cards. For New Year's Eve we decided to have a family party at my sister Nancy's house in upstate New York. I wrote in my diary on December 31st: "Leaving soon to go upstate; whole family wants to celebrate the end of '92 together. Needless to say we are all happy to see the end of this terrible year. I have some really mixed feelings . . . I don't know how to get out of the slump . . . I don't know when this grieving should be over. I feel like I can't make a decision about anything. Part of me wants to make changes and part of me doesn't have the energy to do a thing. I guess I'll just keep hoping I'll crawl out of the hole."

Even though I was unaware of it, a healing process gradually did commence. Responsibilities at work, the passage of time, and the help of friends
and family started to put me on the right track. Eventually I was even able to
look at old photographs and videotapes. One of the videos I watched was of
my parents' 15th wedding anniversary party. There were fireworks, a barbecue, and at the end of the day we produced a "wedding cake" and made
Mom and Dad cut it and feed it to each other. Dad, the comedian, slammed
his fork filled with cake into Mom's mouth and she howled with laughter.
Then we chanted "Kiss, Kiss, Kiss" and they did, for a long time. The entire
videotape is filled with laughter and love.

Suddenly everything clicked; it was as if a fog lifted. I had been grieving
for them, but they were exactly where they wanted to be, together. When I
thought of the loneliness and emptiness that would have been left to the
surviving spouse, I realized that to some extent what had happened was a
blessing. I decided that instead of dwelling on the tragedy, I would think of
what happened as a love story.

Now when we get together for birthdays, Christmas, and other special
occasions, we still miss our parents, but when we talk about Mom and Dad
there is always a lot of laughter. I think we are comforted knowing that our
parents are together and, happily, their love brought all of us together too.
On my parents' tombstone are inscribed the words "Together Forever". Who
could ask for more than that?

CHAPTER 4

SPOUSES, MATES, AND EX'S

People address the impact of losing their significant partners.

The Most Important Day Of My Life
by Cynthia Kuhn Beischel

Almost four years ago, a long-time-in-planning family vacation finally took place. My husband's parents had rented two lovely houses on the beach in Isles of Palms, South Carolina, where all of their children and grandchildren would spend time in reunion. Altogether there were thirteen of us, and much preparation had gone into this event. We had all managed to arrive from different parts of the country within hours of each other. Each family, in turn, had settled into their accommodations. Later, my husband Jerry and I walked together along the beach, holding hands. But, tired from the drive, we went to bed fairly early.

The next day, Jerry, a morning person, and our daughters, who were excited about being on vacation, awakened early. They encouraged me to get up also, but I groaned and said this was my vacation too. The way I wanted to spend it was to stay in bed and sleep late. Though obviously feeling I was going to miss out on the activities, they grumbled "fine" and left the room, with my husband making a final comment that he was going to leave me alone and this was the last time he'd try to do something for me. I called back to him as he closed the door that I didn't think his remark was fair—I just wanted to sleep in a little while.

I got out of bed an hour or so later, put on my bathing suit and went downstairs to fix my breakfast. I visited with my brother-in-law, Edwin, while I ate. I had just taken a swallow of freshly squeezed juice when my older daughter Merritt ran into the kitchen, out of breath, saying Dad and Lindsay needed help. I said okay as I took a bite of toast, picturing their wanting my input on a sand castle design. She became agitated and repeated that they needed help. This time I heard the urgency in her voice, as did Edwin who ran out of the house with me, telling Merritt to stay there and watch his baby.

Within seconds I was on the beach, helplessly watching a scenario in the ocean that I had trouble comprehending. My husband and daughter were clearly in danger as I heard Lindsay's screams, but my legs felt heavy and I couldn't make them move fast enough. I had a coarse piece of whole wheat bread in my mouth that I couldn't chew or swallow. After a blurred sequence in time, during which I was confused as to what I could do to help and then watching some strangers rescue my younger daughter and drag my husband to shore, I held my saved child while other people were trying to resuscitate Jerry. Salt water foamed out of his mouth. Between breaths Edwin encouraged me to talk to Jerry as he administered CPR, to tell him that I loved him and I didn't want to lose him. All I could do was stand there speechless. I rode to the hospital in the front seat of the ambulance listening to the siren, desperately hoping that what they were doing in the back compartment was going to keep Jer alive. At the emergency entrance of the hospital I watched as they carried the gurney in. When I saw his feet, I thought, *Those are the feet of a dead man.*

That day my husband died. That day I, in a very true sense, was born. All the makings of who I am today had been unfolding throughout my entire life, but it wasn't until he left so abruptly that I was forced to really get to know myself, to give birth to the essential me. As with most births, I experienced tremendous discomfort. I believe that my husband was sad to leave us, feeling the pain of any major parting, and then moved on to his new existence. It is my life, however, that I know best and can study for significance.

Our marriage had been a cloak for me, insulating me against harsh environments by providing warmth, comfort, and style. Like all coverings, this mantle was stifling at times and not protective enough at other moments. Sometimes our union felt as if it were made out of the finest linen or silk; other times, it reminded me of horse hair fabric. Nevertheless, our relationship had become a comfortable, dependable and favorite garment, an ensemble I cherished and would not have discarded.

On the day Jerry died, I found myself suddenly standing exposed and vulnerable. However, part of me felt determined to find and show my strengths. Before I was even aware of what was actually happening, I began to tap into my resources, to learn more about what I am capable of handling, and to get more in touch with my purposes and desires. Since that momentous day, I have matured and become wiser and have begun to enjoy the process. At this point in my life's journey, I feel happy about setting a good example for our daughters. I have never asked why this happened to me; instead, I have always asked what I could learn from it. I have learned so much.

I have come to view "important" as a neutral word, which no longer carries the connotation that an event is good or bad, but rather suggests a guidepost or sign to greater significance or consequence. My guess is that most people would immediately assume a "most important day of one's life" would be a positive experience. Looking back I found that I needed to ask what determined the label "positive", which I discovered was based upon interpretation.

Certainly my most important day was filled with and followed by losses. No longer do I have the luxury of looking forward to hearing the back door open at dinner time, taking weekend walks together, receiving back massages, or enjoying being pampered by Jerry's ability to create wonderful meals out of "nothing". What I do have, however, is the ability to still hold onto his belief and pride in me, to sometimes imagine that he is helping me as I struggle with insurance companies, uncooperative tenants, the decisions that come with parenting, and to interpret my loss as an intrinsically personal gain from a different perspective.

Why?
by Eloise Y. Lott

"Honey, you have been working too hard," my husband said, as he kissed me when I came in from work unusually weary. "I am going to take you on a vacation and give you the rest you deserve." He smiled while fluffing a pillow for my neck as I flopped on the couch for a few moments of rest before beginning my evening chores.

Vacations were few and far between in our family. For years I had been fighting a battle with cysts, tumors, and the beginning of a malignancy, which left little time or money to be spent on pleasures. A few days later, however, Etheridge made arrangements with both our bosses for a week off just before school started.

He rented a cottage on the beach in Florida, which had a boathouse with a recreation room out over the water. It was soothing to lounge in this nice cool room, where a breeze from the ocean made our time so comfortable. We enjoyed the hours strolling along the beach, hand in hand, as the children gathered seashells.

Etheridge, Larry, and Steve went deep-sea fishing, while Myra and I went to see a porpoise show. The children enjoyed the fishing from the boathouse, swimming, and building sand castles.

A problem back home kept disturbing Etheridge. There was a high-voltage power line going over a tree in our yard. A telephone line going to the house behind ours ran through the branches of the tree. Sometimes when the wind was blowing we could see sparks fly as the branches rubbed along the telephone line. I had called both the telephone company and the power company about this problem. Several times during our vacation Etheridge remarked, "I sure hope they have that tree trimmed when we return. I am afraid the children might get shocked by it sometime." We tried to push this concern out of our minds, so we could concentrate on relaxing. The week ended all too soon, and we had to return to our jobs, and get the children enrolled in school.

Friday was the first day of September, and it was raining when I awoke. After the children caught the bus for school and I was ready for work, I went to our bedroom to kiss Etheridge goodbye.

"Honey, it is raining and you need some rest, so just stay in bed this morning," I said as I stooped over the bed to kiss him goodbye.

"I think I will," he wearily answered. "I don't know when I have ever been so tired."

He pulled me back to kiss me again and said, "Honey, don't work too hard, and if you need me for anything, be sure to call me."

I promised I would as I pulled the door behind me.

My office work had piled high while I was on vacation. I was deeply engrossed in my book work when the phone rang. As I picked it up, my usual "good afternoon" was interrupted.

"Eloise, call an ambulance and come home quick," Mama gasped.

"What's wrong, Mama?" I cried as fear gripped me.

"I'm afraid Etheridge has been killed."

"Oh no, he can't be dead, Mama!" I chokingly answered.

My boss rushed to my side. "What's wrong, Eloise?" he asked.

"Mama wants me to call an ambulance; she is afraid Etheridge has been killed."

He called Joe from the shop as he dialed the ambulance number, gave him his keys, and said, "Joe, Eloise's husband has been hurt; take my car and drive her home."

"He can't be dead," I whispered as Joe sped down the highway.

I saw a large crowd of people gathered in the yard as we drove into the driveway. I jumped out and ran toward them. Someone grabbed my arm saying, "Eloise, please don't go around there."

"I've got to see about my husband," I cried as I pulled loose.

I froze in my tracks when I saw his limp body draped across the limbs, with one arm dangling through the branches of the tree in our yard. All hopes I had that he was only hurt vanished.

Anguish filled my heart. My strong, healthy husband on whom I had relied for fifteen years, gone so suddenly. Never would I feel the comfort of his strong, loving arms around me again. How would the children get by without the loving discipline of their father? These and many doubtful thoughts flashed through my mind.

"I will be a father unto you." (2 Cor. 6:18) came to mind. But how would I, having one surgery after another, ever manage without him? He had always taken care of things so capably when I was in the hospital. I prayed for strength and wisdom to carry on. The Holy Spirit comforted me.

As I remembered my weaknesses, fear overwhelmed me. I went inside, fell across the bed and sobbed. "Oh God, Etheridge has always been there to help me through all my pains and sicknesses. He took care of the children. Oh how can I go on without him?" He seemed to speak to me. Suddenly, a neighbor interrupted my thoughts.

"Eloise, my husband and I will go to school and get the children."

"Oh, no! Not yet please!" I cried. "Not until his body can be removed from the tree." I didn't want the children to remember the sight of their daddy's limp body in that tree. Soon the Rescue Squad and doctor took him down and stretched him out on the lawn to administer first aid, but the doctor said Etheridge never knew what hit him.

Mama's voice sounded strange and far-away as I heard her tell the doctor, "Etheridge got up after the rain stopped and went out to trim the trees. I called him in for lunch at noon. He ate a hearty meal and went out to trim the last tree. I heard a noise and a groan and looked out the window. The tree and telephone line were on fire. A neighbor ran over and told me to call an ambulance and he would call the power company.

The doctor said, "The groan you heard was air forced from his body as the electrical surge went through him. It was so quick he felt no pain."

I felt so empty and helpless. I had never thought of losing Etheridge. He had been so strong and healthy, and I so weak from the twenty-odd surgeries. I thought of how deeply depressed I had felt about being so much trouble and expense after a series of serious surgeries. He took me tenderly in his loving arms and squeezed me tight as he said, "Honey, stop worrying. Don't you know I love you? I'd rather have you, with all your sickness, than any woman in the world." He was compassionate and understanding.

The neighbors brought the children in from school. They had already told them the sad news. They were as stunned as I was. They cried as I took them in my arms. I tried to be brave as I told them, "Daddy has gone to live with Jesus now. We will miss him beyond words, but he would want us to be strong. We must prepare to meet him by trusting God . . . " We all broke down and sobbed.

I never knew shock could cause so many problems. Shortly after the undertaker left with Etheridge's body, my feet and legs began tying in knots with cramps. Neighbors massaged, I tried to stand, but walking was impossible. The pain was very excruciating and would not let up. It took hours to get them to relax. And, in the following weeks, the children and I experienced many physical complications which the doctor described as a result of the shock.

After Labor Day, I sent the children back to school. I knew the sooner we returned to our regular routine the better off we would be. I stayed home from work a week to take care of the business involved with Etheridge's death. Then I tried to pick up as usual, but life was so different now.

I seemed always to be listening for Etheridge to come home. Many nights I would hear him at the back door saying, "Honey, I'm home." I would jump out of bed and be half way to the door before I realized I was only dreaming. The nights were so hard. All the pain and heartache seemed to flood over me again. There was no warm, tender body to snuggle up to and feel protected by. There was no one to talk to about the concerns of family or work.

We all stayed busy. I worked my eight-hour job and kept the children in their varied activities. Steve, ten years old, was a pitcher for the Little League Ball Team. Larry, thirteen, was very talented in music and was much in demand by the school, church, and social groups. Myra, seven, was beginning the steps in Girls Auxiliary and taking music lessons which kept her busy.

Etheridge's brother told me, "Eloise, you are so foolish. You are killing yourself running with the kids to so many activities they are involved in. Why don't you stop it?"

"Pete, I'd rather run myself down keeping them in worthwhile activities than try to get them out of something they got into because they were not occupied," I replied.

At times the loneliness was almost unbearable for all of us. Etheridge had been a doting husband and father, and we missed him tremendously. I wanted the children to be thankful for the years we had together, without feeling cheated at our loss.

One day when Myra was feeling deeply deprived of her daddy's love, she came to me putting her arms around my neck. "Mother," she whispered, "I miss Daddy so much. Just think, I only had a daddy seven years."

"Yes, Honey," I replied, as I took her on my lap. "I know you miss him. We all do! But think how lucky we were to have had him with us the many years we did."

She hugged me, and said, "He was a good daddy, wasn't he?"

"He sure was and he loved us all so much!" She smiled and went back to play.

While waiting for the school bus, shortly after Etheridge's death, a child stuck a pencil in Steve's hand, which required surgery. Soon after, all my appliances began to burn out. Then the car hood fell as Steve was watching his uncle work on his car. The latch stuck in his head, and as blood streamed down his face, his uncle rushed in with Steve in his arms crying, "Oh God, Eloise, come quick. I have killed Steve."

I put him in the car and rushed him to the hospital. After shaving his head and getting the bleeding stopped, he had a three-inch gash in the top of his head, and they feared a skull fracture. But it healed without further complications. I began to wonder why all these accidents? Why all the years of surgery? Why the loss of my young husband, when the children and I needed him so badly?

I turned more and more to the Bible for support. Praying daily for faith, strength, and guidance, I worked hard at raising our three children. Time passed and my surgeries continued. My daughter, at seventeen, was in a car wreck two days before graduating from high school, leaving her paralyzed from the breast down. She's been in a wheelchair for twenty-five years. Larry contracted a Hepatitis B Virus which destroyed his immune system, and he had cancer and died at age forty-five with AIDS. Steve's wife has been critically ill with cancer, and he has had some serious health problems.

We can't understand why so many things happen in this life, but God promised His Grace to be sufficient, and I don't know of a family anywhere that has had more love, togetherness, and happiness than we have. In spite of all the turmoil, we have truly been blessed!

Out Of The Depths
by Sydnea Miles

After the sudden death of my husband Roy, I found it difficult to cope. Shock! Fear! Guilt! Intense grief! All gripped me in their clutches. Unusual business responsibilities, the necessity of making a living, and the reality of being alone were overwhelming. I was totally unprepared for any of them.

As time went by, I tried to work my way through each ordeal. Gradually I felt my pain subsiding, but through the years I had a recurring dream that perplexed and disturbed me. Although it came infrequently, it was always the same in certain aspects.

In the dream Roy would unexpectedly return home after having been

away for a long period of time—sometimes months, sometimes years. I had
no knowledge of his whereabouts during his absence. He would come close
to me or sit beside me and hold my hand. He expected life to resume as it
was before he left, as if there had been no time lapse. He refused to explain
why he left or where he had been. He gave me the silent, but repentant,
treatment with a shy smile or pleading eyes. I became angry like a jealous
wife who had been deserted by her errant husband.

I always awoke from the dream when I reached the anger stage. In the
black darkness before the dawn, the magnified outrage mushroomed until
the fallout ruined my day and added to my burden of guilt. What was odd
about the dream was that I had never felt angry about Roy's death. I had
experienced many other emotions but anger wasn't one of them.

After years of that repetitious dream, I had one with a surprising difference that filled me with indescribable joy.

Stashed away in an old trunk was a forgotten photograph of Roy dressed
in his National Guard uniform. Wearing his spit-and-polished boots, he is
leaning, with one foot propped behind him, against a sturdy fence post. His
wide-brimmed hat is pushed back at a cocky angle and the big grin on his
face exposes his flawless white teeth.

In the happy dream he appeared to me in the form of that photograph as
if it were projected on a giant movie screen. The scene slid by in slow
motion. As he approached me I began to feel a tremendous love, so joyous,
so penetrating, and so encompassing that I was ecstatic. It was like nothing
I had ever known before.

Before the scene passed from view, I awoke. The intensity of that love
was still present and continued for days. The reality of it remains with me,
even now. I never knew that I could go from the depths of sorrow to such
ultimate joy as I felt in the transforming love of that dream.

Absence Makes The Heart Grow Fonder
by Adrienne Folmar

Someone once told me that I had a good heart, but I could not solve all
the problems of mankind. As just another imperfect human, I knew I could
not save the world. Still, somewhere in my unstable psyche, I believed that

my desperate will was strong enough on its own to keep the man I love alive. I say "love" in the present tense because that emotion did not die with him. In contrast, I find I love him even more.

At only two months since his death, I still count the days. The 26th of every month, I have a flashback to that June evening in the hospital. I see him die over and over again. I put my face next to his and closed my eyes, photographing his face, scent, and the warmth of his touch in my memory. I was nearly asleep when family began to arrive, shattering the moment.

He was asleep when he began the abnormal aspirations that finally ended in one last breath. I was grateful that we did not have eye-contact. In his lifetime, he had melted hearts with those doe-like brown eyes and beautiful smile. I did not want those now empty eyes to be my last memory of him.

I recall the cool feel of his skin as someone eventually pried my arms from his bed. How could I leave him alone? What if he woke up and we were gone? I know the Bible teaches in *Ecclesiastes 9:5* that "the dead are conscious of nothing at all" but, of course, I was understandably irrational.

I had slaved for him. I made his bed, cleaned his room, brought him food, read to him, walked with him, washed his hair, and brushed his teeth. Many nights, I slept on the floor near his bed so I could hear him breathe. I denied myself much for the sake of his comfort, getting by on an average of four hours sleep per night. He called me his "southern comfort" and "extra mile" because he knew what anyone else wouldn't or couldn't do for him, I would. I never had the promise of his ring or the pleasure of bearing his name, but by anyone's standards, we shared a life together. I had his respect, trust, and love. Our six years were an entire lifetime.

Now people say I need to "move on with my life" and "start getting out and meeting new friends". I can barely dress myself some mornings. I wake up at all hours of the night. Some days, I might forget he is gone and I pick up the phone to call him. The pain stabs me when realization sets in. He was the one I turned to in all matters. Whatever joy or pain I experienced in life, he was my sounding board. Likewise, I was his sympathetic ear.

I found true solace, albeit a small amount, in the knowledge that his suffering was over. The pain was tremendous for him; he often begged us to help him. For the first time, I couldn't "fix it".

I wondered if I tried hard enough. Did the doctors do all they could or did they give up on him because he was terminally ill anyway? Did he know what was happening? Did he know the moment he died that it would be my heart that stopped beating and his would now be pulsing inside me?

There is an unimaginable sense of devastation. Daily I experience anger, guilt, frustration, memory loss, appetite changes, insomnia, flawed judgment, and a desire to die. I foolishly think that, if I allow myself a moment of happiness, his memory may slip into the background and I might forget him. I read that letting go of the pain does not mean I love him any less. Yes, I treasure the memories we created together, but, at this point, I am living by means of those memories. To relive those times keeps him alive in my heart.

It has helped to keep a journal. I believe whatever way a person can find a release, do it actively. I find doing good for others helps keep my mind occupied. One day, I believe the pain in my heart will go away. Then, I will breathe again. As I try to regain my endurance and gratitude for life, I realize I am everything I am because Ron loved me.

Each time there is news of a death or I hear a favorite song or see a sentimental movie, I break down as if he died moments ago. We lived life through each other. Now, I must learn to live for myself.

Run Aground
by Linda Vissat

My body jumped and my nerves jangled when the phone rang. I had been in meditation, emptying myself of all the serious current events in my life. The phone call was from Pat, my ex-husband's present wife. Frank had married for the third time. She was it. My instant recall was triggered and I remembered Frank saying, "No, Linda. I'll never remarry. You are the only woman I could ever love."

Though Pat was calling to tell me Frank was ill, the only thing I remember from her thirty-minute oration was her comment, "I've had to put up with you all these years." I was nonplussed by this comment and suddenly felt like a beached whale that received no help because I wasn't an endangered species. Ex-wives are a dime a dozen. I could feel myself searing in hot sand, choking, and suffocating, right next to Frank in his hospital bed. My mind raced, unfolding pictures of the past, present, and future, more quickly than she could talk.

What a blockhead Pat was, I thought, giving me directives on how to run my life, as though when she married Frank, she married me, too. Somehow she got the idea that grieving a loss was her privilege alone. Tears seeped from my eyes. I had been married to Frank for seven years and had his only child. For twenty years now, I had known him and she had known him for only five.

A metamorphosis overtook me. For the last thirteen years, my life was committed alone to Frank's daughter. No other man in my life. I had lived in the land of "Frank and divorce" and would now be forced to move into the world of singles. This was an overwhelming change. I'm glad I was sitting down when the call came; my legs felt like jello.

My child's father was still alive, but on the edge. His plug was about to be pulled. He had cancer and was terminal. The lymphoma had laid siege to the lining of his heart, strangling him. Andrea, our fourteen-year-old, sat in his hospital room holding his hand amid the tubes suspended from his waning body. She sat like a pillar of cement, yet hopeful. Frank had a choice button and full access to morphine. It would have been rare for him to acknowledge his surroundings under these circumstances.

When he learned the cancer had returned after being in remission for six months, he promised he would rest for four months after he finished his next rendezvous with chemo. A confirmed workaholic, two weeks after the first go-round, as the chemicals and radiation did their job, Frank did his. He was a self-employed house framer, jack-of-all trades in construction, and had an appetite for work as voracious as for food, but now he had no strength. Normally one hundred sixty pounds, he dropped forty pounds. Still he refused canes, and, now in pain, he slouched like a man of seventy when he was only forty-two.

Our daughter lived with them during the school year, an in-kind trade since I had seen no child support for seven years. As was typical, Frank wanted everything for himself, his step-family and his daughter. The day he left for the hospital, it had been agreed Andrea would remain there to complete her first year of high school.

Things were not to remain "as usual". In my experience, last requests by the terminally ill are seldom honored; this was no different. In a heated tirade, Pat said, "She needs her mom right now. I'm not her mom and I don't want her here." Then added, "She never does anything to help anyway."

I had visited this household and witnessed their family interactions many times. Frank's other family included two step-daughters, one twenty and contemplating divorce, and another who had just turned sixteen and had a four-month old baby. Plus there was a ten-year old unruly step-son. Frank had my daughter in the middle of this "as usual" environment.

While everyone remained cement pillars on the outside, not allowing external weeping, I would see them crack, pick up the pieces, and resculpt new images of themselves each time. We have all been changing, drifting further away with every day. Vagueness and haze grows, soon turning to darkness. We will never see Frank again, as he will never see us.

Pat told me I can't cry, that I'm giving marriage and divorce a bad name. Her words to me were, "You will divest yourself of all your emotional holdings. Now. He is dying."

My response, in thought, was *I knew that a week ago. It's been twenty years for me and only five for you.* While Pat had been at work, I had gone to visit Andrea at Frank's bedside. He had been resting. While he knew who I was, I hugged him. "I love you, Frank," I said as I broke into tears.

"I'll be all right," he said.

Now, in the hospital room he stared right through me. I said nothing. He was already gone.

Learning Through Suffering
by Joyce Murray

I grew up in a big Catholic family. Throughout all my school years, there was a boy I had a crush on. Mike was the nicest, most handsome, strongest, best athlete, most well-liked, all around great guy. We dated all through high school and into college. When we married I was the happiest girl in the world. We both had good jobs, had a darling little Cape Cod house, and I thought we'd live happily ever after. Our relationship survived and thrived through job changes, lean times and plentiful times, and through the births of four beautiful children.

Each child brought joy and challenges, and so much love. We were one big happy family until I got the worst news our family could have received.

Mike had been out of town on a business trip and had died in his sleep. He was only thirty-four years old.

Our happy home came tumbling down. Mike was the glue that held our family together. And now he was gone? No! I couldn't, wouldn't believe it! People don't die that young, not when they are strong and healthy like Mike. He didn't smoke or drink or abuse his body in any way. No! This couldn't be true. I felt as though someone was playing a very sick trick on me. It had to be a mistake. All I could do was to pray to God to make Mike's heart start beating again. He'd raised Lazarus from the dead; He could raise Mike too, I was certain.

Each time the phone rang, I was sure someone was calling to tell me the good news that Mike had sat up in the morgue and started talking to the hospital personnel. But it never happened.

I wanted to go to him, but no one thought I should; no one would take me. I know people were trying to do what they thought best, but I still wish I could have been with him sooner than I was. I wanted to see for myself, to hold him, to touch him, but that wouldn't happen until a half hour before everyone else started arriving at the funeral home two and a half days later.

Those days were a horrible blur. Others were caring for my children and me. I was in deep shock and denial.

I didn't feel I could go on without the love of my life, my best friend, and confidante, my lover, and spiritual leader and advisor. I was devastated. I had serious doubts about how a loving God could allow this to happen. It just didn't make sense, and I always needed for things to make sense. I longed to understand. Was I being punished? But even if I wasn't worthy, how could He deprive our poor children of a loving father? I was totally miserable, brokenhearted, and felt like a knife was in my chest all the time. I would sigh and felt a painful weight. I didn't know what to do or think.

About three months after Mike's death, Mark, a man who had gone to school with Mike called me. The two had car pooled during college and we had all attended each other's weddings. I never knew him well, but I recalled Mike had thought Mark was a "nice guy". Mark was now divorced and had boys at the same school my girls attended. He called late one night when I was already in bed. It felt weird to be talking to another man while in the bed Mike and I had shared. I remember his ending the conversation by telling me I had to have faith in God and faith in myself. It sounded like good advice.

At about this time, the shock and denial were beginning to wear off, leaving the hideous reality of the situation bearing down on me. I continued going to Mass, although I usually ended up crying. Spiritually I had reached a low point.

The holidays came and I cried every day. I wasn't sure I could survive Christmas because it was so painful, but I felt I had to celebrate the season for our four little children who now looked only to me for everything.

Just after Christmas I came down with a terrible cold and flu, so on New Year's Eve I was home alone while my children spent the evening with family and friends. While getting ready for bed, I talked with Mike mentally as I did every night. I told him I wouldn't mind if Mark called me again. I was contemplating a new year, a new decade, and my life as a widow with four children. I was coming to the conclusion that I would have to remarry. I thought that was the only thing to make everything turn out all right.

The very next day, New Year's Day, Mark called. I saw it as no coincidence. I believed Mike and God were orchestrating my getting together with Mark. He seemed like such a great guy. I took his call as a green light from God to fill the void of Mike's absence, so I called him back a few days later and invited him to celebrate my birthday. In a matter of two months, we set a date to marry the following November and went full swing into making plans for a big wedding. It was confusing, but it seemed to offer the answer I'd been searching for. It seemed for some mysterious reason that Mike had died so I'd be free to marry Mark. I thought it was what God wanted for some purpose.

But way deep down inside, I knew something didn't feel right. I figured it was Mike's absence after eighteen years and Mark's being a different man. It was all a mixture of bitter and sweet, but life had some direction, some meaning again. And we were going to be a family again. I was going to have a man in my life again.

Upon reflection, I don't know if we weren't within God's will at all or if we, with our human imperfections, made it impossible for us to carry out His will. Mark and I had a beautiful wedding and honeymoon, followed by some very bad months together. Almost right away there were serious problems. I began to see a different man emerging. It became evident Mark and

I didn't really know each other. I hadn't seen any hint of his temper during our courtship, but now I witnessed horrible tantrums and violent outbursts. He was abusive emotionally, verbally, and otherwise. He had a chronic personality disorder which he had kept disguised by his great acting ability. When I found out I was pregnant, I hoped and prayed it would somehow help us. Things, however, went from bad to worse and we separated. However, I was still hopeful we could work things out. We just had to.

When I was about seven months pregnant, a friend of mine invited me once again to a Bible study. She had asked me several times before, but I was too mad at God to read His book. Finally, after realizing what a mess I had made of my life in less than two years, I felt desperate enough to attend. Completely broken, I turned to the Lord and began to allow Him to come into my heart.

When Mike was alive, I had experienced God's love through him. Instead of relying on God, I had relied on Mike. When he was gone, I was completely lost. Slowly I began to develop my own relationship with Him. I felt the beginnings of healing and hope and peace through prayer. I also reached a decision: I was going to file for a divorce. I needed time to sort it all out and really heal.

The divorce proceedings dragged by very slowly because Mark disputed me on everything. I was still emotionally needy and hurting so I reached out to him for physical comforting on one occasion because I thought I just couldn't live without "love" any longer. I see now that what we had was just sexual attraction. I wanted it to be love. So, after quite a while, in the midst of a pending divorce, we began to consider a reconciliation.

I often think back on all the coincidences that I took as signs I should marry Mark. When I discovered Mark's birthday was the same as one of my children's, I "knew" that was not just a coincidence. They were meant to share birthdays to signify a bond in our families.

After the birth of my third child, the chaplain had made a wise crack about having three girls. I had for some unknown reasons responded by saying, "Yes, and I bet the next three will be boys." Mike and I had only one son , but Mark had two, so I looked at the fact that, when we were married, I would have three boys.

My cousin had successfully remarried sixteen months after her first husband died. Another of my "signs" was we, too, would be getting married after a sixteen month period. Significantly, the priest, the church, and the hall we wanted were all available on only one day in the fall of 1990, my son's birthday.

Mark had finally gotten a job, and at this point I still didn't fully realize the extent of his personal problems. While I continued to hope and pray for his healing, we began dating again and went to counseling together. I believed things looked a bit optimistic until we tried to confront a real issue, and yet, I continued to hold onto the most minute signs of hope. After months of continuously praying, it became clear to me that sometimes the Lord answers prayers with "no".

In the passage of time since my divorce, I have gained a new appreciation for the role of suffering. In the past I had always naturally sought to avoid it, but I'm beginning to see how there can be benefit in it. Unfortunately, we sometimes learn the most from our painful life experiences. We have a choice. We can become bitter, as I did after Mike's death, or we can become better.

His Shirt
by Christina Keenan

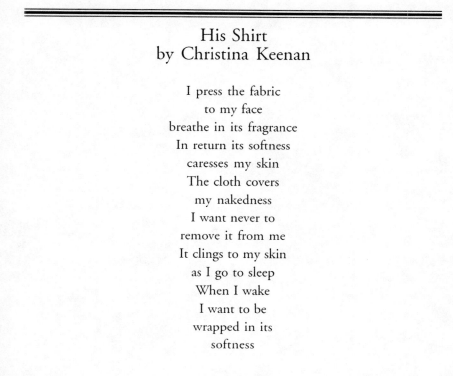

I press the fabric
to my face
breathe in its fragrance
In return its softness
caresses my skin
The cloth covers
my nakedness
I want never to
remove it from me
It clings to my skin
as I go to sleep
When I wake
I want to be
wrapped in its
softness

feeling its weight
against me
always near me
it protects me
from the cold

CHAPTER 5

THE LOSS OF FRIENDS

**Men and women describe the importance of friendship
as they discuss their losses.**

Losing Friends, The Hard Way
by Al Sandvik

I'm in the season when my ranks are imperceptibly but inevitably thinning. More and more, the obituary page becomes an important source of reportage. I like it when newspapers let the family include a photo with the notice. Even if you don't know the person, so often you can see how the face puts meaning to the name, or the other way around. You feel, yes, she looks like a Mildred, one of those good-egg Mildreds. Every once in a while I'm startled by one of those faces saying something back to me because it's someone I know, someone I shared some life with.

Losing friends this hard way, my contemporaries tell me, is something we have to expect and get used to. And we sort of do, at least the formal part of it. But not the bottomless finality of death. That is always a wrench.

When a friend goes, all of us who were close are—no matter how much warning—shocked and saddened. Our first questions, if we didn't know, are always when, where, and how did he die. We need a reason for death other than the one looking us full in the face, that the time comes.

Well, it was a cancer she had, or a bad heart, or an aneurysm, whatever. Dwelling on the cause—how long she had it, how she managed it, or so on—is useful. It gives us a way to talk about death with everyday words and thoughts. If we didn't have the how of it to talk about, many of us might be left wordless in a discussion of the real event: That our friend has left this vale, the door bolted fast behind; no longer here touching and touched; that voice, that smile gone for good.

We wade through the tides of ceremonial grief at the visitation, the funeral, and the burial, trying to remember that it shouldn't be entirely depressing. We summon faith in order to feel some of the promised uplifting aspects of death.

After, on the quiet ride back home or back to work, we wonder how we can keep his or her memory alive. We promise ourselves, we pledge that we will never forget, but, at the same time, we're afraid the forgetting process will begin the minute we get back to the stuff of our own lives: the picking up of a long memo to get ready for tomorrow's meeting, or using a pencil to plan supper for our Friday night guests, or yanking on the mower's starter rope to get at our overdue grass cutting.

But, try as we might to resist, time moves our departed friends farther back in our minds.

My way of trying to not forget is this: soon after it happens, whenever the cloud of sorrow yields a little space, I think through how this person changed my life; more specifically, changed my living. I consider how they affected the way I do, or think about, certain things, how they changed or added to my views and values.

I mine our shared memories, digging for hard ore, looking deeper than the handy, popular physical traits—"Wasn't it wonderful the way she always . . . ?" I look further for what it was he or she and I can hold onto together, a definitive rock of their lives that I replicated for my own.

Once found, after I get back to the self-centered busy business of my own life, I can find myself, even years later, pleasantly interrupted by realizing that I am, at that moment, doing, saying, or thinking something the way he would have and, in that moment, I can recognize a living bloom of our friendship.

Time Stopped
by Sara A. Miller

I stopped writing in my journal the day Elizabeth died. It was as if on that day life's memories became too scattered and too painful to write about. Ironically, though I best express myself by recording my thoughts, I could not do so after Elizabeth's death. Death is such a surreal phenomenon; it is hard to believe that it is being experienced. I felt by not recording my thoughts, I would perhaps awake from my nightmare and find that my friend was still alive. If, however, I wrote about the happenings, there would be concrete evidence that it had occurred.

We were a group of thirty college students on a trip to Bolivia to "save the world"—or at least the mountain inhabitants living six hours from La Paz and any form of modern civilization. After arriving in La Paz and doing some second world sightseeing, we were finally ready to do some third world life saving.

The bus on which we rode was an old rickety tour bus—probably the only form of motorized transportation that had ever traveled most of the roads. As we made our way up the mountains, we dodged goats and old men on bicycles. Our team consisted of twenty students who would construct a health post for the surrounding people, and a medical/public health team that would travel to the homes of the Aymara people to deliver modest medical care and public health advice. Our accommodations were very third world. We all piled into one room to sleep, and our only connection with civilization was by a radio whose frequencies were disturbed by even the slightest change in weather. We were undaunted though, especially Elizabeth. It is funny that when we write about the deceased we sensationalize their personalities and actions. "She was the most enthusiastic, the hardest working, the first one awake with a smile on her face." In Elizabeth's case, however, this was all true.

Our first day of work, we awoke to cloudy skies. The two sections of the team split up. Elizabeth was a member of the construction team, and I was on the medical team. It is an eerie experience to pinpoint what I was doing at the exact moment that the lightening struck. We had arrived at a mud cottage where a little boy who was suffering from terrible pneumonia lived. The child, who even at a young age was modest, did not want us in the house while the doctor was giving him his shot. The three of us who were students stood outside singing American songs and blowing plastic medical gloves into balloons to entertain his siblings. They were delighted, and we laughed as the drizzle began to soak through our fleece team jackets. We had our faces turned toward the children, so we didn't see the lightening strike on the plain below. After finishing at this last cottage, we began the descent to our truck. We heard urgent honking and assumed that our local driver was impatient to return in time for dinner. As we all reached the bottom of the hill, he began yelling in Spanish to run. Our professor, who spoke Spanish as her native language, finally gathered that someone had been hurt and we needed to return to help.

We arrived at the compound to find all of our team members in a state of hysterics. As we stepped out of the van, our team leader, also a student, informed us that Elizabeth had been struck by lightening and killed. Four other team members had been close enough to the blast to be thrown backward and shocked. At that moment, time stopped. I have always felt that the news of a death becomes like watching yourself in a movie. People fell to the ground too astonished to move. Time passed, but none of us were capable of doing anything.

As evening came, our professors made a dinner that wasn't eaten by anyone. The doctors informed us that, even at home, Elizabeth would not have lived through the strike. That night we stayed in the big room knowing that Elizabeth's body was in the next room. All of us were too frightened and strangely repulsed to look at her. Rain continued throughout the night; none of us slept. Those who had tape players put their headphones on in an effort to block out the noise of the rain pounding the plastic roof above us. I have since been amazed at how quickly a phobia can develop. In an instant, thirty-five people had become afraid of rain. We took turns sitting with the others who had also been affected by the blast. During this time, I pieced together the story. The team had worked throughout the day digging out a tree stump from the area where a foundation would be poured. It began to rain, and Elizabeth and another student stood holding a tarp above the heads of the local villagers to keep them dry. The lightening came in an instant. One minute Elizabeth had been laughing at a joke, the next minute, she was gone. A local woman who sat directly beneath Elizabeth had been left unscarred, but the baby in her arms had been struck and died.

Morning finally came and the old adage that things would look better in the morning did not hold true. The dynamics of group grieving is frightening when students who had been virtual strangers the week before were suddenly forced to be each other's support system. My whole life, I have looked to my family for comfort and support. Now in the time of my greatest grief and even greater religious questioning, I was a continent away from my loved ones. I was forced to rely upon people I hardly knew for the sort of comfort that would get me through this grueling time. Tempers began to flare as people's instincts turned to the selfish need to be at home and collapse among those who had not lived through the experience. Because all of us went through the crisis together, we all teetered on the verge of sadness and anger, but many did not express these feelings because there was no objective outlet through which to vent our feelings. The storms had shifted, and the radio would not reach our contacts back in La Paz. A group of friends who had been the closest to Elizabeth finally decided we needed to say our goodbyes.

What a strange, and yet somehow primitive, peaceful experience. She looked at peace though her lips were blackened at the points where the life had been burnt from her. The sheet lay so delicately over her—protecting not her—but rather us, from the horrors that lay beneath: a charred work boot and the shredded leg of her jeans where the energy had been grounded. To this day, I am plagued by the fact that I could not touch the body of my friend. She lay there more beautiful than the waxy, swollen bodies of the dead that I had seen before. Her skin was stretched taut, not from the brushes and colors of the make-up artist, but from not having lost its youthful elasticity.

The smell of death was not present in the room that morning. Instead, there was the smell of charcoal. Not like when a campfire clings to you after an evening, but that virtually odorless odor for charcoal—a cleansing charcoal that purges the poisons from your stomach and had purged her body of life. The room was filled also with the faint odors of homemade antiseptic. Sterile hospital smells did not exist in this outpost. It almost seemed death was meant to be this way. In civilization, Elizabeth would have been pumped, tubed, taped, and left to suffer through the convenience of modern medicine. Here, she lay adorned with white blooms picked from outside the building and grasses placed like a necklace around her neck.

After the initial acceptance that Elizabeth was gone, I felt it would be selfish to grieve for myself any longer. I took it upon myself to help others through their grieving. I began collecting things: tree leaves, the blooms that lay upon her to give to her boyfriend who was still in the States and probably not yet aware of Elizabeth's fate. I worked with our team captain to whittle a cross that would be used as a memorial at the site. Leading the group and offering my support to them was the thing that got me through. I began to feel very little: a strong desire to return home, and much compassion for others, but no feelings of sadness for Elizabeth's passing.

We were finally informed via the radio that our professor had made it to La Paz with Elizabeth and there would be a funeral there as well. However, since we were traveling during their holiday season, they did not think we could get tickets out of the country until the end of the month, our original departure date. Two days passed. Some of our team doctors went out into the village to work, but the students sat at the compound listlessly playing cards and straining our ears for any noise on the radio. Finally, we were given word that the team would return to La Paz and that seven of us, the "high priority" people who had known Elizabeth the best, could fly home the next morning.

The events that followed were strangely ironic. If she had not been someone that I had known and cared for, I would have laughed at the wake that Elizabeth was given. The makeshift viewing was thrown together for the benefit of the team, and her body would be flown back to England to her parents the following day for a proper funeral. The seven early departures piled into a truck. The driver, in attempts to console us, relayed the events of her son's death the previous year.

We pushed ourselves up four flights of concrete stairs. Dank puddles settled into the concrete and the paint peeling off of the walls had turned the color of rotting book pages. The top flat surface of each wall was covered with "beggars barbed wire"—the concrete wall had been dabbled with shards of glass before it was fully dry. Quite an odd thought that someone would scale the walls of this dilapidated building to steal the bodies from this makeshift funeral parlor. Upon reaching the fourth floor, the building did look like a parlor, a fortune telling parlor. The casket was raised to the level of my waist and supported with cinder blocks. The renters of the room had placed red velvet blockades like those at a movie theater around the casket, apparently to make us feel comfortable by giving us separation from our friend's body. The room glowed with a bright glaring purple from the neon blinking cross perched behind the polished wooden box. We hugged and cried, but at this point, I was cried out and numb to the idea of Elizabeth's death. I was crying at the pathetic state of her funeral. We laughed through our tears as we attempted to make things right by saying, "Elizabeth would have been so happy about the cross, purple was her favorite color." I was angered she was buried in her work boots and a sweater with tiny sheep that she had worn in the sixth grade. Still these were the nicest clothes she had with her, since we had all packed for a month of hard labor and medical work.

The next morning we returned to the States early. It was impossible to part with the rest of the team. They had become family. After not having eaten and barely having slept in three days, emotions were heightened and I tried to get them to change my ticket. I felt an overwhelming sense of guilt over leaving the rest to mourn in what had become to me a wretched place. I was forced onto the bus, however, and found myself on a plane going home. Arriving at home, I still could not entirely allow myself to mourn. My family listened and offered support, but they had not been there and could not understand the extent of what I had lived through. I called my fellow team members constantly, grasping for the sense of togetherness that we had experienced in Bolivia. The phone bills piled up, and my sense of peace did not become any stronger.

Two weeks later, after the entire team had returned home, we met in Chicago at the apartment of one of the students. I was excited at being reunited, but felt a sense of unease about what I would face. Sure enough, the evening started off fun and only slightly strained. As the drinks flowed more quickly, so did the emotions, and I found myself in the middle of a breakdown session. Our team captain, who had been so supportive during the length of the trip, began blaming himself for not being able to resuscitate Elizabeth. Others began to join in the "what if" questioning, and the night took a turn for the worst. I suddenly realized that I had no interest in being supportive any longer. I acted concerned, but knew nothing could change what had happened, and each of us needed to come to his or her own resolve about this experience. I was angry and slightly jealous I had not been at the site of the accident and thus could not take part fully in the "what ifs".

A wedge between the two groups, the witnesses of tragedy and those who were affected but not actually present at the actual strike, was driven deeper when we finally returned to school. The Bolivia team was a strange wonder on campus. It is a small university. Everyone on campus knew what had happened and wanted to find out the details. While most team members clung to each other, I could not bear to see but a few of the team members. We had spent four terrorizing days talking and thinking together about one intense incident, and upon our return, I realized the superficiality in most of our relationships. Seeing my fellow team members meant having to fall back into a special connection we felt we were supposed to feel, but most did not.

I sensed that I was becoming easily angered by many things that would not previously have angered me. An article had been published in the school paper claiming Elizabeth was to be honored because she had given her life in the service of others. I was upset because it was not as if a building girder had fallen on her head. She could just as easily have been struck by lightening at home. I was not minimizing her beauty of heart and soul, but I did not like my friend being turned into the poster child for a service organization. I felt as though they were using an unfortunate situation to their advantage.

The team was called together to meet with a "Severe Accident Crisis Team." The crisis intervention leaders, though they were professionals, could not understand the full depth of the problem. They split the team into the two groups for counseling: the strike victims and those who were in Bolivia but did not see or feel the strike. The grieving was intensified by the fact we were made to feel as though our emotions were less important, and less justified, because we had not been present at the time the lightening struck. I felt spiteful and angry most of the time, but I now know all of these emotions were acceptable.

As time wore on, people slowly began to talk less about Elizabeth. I tried to shut the experience out of my mind. I suffered severely from separation anxiety with loved ones. I was paranoid that in leaving anyone, even for a few minutes, it could possibly be the last time that I would see him or her. The feelings lessened for practical purposes as time went on. Knowing I could not spend my entire life not leaving those I care about, I forced myself to go about my daily life.

The anger I felt toward the university and my team members eventually subsided and changed to a desperate need to let Elizabeth's memory live on. We formed a committee with many of the Bolivia team members to collect money for a memorial at the university in Elizabeth's name. I slowly began to feel compassion for those with whom I had been angry. In collecting money and beginning the construction of a theater in Elizabeth's name, I felt that I had finally put my friend's memory to rest in a respectable and comfortable way.

Memories of her still pop up at strange times, but I have entered the period where I can more easily disconnect the terrible memories of Bolivia with the happy memories of Elizabeth that occurred before Bolivia. I am still fearful of lightening. I have been able to resume normal activity and even convince myself most of the time that a person cannot stop daily life when the rain begins. Every time the weather kicks up, however, and every time I see lightening on the horizon, I think of Elizabeth. For this, I am ironically fearful and thankful in the same breath. I relive terrible memories at the whim of the weather, but I have the rain that I can regularly count on to remind me of a dear friend who will always be with me in spirit.

Several months after I returned from Bolivia, I finally began writing again. However, it was not until a year later that I could bring myself to write about my experience there.

Anatol
by Stanley M. Lefco

Anatol and I were brought together through adversity, and our unusual friendship lasted until his death. When I met him, it was 1981; I had been a widower for three years. My wife, who was twenty-nine years old, had died of a brain tumor. I was thirty-four at the time.

Anatol was in his late sixties or early seventies when his wife died of cancer. Our rabbi thought our common tragedies would give us a point of reference. I doubt we would have ever met otherwise. I went to visit him. It was an awkward first meeting. He was a quiet and gentle man. He spoke softly, in his European accent which reminded me of my parents who, like Anatol, had come to this country from Poland. He was still deeply mourning the death of his wife. Her picture occupied a central place on top of his television. As time passed, he mentioned her less often, but I don't think he ever stopped thinking of her.

I would try to call him about once a week to see how he was doing and if he needed anything. I would also try to stop by and see him on a somewhat regular basis. But there were times when several weeks passed when I realized I hadn't called. Rarely did he call me; he didn't want to bother me. In the beginning he was in good health and was pretty much able to manage for himself. He didn't drive, so he either walked or took a cab to the supermarket. Bridge was an important part of his life, and he had a circle of friends with whom he played. I think these friends, whom I never met, were also friends of his wife.

Anatol had no family in Atlanta. His son lived in Mexico and his two grandchildren lived in California. Other family members lived in Europe and Mexico. Except for his son, I never met any of his family. I was introduced to his grandchildren for the first time at his funeral.

Our lives went in different directions. I started to date again, but he had no interest in female companionship. I never asked him if he had any interest; I'm certain he would have thought I was ridiculous. It is difficult now to recall what we did talk about. His family. My family. World affairs. Grocery shopping. I don't think he ever watched television. He would listen to the radio and there was always a newspaper around and a weekly news magazine.

His life for the most part was self-contained. After five years of single life and many blind dates, I remarried in 1983 to a wonderful woman, Jane. Four years later Leah came along and three years after that Michael was born.

While I started my life over again, Anatol maintained his card games and his long distance phone and letter contacts with his family. We were aging in different life cycles. My younger friends and acquaintances were having children. Those closer to my age and older were celebrating their children's Bar and Bat Mitzvahs, graduations from colleges, and marriages. Either they were celebrating milestones of their own marriages, or getting divorced; some were celebrating fortieth or fiftieth birthdays.

Anatol's friends were getting older and some were dying. His circle was getting smaller. As time went by, I slowly watched him age and turn even more inward and become more reclusive.

Looking back, I find it ironic that he lived in a part of Atlanta that is the social center of the singles scene. On weekend nights the streets would be filled with festivity, and a few blocks away, down a street of apartments, lived Anatol, quietly alone.

The day came when the bridge games ceased, for the friends were no longer there to play with. For Anatol, even going out for groceries became a terrible chore. When we first met, he never complained about his condition, but as the years passed he began to talk more and more about his health. It became a preoccupation. Visiting him was becoming less and less enjoyable. Offers to take him for doctor visits were refused. He was stubborn in his way and didn't want to be a bother. I felt somewhat useless in trying to help him.

Yet, he delighted in my children, and there was a sparkle in his eyes when I brought them by. They never left his apartment without a box of candy. I always wondered how he managed to keep them in stock.

As he was able to do less and less and I felt I should be doing more, I contacted the Jewish Family Services. They assigned a social worker to help him. I began to fear more and more for Anatol. Living alone, who would help him if he suddenly became ill? What if he couldn't get to a phone? I dreaded a phone call from a neighbor, telling me that he or she found him on the floor ill or dead.

Then one day the social worker called and said he tried to reach Anatol, but that he was incoherent over the phone. He had gone by his apartment, but he would not let him in. I called, but I could barely understand what he was saying. His voice was very weak and his words unclear and muffled.

I went there and after an insufferable time Anatol let me in. He was lying in bed, breathing heavily. He was weak and pale. I insisted on calling 911 to have him taken to a hospital. He was always against this and, with all his energy, implored me not to do it. I was lost. I tried to reach his doctor and got the doctor on duty, who told me to call an ambulance. But I hesitated. First, I called his son in Mexico and told him that I thought he should come to Atlanta immediately. Then I called Jane and explained my dilemma. In the end I did call an ambulance and, hours later, I found myself at the hospital, answering questions from the admissions staff. In a treatment room Anatol was being fed intravenously for his dehydrated state and given other medication. It was the next morning before I drove home trying to gather my thoughts and understand my feelings.

The hospital staff did all they could to make him comfortable. I tried to visit as much as I could, but the hospital was far from my home. He had been in the hospital only three or four days when I last saw him. I asked him if he needed or wanted anything. Softly and with all his energy, he told me he wanted to die. He had told me that on other occasions, but I hoped his spirit which I always believed he had (but which he would not admit) would fight on. A couple days later when it seemed he was improving and might be able to spend his remaining life in a home or his apartment with supervision, he took a sudden turn for the worse and died. It was only a week after I had put him in the hospital.

I realize that I knew very little about Anatol. I knew he survived the Holocaust and had lived for a time in Cuba. I had once asked him to tell me about his life, for I was certain that it would make an interesting story. But when I pressed him, he declined. I tried unsuccessfully on other occasions to have him tell me the story of his life, but he never would.

I don't know how to describe my relationship with him. At one point I thought he might be a father figure, but our relationship never matured to that. While we were more than acquaintances, saying we were friends might be stretching the meaning of the word. Yes, we were friends; I know he thought of me as a friend, but we were like two ships anchored next to one another. As much as we had in common, there was so much we didn't.

The funeral was on a bright and sunny Sunday morning. His son, his grandchildren, two friends, Jane, the rabbi who brought us together, and I were the only ones there. As the rabbi gave the eulogy and pronounced Hebrew prayers, I looked down the hill and one hundred feet away saw the marker where my first wife was buried.

His passing has left a void. I miss this sweet, caring, quiet, gentle man and know that now he is, at last, at peace.

Jacque's Story
by Joan C. Curtis

This year when the jonquils poked their lovely yellow heads out of the winter ground to announce the advent of spring, I was suddenly reminded of Jacque.

It was a chilly February afternoon the first time I visited Jacque. As I headed across town with the directions on my car seat, I wondered what I would say to her. What does one say to a young, vital woman who has breast cancer? My mind played out scenarios, but each one seemed shallow, lost like the tail end of a sermon with no meaning.

Jacque greeted me at the door with a radiant smile, and my awkwardness fell by the wayside. She measured about five feet two or three. Her light brown hair was cropped short, and her hazel eyes bright, full of energy.

When she talked about her illness and the prognosis, she was upbeat, encouraged, hopeful. Following a bout with breast cancer the year before, the doctors happily informed her the cancer had not appeared in her lymph nodes. Unfortunately they recently discovered the disease went into her blood stream. She now had a spot on her lungs. But, she assured me, as if I was the one needing assurance, the doctors were trying a new medicine. She had a chipper way of talking. Her speech and voice were laced with shining hope.

Jacque was the mother of two young children, ages five and nine. Her greatest fear was to die and leave her children. "I want to see my children graduate from high school. I want to dry their adolescent tears. I want to be there for their prom nights. I want to know my grandchildren." She talked more about her family and loved ones and their pain than she did her own. Her main concern was with her family's suffering.

Beginning with that first February afternoon, I visited Jacque nearly every week. I went as a lay counselor for my church. During that time I watched her deteriorate physically but grow spiritually. I was there to give her support, but I often wondered who was supporting whom. I could do nothing but listen, hold her hand, laugh, and cry with her. After each visit I was more convinced than ever that Jacque would survive this illness. I remember telling my husband, "If anyone can fight this disease, Jacque can. She's determined, like a mother lion protecting her cubs. She won't leave her children."

By March when the cold hand of winter had loosened its grip, Jacque and I had become close friends. I relished her enthusiasm and optimism. During each visit she'd tell me about a new test or a new kind of drug the doctors recommended trying. The following week she'd report matter-of-factly that the drug had failed. The results of one test after another proved disappointing. Jacque was running out of options. She became angry and frustrated with her oncologists. The doctors didn't believe she'd live. They acted as if she was already dead. I mimicked her hope and actually believed it. I prayed harder than I've ever prayed in my life: *God please give Jacque one sign, just one piece of good news.* Was that too much to ask? But my prayers went unanswered.

Spring came and Jacque was put on oxygen. She downplayed it like she did everything, said it was just to help her breathe. She had a new pain in her side, but she felt it was the result of the medication. I began to suspect otherwise, but I didn't tell Jacque. She told me she and her family were going to the beach. "We go every year, and I don't want to disappoint the children." Jacque said she didn't care if people stared at her because of the oxygen. "I'm just going to get my lawn chair and umbrella, carry my oxygen tank with me, and enjoy myself." She grinned at me as if her plan to go to the beach was the most natural thing in the world. We both didn't say what I know we both thought: this might be her last beach trip.

It was harder and harder for me to go see Jacque. On the trip across town, I felt myself getting lower and lower. I feared walking into her house, knowing that her future was so bleak. I feared hearing the next dreadful prognosis. My heart pounded and my stomach tightened as I walked once again up the cement steps to her door.

That day, Jacque's mother was visiting. To have some privacy we talked in Jacque's bedroom. She was full of life. I'd never seen her with so much energy. She sat on the bed, Indian style, and chatted as if we were attending a slumber party together. We laughed and talked. The heavy cloud that was hanging over me lifted and flew away. Jacque talked to me about the out-pouring of love she had been receiving from so many people she didn't even know. "I've gotten cards and letters from all over town. Churches have learned of my plight, and people are sending me notes. It's unbelievable. I've seen so much beauty. I've experienced love at its purest. It's been an amazing journey. I know after learning all this, God won't let me die. There must be some purpose to it all. I just know he won't let me die now."

And I knew he wouldn't either. It just didn't make sense. Jacque was rich with the true meaning of life. She was overflowing spiritually even though physically the disease wouldn't let up. Several times she said, "I wish I could just shed this body. It's wasted."

Jacque's spirit entered me. I left her house that morning with a renewed sense of self. There was a lightness to my step that I hadn't noticed before. I began seeing and feeling things with a new kind of intensity. A breeze blew against my face. I cherished and held onto the pleasure of that moment. When an old man smiled at me, I smiled back, the depth of that greeting riveting me in place. The sky was bluer than ever before and the sun brighter. The flowers had begun to blossom. Jonquils peeked out of the ground; azaleas began blooming. Colors of majestic quality appeared all around me, and for once in my life I really saw them. I saw everything, felt it, smelled it, lived it.

But I wanted Jacque to experience these things, too. I wanted her to share in my renewed sense of life. I wanted to give her everything I was feeling. Whenever I got into my car, drove somewhere, enjoyed a pleasant dinner with my husband, exercised at the Y, shopped for groceries, walked across the street, I felt guilt. Jacque couldn't do these things. Tears filled my eyes at the strangest times and places, once during a concert where the music filled me with sensations I'd never known before and once during a lunch with friends. I couldn't stand living with these new heightened senses while Jacque died.

One afternoon my husband brought me a fistful of jonquils. They were glorious—every possible shade of yellow. I placed them on my kitchen table, and they brightened the room. As I looked at the delicate flowers, their petals and soft buds, each one singing about the beauty of life, I realized that Jacque might never see jonquils again. This would be her last chance. As much as I loved those flowers and as much joy as they brought me, I resolved to give them to Jacque. I had to do it for me, to ease my guilt.

But Jacque had to cancel our next two visits because she went into the hospital. The flowers wilted and died before I could get them to her.

Days later Jacque went into a coma. I watched her fight to the bitter end. Her will to live was amazing. Late in her illness she told me that each morning when she opened her eyes and saw light, she was grateful to be alive. I knew then that Jacque's hope was evaporating. She gripped each day like a precious gift, afraid to let go. But she finally did on May 21, 1995. She was thirty-eight years old.

One year later I still struggle to understand why Jacque had to die. Will her children remember her courage, her hope, her love? The memory of her last days, fighting, battling to hang on, haunts me. Sometimes when I feel overcome by anger and doubt, I remember Jacque's optimism, and I'm ashamed.

Jacque's life touched mine, and her death will never erase that. I remember the day I caught her doing laundry. She told me how grateful she was to feel well enough to do the laundry. Can you believe it? Laundry, that chore we all despise. For Jacque, life's chores became life's pleasures. When Jacque returned from the beach, she handed me a small hand-woven basket. I put it in a prominent place in my home, a place I must pass everyday. She gave me the gift of life. She gave me her spirit and her will to live.

Today, watching the jonquils begin to rise up from the ground, Jacque's spirit clutches me again. I reach down and touch the delicate flower like I would a newborn child. I lift my head to the sky, close my eyes, and when I feel the warmth of the sun and the delicate caress of a spring breeze on my face, I see Jacque's radiant smile.

Maybe God had a purpose after all.

What Does Bird-Watching Have To Do With Grief Anyway?
by Rebecca A. Wright, RN, CRNH

On November 17, 1995, my thirty-five year old best friend died of a massive heart attack. There was no warning, no signs that she had heart disease. She was just there one day and gone the next. The emptiness has been overwhelming at times. I lost my confidant, my cheerleader, and my bird watching partner. It wasn't really the activity of bird watching (I've since recognized); it was the camaraderie and the conversation that made our adventures so enjoyable.

When my friend died, she left behind a large circle of friends who love her and miss her as much as I do. We are all grieving in our own way and in our own time. Periodically, we get together and share memories of the times we spent with our friend. It helps. Although each of our relationships with her is as different as each of us is, and each of us is grieving in our unique way, it is comforting to share our grief and know someone understands. Sometimes, when we are together, I bring a single white rose as a reminder of the one who is no longer with us.

***

Today, I went bird watching alone. The first time since your death. I came home soaking wet and full of mud. You would have loved it. I missed you. I went to one of our favorite places and everywhere I looked, I remembered other trips we made there. I thought, *There's where we saw the Spotted Sandpiper. There's the field we cut across in ankle-deep mud to get closer to the Egrets.* The rain seemed to suit my mood today. It started when I was about a half mile from the car and I decided to not turn back. Instead I let it drench me. It seeped deep into the secret places in my heart. The places I don't show to anyone anymore. It hurts too bad. I thought, as it started to drip off the bill of my cap, that maybe the rain could clean out the pain. Well, it didn't clean out the pain, but I did pass another milestone today. I went bird-watching alone, and I didn't fall apart.

The morning after you died, I sat in the breakfast room staring out onto the deck. I wasn't looking at or for anything in particular, just staring. As I sat there in shock, a little House Wren came and sat on the ledge of the deck and seemed to be peering in through the glass door at me. It was only there for a moment and then it was gone. I remembered how we had visited your sister's house in the spring and saw a Bewick's Wren building a nest near the porch. It was an unusual sight for this part of the country and we were so excited. Three weeks before you died, I gave you a birthday card with wrens on the front of it. Was the little wren who visited my deck trying to tell me something? I remember sitting there letting the tears run down my face and hoping the wren would come back, just once more. Or, was it that I wanted you to come back?

That was almost one year ago. I've gone through lots of "firsts" this year and just last week was your birthday. It is easier to cope now than it was during the first few months. Then, it just hurt to breathe. And the guilt I felt for hurting so bad. I'm not your parents who have lost a child, or your daughter who lost her mother, or a sister or brother. I'm a friend, but I have lost the best friend I ever had and probably will ever have. You were someone who loved me unconditionally, even after living together for three years. You were always there to listen and never judged. You taught me what it meant to be a true friend. I miss that closeness now, that sharing of myself. I only hope that I was the kind of friend you needed me to be.

I've worked in Hospice for almost four years, and I deal with loss and grief issues every day. Nothing, however, that I have learned really prepared me for how I would be feeling after your death. I knew it all from an intellectual side, but now I know it from the heart. I used to step outside of myself and assess what I was feeling. I would think to myself, *That's denial*, or *That's bargaining*, as a particular thought or feeling would cross my mind. I think instead of helping, it made the process more difficult. I was constantly judging my progress, or lack of, and not allowing myself to just feel. People in the community and even family looked to me as "the expert" and to help them with how they were feeling. But how could I help when I was doing a lousy job of coping myself? It's only been in the last couple weeks that I have given myself permission to feel again, and it hurts. I realized that only in living through my own grief can I help others cope with theirs. I don't think the pain ever really goes away; it never just passes. A person can learn to cope with it though, and life becomes easier to live again. Your birthday, the anniversary of the last time we spent time together, and the anniversary of your death are all happening in rapid succession, and I can't ignore my grief any longer. I now understand I have to live through this to get to the other side, and I can't hurry this journey any more.

I never look at one of God's winged creatures now without thinking of my precious friend and I wonder if it isn't my friend somehow looking back at me saying, "It's okay, I'm all right, and soon you will be too. And when it comes your time to die, I'll be back with wings on to help you over to the other side. Then we'll have eternity to spend together." So, maybe next weekend I'll go bird watching alone again.

Martha
by Pat Goehe

"Dear friends of Women's Studies, it is with deep regret I write this memo. Our friend, Martha, is dying and by the time you receive this, she probably will already have left us."

***

I had known Martha for many years primarily through our work with the Faculty Senate on our University Campus. Later, I was drafted into heading the Women's Studies Program as it was being cut by our Provost; I learned Martha had helped start it. We laughed together about all those male doctors she had to put up with over her career as nurse and Associate Dean of the School of Nursing on our campus.

I also learned of some of Martha's health problems. Among other things, she was diabetic and the previous year had been on leave because of the severity of her problems. Returning to work under a new dean, Martha became overloaded and before anyone knew it, Martha was in the hospital dying.

As soon as word came to me, I began daily treks to the local hospital. Most of the nurses giving the care had been trained by her. Colleagues were always there in vigil. She was a wise woman in many ways. She wanted a dignified death without extraordinary measures. She created a living will and spelled out other estate details. Because she believed her sister could not "pull the plug", so to speak, she gave a friend power of attorney and executor status. Each day I would talk with this friend. Martha's condition deteriorated. At appointed times, the friend and I would go into Martha's room where she was plugged up to every machine possible. According to the friend, Martha's doctor said he wanted Martha to die a natural death. "This is natural?" the friend would say to me. We would look at each other, then at Martha, and shake our heads.

When the machines became intolerable, the friend started investigating as to why this was allowed to continue since she had a living will on file. The nurses indicated the head of the hospital would have to make the decision. Well, the chief of staff was Martha's doctor. The truth became known. He was so close to Martha that he couldn't let her go. The friend realized she would have to take legal action. I was learning much about living wills, as well as about dying, and I was to learn even more in the next few days.

I sent my memo out to the Women's Studies group. The friend and I discussed making a special memorial through our group or possibly joining with the School of Nursing who would undoubtedly do something. We decided that the two groups were different and that it was important to recognize Martha's contributions to women through our program. Not wanting to be a dictator, and since I had been a silent supporter for many years of Women's Studies, I asked in my memo for input from the group on their preferences.

I spent that Friday evening at the hospital. As I left, I told the friend that I would be back Monday because I was tied up with family things on the weekend. On Sunday evening I was exhausted and fell into a deep sleep. I dream often and this evening was no exception. In my dream I had driven to the parking lot of the building where I work. As usual, the parking lot was very crowded. I grabbed my briefcase and belongings and headed toward the building which housed several departments. Mine was on the third floor; the School of Nursing took up the second. As I was half way to the building, I saw a woman stop in the parking lot. She seemed to be waiting for me. As I drew closer, I realized it was Martha. I thought to myself, *Oh my God, what has happened? How am I ever going to explain my memo to her? How did this happen? What is going on?*

Face to face with Martha, I couldn't believe my eyes. First, as though she had been reading my mind, she said, "It's okay, Pat." I just stood there not being able to say a word. Never had I seen Martha look as beautiful as she did then. Clothing was not something important to her. Now she was in what my daughter would term a "preppy" outfit. She wore a pleated plaid skirt, a well tailored blazer, a delicately ruffled white blouse. But what really impressed me was her face. Her skin was luminous and her blue eyes long ago faded with aging, now were as bright as a newborn's.

"Martha, you're beautiful!" She smiled at me in her usual way and said, "Thanks, Pat." Then she was gone. So was my dream.

I didn't have to be at school early that Monday, so I casually went about showering, and half way through dressing I remembered the dream. Somehow I knew intuitively what it meant. I quickly tried to call the friend at her department, but got no answer. I rushed to get dressed and on the campus. As I approached my office door, my chairman came out of his. He told me the friend had been trying to reach me. Then he added, "Martha died last night."

I related this experience to a number of people. Some, including the friend, looked at me strangely and said nothing. Others jokingly told me they hoped I wouldn't dream about them. I have had several similar dream experiences since that time. I don't know why. I do know I never take them lightly.

Thank You, My Friend
by Bruce Owens

I thank you for the many times
you got in touch with me
and all your contributions
to my happy memory.

I thank you for the friendly smile
with which you always greeted me
and for the kind and thoughtful
gracious way you treated me.
You were the shining symbol
of a friendship really true,
and a wonderful inspiration
in all I try to do.
You were a soothing comfort
to my very smallest sorrow,
and you instilled the hope
I needed for every new tomorrow.
And so I thank you for the joys
and favors you extended,
and I pray that God will bless you always,
my dear and faithful friend.

I have many, many memories of Jerry. Jerry and his wife became involved with me when I had a lot of questions about life and no one to answer them. I did not understand the sacrifice and time that they devoted to me then, but as I went through college, became a Big Brother myself, graduated, went on to receive a Master's Degree with honors, married, had children, and won a national championship, I realized what type of guidance they gave me. Jerry and his wife answered my questions by teaching me values about life, by showing me friendship, love, how to set goals, dreams, and most of all, how to keep plugging away and trying to do things right at all times.

Some of my fondest memories include the old blue Volkswagen Bug that I thought was a secret agent car because I could push the red brake light and it would come on. I remember watching my first Wimbledon Match with Jerry. I remember that he would sometimes let me help build the deck on their old house.

When I was playing football and missed picture day, Jerry took a whole bunch of photos of me and made me feel great. We won the Cub Scouts Pine Wood Derby Tournament. On my mantle, I still have the orange race car, #19, that he and I built. Jerry helped me build a great chess set out of plexiglass and TV tubes. Jerry and his wife took me to my first Pro-Football game (the Bengals versus the Pittsburgh Steelers), and I still have my ticket stub. I rode the yellow ten-speed bike that they gave me for ten years. I still have it, even though I can't ride it because of a serious knee injury from football. They took me canoeing for the first time, and Jerry and I got into a water fight. I learned how to throw my first frisbee in their yard.

Most of all, I remember the talks Jerry and I had about life. Jerry was a Big Brother, a Father, a Hero, and most of all, a Best Friend to a kid who needed one. Jerry was the most positive influence on my life. I will always love him; I will always remember him; and I will always miss him.

A Laugher's Last Laugh
by Phyliss Shanken

Do you know what I always loved about Mish's laugh? It was the way her nostrils vibrated to the rhythm of her convulsive merriment. Fortunately for me, this earlier study of Mish's laugh eventually came in handy. When she was dying of lung cancer, she could hardly exert the *sounds* of joy, but her undulating nostrils revealed the truth of her mirth, nevertheless. Knowing she had limited time left, eighty-year-old Mish sent word that she wanted to say good-bye to me. As Mish had delighted with me in the comedy of living, now she was to teach me about dying.

Mish was the catalyst to some of my new insights. For example, I learned that when someone is going to die, you don't have to worry about what you are wearing! On the morning of my farewell visit when I was making my wardrobe selection, I had second thoughts—I might have worn this outfit last time I saw Mish. Amused by my adolescent ruminations regarding my appearance, I inherently knew that these were needless worries. She was dying. Where she's going, she won't be judged because of her dearth of fashionable friends! Even if Mish were appalled by my wearing the same outfit twice, her opinion of me wasn't going to last much longer. Mish and I laughed about my internal dialogue when I embellished it at the time of my visit.

That day, I gently touched her emaciated arm, awakening her out of a deep twelve hour sleep. Mish smiled broadly and said, "I'm so glad you came. I wasn't sure how you'd feel. So many people feel uncomfortable about this."

I hated to think of my lovely, fun loving Mish, who had given laughs to so many, being isolated in her dying process because people, reluctant to face the realization of their own death, were afraid to visit.

"Mish, you have given me a precious gift. I am honored that you sent for me."

Her eyes turned from me as if she had urgent business elsewhere. She looked toward the assistant who helped while Mish's daughter was at work each day. "Get Phyliss the bras."

She responded to my incredulous expression: "I have so many bras. Some I've hardly worn. You'll take these bras. If they are too small, you can get bra extenders."

I guess I was prepared. A few months ago, Mish had offered me her shoes and I had responded, "Mish, I'd walk in your shoes any day!"

While the assistant was frantically searching for the bras, we went back to our conversation. In the past, Mish had been hungry to taste the humor of life, particularly embracing my accounts of embarrassing moments. She used to say, "Phyliss, tell me stories." Alternatively, today, I assumed the job of asking questions, and it was Mish's task to muster up all her energy to answer. She needed her breath more than I needed mine, and frequently she stopped talking in order to breathe in more air.

I prompted her: "What's it like to know that you are dying? What kinds of things do you think about these days? Do you spend your time contemplating your life? Do you have any regrets?"

Mish elaborated obediently while relishing these inquiries. Her main regret was how she had treated her husband when he was dying, forcing him to eat, withholding pain medication because the doctors had said not to overdo it. Then she told me about her prayers. She selected one of five prayers each night before she went to sleep. Since I am of a different faith, she recited a few for me.

I guess, at that same moment, some of life's juices returned to Mish, because even though she hadn't been eating, this time, when the assistant asked her what she wanted to eat, she came up with an answer. For an instant, I recognized the old Mish as she requested a scrambled egg sandwich.

"Fry the eggs in butter," she said. "It's okay. They take fat girls in hell!"

Looking as if she had just played a trick on the teacher and was trying to conceal her delight, she opened her mouth wide. There was only a small sound coming from her throat, but I knew she was with me in laughter because those nostrils that I had studied in the past told all. The giggles of her childhood were playing hide-and-go-seek, but we barely noticed the loss.

As she laboriously ate part of her sandwich from her awkward position in bed, she attempted to manipulate her coffee cup. She was clumsily trying to turn the handle around so she could lift the heavy cup, or so I thought. I wanted to be helpful and kept turning it so her hand could lunge for the desired handle, but I found that I was working at cross purposes with her. She was trying to turn the cup the opposite way! She nearly slapped my hand in reproach as we both realized the comedy of the moment. Unlike our past experience, I laughed more vigorously than Mish, but Mish's and my eyes measured the same intensity.

The time came for me to leave. The assistant had found only two bras and was scolded by Mish who assured me that her daughter would find the rest. I pledged to return, although I believed that this would be the last time I would see Mish. I took the two bras, walked to the door, and turned back to view my last portrait of her for my life's memory album. In the car, in honor of Mish's and my whimsical history, interrupted by spasms of belly laughs which willingly emerged from my throat, I cried all the way home.

Clinging to life, Mish lingered on. Ten days later, I returned to a much weakened Mish who could hardly speak without losing her breath and who barely had the energy to smile. She told me the bras had been located and were in the pile over there. I thanked her and moved them to the chair by the door, promising to take the bras with me on my way out.

These days, she hallucinated most of the time. She imagined herself running around in a field, talking and caressing her yearned for but not yet conceived great grandchildren. Despite these pleasant experiences, unlike her usual fun-loving self, Mish appeared to be seriously working on the task of dying.

I determined my visit was too exhausting for Mish and my presence was no longer helpful. I would not return to see Mish alive again. As if in agreement, at the moment of my insight, Mish said, "I'd like to go to sleep now." Longing for sleep, even before she had completely uttered the words, "good-bye", she closed her eyes.

I procrastinated for a moment until I felt secure that she had indeed migrated into her comforting slumber. I languidly planned my exit, turned and once again stood by the doorway to have my very last view of her.

On cue, just before I took the last step into the hallway, she opened her eyes, gathered newfound strength to project her voice and turn up her lips. She commanded, "Don't forget the bras!"

So now, when I find myself grieving my fun-loving friend, rather than envisioning her as weak and dying, I always conjure up that last image. And for further comfort, I tell everyone Mish's and my story . . . "Did I ever tell you about my friend, Mish? The last words she ever said to me were, 'Don't forget the bras!'"

CHAPTER 6

WHEN SOMEONE YOU "HATE" OR ARE ANGRY WITH DIES

Brave women tackle the taboo subject of how one deals with the death of a person they were very angry with or who had caused them great pain.

My Mother Is Dying
by Sara Lyons

My mother is dying. I have not spoken with her for three years now and yet I know she is dying. Her death communicates itself through the crystals of my blood, humming a song so heartbreaking that I think I will go mad.

Her last words to me were left on the answering machine. My step-daughter had the misfortune of picking up the late afternoon message that went something like " . . . you've ruined me, you've ruined the family, why do you want to destroy me? . . . " spoken through a blended whiskey that she had been drinking since probably noon. I listened to it that evening. Not surprised. Her letter the week before had said pretty much the same thing.

I last saw my mother around Christmas, three months earlier. This visit carefully orchestrated by a phalanx of family members and psychotherapists. We showed up at our reunion after an absence of two years, each one of us driving a new gray colored car, wearing the same colors, having our hair in the same style, and wearing an identical bracelet on the right arm. And we each carried a coach bag, although different styles.

What broke my mother's heart was not me, as she contends. If anything, my refusal to go along with her mutually assured self destruction pact was my newfound interest in living. No, her heart was broken decades earlier, long before she could probably remember. She was born into a family that ate its girl children and the fact that she outlived everyone was a testament to her strength.

Mother had survived because she had offered up her own girl-child to the family. Here, take my daughter. And so they did. First her father, then her husband, and then the assorted uncles, and finally the family friends. And when my own daughter came around, she offered up her, too. The strategy, along with lots of booze, sixteen ounces straight per evening, kept her going.

All attempts I made to have a human relationship with her failed, of course. I didn't know that I was challenging her defenses each time I sought her eyes out for just one loving glance of approval. I followed her around like a hungry ghost hoping she would hear me, see me, love me. But like all ghosts in the presence of non-believers, I went unheeded. Slowly over the years I disappeared in even my own estimation.

And now she is dying. Her belief that the magic talisman of my presence would forever protect her is eroding as the reality that I've left her for good sinks into her shattered psyche. I sense the pieces drift away like pieces of burnt fabric in some catastrophic fire. Those colorful shards turn ash gray and drift in the currents of some stifling hot hellish interior landscape.

All I did was look at her and tell the truth. The shock of that act went deep into some interior landscape which until that moment I had no idea existed. I saw the look on her face as the panic raced up her spine and turned her wild eyes inward. She seemed at that moment to expand to twice her size, like a balloon being tested for the boundary of its skin. Then the glistening sweat and, finally, the tears that she held back ferociously. They never came, but I could see them as they welled up in her heart. A floodgate opened, and she began to drown in her own unfelt feelings. And out of her mouth came more betrayal and more lies. Her own heart was cruelly savaged by this monster family lie that she had nurtured for her entire life. It had come down to this. You may live now or you may die. It is simply your choice. I watched my mother struggle for forty minutes as she blocked each loving thought and as she pulled forth the ancestral legacy like a cloak of poisonous snakes and wrapped it around her body. This was it for us.

It has taken three years for the fact that I'll never see her again to sink in. I've had plenty of preparation. First there were all the photos of my daughter and me that she dumped into shopping bags and had my poor dumb brother deliver to me. Then the message that I had been disinherited. Then there was the time I went unconscious and dialed her number. The news that she went ballistic when everyone else in the family flew to California for my daughter's wedding and didn't tell her somehow pleased me. We must have been bitter enemies in our last lifetime and probably we tortured and tormented each other until we dropped dead from exhaustion only to wake up in this lifetime related by the closest ties possible. That is a cosmic joke I can appreciate. But now it's over.

I am at an age where I see my peers begin to agonize over parents in decline. I do not tell them that I had to fight my mother to the death. I do not tell them that there are some mother-daughter relationships that are living nightmares.

I will not go to my mother's funeral. I will not look into her coffin to see her one last time, cold and silent as she had seemed to me so often in our life together. There will be a funeral and a burial and people will come from all over the state to see her one last time. Words will be spoken and family members will comfort one another. I will not be there. I will not smell the overwhelming sweetness of too many flowers filling a small chapel, of the women wearing strong perfumes. I will not see who cries and who falls asleep in the heat of summer (because I believe she would want to die during this season).

On the day of my mother's funeral, I shall say a long prayer to all of the hurt women in the world who have babies they can't and won't protect. I shall say a prayer for all those babies and for the beings who will prey on them. And on the day of my mother's funeral, I shall search the skies for a sign of peace to come.

Moving Past Bitter
by Bonnie Sutton

When my husband of thirty-five years, Jim, died in July of 1992, I wasn't sure of how I was supposed to act because of many factors. First, he had been an alcoholic for all the time we had been married. Second, he had been physically abusive to me in the early years of our marriage. Third, as an R.N., I had learned from experience to suppress my emotions over a patient's death until a later time when circumstances permitted dealing with them. I cried with my kids at the hospital, but I felt nothing.

I went through the normal reactions: shock, bargaining, anger—all those things I had learned about during my nurse's training. Gradually, it seemed that I couldn't differentiate between a wife's reaction and a nurse's reaction. I wasn't really feeling anything at all.

One month before Jim died, my youngest daughter and our niece had a fire that completely destroyed their mobile home. Since they could not find a place to live, Jim and I decided to move out of our nine room home and let them live in it. We moved into a two bedroom trailer on Monday; Jim went into the hospital on Tuesday; and on Friday, he died. As a result, I was dealing with the loss of the home I had lived in for twenty-three years, along with Jim's death.

I don't know if going on spending sprees after the death of a loved one is normal or not. But that's what I did. I rationalized it by saying that I couldn't do it when Jim was alive because I couldn't afford to. Jim, like most alcoholics when they find a new interest, went totally overboard. For instance, bowling. When he discovered he could bowl without too much discomfort, he bought a brand new bowling ball that had to be bored to fit him, new shoes, new bag, and signed up for three leagues each week. Since he was on compensation disability for a back injury, his resources were limited and most went for his hobbies. Therefore, I paid most of the monthly bills.

Until December of 1990 when he was told he had to quit drinking or die within six months, a great deal of his income went for beer. After his death, I had some insurance monies for my use, even after funeral expenses. I had never been able to fix up a place to live on my own, and it went to my head. I bought new curtains, table linens, bed linens, towel sets—all to help me settle into my new trailer. I have always been a compulsive reader and, thus, bought books by the bagful.

Now, four years later, I have accepted Jim's death, finally. I think what I regretted most was the death of my hope that someday Jim and I would have a "normal" marriage without the drinking problem between us. I also regret that our adult children have so many bad memories of life with their dad, but they are gradually remembering some of the good things that happened when they were younger. I just let them talk and reminisce when they are in the mood. Sometimes my nurse persona appears and I tell them, "It's okay to talk about this—it helps to get it out in the open."

The unit that I work on has three other nurses besides myself who are widows. Sometimes we talk about our husbands, how they died, and how we are each handling things now. That helps because we can say things to each other that we can't say to anyone else.

All in all, I think I'm doing okay. I do still get bitter at times about being beaten in our early years together. But I can't change the past, so I try not to dwell on it. My self-esteem has risen greatly, and I can handle just about anything life throws my way now.

Walking Toward Kathy
by Grace Forbes

The only thing my sister Kathy and I could do with some comfort was walk. Our house was over a mile from the main road, and we were always hiking to a bus stop.

Kathy was four years older than me. She had long legs. I can still see her striding, her head down in deep thought, three steps ahead of me.

Kathy needed a lot of space, not because she was fat but because she was angry. She needed a lot of space for her anger.

"Your sister has bone cancer," my mother's voice cracked over the phone one evening. She always referred to Kathy as "your sister" or "that damn kid". When I was very small, I knew my mother loved me. I knew she did not love Kathy.

"Is it leukemia?" I was cold with panic.

"I'm not sure." My mother's voice trailed off.

You're not sure? I screamed silently. *Your child has cancer and you don't know what kind? Am I in the Twilight Zone here?*

"Is she there? Can I speak to her?" I asked.

The line was silent for a long time. I could no longer hear the TV in the background. Mother must have put her hand over the phone.

"Hi!" Kathy said.

"How are you?" I cried.

"I'm fine, how are you?"

A week later I called Kathy at her apartment. She was so depressed that her voice was an octave lower.

"Mom's furious that I didn't call her sooner," she sobbed. "She says the doctor didn't even know I had a mother. She's never going to forgive me."

"Forget Mom's feelings. What about you?" I asked.

"What do you mean?"

"You're what's important. Mom's always running around looking for someone to blame. It's not your fault. You know what she's like."

There was no answer. Kathy would never allow anyone to say anything bad about our mother. Our mother would never allow anyone to say anything good about about Kathy. They'd been that way for forty-four years.

Kathy had always been sick. Family lore says she was born red, ugly, and screaming, and she never stopped screaming. Our mother was a nurse before she married. She used to say, "Your sister was the only patient I couldn't cure." Either Kathy was a bad patient, or mother really should have worked at Woolworth's.

Kathy had epilepsy, tunnel vision, and sinus problems. She could only eat certain foods. She had countless tumors removed. She was in and out of the Cleveland Clinic as often as I was in and out of dance classes.

She never spoke about those visits to the clinic. She came home sad and silent, with little bandages on the insides of her elbows, her hair greasy from the EEG's. Mother did all the talking, explaining to everyone what procedures were done, how they were conducted, and even how Kathy felt about them. Once I suggested she let Kathy tell us about it.

"You can get your own disease," I said. Mother slapped my face.

Through it all, Kathy silently fought. She walked five miles a day until she developed knee problems. She joined the Y and swam ten miles a day.

After her cancer diagnosis, my husband and I visited Kathy at her apartment. We rented a room at a nearby hotel and he suggested a day at their pool. I tried to buy Kathy a swimsuit at the local mall, but she refused. She said she could open a charge account, fill it out, and get 10% off any purchase. I knew when the store saw her only income was her paper route and what Dad gave her, that they would deny her card.

"I get 10% off all the time!" she insisted. I never argued with Kathy. Kathy and Mother were always right.

We changed in the hotel room. We gave Kathy the bedroom and used the tiny bathroom where my husband and I had a quickie as I thought about my sister out there in the next room. I wondered if she heard anything, or knew anything. I knew she'd never even dated a man. She'd spent her puberty in out-patient clinics.

As we walked to the pool, I saw our reflections in the hall windows. For the first time in our adult lives, my sister was heavier than me. When chemotherapy started, Mother had ordered her to eat.

Kathy's swimming days were over, but her pale body was still hard. She could only see well enough to walk around the sides of the shallow end of the pool. I stayed with her, while my husband did laps. Around her neck hung a holy card encased in plastic.

"A scapular," she told me. "It keeps you healthy by warding off sin." The card portrayed Jesus showing off his open heart surgery. Mother and Kathy were the only family members still practicing Catholicism.

I held up the rope of buoys so Kathy could walk under them. She took my hand for balance, hanging on to my hand for a long time.

She's ready to die, I thought. *She just doesn't want to let go of me.*

"Well, she's in good spirits," my husband said on the ride home. "She's positive. She just might beat this thing."

"She's ready to die," I said.

Kathy moved in with Mother and Dad when she started going downhill. She called me weekly to cry about how they were treating her. I drove up there to talk to them. They listened. The next day Dad punched me in the face for standing in his goddamn way. Kathy seemed relieved. It wasn't her turn for a change.

My brother Bill called me. Dad had told him to stop speaking to Kathy, to stop writing to her. She had to be punished because she made them look like bad parents in the hospital.

I called my parents and tried to talk them into letting Kathy move back to her own apartment. They hung up on me. Six months later I received a letter from Kathy, informing me she would not speak to me until I apologized to Dad for standing in his way. The return address was her old apartment, so I called her there.

"If anything happens to you, I want to know," I said.

"I'll have to check with Dad first," she said. Three months later she moved back in with them. I heard nothing for one year. Then I received a phone call from Mother.

"Your sister is arriving Friday and staying with you for five days. Here she is."

"Hi, Grace!" said Kathy.

When I picked her up at the airport, she was surly and uncommunicative.

"Well, you finally grew up," she grunted when we were in the car. "I saw it when I got off the plane. Finally, I said to myself, Grace's become an adult."

"You never went out of your way to spend much time with me, Kathy, so how would you know?"

She stayed in the guest bedroom for two days.

I took her to the public library and we walked through three floors of shelves. She had volunteered at her own small library, and this was Oz to her.

We walked around the lake in city park. Black winter trees were mirrored in the water. It was a raw spring day and Kathy walked with her body curved against the cold. She wore one of my sweaters.

"I've always been jealous of you," she said.

I nodded. *I don't know what I can do about that*, I thought.

"Mom always used to say, `Why can't you be more like Grace?'"

I took a quick suck of air through my teeth and looked away. I didn't know Mom had been saying that. "Well, she doesn't say that anymore, does she?"

"No," Kathy smirked. I had a strong urge to shove her. I let her walk ahead of me. After awhile she stopped and looked at the lake.

"Bill's wife calls me Karen," she said. "Nobody corrects her. Should I be upset about that?"

I was silent for a long time. "Maybe you'll just have a nice Easter no matter what they do."

She caught my eye. She looked shocked. "You too," she said, but she sounded confused.

I had to run into the office for a half day and she called me there. "There's something I have to tell you," she said. There were five people standing at my desk.

"Can it wait till I get home?" I asked.

"I guess so," she said.

I brought her roses that night. She put them on the kitchen table. I took one bud out and put it in her bedroom.

"What was it you wanted to say?" I asked her.

"Oh, nothing," she said.

All through the next morning we chatted by the fire. I sat at her feet and hugged my knees. We talked about God and faith, then we stood up and stretched, face to face. I took her in my arms.

"You are my sister," I said.

The week after she left I received a package in my mother's handwriting. It contained everything I'd given Kathy, the pamphlets from Al-Anon, a recipe book, a pressed rose. At the bottom of one of the pamphlets Kathy had scrawled "I love you. I'm glad we are sisters."

I didn't know then she had only weeks to live. In anger, I threw it all away.

"You're sister's probably not going to live through the night, but we don't want you here," my mother screamed into the phone.

"Then why did you call me?" There was a pause.

"Your father and I are so fragile; we just cannot stand another one of your attacks." I could tell she'd said that many times to others.

"How's Kathy doing?"

"What do you mean?" she asked.

My husband drove us to my parents' house. The sky was metal gray. I prayed, "What should I say to her, God? What would be the best thing to say last?"

Suddenly I was filled with a Knowing.

"Oh, God," I sobbed. "She's already dead."

My husband had pulled into a rest stop. "Do you want me to keep driving?" he asked.

"It doesn't matter now," I said.

Mother opened the door and greeted my husband effusively, pretending I wasn't there. I climbed the stairs to the room I had shared with Kathy. My husband, who comes from a culture where you don't criticize your mamma, lingered to chat.

"Honey!" I shouted, with much meaning.

"Gotta go," he said.

Kathy was on the floor of our room where she had built a nest for herself. She must have grown too weak to climb back into bed, and no one had helped her. Her lips were white but she was still warm.

My husband came up behind me, followed by my mother.

"She's dead," I said.

"I was just talking to her," Mother said, but I knew she was lying. The phone rang. I could tell by my mother's voice it was Dad. He had gone to get the oil changed in his car.

"We have a problem here," Mother said, vague as ever. "Call me back."

While she was dialing the ambulance, I whispered something a patient in a nursing home once said to me. "Give Jesus a big hug for me," I said, stroking Kathy's hair.

"I will," my husband said.

My husband performed CPR on Kathy until the ambulance arrived. I stayed in the living room and held our three-year-old son on my lap who wiped tears off my face and patted my cheek.

"She'll be all right," my little boy said.

My mother darted into the room. I could hear my husband counting and pounding on Kathy's chest.

"I'm so upset," my mother said. I looked at her and waited for her to finish. She didn't sound upset. She ran off into the laundry room as if I'd slapped her. My son felt warm against my stomach. Upstairs, I could hear the staccato creak of Kathy's death rattle.

The EMT people arrived. A young woman was snapping on white plastic gloves. "Has she thrown up yet?" she shouted. I shook my head no and stepped aside. They pounded up the stairs.

"Has she thrown up yet?" I heard the woman yell at my husband.

I took my little boy out to the front porch. A chubby lady came across the lawn. "Hi, Grace," she said. I'd never met her before. She didn't introduce herself.

"I just wanted to know," she said, a huge grin on her face, "is Kathy dead now?" I nodded and looked with hatred at her. She quickly turned and picked her way back across the grass.

I walked down the street, my son holding my index finger. I didn't want him to see Aunt Kathy wheeled out. A new house was going up at the end of the road. We watched a dump truck groan and haul chunks of debris from one side of the lunar landscape to the other.

"This is neat," my son said. We stayed as long as we could.

My husband was standing on the porch, watching for us, his shirt stuck to his chest. I put my arms around him and our son hugged our knees. We went back indoors and sat on the couch.

A man who had worked with my father appeared at the front door. The man assumed my black husband was an EMT person and began ordering him around. My husband sat down next to me and put his arm around my shoulder. Mother appeared and introduced the man.

"Do you want to sit down?" the man asked her.

"Not with that," she muttered, gesturing toward me. The man looked uncomfortable.

Their talk swirled above me. A shaft of light slanted in from the window and landed at my feet, centered by a brighter light that flickered and wavered, like sunlight on water.

I know what this is, I thought. *I can't bear to look at it.*

At Kathy's wake, my brother followed around behind my father, talking about overtime and IRA's. He sank into the chair next to me with a loud sigh.

"I hope all this will fade in time," I said to him.

"All this what?" he asked.

I wandered into the kitchen alone. I could hear my relatives partying on the back porch. My mother walked in.

"This last week, your sister begged us to take her to the hospital, but we just couldn't. This is the week we get the oil changed in our Cadillacs. I think your sister should have known that, don't you?"

I went to find my husband and asked him to take me home.

A year later I visited my parents. They were gracious and extremely cautious. Mother took me up to the bedroom Kathy and I had shared. The room was rearranged. There was only one bed now. Kathy's high school picture was in a silver frame on an antique child's desk, just inside the door. I couldn't walk in.

My mother touched my arm. "I miss all my babies," she said, tears in her eyes.

I turned away, and I haven't gone back.

"You expect too much of people," my brother said. "Some people just like to take it out on the patient."

"I don't," I said. "I've never seen you do that, but maybe when nobody's looking you put down that Bible you quote so much and beat up an old bald guy."

Getting over losing Kathy took me two years of long walks. I went to the doctor with heart palpitations. He said it was just stress.

Some of my anger for my family has dissipated. I'm beginning to think about the gifts I inherited from them: my mother's love of good books, my father's love of hard work.

I hear my dad is drinking heavily now, and he's become so angry he's had to give up golf, but he loves his garden.

None of my relatives ever talk about my mother.

I still wish them both a good day in my mind.

A woman at work once said to me, "You're so right. You do every thing right." I'm sure she meant it as a compliment, but I cringed.

I don't want to be the one that's right. Let someone else be right for a change. Being right is lonely.

Part of me wants to help my family, and part of me says child abusers don't eat at my table and grin as if they got away with something. And they are not ready to change.

Someone once said:

"Your sister is your enemy and your mirror."

CHAPTER 7

DEALING WITH "UNNATURAL" DEATHS

Deaths of children and adults by murder, suicide, and accidents are reflected upon by those who were close to them.

Kevin's Story
by Frances Davis

The TV Sunday evening newscaster was reciting the usual litany of destruction and murder. I half listened as I prepared the coffee pot for the next morning. "Three people died in an apparent double homicide-suicide this evening in a Northwest Phoenix apartment. A four year-old boy escaped from the apartment and ran over to a neighbor's house. He told them that his dad had shot his mom. Names are being withheld pending notification of next of kin." An uneasy feeling settled over me and I murmured to myself, "When are people going to stop using guns? Will there ever be peaceful coexistence among us?" Little did I know we were the next of kin. Late that evening my ex-husband was notified by the police that our son, Kevin, was one of the victims. He and his lady friend, Christie, had been shot by her ex-husband, Phil, who then turned the gun on himself.

968-BEIS

***

Kevin, I didn't learn about your death until Monday morning when I looked up to see your sister, Barb, standing in front of my desk at work. With tears streaming down her face she sobbed, "Mom, Kevin is dead." I mumbled something incomprehensible to my employer, gathered up my purse, and followed Barb out the door. As she drove me home I kept telling myself, *This can't be happening.* My mind was numb but threads of fire coursed through my body and a huge vise squeezed my brain. This was my child whom I had carried and who had been formed from my body. I felt as if a part of me had been killed.

I kept asking myself, *Why now, Kevin? Why now, when you were doing so well and had finally found direction in your life?* You had drifted into a world of drugs when you entered high school. Always searching for identity, you were vulnerable to gangs, drugs, and escape from yourself. Your dad and I thought that when you married Debbie and had your son, Leif, that you would straighten up. Your marriage failed when, fogged by drugs, you struck Debbie during an argument. Although you tried working at many jobs, they never lasted.

Remember the time you called and asked me to take you to a Detox Center? I know now it was a cry for help but I distanced myself from you, saying that you needed to straighten your life out. And you did when you joined Narcotics Anonymous. For two years you stayed "clean". As part of your recovery you were required to complete a moral inventory. When you confronted your father, old hurts, disappointments, and hidden anger were revealed. It was not an easy time for either of you, but your dad said later that it cleared the air. Then you came to me. A lot of hidden demons surfaced during our conversation, especially your search for self expression and my need to control. When it was over, I held you close and felt your sobs. My tears flowed too.

Your dad and I were so proud of you and supported you as you struggled with the "dragon of drugs" that held you captive. Remember the picture we gave you when you passed your first year of sobriety? A graphic artist friend of ours drew a dragon being slain by a knight, with the caption under it saying, "Kevin, you've slain your first dragon." The whole family had signed it on the back. You told us later how much it meant to you to have us support and encourage you.

Why now, my rebellious son, when we could finally be friends? You were my firstborn, a beautiful, curly redheaded baby, delivered by C section after a long, difficult labor. Instead of crying at your first breath, you sneezed and doubled up your fists, ready to take on the world. And you did! You were determined to have your own way regardless of the consequences. That shock of red hair set you apart and whenever there was an altercation at school you were the first one questioned. School eventually became such a battleground that you never did complete your education.

You had everything to live for. Only a week ago you signed up for college classes. Your goal was to become a substance abuse counselor. You had already served your internship at Tempe St. Luke's Detox Center. How many hands had you held as they went through the first twenty-four hours of withdrawal? You became my guide when I revealed my prescription drug addiction to you. Although you encouraged me to attend an Narcotics Anonymous meeting, I wasn't ready to "come clean" to anyone else. Now you're gone and I am lost. I don't know who to turn to for help.

The night before the memorial service I wandered through the house tortured by the idea that there would be nothing to remember you by. Sleep was my enemy. Since you had never attended our church, I worried that our minister would have no idea what to say about you. I started writing bits and pieces of your life. As I wrote, I felt a great release. Those words became a great comfort to me later.

Your memorial service was scheduled for 4:00 PM, but people were still entering the building a half hour later. The only things placed on the platform were the flowers and the dragon picture. For someone who had no friends two years ago, over two hundred came to pay you tribute. Many of them told us later that they were members of Narcotics Anonymous, and you had saved their lives. My heart filled with pride when I heard of all the good you had done.

Just before the service I handed my scribblings to Rev. Joel. He read them and asked, "May I use this just the way it was written? I don't know if I can get through it, but I'll try."

Kevin's Eulogy—August 30, 1989

Kevin Jerome Mackey made his transition Sunday, August 27, 1989. He left, not in defeat, but as a glorious warrior championing the battle to protect his fair maiden.

Kevin fought many battles; some almost defeated him. He had an iron will. When he made up his mind nothing could change it and he pursued his goals with every ounce of his being. Sometimes he chose less desirable goals, but he never, as far as I knew, did them with a malicious or dishonest intent.

There was a long period when he was not master of himself and was controlled by other substances. When Kevin finally determined the course of his life, he decided to accept and conquer his greatest challenge. Guided by a Higher Power to know, he became a whirlwind, spinning in a wider and wider circle to touch as many lives as possible—until his time on this plane was completed.

He was endowed with an uncanny sense of humor, a contagious laugh, and an ability to tell a joke that would rival Eddie Murphy.

He was a tease—oh, how his little sister, Monica, dreaded the "snake" he kept hidden, that always exploded into her lap or hand at the family gatherings.

He was a dreamer. Many times a faraway look and a soft smile would cross his face, but no one could penetrate the mystery of his thoughts.

He loved people. He could inspire and aggravate all at the same time. I remember how exasperated I would be as he dawdled getting ready for school. He was also a willing worker and put long hours into his tasks.

I think of him as my son, but he was not mine to keep. We had a great many challenges in his growth to manhood. He came into the world fighting it and didn't change his direction until two years ago when he shed the manacles that were binding him.

From the day he chose to accept his final challenge, he pursued it with all the vigor of a saint storming heaven's gate. He was named after St. Kevin, a noble Irishman, and Jerome, the middle name of his father and grandfather.

I am just beginning to realize the wonderful ways he touched other peoples' lives and am overwhelmed by the number of people he has helped. He was exactly where he wanted to be, doing what he wanted to do. To feel anger over the circumstances of his passing would sully his memory. He knew that he was living amid dangerous and irrational people, and he accepted it. We can only honor him for his convictions.

We will always carry special memories of him—I, his mother; Brian, his brother; Barbara and Monica, his sisters; Roger, his father; Bill, also his father; Leif, his son; and the rest of you, his friends.

Kevin is. His transformation only takes his physical body from our sight. I feel that his spiritual growth became so accelerated during the last two years that he has been propelled into a greater opportunity, somewhere else, to guide and counsel.

I miss you, my son. There will always be an empty place at the table, but my heart remains filled with your presence. Goodbye, my warrior knight—you fought your greatest dragon and won.

Love,
Mom

***

Ten years have passed since Kevin's death. I vaguely recall the first year. There were pain drenched days when I couldn't even get out of bed. Where did all the tears come from? I thought they would never stop. Sometimes a craziness swept over me and I wondered if sanity would ever return. Sleep was my enemy. If I closed my eyes, the nightmares would appear. I would prowl through the house, desperate to talk to someone but not wanting them to answer me. Who would listen? Who would remove the pain, the guilt, the torture of living? I quit my job, stopped going to church, and became reclusive. My daughters and remaining son called often; we needed constant communication to reassure ourselves that life continued for us.

I never knew how much this affected my husband until we were asked to share our experience at a Death and Dying Class at a local college. Bill told about the times when I would say, "Just hold me," and then push him away. I could see the pain and confusion in his eyes. He said he felt like he was married to a stranger. The woman he loved and cherished was only a shell. Intimacy and sharing had disappeared. He said he felt so helpless during that time, but he patiently stood by me.

After I had passed the first year of intense therapy with a special counselor, I began to respond once again to Bill's love and tenderness. It took a great deal of patience and understanding, but our love has survived. With every passing day we realize how fragile love is and how carefully we need to nurture it.

Among the sympathy cards we received was a note from the grandparents of the little boy that ran from the apartment. Christie's son, Luke, went to live with his maternal grandparents. Over the years his grandmother, Joanne, has sent pictures and letters telling me of his progress. In one letter she said that when I was ready Luke would share what happened that night. I don't know if I will ever be ready. When loved ones die we form a mental picture of them which we guard zealously. Anything that would alter that picture might shatter our sanity. Sometimes that is the only way we can cope with the loss.

We keep Kevin's memory alive by including him in our conversation. The first Thanksgiving we sat around the table, each one afraid to mention his name for fear of opening the wound of his absence. Finally, I said, "Let's toast Kevin wherever he is." I lifted my glass toward the bronze box containing his ashes that sat on the fireplace mantle. With that the floodgates opened and we spent the next hour sharing our feelings, fears, and family love.

His physical presence is the only thing missing. His essence remains with us, even today. Sometimes he appears in my dreams, such as the time I entered a room and saw him sitting in a big easy chair. "Hi, Kev, what are you doing here?" I asked. He smiled, shrugged his shoulders and replied, "I'm only visiting." He was very close to his youngest sister, Monica, who is also a redhead. Just before his death she had barely survived a ruptured tubal pregnancy. Late one evening, he walked into her hospital room. She told me later that he had an angelic glow surrounding him and said to herself, "He's too beautiful to be real." Three weeks to the day he was dead.

If I could share one thing with those who have lost a child, it is to live for the loved ones still with you. The child of your heart has completed this earth's journey and is on to wonderful new adventures in another existence. It is okay to grieve; it is important to retain and honor his or her memory. Walk your walk through the valley of the shadow, however long it takes, but keep moving until you reach the other side. Remaining in the shadow will inhibit not only you but everyone around you. Release your loved one to journey on their spiritual path wherever it is. Nurture yourself, seek counseling, write a journal, take time to heal. Later you might share your compassion with others who are suffering. I studied everything I could about the grieving process and presented seminars on Death and Dying. Not only was I able to help myself, but others who were still grieving. Eventually I completed ministerial training and am now a pastoral counselor, specializing in pet loss grief support.

I know now it's not what happens to you that counts as much as how you learn to handle it. Almost fifty years ago my little sister, Janet, drowned in the family swimming pool. My mother never recovered and died ten years later. I lost not only my sister, but my mother, my childhood, and my memory before the age of nine. I grew up believing that I had caused Janet's death and an avenging God was punishing me by taking away everything I loved. For years I distanced myself from the God of my childhood. When I met Bill in 1979, we attended a New Thought church and there I learned about a different God, one that loved me unconditionally and never judged me. It changed my life and my understanding of God. Otherwise I'm not sure I could have survived Kevin's death.

What have I learned? Compassion most of all; forgiveness, not only for others but for myself; patience and acceptance. I tried to focus on something good that would come from this devastating incident. Sometimes it took a lot of searching but the more I could find something good, the faster I was able to recover. I thank God for all my blessings—my husband, my family, my friends, and my faith. Without them, I never would have survived.

My Life Has Changed
by Lydia Frescaz

Dear Angela,

I just lost you, Angela. You were only twenty years old and five-and-a-half months pregnant. Oh my God, this is not supposed to happen; please tell me this is a dream—that I will wake up and all will be fine. But this isn't a dream, and I'm supposed to be okay.

You were murdered by your estranged husband. You were supposed to fulfill your dream. It's not fair; you didn't have a choice in this matter. Your rights to live were taken away from you.

How do I go on, knowing a piece of my heart is missing? How do I cope with people trying to tell me everything will be all right? How can they say that?

I just lost my daughter and I am supposed to be all right with this? Sometimes I feel like saying, "What would you do if this was your child?"

I go to bed, knowing that restful sleep will not come my way, for I know you are gone forever.

I am in shock, in total denial, thinking this is not happening to us.

You were at the hospital under care for ten days until you died. Here comes the realization of your funeral. I called the funeral directors in my hometown, and they knew that my heart was breaking and under so much pain. They made sure everything was in order and made the process easier for us.

During church services, just hearing the music can tear me apart. I am comforted by the words which I need to hear and by knowing that God will take care of my Angela and her baby.

We come home away from all our friends and the rest of the family to be alone, just to sit and remember you as a happy loving person, because they still don't understand our loss.

I have discovered that when someone dies, I am supposed to go on with my life. Well I sure wish somebody could wave a magic wand, but that won't ever happen.

I also have found out that people tend to shy away from me for they don't know how to handle my loss, so they just find excuses to avoid me.

I still talk about you, Angela, like you were alive and here. I talk about you being a wonderful person who was a good mother to the baby that you left behind. What do I tell Bradley when he gets of age? Not only do I have to cope with your death, I have to cope with the horrors of a monster that is in prison for life, but that doesn't help matters for he will probably come out and try to see Bradley.

Our lives are not the same since you died. Our holidays are filled with a void. You are missing and we hurt inside and out.

Why is it hard for people to accept that we will never forget you? I have discovered that everything has changed here. We try to live each day to the fullest for we will never know when our time will come.

I used to have a gleam in my eye that shone when I spoke to people. Well, that gleam is gone for now; maybe it will come back, I don't know.

Yes I can laugh again and I know that you wouldn't want me to cry everyday, so I try to keep busy by writing what needs to be written to help others like myself to encourage them not to give up, to keep memories alive, and to avoid letting people try to influence the feelings of every day life.

I live each day as it comes, and I do pray to God to give me the strength I need. I know I can't do this alone. Everybody needs a good loving friend, a good family member to be by our side when we are having a bad day. God is always there, always available.

It has been four years, and it seems like yesterday for me and the rest of the family. We are a close family that has not drifted apart. We comfort each other, for everybody has different days.

Sometimes I can't find the words to express my feelings. I wish my heart would quit hurting but, being your mother, that is impossible for me. I continue to have all the symptoms of coping: anger, sadness, sleep deprivation, struggling.

I will go on with life, but I am not happy. I know what a wonderful life we all could have had if somebody hadn't taken action and destroyed your life. It just isn't fair.

I will always miss you Angela, and I will always love you.

Your Mom

A Letter To My Sister
by Isabel Meisler

Dearest Ann,

I think your death really began for me that Monday morning you phoned from your home in Florida and in a loving tone told me a disguised goodbye. "Stay in the Light, Issie", you said. "You have worked so hard all of your life to stay in the Light." Alarmed immediately, for you had been struggling in and out of clinical depression for two years, I directly asked if you were planning to take your life. You denied it, laughed, sounded strong, not sad, and perhaps I should have known that a strange inner peace is sometimes the precursor to suicide once a firm decision has been made. Soon after our conversation, I called your psychiatrist, part of me fearing your reaction to this lack of trust. Refusing to let me speak to the doctor directly, which is policy I know, the secretary conveyed to her my concern and your words which so frightened me. I felt perhaps you should be hospitalized. The reality I was told was that you would have to agree and want that move. Later you phoned me, again so lovingly, telling me your doctor had phoned. You thanked me for my concern and reassured me that all was well; you had no intention of suicide. By Friday you were dead.

How I later agonized over those days, seemingly wasted between Monday and Friday, when I thought I might have flown to you and prevented this tragic act. I finally became convinced, though not until several years later, that almost certainly it would have only meant postponement; that even in hospitals, determined patients find a way to end it all. You were certain of your choice and I now believe there was no deterrent to be had, from caring husband, children, or me, your sister and closest friend. We were helpless in the face of your decision, a determination somehow graphically accented by your choice of a gun to end it all. Later we discovered your careful planning; how you stopped medication several weeks earlier, purchased your weapon of choice, meticulously went about putting your life in perfect order; every drawer, every bill, every file; finality in everything. This was no dramatic irrational act. This was choice, and on some level I knew we had to respect that.

Fatefully, and a circumstance for which I will be forever grateful, on the day you phoned to say "good-bye", a woman full of wisdom came by. I was taking her to the airport after her completion of a dynamic workshop she gave on the weekend. As I shared my fear and pain over your words she told me, "Remember this: everyone who takes their life leaves behind a gift for each person they loved." How strange that sounded to me at the time, not absurd, but unfathomable. The healing truth in them was nothing I could hear that first year of horror, agony, and loss.

From the beginning I ran the gamut of emotions, yet I never felt anger at you over your choice. I felt rage and anguish at being abandoned, for who was closer than we with our almost daily phone fix, our laughter, the iron bond formed in our twenties when we both realized what deep wounds we were hiding and could finally share. I had been told from sources I respect that the one who dies is still near for awhile. I wanted to believe that and the night of the day you died seemed to confirm it for me. I was sitting on the bed, numb from shock, exhausted from my reaction to the terrible message conveyed by a Florida policewoman. For I couldn't stop screaming. It was as if screaming would somehow keep those words, that lethal reality, at bay. Finally, I could scream and cry no more. I became silent. Suddenly I began to spiral down into a place of such living hell that it was horrendously clear the only choices would be to rush to a hospital for pain-numbing drugs or die. It was the most extreme moment of my life and lasted only seconds. I knew that this was not my pain, for I surfaced quickly. Instead, I knew you had allowed me experientially to know why you chose not to continue; no one could continue living with such unspeakable darkness. I spoke aloud saying to you, "I understand." And so my anger is never at you dearest one, only at the hole left when your beautiful presence departed. I mourned me, in my newly amputated form, and raged only over what might have been.

Shortly after you left, the legacies of suicide began. First, what to tell people. In my raw woundedness I needed to share, to speak of my loss, and when questioned to speak the truth of how you died. I couldn't break through to the reality of your being gone unless I stayed with truth. But mother was from the old "hide and survive" school. Remember, more than thirty years ago how she told us, when I was twenty-two years old, and you were twenty-six, "Do not cry today at your father's funeral. You can cry later, in private." For two years after that, I was often awakened by someone shaking me to tell me I was crying in my sleep. And so our poor mother implored me to tell everyone that you had a heart attack; "to honor your memory" by hiding this choice you made.

Thus we each had little help from the other during those anguished three months she survived your death. For hide and survive does not work well when it comes to grieving. Apt is the timeless wisdom of Shakespeare: "Give sorrow words" Malcolm advised Macduff, "the grief that does not speak/ whispers the o'er fraught heart, and bids it break." Mother was trying to protect you, and all of us, for survivors are still struggling against centuries of stigma. I found help in reading books, such as *The Enigma of Suicide* by George Colt, but mother's heart did break and by April she had succumbed to a stroke and died. I had lost you both.

The two of you had been essential scaffolding for my existence for you were all that was left of our tiny original family. It was more than I could take in, so I unwisely copied mother and shifted into "strong" mode. I learned much later from a hospice worker that this is not unusual and that one's strongest quality often gets exaggerated after loss. I became inappropriately competent: arranging mother's funeral, selling household goods, settling her estate, unraveling the endless red tape of insurance, grieving little. As numbness lifted and depression set in, I found myself not at all sure I wanted to survive the two of you. By February, a year and a month after you died, a tumor was found in my neck. Within the year I lost my thyroid to cancer. And then the shift began. I finally realized I couldn't do the strong act any longer. I deserved an A for effort and an F for results. After more than two years I began to reach out.

I took a local course on grieving. I discovered I couldn't even speak when asked to tell my story. Not the first week, not the second. A solid lump of unspoken grief blocked my throat. I listened and found out how normal it was to have run to answer your phone call weeks, even months, after you had died; or to pick up the phone to call you so many mornings; to literally panic when I thought I had lost the earrings your daughter gave me that belonged to you. Perhaps not so normal was my prolonged reaction to the photo your son Billy had given me at your funeral that he took at Christmas, capturing your wonderful smile. His precious gift was part of his healing I am sure. But for me it created searing pain. And in the beginning the pain is absolutely as physical as it is mental. Only when the grieving class required that at the end of six weeks we bring in a picture of our loved one was I able to risk looking at you. And even after that, I had to put you out of sight. It was all, still, too fresh for my anguished heart though it was more than two years after your death!

I reached out further and began to see a therapist. I was helped to understand better the dreams where mother was drowning and I couldn't save her; the elevator dream where my joy knew no bounds when the door opened and there you were. I moved to join you on your way to the "rooftop", but you sternly shook your head and closed the door. I wasn't welcome. I had to let you go, honor your choice to ascend alone. I was helped with the strange and guilt-incurring reality that in spite of three wonderful sons and a loving husband, I just wasn't sure I wanted to live on without you, so entwined had we been in our love, lives, and laughter. I was helped with another aspect of my covert preoccupation with death: the frequent fear that one of the children would have an accident, that Arnold would die. I learned that all of this is normal for suicide survivors. How essential it is to learn such things and to seek help through books, people or groups. For suicide is too unnatural a path and no one really knows how to handle it alone. We can so easily get lost in a morass of guilt, pain and bewilderment; we can even die. The mere passage of time is not enough. It helps, but if we do inadequate grieving, lock away our pain within, we lose not only the one we loved, we lose part of ourselves.

But the healing journey had finally begun. And I remembered those words that somewhere there was a gift to be found. No longer resistant to the idea, I became curious. Nothing occurred to me but now I was at least open, shifted to a more positive place. I began to think about our lives, how we mirrored each other so well. Educational products of the 1950's, housewives and mothers in the 1960's, we laughed and sympathized continuously about our lack of organization. "You're sure no balaboosta", my Yiddish speaking mother-in-law used to say, although she always kindly followed with, "Somebody doesn't like it? Let 'em clean!" Which she did. I remember my hurt, which you helped convert into hilarity, when my father-in-law found me washing the kitchen floor on hands and knees and remarked, "Nu? So what's the holiday?" Laughter tainted with self-hatred informed our hectic lives, the unfulfilled lives of you, the gifted artist, me, the would-be writer. How we shared dreams of using these talents. But we were stuck in our fear. Maybe it was fear of failure, perhaps fear of success. It doesn't matter; we never managed to quite get our gifts out there. You kept taking art lessons, long after your teachers told you that you should be teaching them. I kept reading "Writer's Digest", the subscription you gave me each year. We laughed a lot, we supported each other's longing for expression and, somehow, each other's inertia. So many excuses. So many people to take care of.

Finally I began to look closely at our closet talents. Your beautiful art had been hung in the homes of your children, admired by all, and I mourned what might have been. Slowly I began to believe I could make some amends for those years of aborted creativity. I began sending out small articles. Back came the usual rejections, a few unpaid acceptances, then my first paid acceptance. Joy grew in this new doing but I suspect not one step would have been taken had you not left me this strange legacy I was uncovering, creating a deep need and aching desire to "do" for us both. No more silent voices. I could speak for us by writing and this gift of release was from you.

And there have been other gifts. I, so unschooled in grieving, have been able to clear walled off pain from past losses: my roommate Ilse's suicide, our father's death, our beloved step-father's death, our family friend Jim's suicide, and more, so many more deaths. For I've learned that grief relates to all the losses we've had in life, to grieve for one is to grieve, finally, for them all. And then there has been the gift of removing historical masks in the family. This has been a most difficult challenge. For I've been our mother's daughter, our mother who wouldn't even let me tell her closest friends when she was unwell. We had to always pretend to be strong, in tight control of everything. How exhausting that has been. I had so little knowledge of our family, mother being an only child, our father having one sibling, and you my only one. Such a little family and with the two of you gone I suddenly lost access to our history. But I had begun to wonder and to reexamine many things, for therapy had confronted me with my lifelong pattern of mood swings. You had completed suicide, and your son has had to struggle so long, but so bravely and well, with his mental illness. Mother's family were all long gone, but there was an older cousin by marriage left on our father's side. I wrote her asking if there was a tendency towards bipolar illness, depression, whatever in the family. "Oh yes," she wrote back. "My husband, your father's nephew, struggled with depression. I knew it when I married him and didn't care as he was so wonderful. And yes, several of my children have had to deal with forms of depression," she wrote. "One had to be hospitalized for awhile, and one is a recovering alcoholic." I really didn't want to know this. It's taken me a long time to come to terms with it, accept it, gather my tools for dealing with my own mood swings, and finally, the hardest, to tell my three sons to remain alert in their lives for signs, just in case they are vulnerable to this chemical inheritance. But the upside is that so much more is known now. There is more help and understanding than ever before as we make new discoveries about the brain. So dearest, this is actually another gift that emerged from your illness, a gift of knowledge to the entire family, for indeed forewarned is forearmed. I suspect there will be more that I discover, gifts that emerge. I promise to be open to them in honor of you who so enriched my life while you lived. Just like in Brer Rabbit, you were my "laughin' place". So many happy memories. And though I will never stop missing you, I choose to focus on these now for they will enrich me all the rest of my life.

I love you,
Issie

Cry Uncle
by Gabriel Constans

This piece previously appeared in Bereavement Magazine *(June 1999) and* Challenges *(January 1997).*

"Yep, there's been lots of bears out here. Your dad and I almost got eaten alive once. Remember that, Jerry?" I was with my Uncle Danny and my father walking noisily along a woodland creek when he started in on one of his famous tales.

"Sure do," my dad replied. "I thought we were dead meat."

"Come to think of it, it wasn't too far off from where we are now. We'd just walked around a blind corner of trees when out of the blue comes this nine foot, growling grizzly. It stood straight up, roared, and charged at us full speed!"

As I listened my feet began to feel like they were stuck in mud. I finally got them to move a few inches and strained my neck to see the upcoming bend. He must have relished my increased apprehension as he continued his hair-raising story.

"Yep, it was scary alright."

Reluctantly I stuttered. "What happened Uncle Dan? How'd you get away?"

After a long pause and knowing glances between him and my father, he replied. "Luck, Gabe, pure luck. We turned and tried to run, but your dad's so darned slow. The old grizzly was right at his heals, licking his chops! I picked up a rock about so big (he picked one off the ground the size of a baseball and displayed it as evidence), closed my eyes, and threw it with all my might towards his gigantic jaws of death. The rock hit that crazed bear right between the eyes. It didn't really hurt him none, he was so big and all, but it stunned him just enough for us to scramble up the gully to our jeep and tear out of here."

"It was luck alright," my dad interjected. "You throw about as good as you jive. You couldn't hit the side of a barn from twenty paces. It's still hard for me to believe." He was grinning from ear to ear.

The rest of that "pleasant day in the country" was a total wash. I was scared of my own shadow. My uncle didn't give me the slightest clue or indication that he was telling a tall one. I fell for it hook, line, and bear claw. It wasn't until I'd turned sixteen that I had the nerve to ask my father if Danny had really saved him from a bear. Much to my embarrassment, he began to chuckle. "A bear? You're kidding! Maybe a deer or a raccoon, but a bear?" His laughter said it all. "You don't know your uncle very well, do ya?" I guess I didn't, but I wish I had.

That was the first, but not the last, time my uncle left me wondering which way was up. As I got older I learned that he was notorious for his inventive and intricate shenanigans, which he played on both family and foe. It may sound masochistic or foolish, but I'd be thrilled to have him pull the wool over my eyes again.

I always envisioned my uncle as a free-wheeling, fun-loving spirit who made the most out of life. He had a beautiful, intelligent wife, Aunt Sharon (who I had a crush on all through adolescence); three bright, good looking kids; was financially successful; and enjoyed a variety of activities and pursuits.

As I matured, so to speak, Danny and his family moved out of town and I didn't get to see him very often. Once or twice a year we'd cross paths or I'd hear about their latest adventures from my mom and dad. As far as I knew, they were living "happily ever after". Their kids were all grown, married, and had munchkins of their own. Long after I'd left the roost and gone south to greener pastures, Danny and Sharon moved back to my hometown for good.

My wife/partner, Audrey, and I remember running into Dan and Sharon several times in the last few years. At my mother's sixtieth birthday celebration, Danny told us about the judo tournaments he'd entered, their children and grandchildren, and continually complimented us on our family and our work. He mentioned, as an aside, that he'd stopped drinking, was going to a counselor and "making progress". I remember answering "that's good," as if I'd known all along that he had a drinking problem or was getting counseling.

After the party I asked my mother about his remark and discovered that Danny had been drinking off and on for years and was seeing a psychiatrist to help with his "problems".

"Drinking? Problems? He seemed fine to me," I exclaimed, feeling like the last man on earth to see the elephant in the room.

"Yes, drinking," she replied. "He's had difficulties for a long time. He's doing much better now."

Difficulties? I said to myself. For some reason I didn't inquire as to what those difficulties or problems were. Part of me didn't want to know. I wanted to keep my childhood image of the fun-loving uncle who always had a joke or aside for any occasion. Any other reality was unacceptable.

Several years passed until I returned home last winter for a medical emergency. My father had a heart attack and successful bypass surgery. A few days before I was about to return home, I ran into Dan sitting in my parents kitchen.

"How you doing, Gabe?"

"Pretty good, how about you?"

"Okay. Boy, you've really grown. You seem like a real man now."

"I've been grown for sometime, you know. I'm forty-one."

"No, that's not what I mean. It seems like you've really come into your own, found yourself, feel good about who you are. You know what I mean?"

"I guess so. How's Sharon and the clan?"

He smiled contentedly. "They're great. I've got the most wonderful children and grandchildren anyone could ask for."

"It's still hard to think of you as a grandfather. You seem so young."

Grinning sheepishly he replied, "Well, that's what happens when you have such a great wife. It seems like you've found your match, too."

"No doubt about it. I couldn't be happier if you gave me a million dollars. Well, maybe a little happier."

"Yeah, it helps, but it's no panacea. It can't give you peace of mind."

The smile quickly left his face as he drifted inward to some dark, foreboding cave.

"Danny . . . Danny?"

He didn't answer. Suddenly, he got up and started to leave. Then, just as abruptly, he stopped. "Why don't you and Audrey come over sometime? How about tomorrow?"

"Thanks, but we have to head back home in the morning."

"Okay. See ya later."

He shook my hand firmly, turned, and left. I never saw him again.

Two weeks later my dad called.

"Gabe."

"Yeah."

"Did your sister call you yet?"

"No. Why?"

"Well . . . I've got some bed news."

"Are you okay?"

"Yeah. It's your uncle."

I couldn't for the life of me figure out what was going on.

"Danny?"

"Yeah," he stated flatly, followed by a long pregnant silence.

I took a deep breath and asked, "What's happened?"

"Danny's dead."

"What!?"

"He killed himself."

"Come on, quit joking around."

"I'm not kidding."

"When?"

"Yesterday. He shot himself."

"Oh my God! Why?"

"He'd been depressed for a long time. I'm not surprised."

"Well, I am. Are you okay?"

"Yeah, I'm fine."

"How's Sharon and Mom?"

"They're hanging in there. They weren't totally surprised either."

"I just saw him a couple weeks ago; he seemed fine."

"Well, he's had problems for a long time, you know. He's told me several times over the last few years to not be shocked if I found him dead someday."

"Didn't he get any help or anything?"

"Oh yeah, he'd been doing everything. He was on medication for his depression, attended Alcoholics Anonymous, and saw a psychiatrist regularly."

"Depression. I didn't know he was depressed."

"Oh yeah. That's what's been eating him for so long. He just couldn't shake it. He tried everything."

"Man, I still can't believe it. Did Sharon find him?"

"No, a neighbor did."

"Is there anything I can do? Do you want me to come up there?"

"No, we're okay."

"Are you sure?"

"Yeah, thanks."

"There must be a local support group or something. Do you want me to call and find out?"

"No. Not now. Maybe later."

"I'll call you tomorrow."

"Okay. Bye, Gabe."

I hung up the phone and sat silently in shock. How could this kind, gentle man have killed himself? He had everything. He helped countless young people, including my nephew, to do things they'd only dreamed of. He'd never hurt anyone. He was always trying to make other people happy. Why was it so hard for him to give himself what he gave others? Questions, questions, questions. My mind tried to bend around the unanswerable.

As soon as I told Audrey about his suicide, she asked if I was okay.

"Yeah, yeah, I'm fine. If I could just figure out why he did it. I don't understand. Why didn't I see it coming. It's like I was totally blind or something."

"Yeah, it's weird. I wouldn't have guessed in a million years."

Weeks passed. I kept in touch with my parents and heard about the hundreds of people who attended the funeral, the kind words, and how everyone was reacting, especially his wife and children. I thought about his death day and night: how he died and the questions which arose in its wake. I told some people at work, and they gently asked how I was coping. As usual, I replied, "Fine, just fine." Or so I thought.

Three weeks after Danny's suicide I found myself crying at the drop of a hat, easily fatigued, and having difficulty getting up in the morning. At first I couldn't figure it out. *I must have a flu bug or something,* I'd tell myself. When the "flu bug" didn't go away after five days, I told a friend and she pointed out the obvious. "Maybe the loss of your uncle is catching up with you."

Of course she was right on the money. I'd been ignoring the obvious, like someone who thinks they've lost their glasses and they're right on their head. I slept in a little longer, took an extra couple days off work and let my tears fall whenever they came. My energy gradually returned, but I still felt like a dunce. "Why hadn't I known he was depressed? If I'd known, maybe I could have said or done something to stop it."

Such magical thinking did nothing to alleviate my feelings of helplessness. I was desperately trying to establish some control over a situation that was beyond my control. I thought if I could figure "it" out, I'd be resolved of any guilt feelings that lay festering below the surface. In fact, what I needed most was to stop intellectualizing or telling others "how to get support" and allow the sorrow and sadness I was pushing down to break free.

His death sparked my fear as well as my sadness. It reminded me of a time or two when I'd felt overwhelmed or depressed, and the thought that I could have taken the same path was unnerving. Though it's a choice anyone can make at any time, his actually doing it made it so concrete and real. Most of us look at suicide as unacceptable, but when it hits close to home it can become a less forbidden option. Although I had no intention of taking my own life, for any reason whatsoever, the suddenness of his departure brought up many questions and made me a little less sure of my secure, predictable existence.

I thought I knew Uncle Danny, but I only knew the aspects of his character that were easy to digest. I think I know him a little better now. I don't believe he was ever able to experience real joy or happiness in life and that's a hard fact to swallow. Whether his depression was a biological/chemical imbalance or a combination of personality, circumstance, and alcoholism is in some respects irrelevant. It doesn't detract from his good nature, endless compassion, or irreverent humor. My only regret is that I didn't "really" know him when he was living. He had to die before I began to see his valleys as well as his peaks.

If I could talk to him now, I'd remind him of the many lives he touched— for the better. I'd tell him his life had meaning and purpose. I'd tell him he's missed beyond comprehension. I'd let him know, in no uncertain terms, how much he'd loved and been loved by his family and friends. I'd tell him about this time my father and I were walking in the woods and were attacked by a giant grizzly!

Requiem For An Unbroken Love
by William Cummings Kern

Thanksgiving.

Raindrops pelted the cedar siding of our house with an incessant clatter. An eerie silence roamed inside, ignoring the blustery patter of rain carried on an irascible wind. In the family room, the glass doors to the fireplace were pulled back; several split, fir logs were stacked on the grate. A cold wind whistled into the room, whirling down through the tall, brick chimney. The parquet dining room table was bare except for a scattered newspaper and two ivory-colored, half-burned candles. Slender, tapered, and pure, the candles were elegant symbols of our many romantic dinners together at this table. Amid the dusk of candlelight, Margie and I.

The air in the house smelled flat and ordinary, like yesterday's or the day before. It longed for the aroma of a roasting turkey, or pumpkin pies baking in the oven, or the scents of people, perfumes clashing with colognes. The kitchen was still and empty. The lights were turned off. Two bottles of Chardonnay waited on the counter, like chess pieces waiting to be moved. No people would join us this day. Once again Margie had received no wishes, no cards, or phone calls for a "Happy Thanksgiving". Not from her mother, her sister, or her two young daughters. And no invitation. Deeply hurt, she had escaped, upstairs to her study. She had shut the door.

"I just can't pretend anymore that everything's okay and walk around with a smile," she told me days before. "The holidays are going to be really hard for me," she had warned me earlier.

Concerned, I talked about plans for us to leave town for the holiday. "Let's go skiing at Whistler," I tempted her. "A weekend at the Four Winds Inn in Seaside? A cabin at Timberline Lodge on Mount Hood?"

She said "No" or did not respond at all. I tried again. After several days I gave up. In her state of mind, there was no return to happiness. Her family, her children, had for too long perniciously and relentlessly abused her. Even today they had turned their backs. With cold, impervious, and remorseless faces, they ignored the already fragile spirit of their broken, aching daughter, sister, and mother. Despite my unrequited love, I could not erase four decades of rejection.

In the darkness of this night, without a clue, without a goodbye, without one word, without an "I love you so very much", without an "I'm sorry", without an explanation, Margie, my wife, took her own life.

No single word can portray the ruin Margie left behind. Her one single mistake, executed in a second, mutated my life. There was no going back; as hard as I tried to turn back time, her death remained an immutable event. My world collapsed.

I felt torpid. Languid. I could not get out of bed or lift myself from the sofa. I couldn't eat. I lived on one coffee drink a day. I could not make myself read or write the simplest sentence. For weeks I sat in my blue leather chair by the patio door gazing outside, watching nothing. Even in the dark of night, I stared outside. Sometimes, something would catch my eye. A last bloom of Margie's Caribbean rose tree suddenly appeared, early during that mild, wet winter. It was bright orange and yellow, the color of aging maple leaves in the fall in Vermont. I took my pruners, cut the flower, and threw it on the ground. "Damn you," I screamed into the rain. A last maple leaf, discolored a moldy purple, clung tenaciously to a branch on our anniversary tree, a Norway Maple. The tree looked barren, just thin, gray sticks. I wanted to cut it down with the largest chain saw I could find, but never did. I never look at that tree anymore. Squirrels, clasped upside down on Douglas Fir trees in our backyard, chirped, begging for bird food. I yelled at them, "Get lost" or "Shut up!" I didn't care. I cared about nothing. Nobody. I just sat in my chair. My pain was so great I wished to die.

Guilt descended violently and overpowered me, like mountains crushing my chest. Guilt set me adrift on a turbulent and anguished sea, and sentenced me to a raft of logs tied together with a thin rope, a tattered fig leaf for shelter and sail, leaving me in irons, and exposed and vulnerable, in endless pursuit of questions, in endless defeat of answers. Only the breath of guilt stirred the raft along; it was as powerful as the wind, and the tides, and the currents.

The fragile raft crested and plunged with the swells of guilt as I relived and examined our life together, over and over, asking questions, looking for clues and answers. I became a detective obsessed with finding that one question, exploring every detail of every second of our short life together, every vignette, every event, every extraordinary moment. *Did I tell her "I love you" enough?* I questioned. *Did I hear her cries for help? What did I do wrong?*

I turned over every clue, every bit, every morsel, every orb that I could find, looking for any answer. *Why did she do this? If she hadn't married me she would not have done this! I must've done something wrong!*

I never learned even one answer. Obsessed and poisoned by guilt, I continued my endless journey, exploring every detail, over and over and over, in endless circles of questions. I needed help.

My first counselor, Janine, a young and soft-spoken psychologist, working in a corner office with huge windows, oak and leather furniture, and thick carpeting, saw me for fifteen sessions. A cup of freshly steeped cinnamon herbal tea, placed carefully on the armrest of her green recliner, was her constant companion. With the clockwork of a parking meter, fifty minutes was all she ever gave me. At fifty-one minutes, her eyes glowed "Expired".

Inside, my body felt grated and raw, flesh abraded on granite rock. My hands and legs trembled. I had lost twenty-five pounds. My skin looked sick, the color of bruised apples. I was still not eating. One friend told me that I smelled like acetone. "From the breakdown of muscle," she said. She gave me some stress vitamins and brought me lunch. My blue eyes looked dull, cataract. My speech was incoherent and I wailed and blathered through each session with Janine. Soon, I began to notice her frustration with me. She would consider the gray sky from her huge picture window or study the floral pattern in her homely dresses whenever I talked. At the end of the fifteenth session, she told me she couldn't help me. She fired me as her patient. It didn't matter. I felt no pain anyway. I was numb. I dreamed of being with Margie.

Thirty-one days after her death, after Christmas dinner, I ran outside from my youngest daughter's home in Oregon, my breath crystallizing in the minus ten-degree temperature, wailing, as I begged and pleaded my family to end my misery. "Shoot me. I want you to shoot me," I yelled at my daughter. "I know you have a gun. Get it. Please! Kill me. Kill me. I want to die." Neighbors gawked in horror from their frozen windows. Dogs howled. None came to my rescue; I was but a diminutive, pathetic shadow crouched in the middle of the street, surrounded by ice and mounds of black snow. I *had* to escape my pain. I no longer existed. My soul, my spirit, and my dreams for a life together had vaporized. I was but a skeleton of life. A bullet could destroy nothing more.

My family did not oblige. Like sentries, they stood watch, and froze with me, standing in the snow, braced against the howling, icy wind. Helpless, they finally carried me back inside.

Later, I told Courteney, my new counselor. She lost her husband to suicide a decade ago. She understood my pain. She was a gentle woman, but of confident character, and I wished she could have been my mother then. My mother passed away a long time ago. Courteney's straight silver hair shone like a star. She pulled her gentle face into a stern countenance and directed a firm rebuttal at me, "Margie's pain was not about you. Her decision had nothing to do with you. You must stop feeling responsible! Your guilt will destroy you." I don't remember her words even reaching my eardrum, back then. I wanted Margie back.

For weeks, I attempted to secure a bargain with the devil. God had ignored me when my little brother died, years ago. I wouldn't bother with him again. Beelzebub, on the other hand, I thought, was a figure I could bargain with. As my head hung listlessly over my cereal bowl, I appealed to him every morning during breakfast, while I drowned Wheaties with my spoon in the milk in my bowl. "Take my soul," I sobbed. "It's yours. Take whatever else," I pleaded with sinister contempt, "But, you must let Margie come back. You must!"

I entreated him to respond immediately. I told Margie to phone. I wrote down our phone number and affixed it with tape to the oak kitchen cabinets by the telephone. I told her to call collect. "We'll start a new life," I promised her. "We'll change our names. No one needs to know. Everything will be just fine. I'll meet you wherever you are." Neither the devil nor Margie ever called me. I even extended the deadline. Several times.

Later, I told Courteney. She only listened and silently acknowledged my journey through insanity. Her blue, sage eyes told me she understood. She drew a narrow smile, just barely revealing her peroxide-white teeth. She asked, "Bill, what are you going to do to stop your guilt?" I shrugged. Silently I told myself that, more than ever, I wanted to be with Margie.

In late March I hiked Four Peaks, a solitary mountain just east of Phoenix, on the fringe of the Arizona high country. My best friend, David, had insisted. I warned him that I had not moved a bone since November and that I would be happy to stay in his Jeep, right where we had parked. He insisted I go. "Come on, Mr. Bill. You're burning time," he admonished me. "It's only a thousand feet straight up!"

In the three days I had spent with him prior to the hike he never could grasp my pain. He empathized, but he skillfully deflected my pain with jokes of harsh reality. "Move on and find yourself another woman," he said. "Take off your wedding ring and start having some fun." That nearly cost him our friendship.

I was surprised at my strength. We reached the top of our hike, at some seven thousand feet elevation, in mid-afternoon. I was still angry at David. I rested briefly, alone, standing amid Ponderosa Pines, breathing the crisp, dry alpine air, under a cloudless, azure-blue sky. I could see forever.

At that dreamy moment it suddenly occurred to me that David, like everyone else, could see me hurting, but only in a bewildering two-dimensional plane, flat, like on a movie screen. He, just like others, had no knowledge and no idea of, nor interest in the shape, the depth and perils of my world, and the lethal pain that reigned there.

People showed genuine concern and frustration. They told me they *wanted* to walk the path of grief with me and they *offered* to take some of my pain away. But they could not. They could not cross over into my world. Sometimes I doubted their sincerity, but in the end I had to believe in their genuineness. Even my mighty "companion" in this journey, my counselor, Courteney, could only drop me off at the gates and wave me off with a "Hang in there." Platitudes and cliches were everyone's most sincerest form of comfort. They wished for me to feel better. It was the best they could do.

In Courteney's small office, no larger than my life raft, I told her, "I feel so unheard, so isolated, so unreachable, like the man on the dark side of the moon. I ache to have someone in my world, to help me face Margie's skeletons and my guilt." She spoke authoritatively, repeatedly pointing her middle and index fingers at a point just in front of my knees. "Bill, healing has to come from within you. You have to be good to yourself. You are a wonderful, sensitive man. A good person. Guilt is something you place in your mind. You can also take it out. Don't let Margie pull you down. You were not responsible." She promised me things would get better. Soon.

She was right. There are no potions, no incantations, no prayers, and no antidotes. It was my work to do. Hard work. I did not believe things would ever get better. I could not keep on carrying the burden of this cross. I had no idea how to get my life back together.

The logs of my raft roiled against the endless turbulence of water and began to break away from the single rope holding them together. Demons rose up from the surface of the water, like leviathans. They sneered and taunted me, blamed me, accused me, cursed me and told me, "It was all your fault." I was so defenseless I let them tell me. I plowed the water with my hands, but it was like moving air. I could not make the raft move away. I lay in irons.

My wish to escape my pain intensified; it became a self-fulfilling mandate. Although Margie had always said she wanted to die before me, I had always wanted to die together. I never understood why she always talked about that. But so it would be. I let my raft come apart. I dissolved into the sea. Before I went out to the garage I placed on the dining room table my Will, directions for my memorial service, a farewell poem, and a letter to my daughters. I put the cats outside. I sat down in the car and held a picture of Margie to my heart. I nestled the urn holding her ashes on my lap. Curled up in my seat, I relived our extraordinary wedding. Margie looked so beautiful. Her ivory-colored wedding dress a perfect companion to her smooth, olive-colored skin, her dark brown hair, and green eyes. She walked down the aisle toward me, smiling that broad, perfect smile that first attracted me to her, her innocent, big eyes, glowing with love, focused on me. I read part of the poem I wrote for our engagement:

> *"Margie, words can only fail all I wish to tell you.*
> *Thus I can only paint for you with the imperfection of words*
> *the sincerity of my true love for you and*
> *the wisdom of this love that there is no other.*
> *This is the shore I longed to reach.*
> *Lest the peril which befalls the flower,*
> *I promise to cherish and nurture always the 'specialness'*
> *which brought us together . . . "*

I did not want to live without her . . .

I felt Margie place her soft hand on mine. Seconds before it was too late, I turned off the ignition.

"Where to from here?" I whispered into the tropical wind as I savored the early May sun on the balcony of my hotel overlooking the glistening waters of Bahia de Mismaloya. I had not come to Mexico to run away; I already knew that the invisible wounds of this trauma would last my lifetime, wherever I went. Instead, it was a promise to my teenage daughter for us to escape the gray winter of the Northwest. I kept my promise to her.

I keep my promises.

And so had I promised to Margie at her memorial service,

> *"Margie, I will not forget you.*
> *I will not let your name perish.*
> *I will not let your memory fade.*
> *I promise that our love will outlast the skies, the trees and*
> *the oceans.*
> *I will love you until the end of time."*

In my many sessions with Courteney, she had told me so often that I had "such a wonderful ability with words".

In June I told her I had started writing again. Her face pulled into a warm smile, one that reminded me of sitting on my grandmother's lap as a lad. "I am writing a play," I told her. "About Margie." She looked at me curiously from her bulbous, rose-colored recliner. I swallowed hard and continued, "The greatest honor I can give Margie is to remember her. True love, as they say, is, after all, practical concern. My love must take another form. One that embraces life today." Courteney remained silent.

"I want the world to know about Margie through my writing. She had a story to tell, but she couldn't tell it." I described the story line of my play. I watched bumps travel on her tanned arms. She smiled that warm smile again and said softly, "This is wonderful, Bill. Your story, your play, will touch so many people's lives. And, in such a healing way."

Thanksgiving. A new year.

It will soon come. I whisper familiar lines, "The holidays are going to be hard for me. It's hard to walk around with a smile on my face and pretend everything is okay." I try to look past the present. I shoot bad memories from the sky, like clay pigeons. I work on my play. I hope that the flowers will bloom again.

I write. I remember. My love.

Unbroken.

Fat Danny
by Sylvia Beddoe

As a child, he was nicknamed "Fat Danny". He was always extremely over-weight, round and soft, and he reminded me of a young version of Santa Claus, without the white beard. Danny loved food, and his favorite food was candy. Chocolate, vanilla, strawberry, cherry, grape—it didn't matter—he relished every mouthful. He always carried candy with him. The pockets of his clothes looked like a squirrel's cheeks packed with nuts for the winter. He was teased a lot about his weight and the more he was teased, the more Danny ate and the bigger he became. That seemed to be a pattern he would follow throughout his life. The worse things got, the more Danny ate. Soon, eating was his only escape.

It seemed to me that my brothers and I never did anything right in the eyes of our mother. Over time, I began to realize that none of us were as perfect as Mama would like. Danny never did understand that, and as a child he kept trying to please her and the harder he tried, the worse he failed. Mama's own insecurities fell onto us and the pressures were great, and have continued to be throughout the years.

As the years passed, Danny became more insecure within himself and, in his words, he saw himself "as a complete misfit and failure in life". He was the man of the house while Mama was on her own. I can remember Mama going to work, leaving Danny in charge of the house, my brother Jake, and me. The day would begin with Danny tying an old blue-checkered apron around his plump belly and then pulling it up under his arm pits so it wouldn't drag on the floor. He would pull the old yellow step-stool to the counter and slowly plant both feet firmly on top of the stool and begin washing the mountain of breakfast dishes. Bubbles flew and water dribbled down the sides of the cupboards as Danny hurried to finish, only to begin another chore. When Mama would return home, the only things she seemed to see were the dried water dribbles and what had not been done. She never praised the work Danny had done.

There were times, later on, when Danny would be taken over our stepfather's knee and strapped with a thick leather belt for doing something that was not approved of, or for not watching Jake and me as closely as was expected. He would hold in every tear and, rubbing his chubby bottom, would walk, head hanging low, to the bedroom to sob into his pillow, all alone, in the dark.

Danny told me of times he would proudly display a piece of artwork, only to be criticized by Mama who said, "The sky isn't purple; it's blue." He recalled the many times she said his homework could have been neater and asked why he had gotten only B's and not A's. His best was never good enough. Even though through the years he tried harder and harder, things remained the same.

As a result, at the age of sixteen, Danny began to drink heavily, which only added to his already portly appearance and low self-esteem. The booze began to control his mind as well as his body, yet it wasn't enough to control the pain in his heart.

My recollections of an evening when I was about twelve are vivid. Danny's girlfriend ran screaming across the courtyard of the motel my mother managed. The kitchen door flew open and slammed into the wall. Marlene rushed in with Danny on her heels, a plate of steaming spaghetti in his hand. Danny hurled the heavy pottery dish, missing Marlene's head by only inches, splattering the kitchen walls with noodles and bright-red sauce which looked like bloody worms sliding down the walls. As abruptly as he had entered the room, Danny suddenly collapsed and fell on the cold, hard linoleum floor.

None of us had any idea what had started this insane moment, nor had we any idea why he had passed out. Mama rushed to call an ambulance and as she frantically dialed the phone, Jake and Marlene tried to help Danny regain consciousness. I stood in the background fearfully watching as they tried cold water on his brow, shook his body, and slapped him in the face to arouse him, but there was no bringing him around. There he lay, nearly dead.

Nearly dead. How very true that was. The doctor told us Danny was diabetic and had gone into insulin shock. Worse, he had massive amounts of heroin in his system as well. The mixture of fear, anger, pain, and disgust on my mother's face said it all.

Within a matter of days, Danny was home again giving himself insulin shots as they were needed. He told me once that he felt "like a human pin cushion". Despite warnings, he continued to drink heavily and, unbeknownst to the family, insulin was not the only thing being injected into his body.

Ten years passed and the situation worsened. Following a marriage that ended with Danny's wife being committed to an institution for the mentally ill, and two children taken away and put into a foster home, Danny lived with Mama. He stole from her on a daily basis: money, jewelry, family heirlooms. Nothing was exempt from his grasp; he had to have money to buy the food to feed his habit. He didn't just frequent the local bars, he nearly lived there and was rarely seen at home unless he was in a drunken stupor or so high that he didn't know anyone, even himself.

I stood paralyzed with fear in the corner of my mother's bedroom the night Danny pointed a loaded pistol at Mama. He was yelling at the top of his voice, and looked like the devil himself waving the pistol in the air and demanding money to support his habits. The frail appearance of my mother at her five foot seven inches and mere one hundred pounds seemed to be no match for Danny's five foot ten, nearly three hundred pound figure. Yet, despite the difference in their sizes, Mama had a strong will and a stare that could put the fear of God into anyone. She glared straight into his eyes, reached up quickly, and snatched the gun from his hands. Instantly, he fell to the floor, sobbing and begging forgiveness and help. That night he was in the hospital, again, beginning what would soon become one in a series of frequent, unsuccessful stays.

I don't think any of us realized until after his death nearly nine years later how much pain Danny had been in, mentally as well as physically. By the time of his death, he had gangrene in his right leg, and had lost nearly two hundred pounds. Food had become one of his least favorite things, having been replaced by heroin, cigarettes, and beer. Antibiotics were used but none helped, and it was only a matter of months before the gangrene moved up from his foot, reaching his hip. The pain was rapidly becoming more than Danny could bear, even in a drug induced state, and the doctors said it would "only be a matter of time" until he died.

Danny also had Alzheimer's disease by that time, and generally didn't know what was going on or who he was. Mama slept on the living room couch so she could hear him if he tried to wander out in the night. Many times she would have to hunt the town in search of him. He was like a child who would wander off if out of sight for only a moment, and then he was unable to find his way home. He regressed to nearly an infant stage, being spoon fed and wetting and messing his bed at night. He had to be taken to the bathroom, and at bath time, he had to be undressed and watched intently so he wouldn't eat the soap or try to drown himself. Yet, even in all this, there were moments of what we could have called sanity, adulthood, or reality. It was in just such a state that Danny "chose to leave".

Several months after my brother's death, Mama found poetry that Danny had written twenty years earlier. He was an avid writer, yet sadly, the poem, as well as the majority of his works, dealt with death, darkness, sadness, and undying grief.

Six weeks before his thirty-fifth birthday, my brother took his life. Early that morning my mother went into Danny's room to see if he had tried to give himself his morning shot of insulin, or if she had slept through his usual noise of stumbling around on his crutches. It was then she found his cold, gray, lifeless body in his bed; he looked as if he were sleeping. On the nightstand was an empty bottle which had once held heroin, along with a needle and syringe, a half-full bottle of insulin, an empty bottle which had held a dozen strong pain killers and an empty beer bottle. No note, no goodbye, no farewell. Just signs of how he had chosen to leave.

I loved my brother, yet strangely his death did not seem to affect me at all. I did not grieve—outwardly or inwardly—but I did not deny the fact he had taken his own life either. I did not cry, become depressed, hide away, or lash out at the world in anger. I simply resigned myself to the fact that he was dead and I would never see him again. Period.

Five years after my brother's death, I began the college education I had always dreamt of. During an English course, we were required to write of a personal experience which had affected us deeply. I have had many experiences about which I could have written, yet as odd as it sounds, the first and only thing that came into my mind was my brother's suicide.

As I began to write, I realized how creative and loving a little boy my brother had been and, as a man, how lonely and filled with pain he had grown. The more I wrote, the more I realized what he had meant to me. He had not only saved me from drowning when I was three, but he had taught me the value of life.

It's been seven years since I wrote that paper. Seven years in which memory after memory—good and bad alike—have popped into my head. I am only now beginning to appreciate who Danny was and what he meant to me.

Did he meet his destiny? I'll never know. And even though the autopsy listed several "possible causes" of death among which were gangrene, lung cancer, heart failure, blood clot, insulin shock, drug overdose, and others I was not told of specifically, I often think he simply died of a broken heart.

Daddy's Death
by Suzanne S. Craft

Imagine a peaceful summer morning in June. The children have just gotten out of bed and are still in their pajamas. My husband, who works nights, has just gotten home. I've just put a load of clothes in the washer. The day has started out just like every other day. And then the phone rings and a nightmare begins.

When I answered the phone, I didn't recognize the other person's voice. I finally realized that it was my mother calling, but she was so hysterical that I could hardly understand her. It finally sank into my head that something terrible had happened to Daddy. The only words I understood were "tractor" and "at home".

I slammed down the phone and shouted at Bill to get the baby some diapers. As I ran through the house trying to find a pair of jeans, I told our two girls to run and get in the car because something was wrong with their Papa.

All the way to my parents' house I kept telling myself that Daddy was hurt badly, but I was sure that he would be okay. When we topped a small hill a little ways from their home, I saw people everywhere and two ambulances in the field beside the house.

As soon as the car stopped I began to run toward the field. I remember screaming, "Daddy, Daddy!" When I got about halfway to where the paramedics were loading him into the ambulance, my family's pastor caught my arms and began to shake me. He kept telling me, "He's alive! He's still alive, and your mother needs you at the house."

I got back into the car and my husband drove me to the house where my mother was waiting. As I helped her to dress, she tried to tell me what had happened.

My father was on the tractor cutting hay. Mother had made coffee and had gone onto the porch to wait for him so she could take him a cup. Daddy drove out of her sight behind some gardenia bushes in the yard. The tractor came back into her sight, but Daddy wasn't on it. She threw her cup down and ran into the field toward the place she had last seen him. She found him lying on the ground with cuts all over him. He had somehow fallen off the tractor and the hay cutter had run over him. He was still alive, though.

She had to leave him while she went back to the house to call 911. She was also able to collect her thoughts enough to call her pastor and me.

The ambulance carried Daddy to the nearest hospital, but it was only a small one and was not equipped to do the major surgery that Daddy needed.

By the time we got to the hospital, my mother's blood pressure was so high that the nurses could not even get a reading. My brother had been called at work and had been brought to the hospital. He was almost as hysterical as Mother. The doctors told us that Daddy would have to be airlifted to the nearest large hospital so that he could get the treatment he needed. One family member could ride in the Army helicopter with him. He told me that I needed to realize that my father might not even make it to the other hospital. I thought he was crazy. I was sure that now that the doctors had stabilized him enough to move, he would be fine.

When the helicopter landed at the hospital, Daddy was immediately taken into a trauma unit for his condition to be better evaluated. The doctors sent me into a small room to wait. I have never felt so alone. Bill was driving my mother and brother to the hospital, but it would be at least thirty minutes before they arrived.

About ten minutes after the arrival of my family, a doctor came in to talk to us. He said that Daddy had two skull fractures that they thought were his worst injuries. They had already taken him to surgery to begin working on them.

A few hours later the doctor came back to tell us that they had completed the surgery on my father's head and that his condition was stable. They would wait a while and then begin doing surgery on his other injuries which included several major cuts on his back and legs. Both of his legs were broken in several places. His left shoulder was gone and his left arm would possibly have to be amputated. They didn't know how much, if any, brain damage there was.

It seemed like hours, but was actually not long, before the doctor came back. This time his news was worse. Daddy's condition was no longer stable.

His blood pressure was dropping and the blood they were giving him was no longer clotting.

Through that long day and even longer night we prayed and cried and prayed some more.

Before daylight, the doctor came to us again. He told us that we could go see Daddy if we wanted to, but his condition was not improving. A little while later, my daddy died.

I simply cannot imagine the horror Mother must have felt when that tractor came into her sight without Daddy on it. I imagine she might still have nightmares about it. I know that God has given her strength, living daily in His presence.

I can only wonder how my brother feels each day when he drives home from work and Daddy isn't sitting on the porch. I think it would be worse if he had to drive up and see Daddy sitting in a wheelchair without an arm and maybe paralyzed.

I only know how I, Daddy's little girl, felt and feel. I cried myself to sleep every night for a long time. Sometimes, I still do. If it had not been for my children, I would have closed myself in a dark room and stayed there. I didn't want to eat and was afraid to sleep. Each time I closed my eyes, I could see my daddy in the helicopter or the hospital. I could feel the panic that I felt when I answered the phone that morning.

My depression finally got bad enough that it affected my husband and children. I screamed at the kids all the time and argued with Bill over nothing. If anyone said I needed help, I snapped at them. I felt like I should not ask anyone but God for help. He was the one who had taken Daddy from me, and since God doesn't put burdens on us that we can't bear, I felt that He would give me the strength to bear my grief. My husband finally convinced me that going to a doctor for help with this problem was the same as going to the doctor for any other illness. He said that God gave the doctors knowledge to help us and there was nothing wrong with asking for help.

I am better now, although there are still days when I cry all the time. We, as a family, have been able to go on with our lives. We go to the places we went with Daddy and we even do some of the things we enjoyed doing with him. We have learned to remember all the happy times we had while he was still alive and to be thankful that we had so many happy years with him.

The shock of my father's death has worn off. He will have been gone a year on June 12, 1997. I sometimes still miss him so much that I get a sick, empty feeling inside.

I know that God has a reason for everything He does. I may never understand why He took Daddy when and how He did, but I know that His will was done. I just have to keep in mind that God knows what He is doing, and pray for Him to give me the comfort and grace to accept and live with it until we will be with him again.

The Drowning
by Su Ready

This piece was previously published in Ascent *magazine under the name of Su McDonald.*

Your drowning embarrassed me.
I never showed off the official photographs
of you, wet and showy at the water's edge.
I promised your remaining boots and shoes
that nothing would be told.
Every decision is a moral one. Don't
peek out at me from behind
the fortune teller's cards. Don't whisper
to me from the back seat anymore.
I can handle a stick shift.

You stood in the canoe and rocked;
the rapids released and orderly
collected you and bore you away.
I turned and saw nothing.
I am single now, a creature of habit,
washing diapers, rinsing skillets and my hair.
For a long time I looked for you in running water,
in every glass of water, in every ice cube.
But you were dissolved, spilled, and evaporated;
you retreated like a resting stain.

Derek
by Gail Lewis

Smelly high top sneakers lay where they were carelessly tossed by the door next to the backpack full of schoolbooks. Black fingerprints marked where Derek touched the wall after delivering the newspapers on his neighborhood route. Dirty dishes were piled up in the sink. Everything looked normal, but Derek was dead. He would never again walk in the door shouting, "Hi Mom, I'm home." At fifteen years of age his life ended, and my husband and I realized that our lives, as they had been, had ended as well.

The calling hours at the funeral home were a blur, as was the endless line of people who visited. People filled our house bringing food, and the phone rang again and again with calls of condolence. After the church service, it was all over. I threw away the flowers that made my house look and smell like the funeral home.

With everyone gone, I didn't want to dwell on death anymore. I wanted to make a new start. The way I dealt with Derek's death was to use every bit of energy I had to clean it away. I bought a large plastic bin and packed Derek's mementos, awards, and special things in it. Then I put the bin away in a closet. Everything else of his went to the Rescue Mission's thrift shop, along with the funeral food that I was too nauseated to eat. With a vengeance, I scrubbed the house until my hands were raw and every trace of Derek was gone. Gone were his fingerprints, shoes, books, games, clothes, everything that reminded me of him. Still the house was full of him, and too empty to live in.

I couldn't go back to work as a part-time clerk in a card and gift shop. How could I sell Christmas cards and gifts to happy shoppers when there would be no Christmas for us? I quit my job and did volunteer work at the hospital in order to keep busy. My husband tried to return to his job as an insurance agent. He found himself having to pull off of the roadway while driving to customers' homes. He wasn't much good at selling insurance since Derek died. His company put him on disability. The stress was getting to both of us. We both felt like we were going crazy in that big, empty house all by ourselves.

We needed a new beginning, so with the help from my family we moved to Florida. We began our new life in a small house in a city where the sun shines. We can take long walks on the beach when we feel depressed, and that helps. All that we have of Derek is the bin of mementos and photo albums. In this house, we do not hear his voice and see things that emphasize our loss and emptiness. We never have to worry about seeing Derek's friends grow up or being around people and places that remind us of him.

It has been almost six years since Derek died. I think about him every day. Sometimes I think about how he would have been going to college now, starting his senior year. What would he have studied? He would have been so intelligent, so handsome.

Derek's death changed the course of my life, and that change has led me in the direction of going to college, pursuing a degree in elementary education. My husband has a new job in social services which he loves. We have made new friends, done new things, and doors have opened in our lives. Every day as we move forward, the empty place that we feel inside of us grows smaller, but we still grieve for Derek and always will.

***

Derek Lewis died on October 27, 1990, of auto-erotic asphyxiation. He was an honor student in the tenth grade, played tuba in the high school marching band, was a Boy Scout, and was earning money for college by delivering newspapers.

CHAPTER 8

CHILDREN'S PERSPECTIVES

The feelings and impressions of death are revealed through the eyes of children.

From Grampa With Love
by Elysha Nichols

Some of my best and most important memories of my Grampa are from times that I spent with him. Many times I was invited to eat breakfast with him at his favorite restaurant.

Vandalia's just a small town, and it took us no longer than five minutes to get to Robbin's where Grampa was to meet "The Men". They were old friends who ate breakfast together and talked about their many interests. We sat down at a table for six. I was on the right of my Grampa. The waitress came for our order. Grampa got some coffee and asked for a pack of cigarettes. I ordered my meal. We sat quietly until the waitress brought Grampa's cigarettes. He smoked silently. I looked at his warm, wrinkled face as he sat there. Grampa was about seventy, and he really looked his age. He had wrinkles under his quiet eyes. Grampa wasn't one to shout or scream; he was the soundless, loving man that I was going to be like. Whenever he touched me with his soft hands, I would squeeze him back with love.

One of Grampa's friends strutted into the restaurant. He sat down across from Grampa and bellowed a warm hello. We exchanged glances and then they started to talk. Other men came in and sat down with us. As they talked, I received my breakfast. After their conversation was over, Grampa's friends left. Grampa asked me if I had an enjoyable time. My reply was a very certain "yes". We stood up, hand in hand, and left.

Now Grampa is gone. I really loved him with all that I had in my heart. He was very special to me and I was also special to him, for I was the last person he asked to see.

Only Fear And Grief
by Tim Lanham

This piece was written at the age of seventeen, describing an earlier event.

***

I see my mother lying there encompassed by the cold steel casket and the white silk pillows that surround her. She's dressed in a long pink nightgown as if she were ready for bed. Her lifeless body looks like it's never looked before, so thin, so pale, so troubleless. She doesn't look as I remembered her. It's as though she were not real, maybe nothing more than a mannequin you'd see in a store window. Yet she's as real to me as a flower you can see and touch. A flower that is happy because of the new life the sun brings to its roots. But there's no sun or happiness here, only fear and grief.

Why do people fear death? Why can't I, a boy of nine years old, hold my dead mother's hand and not understand the coldness and lifelessness of that touch? I shouldn't doubt God's power of life over death, for it is God's right to give the gift of life and his right to take it away.

I remember learning in church that the spirit is everlasting. When we die, our soul goes on living eternally in the Kingdom of God if we're good and in the Damnation of Hell if we're bad. But that still doesn't explain to me what death is. The coldness and stiffness of this dimly lit room with all the flowers from people who don't really care, is this what death is? Or maybe I'm living now the death of a past life. I wish it could be explained to me more clearly but, since we live on past experiences, maybe I must experience death before I know what it is. Just as there can be no solids without space, there can be no life without death. It's a necessary end to make way for the new life that is coming.

I just hope, as I leave the funeral home, that God will care for her soul wherever it may be and that he will give her new breath and new life, show her the joy that she gave to me as a child. I hope that God will put on earth in her place a person who has as much kindness and lovingness as my mother had so that the whole world may benefit from it.

The Gift Of Sacrifice
by Loren Bondurant

My grandpa's name is Ronald McMaster. I want to tell you about how great he was and how his death affected me and my family. He was born in 1932 and grew up in a small town in Nebraska. The Army was his career. He retired with the rank of Colonel in 1989.

Every summer we would fly from our home in Florida to visit my grandparents in Indianapolis. Grandpa would spend a lot of time with me. He taught me everything from fishing to shooting a rifle. I still remember when he took me to the range to shoot and I got a bullseye. He was so proud. I went on trips with my grandparents, and Grandpa said I was his #1 traveler. He was a strong supporter of my music, and I loved to play for him. When we moved to Richmond, he would come over every couple of weeks, and I would play some "Boogie Woogie" for him on my piano. At those times I never dreamed of something horrible happening.

On October 23, 1996, my grandpa was diagnosed with terminal lung cancer. I felt confused and sad. I knew something was starting to eat away at Grandpa's body, but I wasn't sure how this would affect him physically, and I wasn't sure when he would actually die.

At first, it wasn't so bad. He could still get around, see us, and do all the regular stuff he always did. In April 1997, my grandparents took my mom, brother, and me to the Dominican Republic. Grandpa enjoyed us enjoying everything: swimming in the ocean, boogie boarding, riding horses along the beach, playing tennis, and doing all the carefree things one does on a trip.

In the summer, we would go to see him. While we were there, I would sometimes bring a book along and sit on the bed next to Grandpa and just read. Other times I would just talk and hold his hand. On some occasions my brother and I would take our violin and cello and give Grandpa a mini-concert. My mom was going to buy us electric guitars for Christmas, but my grandpa had a way of finding things out, and he bought them for us to have before Christmas. We took them over, along with a thank-you poster we made, and played the only song we knew how to play—"Wipe Out". Grandpa loved it! It was a good feeling to know he could still share in our life even though he was so sick.

Sometimes we would go over when I didn't want to. Friends would call to arrange a movie or something, but I had to turn down their offers. I can remember when I was actually angry that I had to go to Indianapolis. How stupid of me. My mom was trying to help me take advantage of the time left.

One day in late summer my grandpa had a brain seizure. We rushed over. My dad, brother, and I were going on vacation the next day. I was worried something worse would happen while we were gone. My mom told us now was the time to tell Grandpa how much we loved him and how much we would miss him. He looked a little skinnier than he did in the spring. I told him how I felt, and while doing this, Grandpa nodded. I looked in his eyes and he was saying "I love you" and "Please don't cry" at the same time. Even though it was sad, it was a kind of gift to be able to tell him what I thought, because that was the last time he could talk with me.

During the last few weeks of Grandpa's life, my mom wasn't around our house much. She was in Indianapolis helping my grandparents. We would stay with friends after school. Our routine was so different. Some activities suffered, but I understood it was okay because we knew it was only for a short time, and we all had to do our best in spite of the circumstances. The Saturday before Grandpa died I saw him for the last time. He was very small, and for the first time I thought he looked very tiny in a weird, scary way. It felt as if I only saw him for an instant and then Dad took us home.

My grandpa died September 17, 1997. That night I was in bed, and my dad was reading a Bible story to me and my brother. Afterwards, Dad told me kind of quietly that Grandpa had died. When he told me, I couldn't believe it. I asked him to repeat what he had said. After he said it the second time, I felt like a bomb exploded on me. I lost my voice. Grandpa was gone from earth for ever and ever. I was very sad. My dad said it was good that Grandpa died because he was now free from pain, but that didn't stop me from feeling terrible. Ten days later we had the memorial. I saw so many people there. I was amazed at how many lives Grandpa had touched. Most of them were direct friends of my grandparents, but I saw my friends there too. I thought it was really nice of them to be there since they didn't have to be.

I learned that everybody makes sacrifices in a family. Not because they have to, but because they want to show their love and gratitude. I think that applies to everyone in my family. I know that it will never be the same without the physical presence of my grandpa. All the things he did for me and said to me will always be in my heart. I wish that I could see him again, but I am glad that he is in a better place.

Sometimes now, when it's quiet, I'll think about Grandpa. I think about how much he loved me and how much I love him. I miss him very much.

How I Accepted Death
by Chad M. Bice

I can remember my grandfather's death like it was yesterday even though it was several years ago. I can remember thinking on my way to the funeral home that I wasn't going to cry. Men don't cry. When I arrived, I walked in and began to talk about Grandpa with my relatives. Actually I didn't speak for some time. I didn't know what I should say or do because it was the first funeral I'd ever been to.

After observing my peers carefully, I decided to talk about what I would miss most about him. That was an easy subject. Grandpa was a retired mechanic of thirty years and, when he did retire, he ran a small business out of his garage for several more years, fixing peoples' cars, trucks, and vans. I used to love to go out and watch him fix all of those automobiles. I stood in awe as this man picked up whole transmissions by himself. It was unreal to me that he seemed to know everything there was to know about cars. And his seemingly endless collection of tools—he knew where every one was and exactly what it did. There was always that smell of gas and oil mixed together that hit me as soon as I walked into the garage. It was with that memory I felt my first bit of heartache over losing him.

There were a lot of friends and acquaintances that my grandfather had made over his lifetime; I couldn't believe how many people came to the visitation. After what seemed like an hour of conversing with my relatives and others, I finally went up to see him. When I laid my eyes on his still face, all I could do was stare. As I stood there, I could feel a huge surge of tears working its way up from somewhere deep inside me.

No, I thought to myself. *I'm not going to cry.* But it was no use. They were coming and there wasn't anything I could do to stop them. I made my way outside as fast as I could, trying not to look conspicuous, and just as I got out the door, the tears came. They kept coming for another twenty minutes before I was finally able to get myself under control again. I was very hesitant about going back into the parlor where my grandfather lay. I honestly did not know if I could handle it.

I knew, though, that I had to see him. I had to go in and see him one last time because I knew it was apt to be a very long time before I ever saw his face again. After I had mustered up a little courage, I finally went back, pacing myself, taking it as slowly as I could, hoping that I wouldn't lose it once again. As I approached the coffin, my eyes stared fixedly at his face and, when I finally reached it, I noticed something there that I hadn't noticed before . . . peace. I realized a moment later that I didn't need to try and control myself anymore; control was already there. It came from the idea that my grandfather was at rest at long last.

For the days to come, I reflected on the whole experience again and again, trying to make the pieces fit properly once more. Not the pieces of my heart, although that was part of it too, but mostly the pieces that surrounded the now empty hole in life where Grandpa had once been. I found myself getting teary-eyed on several occasions when I drove by his house and many times when I thought about him lying sick in bed, helpless to do anything.

My mother and I used to go visit with him almost every week, and even more frequently after he became ill with Parkinson's Disease. We had all gotten pretty depressed during that period, seeing his hands shake uncontrollably. It was very difficult watching a man who had been so strong, so kind, and so loving afflicted with a disease that took away all of the control he had over his body and all its functions, but left his mind intact, trapped in a worthless shell.

We all knew, eventually, we weren't going to be able to take care of him and that he would have to go to some place where he could be cared for on a daily basis. When his disease finally progressed to that point, we ended up taking him to a veterans' hospital in a nearby town. He had family visiting him all the time, nearly every day, and that made us feel a little better because none of us had really wanted to put him in a home of any kind. The veterans' hospital had a nice guest house that we would stay in from time to time on our visits. We all watched him slowly deteriorate. Then, after a few weeks, Grandpa developed pneumonia. That is what finally did him in.

Things went from bad to worse very quickly. The worst thing of all was watching him suffer. Not for a week or two, but for five or six. I remember him asking us at one point if we would take the feeding tube out of his throat. By then, he had barely been able to move. The pain he felt must have been unbearable, but what could we do? We were hoping against hope that he would come out of it all right. When he realized that no one was going to help him take out the feeding tube, he laid his head back down against the pillow and began to weep. However, he was so dehydrated no tears came. Seeing that really tore me up inside.

Twice after that time he tried to pull the feeding tube out by himself, but to no avail. The nurses always caught him. A part of me actually hoped he would succeed and his suffering would end; it was so hard to watch. I suppose I should have been thankful that he died after that kind of suffering. If it had been from Parkinson's, he would have slowly deteriorated and suffered so much longer, unable to do a thing about it. This at least was quicker, but I couldn't find happiness anywhere within me, not after seeing him like that for a month. When he died, the only thing I was thankful for was that it was finally over. He was no longer suffering.

Then came the funeral where I said my last goodbye. It was after the funeral that I started taking a bit more interest in Christ and the Bible. The Bible made me see that heaven and the presence of God and His love was so wonderful that the suffering my grandfather had experienced would seem completely forgotten in comparison to what he must be experiencing now. Then, I came to the conclusion that death isn't something we should feel bad about or fear. On the contrary, it is a release from this existence that can seem like hell so much of the time. I knew Grandpa was safe up in heaven and that he would never feel such horrible pain again. I was finally able to make my peace with that. I knew God would take care of him.

Carrying On
by Merritt Ann Beischel

June 7, 1992
Sometime late morning, or maybe early afternoon,
when the sun casts down its heat, spreading daylight past the horizon
presenting a overall delightful day
I played frisbee on a South Carolina beach with my dad and sister. Time
passed with the flings of the disc until we moved
possibly without thought
to wade in the water,
to swim, stroking and being stroked by the waves,
and I felt I wasn't advancing away from shore because the ocean ahead
didn't seem any closer than before.
We three swimmers, along with people oblivious to us who continued
sunbathing, tossing sand, and hibernating on the beach, were generally
unaware of anything other than the effect of the elements on our skin.
I don't recall looking back towards the house where my dad's parents,
siblings, and families were staying for the week,
celebrating the first time the Cincinnati Beischel clan were all together in
years,
having moved in just the day before,
having had only one group meal when we all ate black olives off the
condiment tray
before the food was put on the table.
The house couldn't be far behind.

Two clocks, one racing the speed of light for some galactic Olympic gold
medal, the other moving only after heavy deliberation, took over whatever
pace existed before,
that I had taken for granted.

I am unclear now, and may have been then too, as to whether
my head snapped back physically or if I just imagined the sensation
or if it was tethered to Dad's.

He was bobbing up and down
even though his eyes were fixed, locked, focused, directed, tuned, looking
at me.
Did he speak aloud over the crashing
or did his glance go directly to my inner ears?
get help go back
How could normal sound waves from his throat have overpowered the
tidal wave?
get help go back
I didn't see Lindsay in the foam but that didn't cross my mind.
get help go back
I'm not sure I could have seen anything else.
The wave didn't reach me
and my eyes didn't look like Dad's
and my arms and legs worked.
They worked to shore despite my lack of direction
maybe someone else had a map to the beach
where the sun was still beaming, where people still were oblivious.
Salt water, air, and my voice were all caught between my head and my
slushing stomach when I tried to talk to the first person to walk by.
"I need help . . . "
"What is it?"
"My dad . . . "
"Are there . . . "
" . . . and sister . . . "
. . . sharks?"
"No, I mean I don't think so—they need help . . . "
"I don't swim real well."
"Just get help . . . "
While Lindsay, I found out later, was clinging to Dad's body,
—I'm not sure if his spirit was still in it or not—
I, again with legs that for all I knew could have been another person's,
made it to the kitchen.
It had to be morning—
Mom was eating wheat toast for breakfast with an uncle I hadn't been
particularly close to.

She stopped chewing
my uncle appeared electrified
someone screamed
maybe all three of us
somehow an ambulance was called
somehow my uncle reached the water's edge, the water, Dad, Lindsay
clinging to Dad's unconscious body.
However I got back to the beach included a stop on the porch of the
house to scream to the ambulance workers where they should go. On the
beach people had gathered around Dad,
watching him being pumped, poked, CPRed,
and I yelled at them in my head.
Why the hell are you here don't you have anything more entertaining to do
on this sunny day why do you need to see my father unconscious why do I
need to see this?
Mom left with the ambulance
Dad had probably already left
and Lindsay and I stepped in the shower,
attempting to wash away one water with another and
thinking that if the water from the faucet was dripping onto my face I
could prevent the tears from wasting their time.
We were trying to convince each other that Dad had to
—he had no choice—
be around for our
graduationsweddingschildrentradionalurbanceremoniesthat
bothparentsaretoattend
RSVP not needed.
The two clocks were still ticking through the time it took to go to a
hospital I was unaccustomed to and wouldn't have to see
again.
They stopped and nothing took over when Mom, wheat toast by then
heavily lodged in her stomach, came into view
still wearing her bathing suit cover up she had put on to join in the family
beach playing.
In case Lindsay and I needed a translation of what Mom's sobbing meant,
Dad's dad told us.

I thought the old were supposed to go first.
"They did all they could do. His heart stopped. We may never know why
it happened, but it's God's will"
or some similar words that infuriated me.
A car ride back to the house was driven by someone still functioning,
followed by sleep on the floor in the room both my parents slept in the
night before.
If I dreamt, I wouldn't be able to say of what, but I woke feeling
nowhere near great, not at all thoroughly rested,
but as if the sleep put a Band-Aid over some aspect of what had happened.
If Dad had visited me in a dream, I kept questioning in my head, wouldn't
it be vivid?
I would have bet so, but it wasn't.
I just felt better.
Ready to assume my new position of one who moves on while Mom and
Lindsay work through the grieving more slowly than I wanted to consider.
I was the strong one, after all.

Three years before, on a lake, I watched Dad and Lindsay floating in a raft
as I sat on the dock
until I fell in the water after loosing my balance.
They were facing another direction, away, and didn't turn around until
after the shock of water, not air, around my head diminished and I pulled
myself back up.

We didn't buy wheat bread for a while.

***

Late 1992-
The Magnificent Morphing Mother appeared after Dad died, transforming Mom into two parents, financial expert, landlord and real estate guru,
insurance wrangler, driving instructor, homework resource, only discipli-
narian.
She, as many going through a job change, stumbled at first,
a toddler taking uncertain first steps while testing out her new found purpose.

The household is slightly chaotic,
not what many would describe as orderly;
dust is a surface decor of choice,
more likely circumstance,
the yard is left as a nature preserve and when my aunt, Mom's sister,
comes to town she feels obliged to offer, as a deliverer of beauty and
justice, to trim our shrubs
"Your neighbors were thanking me as they walked down the street",
and there is little time in the day set aside for the preparation of a three
course meal that Donna Reed or Martha Stewart would expect.
And Mom doesn't seem to care much.
"These things aren't priorities to me," she points out when her sister
makes comments,
"It's taken fifty years to be able to (and I'm still working on) do what I
want, what I think is important."
No longer living strictly under the guidelines of her parents, she's creating
her own path to show her daughters and herself in the process that it can
be done.
She even uses a college student as a sounding board who's credentials are
limited to having been raised by her and feeding off of her own metamorphosis.
And yet, the toddler learned to walk alone
stepping farther from needing assistance
making sufficient headway to progress individually
before, around, and with me, showing emotional strength I never truly
appreciated.
And I thought I was the strong one.

We Were The Best Of Friends
by Corrie Lynn Hausman

And then my father said, "Your grandmother has cancer."
A moment earlier, he had been talking about the recent snowfall. Now,
with a stoplight glowing red through the windshield, he turned from the

steering wheel with an almost pleading expression and told me that my grandmother was going to die.

When I look back at what has been a relatively tranquil existence, only
my grandmother's illness stands out. In a way, the hardest challenge in my
life has not been my own. I was not the one who went through radiation
treatment. I did not lose forty pounds in five weeks; no one fed me morphine. I was just the one who had to live after Grandma died.

Grandma and I had been, according to family legend, the best of friends
since I learned to walk. We talked about everything: religion, cooking, art,
history, and why lettuce tasted better fresh from the garden. She taught me to
knit and how to live like a decent human being; I taught her how to run a
VCR. Every weekend we would do something new; I always eagerly anticipated these times we spent together.

But now, for the first time ever, my mother had to beg me to come to
Grandma's house. "Please," she said, "do come. I want you there."

"I will," I promised. A promise is so little, and though I made this one
over and over, it was grueling to make myself appear at Grandma's house,
with a cheerful face and arms full of useless presents. I did not want to see
my grandmother, whose body was now wasting away and whose face looked
as if it had caved in suddenly one morning.

I felt an odd aching emptiness that begged to be filled, just as Grandma
was filling her once-tidy bedroom with possessions to be given away. I thought
I could fill it with books, with writing, with anything but Grandma. I knew
we would not be able to work in the garden or cook together ever again.

"What do I do?" I asked my mother.

"Just talk to her."

"But what if she wants to talk about . . . well, death?"

"You'll know what to do," said my mother, smiling and crying at the
same time. "She's your grandmother. You'll know."

So I went, and I cleaned, and I kept my young cousins occupied with
silly games. I sat by my grandmother's sterile bed and held her hand through
the railing. All the while, I denied death and tortured myself with the reality
of it by turns. I went for long walks to the end of Grandma's short driveway,
sometimes taking an hour or more to get the mail, deciding which letter
Grandma would like to read first.

In my dream world, Grandma would easily read her mail, but in real life, she was always exhausted and often times delirious. The violent break in her body had stunned her, left her scattered and confused, like leaves shaken from a tree.

"I have to cook the turkey," she kept whispering, evidently thinking of some long-ago dinner party. "The guests will be here soon."

"Grandma," I said finally, desperately. "You're in your bedroom. See?" I lifted her hand towards the pink-flowered curtains. "See, Grandma? We've already had supper. You're in bed."

"No, no. The turkey isn't done. And the house is a mess."

My grandmother couldn't stop worrying. In health, she was an impressive hostess, frugal and neat, and her house was an oasis of cleanliness. She taught me how to keep order in my life. But now, from sitting still, she had filled the room with herself. She filled it with pills and syringes and bottles, with dreams that rolled and tossed in the middle of the night, while she herself seemed to be diminishing into nothingness.

My grandmother lay there, as still as the hot summer air outside, and yet she was leaving us. Death, itself, could not be touched, could not be handled. Dying was not to be talked about, although the relatives whispered in the hallway and I knew that death was their subject of conversation. *What will we do when it actually happens? Does it hurt? Do you remember when Aunt Grace died, and . . .*

One morning in June, the phone rang at seven in the morning. Silently, I went into my parents' room, waiting for my mother to say it was a wrong number. There was only silence. Then my mother started to cry, hanging onto the phone receiver with both hands. I felt my legs begin to shake, but my head and heart were strangely calm. "Is . . . is she . . . "

My mother nodded.

And that was how I found out. I always thought it would be one of those middle-of-the-night emergencies, an emergency trip to the hospital at three in the morning, but it wasn't.

That morning at my grandmother's house, the Hospice nurse spoke into the phone like a woman ordering eggs and ham, business-like when we most needed it. I hid in Grandma's big orange recliner, and my cousins played computer games.

I looked out the grid of window panes instead. The world was divided up into neat squares. The panes blurred and the sadness was so great I could hear it in the television. It became the doorknob on Grandma's front door, it became magazines on the floor, a bookshelf, the sofa. It became my aunt's perfume, climbing through a chapel of house plants. Where it was did not matter. Grandma was dead.

I avoided her bedroom for as long as I could, but eventually I had to go in to say goodbye one last time.

It was Grandma, but it wasn't. She looked so . . . fragile. Not like the grandmother who always gave me crosswords, Chinese puzzles, blocks—pieces that finally fit into some kind of order. The grandmother who had helped me to work it all out mathematically. Oh, no, this couldn't be the same grandma. Grandma's hair was pure white, wild; she had trouble combing it. She could answer any question.

Now, my grandmother didn't answer. Not this time. I noticed her chest wasn't moving, and saw that her hair was matted and squashed. And, all of a sudden, Grandma's face looked handsome and gallant.

I looked at Grandma again, at the corpse, and stumbled outside to her hard little cement porch, studying the screen door so I wouldn't have to examine my own thoughts. I looked at this plastic door, which would never decompose, and my arm, which would. After a while, I heard the hearse sliding over the driveway to take Gram away. Morning came and went. I didn't notice. I was too wrapped up inside myself to see anything but Grandma's face. It was easiest just to sit on the porch and not think.

From where it had been dark for so long, the tears came. I cried against the cold wall, crying for everyone, the weakness of their bones, their fragile skin, and then even crying for the sun, as the light began to come through the clouds. I washed myself clean with sorrow. Then the rest of the relatives arrived, there was lunch, and I too went in and began to live again.

Body
by Katherine McDonald

Afterwards, I lay my head under the hood of a car to see what it was like for him. I saw his body. No bruises, because the blood had stopped pumping. That bothered me for weeks—why no bruises? I would lie in bed at night, very still, letting my heart slow to a dull rhythm. And I would try to imagine being dead, to be just a body. Under the hood of the car, I felt the weight of my bones against the concrete: I saw the rubber and metal that must have had bits of his hair and flesh stuck to it. Someone once told me, "He's watching you from heaven." But no. He is not watching. His eyes were sunk into their sockets. He is gone, not somewhere else. The only thing that remains was slammed to the ground and then buried in it. A body that once carried itself, touched, breathed, and slapped its knee when it laughed. It danced its last dance. A marionette on the slick pavement. I wanted to know how it felt for him, on the ground after the impact. But I couldn't ask because his lips are sewn shut as he sleeps without dreaming. I cannot ask, and he cannot tell. Body cannot speak, body cannot heal, body cannot carry itself. No bruises, eyes sunk with nothing behind them. I picked myself up off the ground from under the car, and carried myself away, still more than body, still a part of my father's body.

I Love You, Dad
by Julie Seier

Dear Dad,

It seems as if I realized too late exactly what you mean to me, or did you know? I hope you realize that though I may have seemed cold or distant at times, it was never you. I honestly never meant to cause you pain in any way, but some part of me was still that little girl who was so terrified of your anger.

Maybe I should have remembered more often the times when you held my hand when I was going through pain. Or the times you tried to protect me from the harsh world. There are times when I should have said, "I love you, Dad," but the words never came.

I think I should have seen more of the happiness and pride in your eyes when I asked you to join me in some project or activity.

I just hope that as you obtain your final peace you know, despite the times I couldn't stand you for the pain you caused yourself and others, I loved you. And I respect you for trying to do what you felt was best for us all.

Perhaps I should have looked beyond your weaknesses more often and instead seen the man who loved his kids more than they knew. I don't know. I only know you loved me and I you.

The Child And Death
by Rabbi Earl A. Grollman, DHL, DD

This piece was previously printed in Canadian Funeral Director, *March 1971.*

Instead of presenting a learned paper on the subject "The Child And Death", let me attempt to allow the youngster to speak for himself. Role playing truly affords an insight into the child's expectations and anxieties. By assuming another point of view, one is enabled to see things from the "inside out" and better understand the youngster's own interpersonal tensions of life and death.

So by the flight of fantasy and the miracle of imagination, I want you to forget that I am an adult writing for a professional audience. Rather, I will assume the role of a young man of nineteen who in a developmental way is recalling his childhood and the traumatic experience of death, especially in recalling at the age of eight, the memories of his grandfather.

I am now the youngster. I speak to you—the adult world. Will you listen to what I have to say?

You call me *your* child. You have laughed over me and you have wept over me. You have scolded me, and yet smothered me with attention. You have sometimes shouted blame and whispered praises. You have talked about me, and talked to me, but never forgotten that I am your child.

And yet, did you ever stop to think of what I mean to myself? Do you realize how often I ask myself: "What am I?" or "What am I to be?" or "What is to become of me?" Do you ever ask yourself what my thoughts and feelings about myself may be? Of course, I am your child, but your child is me and I have meaning to myself other than that which arises from the undenied fact that you gave me life.

Since I was a little boy, I played games. It may surprise you but some of them involved death—your dying, Mother, or you, Dad, or my grandparents, or even our dog. Thoughts of dying have been part of my daydreams and even nightmares: I tried to discuss these fears with you: "Mom, what happens when someone dies?" I asked. You always put me off. You said: "You are too young to understand." What you really were trying to do was to protect your precious offspring. But you failed: For these thoughts were part of me and there was no one—no one—with whom I could share my innermost feelings. Don't you realize that just as you cannot protect yourselves from pain, so you can't protect me? Don't you understand that the real experiences of life belong to both adulthood and childhood? Tragedy is the heritage of us all!

Sunday School was not much better. I guess you can relegate to teachers instruction in math, or science, or driving. But you cannot wholly delegate attitudes to religion, or attitudes to justice, or the terrible task of explaining death. These must be developed in the home—in day to day contact with people you live with and really love! Sure, I heard the words the teachers said. I just didn't know what they meant. One talked about "ultimate reality" and "absolute ground of being". It was just too confusing.

So much didn't make sense. When a girl's young father died, the minister came in and said that God takes good people because God loves them. But I asked myself: "Why be good if God may reward us for our goodness with death? If one lives longer, does this mean that he was not so good?" I hated this kind of selfish God who takes people away from his family because He loves them. I became frightened and thought: "But God loves me also; maybe I'll be the next one He will take away."

And this "heaven" bit was also hard to understand. I was told that when you die, you go to heaven. When I was very young, I even questioned why they bury a person in the ground. "He's heading in the wrong direction," I thought. Every time it rained I was afraid some dead person would drop down from the sky. Boy, was it scary!

Then Grandpa died. I was eight years old. When I asked about him, you said that I shouldn't cry and just pretend that he was away on a long journey. Now I know that you wanted to help me by easing the strain. But it was there anyway. I was mad at Grandpa because he left for a trip without saying goodbye. Didn't he care about me? Why did he stay away so long? If he went on a long journey, did that mean he would return? And if he went on a little trip, then why was everybody crying? The last time Grandpa went to Florida every one thought it was good for him and was so pleased. Now he takes another voyage and everybody is all shook up. Does *that* make sense?

When I saw you crying, you confided in me for the first time. You said that he died because he was sick. I became frightened. If I have a cold, or the mumps, or the measles, does that mean I will die? Children, like adults, mistake the meaning of words and phrases.

"But, Mom, how does a person look when he's *dead*?" I kept asking. Finally, you answered in disgust, "It is just like *sleeping*. Don't ask me any-thing else!" I now know that when a person dies, his eyes are closed so that he looks like he is asleep. But I was confused because you never explained the difference between *sleep* and *death*. For a while I had a horrible dread of bedtime. I would just toss and turn all night, afraid to close my eyes because I might never wake up again. I was fearful that I might fall off to Grandfather's *type* of sleep.

I guess it is easier for parents to respond with fictions and half-truths that make them appear to know all the answers. Maybe I would have been shocked to discover that you, my mother and father, did not have all the answers and that you yourselves were frightened of death. But I learned this anyway as I grew up. My curiosity was not satisfied by fantasy. Deception is worse than real life.

I asked if I might attend the funeral. Once again, you wished to spare me. But no amount of secrecy could hide the fact that something important and threatening had happened. I just could not help being affected by the undercurrent tones of grief and pain. All of my childish emotional reac-tions—sorrow and loneliness, anger and rejection, guilt, fear for the fu-ture—all of this might have been considerably lessened if I knew what was going on, if I attended the services, and that you, my parents, were not trying to hide things from me.

So you intended it as a kindness when, during the funeral, I was sent to play at my friend's house. I was both relieved and sad. Maybe a little relieved that I was spared whatever took place in the funeral home, but frightened about the unknown and deprived of the reassuring presence of the family. I felt abandoned!

I know that funerals can be painful—but wasn't it an important occasion in the life of our entire family to pay our final respects? Didn't Grandpa also love me? Could I not have expressed my *own* love and feelings?

You should not have waited for a death in the family to explain what happens when a person dies and what takes place at the funeral home and the cemetery. This should have been told to me when I was young and when I started to ask questions. I tried to visualize what was happening the day of the funeral. You want to know something? After I actually went to a service later on, I was less disturbed by observing the funeral than by the fantasies made up by my fertile young mind.

I should have been allowed to participate in some of our religion's ceremonies of death. Isn't religion "experience" as well as "belief"? Perhaps the customs could have helped me to realize that grandpa was dead. I would have joined with others who might share their traditions of love, affection, and understanding. Maybe, by carrying out some of the rituals, I would have felt that I had regained the love I had lost and also been relieved of some of the feelings of guilt because I sometimes could have been nicer to Grandpa. By following these ancient customs, I would have been doing something for the dead, and just as important, I would have brought relief to myself.

Something haunted me. Did Grandpa die because I was naughty? I thought of the terrible things I had done. One time, I even said, "I wish you were dead." When you are young, you still believe in magic. That is, if you wish someone harm, the belief will bring results. Doesn't wishing make it so? I felt that *I* was being punished. Maybe Grandpa died and left me because of what I did to him. *His* death could be *my* punishment.

When I began to cry, you, my parents, chided me by saying, "You have to be brave. Be a man." At age eight, how does one suddenly become an adult? And what's wrong even for grownups to cry? We feel badly. We all hurt inside. We miss Grandpa. We wish he were still with us. Aren't tears a natural way to express our emotions?

The people who came to the house were not any better than you, my parents. I only heard part of what they said because you thought it better for me to play outside with my friends. But what I did hear was strange. No one even talked about Grandpa. They spoke about everything else that had no meaning at that time: trips they were going to take for their summer vacation, the condition of the stock market, the latest fashions, the chances of our baseball team to win the pennant. They didn't leave out anything, except Grandpa. He was the excuse for their coming, and then he became the uninvited guest. Luckily I had a friend in whom I could confide. Tommy didn't say anything, but he helped me just by listening. I told him all about Grandpa: how I loved him, even how angry I was at him for leaving me, and how mean I sometimes was to him. I needed to talk, not just be talked to, or talked down to. At first when I told Tommy about some of my pleasant and unpleasant memories, I felt a little bit better as I talked and cried. I got some of my feelings out of my system. I said the words for the first time. "My grandfather is *dead*." I cried some more, but as a result I at least understood that he would never come back to life again, and making up stories about his being alive was just make-believe.

I had said it. *Dead*. The word has taken on new meaning as I have been growing older.

When I was much younger, I didn't believe death was real and regular and final. Tommy and I used to talk about death freely as we would play with our guns and pretend to shoot each other. Bang, you are dead, but you come back to life again. Or taking a journey: you are gone, then you come back. Death was like you, my mother, going to the store and my feeling frightened that you would never come back. But you always did.

As I grew older, I knew people died. I imagined that somehow these dead people were conscious, but helpless in their caskets. Somehow I didn't believe death could happen to me or people I loved liked Grandpa. Headlines in the newspapers were about others, not those close to me. The notice in the local paper about my grandfather's death just didn't ring true. "It must be somebody else with the same name," I thought and even dared to hope.

Now I know that Grandpa did die. That someday you, my mother and father, will die. I don't even want to talk about it. Yet I guess I have to. I want you to know about my fears, my thoughts. I think of your deaths. Who will take care of me? What will happen to me? Where will I live? Maybe I'm selfish, but aren't we all little constellations about which everything in the universe revolves. So even now, I ask the exact same questions: "What is death?" "What makes people die?" "What happens when they die?" "Where do they go?" and always "When my loved ones do die, what will happen to me?"

I am now older; yet, I still have some fear of death. Maybe we all live in dread of dying. If I have criticized you, maybe I expected too much. For death is a subject on which no adults—even parents—are experts. No one has yet pierced the veil of its mystery. There are no simple, foolproof answers to the most difficult of all questions.

I now realize that it is the parents who communicate feelings about death, both consciously and unconsciously. Perhaps, I have finally learned the secret. The real issue is not how to explain death to children, but how adults can understand and make peace with it themselves.

Just know that I love you and am trying my best to let you know what I am and what I yet hope to be. For you and I look at me with different eyes and different backgrounds. Believe in me and have faith in me that I may continue to develop and learn about subjects that are difficult and painful. I do not promise even myself, but I believe I have the necessary stamina to face crisis if only you speak to me honestly and forthrightly.

You have been young, in another age, but under different social and economic circumstances. I pray to God that I will never forget that I am your child, and I also pray that you will never forget that I am also myself.

CHAPTER 9

THE "KNOWN" FEELINGS

The raw emotions are expressed that appear in the various stages of grief: shock, denial, depression, anger, guilt, and forgiveness.

Alone
by Christina Keenan

In the early morning moments, I awaken. It is still; quiet surrounds me. I can hear the children's rhythmic breathing, the sleep of souls, small and vulnerable.

The clocks tick, and I am alone. Always in the morning, I am surprised by this fact. I am alone, waiting for the gray to come as it has before. I am face to face with each morning's reality. How many hours will pass until I feel normal again? Why me? Why this cruel punishment?

The grayness is here now, all around me. I ache, and my body aches with pain and loneliness. Tears sting my eyes, and I can hear my heart beating in my ears.

Mornings are always the worst. Turned away from the side of the bed he no longer occupies, I lie and watch the parade of disappointments in my head. All in a row, they present themselves.

There is no choice but to watch this bleak newsreel of my life. Tears flow freely, and I let them roll down the sides of my face to settle in my hair. Even the tears can't release the pain.

This mass of steel I carry inside me is too heavy; I can't bear the weight of it. Each day I try to destroy it. I chip away, but I don't get far before the fatigue settles in.

I feel as if I am using a spoon to carry away this mountain of wreckage. The task is tedious and exhausting. In the presence of others, I just cover it up. The tears and fatigue seem to be too much for others to see. I find myself concerned that I am upsetting other people.

Grief is solitary. I have been totally alone in my grieving and now find I need others to help me fight this gray monster. But others can't seem to bear the burden with me. Sometimes I feel angry because no one seems to know just what to do with death. No one knows what to say, so they say nothing, or they say the wrong thing.

I cover it up for the children as well, so that they might heal and start to feel confident in me as their singular parent. I force myself to take the pain and fear out of my face when I am with them.

Then, when I am alone, I start this heavy work again, digging and chipping away at this heavy weight, because it won't leave me. It claws and burns me when I try to ignore it. I can't breathe for its heaviness, and I pray that maybe tomorrow, in the early morning when I awaken, it will be gone.

A Father's Cry
by Todd Skugain

We all know those who are young and foolish. I, myself, was the epitome of that picture. I was more than foolish—outright stupid and utterly selfish may have begun to describe me. I've been perfectly behaved since the day I was married over twelve years ago, don't get me wrong, but before that . . . well . . . I did a lot of terrible things, the least of which was having a three year affair with a married woman. Her husband was "fixed", so you can imagine how awkward it was when she became pregnant. Her husband loved her dearly and stuck by her. She loved me, not him. Myself? Any ability to love had long been overruled by drug and alcohol abuse. How could I love anyone if I couldn't even love myself? All of this, with a child now in the middle. I was too addicted, stupid, and immature to accept even minor responsibilities, let alone the burdens of fatherhood.

When our child was eleven, the three of them, my mistress, her husband,

and the child he treated as his own, moved to Florida and went on with their lives. By then I was married to my beautiful wife, Cathy. She was leagues different from any other woman I had ever met. I could "read" other women's thoughts by their body language or facial expressions, but not Cathy's. She was (and still is) a mystery. Intrigued, I became addicted to her, and with her help, I stopped taking drugs and reduced my drinking to all but a rare treat.

As chemical dependency ebbed away, the capacity to experience emotions slowly returned. I started to act and feel like a human.

Years swept by. Cathy gave birth to our beautiful son, Justin Fletcher. Fletcher was my grandfather's name, and he was a man I loved deeply. When Justin was an infant, we shot a roll of film every day. At some point I came across baby pictures of my daughter. I held them and began wondering how she was doing. Comparing those photos with some of Justin at the same age, a little flutter twinged in my stomach. Remove the gender labeling pink and blue, and the babies looked identical! I put the pictures away, but the flutter remained until it grew into a nagging deep pain in my head. Deeper and deeper it went, haunting me unceasingly. Being now the responsible father, I knew that the origin of this demon was what I denied myself all those many years ago returning to haunt me.

I longed to know my daughter's thoughts and fantasies, her dreams and failures, her actions and emotions. How could I have denied myself such joy? Sometimes I cried and kept saying to myself, "Maybe someday I'll know her . . . maybe someday."

Then she was murdered.

Not by a misguided stray bullet, the intoxicated blindness of a drunk driver, or some freak act of nature, but savagely, mercilessly. An apartment painted with blood, forty stab holes, and all for what reason? No one will ever know. The authorities were never able to establish a motive. Her death was meaningless!

Every horrifying emotion imaginable assaulted my mind.

"Who could do this?" I cried. "Who would commit such an insane, barbaric savagery to this flawlessly beautiful seventeen year old girl?"

Most of all I was angry . . . angry at the murderer, our violent society, the pointlessness of an innocent life robbed, and finally I poured all of my anger into myself. Guilt crept in, overshadowing all my other emotions.

"What have I done? What have I done?" I endlessly asked myself. If only

I'd led a more responsible past I would have honored my mistakes. My daughter created so long ago would have never moved away. In my mind, there is no question she would be alive today. How could I have denied my own child? My deepest, most primeval parental instincts failed me so long ago, only to return exponentially.

The echoes of this reality rang endlessly in my head. I fell into deep depression and began thinking through plots of suicide. And yet, before my own eyes, my son is growing . . . always happily accepting me as his loving father, his playmate, confidant, ally, and friend.

At age nine he still sits in my lap, bubbling enthusiastically about his latest karate move, or snuggling during the scary part of a movie. If I had earlier arranged my life so that I could have raised my daughter, he would not be alive. How do I deserve him when I'd been so blatantly selfish before?

I would have continued using drugs, and I myself might be dead from an overdose, or perhaps even have AIDS. Would that have been so bad . . . to step back in time and die so my daughter might live?

And my wife Cathy . . . who I love so dearly? We would have never met. She is such a frail, little flower. She has the mind of a scholar, the courage of a lion, and yet she is handicapped, her body damaged from a sick childhood. If my life had taken any of numerous different courses, who then, would take care of her?

Cathy risked her life to give birth to our son, though the best fetal-paternal obstetricians endlessly warned us against having children. Since the day Justin was born, the dangers she endured seemed to have created a magical bond between them. Their love vibrates like the colors of an ocean sunset.

Soon after Justin entered the world and I began wondering about my daughter, I vowed that this time around things would be different, and they are. I love him two times more than any other father could love a son . . . no . . . it's closer to a hundred times more. I promised myself I'd spend time with him every day, and I still do. We talk, we play, we're best friends.

I often ask myself, could a love this incredible exist if I never met my wife? If I had raised my first child like a father should?

The answer is no.

So my depression stumbles. I have helped create another life, yet in doing so I have contributed to the senseless massacre of a beautiful girl and the destruction of the continuing joy felt by those whose lives she touched. If I had been a drug addicted father of this girl who would be butchered because I chose to reject the offerings of my drug-crazed lust, then the love I share in my home today would never have been born.

Psychotherapy and drugs have eased the intensity of my inner turmoil. My emotions are numbed and my mood-swings have evened out remarkably, but I don't think I will ever reach a plateau where I don't blame myself for my hand in creating the circumstances that took my daughter away from me and led to her death.

Her killer has never been caught. There were no witnesses and no known motive. She had only friends, no enemies.

I never did anything for her, though with all my heart, I wanted to. She did something for me though, something truly great and wonderful. She taught me fatherhood is a privilege, a joy to embrace every day. This is a lesson I'll always honor, and for that I am eternally thankful.

Metamorphosis
by Anne C. Watkins

I feel like I will never be happy again. I am numb, have no appetite, am not interested in any of the things I once enjoyed. I want to crawl into a deep, dark hole and never come out. When people call to see how I am doing, I lie there and listen to the answering machine but don't pick up. I get sympathy cards, notes from friends who are concerned, and messages relayed to me by family members. I do not respond. All I want is to be left alone.

A tidal wave of blackness has flooded my soul. My grief is physical as well as emotional. Something is in me, something too monstrous to fit. My head hurts, my body hurts, my heart hurts. My soul wrenched apart, I scream, cry, and pummel my fists into the floor. It changes nothing.

I am in shock and need time to process my feelings; I can't be hurried. Someday I will be okay. Right now, I have to have time to sort things out, time to adjust to the loss, time to heal. It is something I have to do myself.

Relatives and friends have written poems about their feelings for our missing loved one. Others take small tokens of love to be discreetly slipped into the closed casket by the funeral director. A friend sings at the service. I can do none of these things. Perhaps something is wrong with me.

I can't rest. To sleep is to let swing open the door that allows images, unpleasant images, to slip into my thoughts. Images of fires, small cars, big trucks. The hateful, artificial sounds of a respirator. Beeping machines, unconscious moans of pain, of looking into a beloved face whose eyes will never gaze into mine again. Of a tall figure in a white coat, saying, "I'm sorry. There is nothing more we can do." Groups of relatives gathered, united in sorrow.

There are other images, too. Images of a beautiful, lively young woman, smiling, saying my name in a soft, sweet voice, a voice I still hear. An expected baby we were so excited about. The nursery, waiting for a tiny sweet babe who will never sleep in the crib, never play with the toys, never wear the soft little clothes. It is too hard to bear.

There are too many bad days, days that drag me under. I feel like I'm drowning. I claw to the surface, struggling to breathe. I have to *want* to make it, to *want* to keep working to break free of the undertow.

People, *normal* people, laugh and talk, chat about their lives, about their dreams for the future, about their children's futures. It hurts to be with them. I am grieving and they are not, but I couldn't wish this pain on anyone.

There are days when I wonder *Why? Why her?* Days when I find myself exploding into unexpected tears. Dark days when all I want to do is sleep. Days when the pain is as fresh as when it was new.

The only thing that alleviates some of the pain is to talk about *her*. Funny things she did and said. Good times we had together. How thrilled she was to be pregnant. Remembering is to have her back with us for a little while. These memories are sweet, comforting. They help.

A surprising thing is happening. I am gradually beginning to have good days! Days when I am hopeful, days when I am happy. Good days slip through the fog of grief more and more frequently. I discover sometimes whole hours pass without my feeling the wrenching ache of grief.

I feel guilty for feeling normal. Then I remind myself that my loved one would want me to be happy—to celebrate her life. I force myself to allow these feelings. I give myself permission to heal. It does not mean that I have forgotten. I loved her and she loved me. I will never forget. And that will get me through. It is enough.

Anger and Forgiveness: Natural Parts Of Grief
by Jo Seier-Doofe

A short time ago I spoke with a man who had been widowed twice. The most recent death occurred more than eight years ago. Carl talked about his first wife's long struggle with cancer and the pain she endured. He talked about her moodiness and her lashing out at him. He emphasized, repeatedly, that he was not angry at God "because God has the right to call us home at any time."

When Carl talked about his second wife's death, he called it a cerebral accident and again reiterated, "I am not angry." While Carl was informing me he was not angry, his fist was pounding the table. I (bang) am (bang) not (bang) angry (bang). I don't think Carl knew his body was admitting what his mind could not.

Carl's lack of personal insight is probably not unique. To illustrate, let me share a bit of personal experience with you. In May of 1973, we lost a thirteen year old son in a drowning accident. It was springtime, flood time in our part of the country. Our son, Jay, had gone with four other boys to Duck Creek. We gave them permission to go because we thought they intended to go to Duck Creek Plaza. The boys intended to go to the creek, and they did. Apparently Jay was walking along the bank of the creek when it gave way and he fell into the swift moving water. His friends were unable to rescue him— and it was ten days before his body was recovered.

I was stunned, unbelieving, torn, tearful, sad . . . everything but angry. Why not angry? He was an innocent child who lost his life almost before it began. He was with four other boys. Why my son? Not having any answers, I swallowed hard and accepted.

We tried to hide our grief from one another. I spent most of my crying time in the bathroom late at night when everyone was asleep. We ran this way and that, all summer long, trying to prove to our remaining children that we were still a family and that life would go on. I never talked with them of their anger, frustration, or how deprived they must have felt when he disappeared from their lives. We seldom talked of Jay and never about anything except how good he was. In making him a plaster saint, we lost his memory.

Years later I can say we handled his death very poorly, but we did what we thought best at the time.

Nine years later, through a haze of words, I learned that we had lost a second son when he was pushed off a sea wall into the Mississippi. My first reaction was shock, and I had trouble focusing on even the most basic things. When asked how to reach our other children I could not remember even one phone number. Later, when allowed into the emergency room at the hospital, I found medical personnel shocking his body with electric paddles. I was angry. It was an anger so deep I felt as though all emotions had been flash-frozen. Maybe they were. Maybe that was how I got through the early days of grief.

I'm not sure I can list all of the reasons for my anger. I'm sure I was angry because Jack was dead. Angry at Jack because he had been drinking. Angry at us, his parents, because drinking was acceptable in our family.

It may have been fortunate there was no way to deny this anger. I had to find a way to deal with it. I did a lot of walking in those early weeks of grief. I couldn't do much else. I had no concentration. I couldn't work. I forgot appointments, forgot to eat, didn't really want to face life without our beautiful, gifted son.

Parents who lose children often become angry at each other. We fall into the blaming trap. I believe we need to say, "I am angry, so very, very angry."

My personal grief experiences have taught me there are many things which trigger outbursts of anger after the loss of one we love. I realized anger is a natural part of the grieving experience and that it is better to accept anger and deal with it, for anger turned inward becomes depression. Anger/depression for a limited time is normal. After some time, I had to be willing to let it go. If I didn't, or couldn't, I'd lose again.

Oddly enough, I never felt (or was conscious of) anger toward the young man who pushed Jack off the wall. At the wake, among all the friends and family, I noticed a young man, a stranger to me, come in alone and sit apart from the other mourners. He didn't go to the coffin, he just sat and cried, allowing tears to drip from his face as though he was not even aware of them.

After a time, I went over and sat beside him. He turned to me and said, "I'm so sorry, Mrs. Seier."

"Thank you," I replied. "I keep thinking no matter how bad I feel there is someone out there who feels even worse. That is the person who pushed

Jack off the wall. It wasn't done maliciously or with any intent to hurt Jack, but it was such a stupid, thoughtless thing to do."

The young man groaned. He seemed unable to stop crying.

In an attempt to comfort him, I told him that I believe love does not die when someone we love dies and that we are never totally disconnected from them. I put an arm around his shoulders and asked if he thought that might help. He nodded, thanked me, and left.

I believe this nameless young person was the one who pushed Jack off the river wall. I also believe God worked a miracle of forgiveness in those few moments. The miracle didn't make my grief any less, but it did encourage acceptance, a lessening of anger, and a greater sense of closure. It was the beginning of the healing process.

You're Not The One
by Ruth M. Zellers

How can I expect you to understand my pain?
You're not the one who lost your spouse,
your best friend, lover, and soul mate.
You're not the one he fell in love with,
slow danced with, sang to, or surprised with gifts of his love
and whose hand he held while driving to a weekend getaway,
or snuggled with on the couch on chilly evenings.

You're not the one he loved no matter how much you weighed,
what clothes you wore, or what mood you were in,
the one he stood up for, encouraged, supported,
challenged, and believed in,
the one he tucked in at night,
the one he held tight to keep warm.

You're not the one who tasted his mouth
as he kissed you passionately;
who felt his skin touching yours,
who buried your face in his hair

and listened to him breathe
while he peacefully slept beside you,
the one who would drown in his longing gaze
which would take your breath away.

You're not the one whose heart rejoiced
at the sound of his voice, his mischievous laughter,
who stayed up all night with him in deep conversation,
the one who cried for him when he was hurting.

You're not the one who felt his head on your stomach
as he would talk to his unborn baby
and watched the smile come across his face
as his unborn baby kicked his hand,
the one who delighted
in seeing him watch his son being born into this world.

You're not the one who watched him hold his son,
feed and play with his son,
the one who saw his son running to him
with tears in his eyes, screaming for Da-Da
and watched him stay up all night rocking his sick little boy.

You're not the one who's cut off from him,
withdrawn from him and
trying to go on living without him,
the one whose world has shattered
and feels as if it has been stopped,
whose hopes have died
and whose dreams have turned into nightmares.

You're not the one who's working, struggling,
trying to raise his two-year-old son,
the one who feels this intense ache, longing, needing,
rage, anger, sadness, hopelessness, helplessness, loneliness,

and screaming within yourself
and has to decide if each minute is worth living for.

You're not the one who watched your everything
ride off on a motorcycle that day.
It wasn't the father of your child—your husband—
that never came home.
How can you expect to understand my pain?

Vultures
by Cynthia Kuhn Beischel

In the animal kingdom, vultures are known for circling the dying, swooping down, and feasting upon the dead. It is their job to eat carrion, and by doing so they actually provide a very worthwhile service in the chain of life by removing the putrefying remains. In human society we have vultures of another kind—the greedy, unscrupulous types who metaphorically eat and grow fat on the loved ones of the deceased. They present themselves as being helpful and providing a good purpose, but from my personal experience, I have come to consider insurance companies as dangerous.

My husband had been dead for about one month when the "death check" was delivered. I was, of course, very grateful that my husband had had a life insurance policy and that we would be receiving a fairly large sum of money from the company. As the representative sat with me, giving me his condolences, the subject came up concerning my buying a policy on myself for the future. This was something I already felt I should do for my daughters, so the representative was certainly not twisting my arm. He left several papers for me to go over that would help me make a choice as to the type of insurance I would buy.

A few weeks later, the man came back out to my house to discuss my purchase more seriously. I had asked my father to be with me. During those early months following Jerry's death, I felt very wobbly about standing on my own and certainly about making major decisions. I wanted the moral support and also to have someone else present to hear what was being said because one of my other symptoms of being newly widowed was an inability to sometimes think clearly and to hold onto facts.

My father and I went over the information with the salesman, and sometimes references were made to the type of insurance my father had which had dividends that had grown over the years and had helped pay for the policy. It sounded perfectly logical then to accept the idea that was presented about giving the company one large sum of money up front for a whole life policy and never have to pay any more. That fact was stated more than once. It was explained to us that, if I had a paid-up additional rider (PUAR) with my policy, the money taken from that plus the dividends that would be accruing would make all future payments; I would never have to make any additional payments in the future. Since I had the money available to me at the moment because of my husband's policy, I decided to take out my policy according to the PUAR arrangement.

I put the decision behind me and didn't think of it again until the following year when I received an anniversary statement. It looked as though I was being asked to put money into my account. I immediately called and spoke with the representative, saying that I had understood when I bought the policy that I'd never have to give them any more money. He assured me that that was correct, that the statement was providing an option in which I could put additional money in the rider but that I didn't have to, and he would send me a paper to sign which would tell the company to use the money I already had given them. He did so and I returned the signed copy.

When the next year's anniversary statement arrived, I wasn't surprised at receiving it as I had been the year before, but I called him again just to check once more that I understood what was going on. He again assured me that yes, indeed, I had bought a policy with an initial, one time large payment and the future payments would come out of the rider and dividends. He again said he'd send me the paperwork and I sent it back signed.

Sometime before the third anniversary papers arrived, I received a letter from the company telling me that my representative was no longer with the company and that he would no longer be able to help me with any future dealings but that I could call up for a new representative. During that year, I also received a letter telling me of a change in the tax laws and that if I wanted to avoid a tax penalty for withdrawing my money, I'd have to do it by a certain date. A third mailing came during this time period, a pamphlet explaining why it would be a bad idea for me to switch insurance companies and that if ever someone approached me with that suggestion, I should be sure to call them. Being trusting and naive, I had no reason to think that I'd be taking out my money or switching companies, so I filed the papers away and went on with my life.

I did, on the third anniversary, once more call the company because a different paper had arrived which said I could no longer in the future make payments to the PUAR if I did not do so that year. The privilege would be taken away. I understood that to mean that I couldn't buy any additional insurance in the future, but that my original policy would remain the same. To make myself more comfortable, I spoke with a new representative and went over what I had been told in the past. She agreed that I could just let the rider and dividends make the yearly payments. Once more I had been reassured. As the next two years came and passed, I filed the anniversary statements away, "knowing" that all was well and it was just yearly paperwork.

This past year, the sixth anniversary, I received the annual statement, and something new caught my eye. I was now being told that if I didn't start putting in a yearly amount of $1494.00, I would no longer have any coverage at the end of four more years. I was stunned. What had all the phone calls been about? Not once when I called up with my concerns had either of these people said that they wanted to make sure that I understood that if I did not put a yearly payment towards my policy that within a few more years I would not have a policy at all. Neither representative had explained that the dividends were not coming in strong enough to make my payments. I felt sick to my stomach. I felt I had handed over what for me had been a huge amount of money to scam artists. If some change did not occur, within another five years I would have absolutely nothing to show for the $12,350.00, while the company on the other hand would have had my money to work with for over ten years. I felt I would have done better to stick the money under my mattress!

Anger can be a good emotion. Along with pain and hurt, my rage got me up and moving. I didn't know what my chances were against a huge industry which just happens to be the only one I know of that doesn't have to answer to federal regulations, but I was going to try to clear up the mess I found myself in.

The process started in August. I began by once more calling the insurance company's office to make sure that I had understood the most recent announcement correctly. The woman I spoke with verified that I would lose my policy within a few years if I did not start making premium payments.

Following that I called everyone I knew who had friends or relatives who worked for insurance companies in order to ask questions of people on "the inside". For the most part, I came up empty handed, but one approach was suggested several times: I was told to contact the state's Department of Insurance. The library was helpful in providing a phone number, and after a few calls I finally reached the correct division.

Fueled by the energy that comes from being on a mission, I immediately sat down and wrote a letter to the insurance company expressing my great disappointment, displeasure, and disgust at the misrepresentation of my policy, concisely laying out the facts that had occurred over the years since its purchase. I also informed them that I was sending a copy of my letter to the Director of Ohio Department of Insurance, the Director of the Life Insurance Division, and my lawyer.

In September, I was introduced via a letter to the man who was to be the analyst handling my case. Over a period of months, I heard from Michael several times by phone and mail. In December, I sent him papers he requested: copies of pages from my policy, letters explaining my payment arrangement which I had received from the representative who had sold me the policy, and a list of the dates, times, and persons I had spoken to over the years. This was one case where my being a pack rat had come in handy. I was extremely grateful I had kept a file with all the paperwork involved. More time passed during which I would occasionally hear from Michael, informing me that my complaint was still being investigated and that the consumer services division appreciated my patience.

In January, five months after I initiated my complaint, I received news from the insurance company that in response to the request from the State of Ohio Department of Insurance for reconsideration of the request for a full refund of premiums applied to my policy, they were going to resolve the matter by agreeing to refund the premium amount. I had fought the big guys and won.

During the time of my investigation and since, I have learned that many of the major insurance companies have had similar complaints and problems reported and, that as a result, there are quite a few class action suits in progress. Perhaps with the news coverage, such policies will not be repeated. Perhaps we won't need to worry about vultures anymore while we're grieving.

Dealing With Dad's Death
by Jacki Webb

My father died four years ago from heart disease. When I was younger I always thought my parents would live forever. My fantasy world was shattered. We knew my father was on borrowed time; he had already suffered three heart attacks in three months. In the back of our minds, we were in denial. We thought we had years, not months, with my father.

We were all by his bedside when he passed. This was the hardest moment of my life. I was angry because he was dying, and there wasn't anything I could do to help him. I also for a moment lost faith in God. I had so many questions running through my head. *Was my dad giving up on us? Why didn't God save my dad? Why, now, as we were just getting to be friends?* The more these questions rambled on inside me, the angrier I got. At my father's visitation all of my anger erupted, and I had no control over it whatsoever when relatives and friends said, "We're so sorry; we know how you feel." I found myself saying, or rather yelling, "No, you don't. You have your fathers; I don't. You don't have a clue as to how I feel." At that instant it was reality instead of a nightmare from which I hoped to awake. I realized he was really gone. I hadn't slept in about two weeks; I didn't feel like eating. Every time I closed my eyes, the hospital scene replayed itself over and over in my mind. Emotionally, I was out of control.

I took two weeks off from work. I wanted to make sure my mom was okay. I just suppressed my own grief and focused totally on her. After six months my mom was okay, but I was falling apart. Everyone in my family seemed over their grief, and I was totally alone. No one was there for me when I needed them. I would cry for no reason at all and argued with everyone in my family. They all thought I was doing it for attention. No one was considering that I had never grieved properly.

Because my dad and I had gotten into a big argument the night before we took him to the hospital for the last time, I felt guilty. The last thing my father said to me that night was, "Maybe I'll go to bed and not wake up in the morning." We didn't say another word to each other until the day before he died, when I walked into his ICU room and told him I loved him and I was sorry. My dad just nodded and we both knew that we had always loved each other.

That guilt stayed with me for about a year. My depression lasted a lot longer. Three years after the death of my father, I finally sought help. I went to a grief counselor and worked out my anxiety, guilt, anger, and depression. My counselor gave me a closure exercise to do. I went to the cemetery and had a conversation with my father. By the time I left there, I felt a lot better.

It's been four years; the pain is gone, but there is still a hole in my soul. Not a day goes by that I don't wish my dad was here. I still feel cheated because when I get married, he won't be there to walk me down the aisle, nor will his grandchildren get the chance to know him.

The one thing I learned from this experience was that no matter how difficult the struggle, we all have the inner strength to make it through a very difficult process. It takes effort and is very frustrating, but with time it does get easier. Holidays are still tough for us, but being a close-knit family we feed on each others' strength, and we're always saying, "Remember when Dad did . . . " I may not have him in body, but I always have the memories.

Silent Guilt
by Tracy A. Rose

When I first returned the phone to the receiver, I didn't feel anything. I was numb. The shock of what I'd just heard disabled my brain from processing the information.

When the phone rang again, it was my sister. I calmly explained to her that I had just been informed that my editor had committed suicide and my article wouldn't run until Friday due to a special issue devoted to his death. As I repeated the few facts the senior editor had given me, my eyes filled. At that point, however, I was in complete denial and insisted that someone at the newspaper must really hate me to play such a sick joke. My sister couldn't understand my reaction and told me it must be true.

By the time my dad called a few minutes later, the truth had started to sink in. By saying the words out loud, they seemed more real. I tried to tell him what happened, but my voice cracked. Soon I was crying so hysterically that I stopped trying to talk altogether. The front of my shirt and my whole lap were wet; the tears continued to fall uncontrollably.

My family decided to drive up to see me and offer their support.

The hour it took them to reach me seemed to last forever. I've always been short of patience, but the situation made me especially edgy. Meanwhile, I used an entire box of tissue going over the alleged facts with my roommate and reading all of the friendly notes of thanks and encouragement he used to leave on my board in the newsroom. I tend to be a pack rat, and in this case, I'm glad I did save everything. Besides a few pictures of him and the times we shared, these notes are all I have left.

I'd been a reporter at the school paper for about five months. He was the only one on the entire staff I really had contact with. He hired me. He encouraged me, and I learned a lot from him. I never had the opportunity to tell him what a big influence he had on my life. Looking at his handwriting scribbled on post-it notes about my hard work and dedication only made me hurt worse.

My family came and went. I didn't want to talk to anyone. I needed to be alone. That night I didn't sleep much. First thing in the morning, I ran to the newsstand. From a distance, I could see the blank front page and my emotional pain was crippling. My heart raced and it felt very heavy, like there was something above it, applying pressure. The cover of the paper contained two small lines telling of his sudden death, as well as several pictures of him. Inside was a short article which lacked a lot of important details.

I stared at these pictures in disbelief. It frustrated me to think how a twenty-three year old man with so much going for him could take his own life. What pushed him to the point where the only answer he could find was to wrap an extension cord around his neck and squeeze the life out of himself?

I soon realized that his death was going to affect all aspects of my life. Losing someone to suicide is different than losing someone to an accident or by natural causes. I sat through classes that week, unable to concentrate, and listened to classmates pass judgment on him for committing suicide. The fact is that he's gone now. It is too late to save him or to get help or to argue over his motives. I'd noticed a drop in his enthusiasm around late October. But everyone around him knew he hated the winter and always got depressed during these months. He had always been upbeat, laughed through the stress, and was strong for everyone else.

One thing I'll never be able to forget is what he described as a great Thanksgiving. He spent it alone with his girlfriend in an apartment, where he fixed them both TV turkey dinners. He said it was nice to get away from all of the stress for a few hours. This was only a few weeks after my grandmother had passed away, so I was preoccupied with my own grief, and he put his own problems aside to help me through that rough time.

He called me often at home, about stories, or just to talk. The night before his death was no different. It was around 10:30 PM, which I thought was odd, being somewhat late to call, but he always kept late hours at the newspaper. He asked about a Valentine's Day spread I was working on; then there was a long uncomfortable silence on the line. He obviously needed to talk, but for some reason decided not to. I will always feel guilt over that phone call. Maybe if I had tried harder to reach out to him . . .

For me, the crying didn't stop the first night. I cried myself to sleep for many nights afterward. I couldn't even force myself to go to the funeral home. The thought of seeing him lying there, the purple and blue bruises covering his neck, was too much for me to handle. My emotions took on a life of their own.

For months and months after his funeral, I woke up each morning hoping that it was all a horrible dream, that I would be able to see him. Every day I had to convince myself he was really gone, and with that a big part of me went also. I didn't want to hang around with my friends anymore but wanted to withdraw further and further into myself. If I didn't think about him, I felt guilty, as if I would lose my memory of him.

I threw myself into my other job and my heavy class load. I needed to keep my mind occupied on something, and in terms of my grades, it was my best semester ever—a healthy way for me to channel my energy and anger.

The loss of this close friend left a wound on my heart that will never completely heal. The wound gets smaller over time, but occasionally it is still difficult to deal with. Now I am able to think of him and remember him fondly without breaking into tears. When people make thoughtless comments about suicide, it is like pouring salt over that open wound—it stings a little.

I often wish none of this had ever happened, but I am thankful for having known him. I consider myself lucky to have had him as a friend and a mentor, even if only for a short time.

Didn't I Close That Chapter?
by Desconocido

Long ago a terrible chapter of my life opened. It started when my grandmother decided to have open heart surgery to correct a defect that had been bothering her. I couldn't figure out why she decided to submit herself to such a delicate procedure. Although weak, she never showed signs of having any chronic disease and had never been admitted to a hospital before. Considering her condition, it was hard to believe doctors would make that determination, but they insisted she needed the operation. They emphasized the importance of taking action quickly.

Some family members agreed with the doctors and supported their decision. On the phone, Grandmother's daughter gave me accounts of how essential heart surgery was for Grandma. According to my aunt, there was nothing to worry about. "If patients well into their eighties and nineties are going through the procedure successfully, why couldn't Grandma take advantage of it as well?" my aunt said. The cardiologist had said the preliminary tests performed on Grandmother indicated she was in optimum conditions for the operation. She would be back home in a matter of days.

However, it became obvious that Grandma wasn't going to leave the hospital soon. Almost two weeks after the operation, she was still in the intensive care unit. Deep inside, I was certain things were not turning out to be as predicted. I started to blame myself because I never initiated a conversation with Grandma to warn her of the procedure's dangers. But who was I to try to talk Grandma out of this? After all, it was her decision. I would've felt terribly guilty if she had died and not had the operation. Perhaps my grandmother's condition was indeed serious. I didn't have the right nor the evidence to think otherwise. My aunt was living with Grandmother and knew her closely and everything she went through. I didn't have any choice but to trust Aunt's word, and according to Aunt, things were alright.

But days went by. The waiting to see what could happen next kept getting longer and more frustrating. I called the hospital several times, but no one could ever tell me about my grandmother's condition. Being far away made it extremely difficult to find answers. I had to be there.

Soon, I began to hear discouraging news. There is always someone in the family who is realistic. I don't remember who this person was, but she or he told me that chances of Grandma surviving were extremely remote. But, even when people strive for honesty and objectivity, their information can still be sketchy.

Because I was tired of waiting for someone to tell me something, I decided to fly home to investigate on my own. When I notified my aunt of my intentions, she emphatically disagreed. My aunt said Grandma would feel guilty if I took time off from my new job to visit. News and sudden emotions at this point would be detrimental to Grandma's health. Aunt convinced me not to travel, claiming there wasn't a reason to and reassuring me everything was marching smoothly.

Two days after canceling my emergency trip, I talked to my mother on the phone. What she told me revealed much of the truth about Grandmother's fragile situation. She told me all the grandchildren under twelve years had been allowed to enter the intensive care unit to see their grandmother. *"Why were the children seeing Grandma?"* I asked myself. *"Was there something wrong?"*

Overwhelmed by fury and suspicion that Aunt was lying to me, I immediately called her to confront her. What she told me sounded even more promising than before. She tried to explain in scientific terms the alleged improvements the surgeon had noticed. I became suspicious and asked to speak to one of her brothers to verify Aunt's version. What he told me felt like a knife tearing my heart: "I think you should come as soon as possible." He didn't say why. I was afraid to ask anyway.

My aunt wasn't intentionally lying or misleading me. Everything she had been telling me ever since day one wasn't meant to create false hopes. But I realized she was in a dangerous state of denial. Aunt refused to see what was coming and it prompted her to persuade me to embrace that optimism. What could we expect in a situation like this one? Grandmother was all she had. No one could blame her for reacting this way. In all my prayers, I begged God not to take grandmother away from my aunt. She would be lost if He did.

Following my uncle's recommendations, I flew to Puerto Rico the next day. During the entire flight, I battled ambivalent feelings and tried to prepare myself for Grandma's possible death. On the other hand, I couldn't give up on her. I had plenty of unrealized dreams. I wanted her to visit me and see all I had accomplished. I wanted to share precious time with her, to let her know how much I loved her, to hug her tight with my arms, to kiss her, to tell her she was the best grandmother in the world. I wanted to let her know I was going to be there for her. I was firmly opposed to letting those dreams vanish. Like my aunt, I also had to hang on to that very last shred of hope. And, like my aunt, I was in denial, pretending everything was alright, refusing to accept that events could've been turning worse.

My sister and her boyfriend picked me up at the airport. I asked to be taken straight to the hospital. Last time I saw her was during Christmas of the prior year. Once we got to the hospital, my sister warned me that I might not be able to recognize Grandma. This warning was incomprehensible. *Why wouldn't I be able to recognize her? She was my grandmother.* But I didn't ask my sister why. All I cared about at the moment was that I could see my dear grandmother.

We finally reached the intensive care unit. I was extremely nervous. My hands were sweating and my heart wanted to get out of my chest. We entered the room and my sister pointed me to where grandmother was lying. Where was grandmother? Where was the beautiful lady I used to know, the one who always shined in the family pictures? Where was the serene, fine-looking face, the brilliant eyes, the smooth gestures? Where had her lovely smile gone? What I saw was disheartening. I wanted to say something, "Grandma, I am here," but I was paralyzed. It was a scene taken out of a somber tragedy. A scene perfectly scripted to stir up the most unsettled emotions. A degrading picture so fixed in my mind I would never forget it. It was so hard to believe I was looking at my grandmother. What had they done to her? I needed to get out of that room.

My sister took me to the home where I used to live with Aunt and Grandmother. All I could think of on our way home was Grandmother. I was so angry. Then I realized Grandma was far from recovery. Only a miracle would save her. But, perhaps, this wasn't the most shocking part. Everyone in the house talked and joked about everything. Not a single word about Grandma was heard. That really shocked me and made me even more exasperated and resentful. Then I realized why they were participating in this masquerade. My family never felt comfortable talking about feelings, especially when those feelings were negative. This time wasn't going to be the exception. It was denial. It was easier for them not to face the reality, not to confront each other with the emotions they were feeling.

After everyone left, I thought my aunt and I were going to have the opportunity to be honest with each other. The image of Grandmother in the hospital kept popping up in my mind and that was enough to shatter all my hopes. But I discovered that ever since Grandmother came out of the operating room, Aunt had refused to see her. She didn't have any indication of Grandma's painful physical conditions. Therefore, it would've been a waste of time trying to deal with the feelings because I, even after seeing Grandma, was still determined not to give up all my hopes.

What made me not give up when apparently I had seen the worst? It was the unfulfilled dreams and the flush of memories triggered in each room of the house, because in every room Grandmother was present. Every memory was so real—right before my eyes. And for a moment I paused to wonder why I was thinking of these images as memories. Grandmother wasn't dead. Things would be back to normal as soon as Grandmother got out of the hospital. God had to let me realize those dreams.

Next morning, I visited Grandmother and to my surprise she was awake. When I spoke to her she even responded by staring at me and making gentle movements with her mouth. Although she obviously couldn't talk because of the respirator, she wanted to tell me something. I looked right into her eyes and all I sensed was desperation, agony, and sadness. She didn't want to go, but the look on her eyes told me that she knew it was inevitable and I had to be prepared for that moment.

The next day I had to return home. I stopped by the hospital to say goodbye . . . not the kind of goodbye people say when they see each other for the last time. It was more like *I'll see you soon*. Before I left, I promised Grandmother I would come back as soon as she went home for good. She apparently wasn't listening to me. Rather, she kept staring at some point in the room the whole time, so focused and concentrated that she wasn't moving or blinking her eyes. I was surprised by the different state of being she was in. She was breathing normally. The brightness of her eyes had returned and even though the appearance of her face was still disturbing to see, at least she didn't look as bad as she did the first time I saw her. I surmised she was resting and relaxing which I took as a sign of recovery. I left the hospital saddened but yet hopeful she would recuperate.

This was the very last time I saw Grandmother. Later that same day, the telephone rang. A friend of my sister called to tell me Grandmother had passed away.

The ordeal was over. No more half-truths, no more biased assessments of Grandma's condition, no more hiding real facts, and no more hopes or dreams. Grandmother was gone.

I was in shock. In spite of my efforts to be objective and prepare myself for the worst, I had been hopeful. After my sister's friend called me, I called Aunt. She couldn't believe her mother was gone. Her frenzy was such that she even reassured me Grandma wasn't dead, that she was going to visit her, that Grandma couldn't leave her this way, all of a sudden.

In the midst of shock, denial, and confusion, there was also clarity. The serenity and the sparkle in Grandmother's eyes hadn't been signs of recovery. They had been signs that Grandma had initiated the peaceful voyage to eternity. Once she saw me for the last time and tried to warn me about her inevitable departure, it was time to go. She hadn't wanted to die until she saw her grandson. That's why she'd been was so restless, begging God to give her a last chance to see her grandchild. Was I naive? Why hadn't I seen it? I had talked to her about getting well, but she'd known that wasn't going to happen. She had tried desperately to tell me not to embrace hope. Then I understood why no one wanted to talk about Grandmother. There hadn't been anything good to talk about.

I began to feel responsible for Grandma's death. At times I felt guilty because I thought that if I had been there for her, to advise her and keep her from going ahead with this fatal surgery, I would have saved her life. My anger turned towards my family. They had been there. Why didn't they tell Grandma this was too dangerous? The least they could have done was talk Grandma into getting a second opinion. But, we all did nothing because the doctors were "right". They knew what was best for my grandmother. Then my anger turned to the doctors. My grandmother was seventy years old. Why couldn't they let nature follow its course? Why accelerate the process of dying? Let God take care of that. My anger next turned to God. Why did He take her away from me? Couldn't He have waited for just enough time to tell Grandma all those nice things I planned on telling her. What was the hurry? He knew we had a lot of dreams. He shattered them.

I was most angry with myself. I decided not to go back to tell Grandma goodbye, the kind of goodbye when people see each other for the very last time. Moreover, friends kept telling me that I wouldn't accomplish any-thing. Nothing was going to bring her back. Friends tried to comfort me by telling me I ought to feel proud of myself for providing Grandma the oppor-tunity to see me before she passed away. They were also convinced that she hadn't been able to leave until she fulfilled her last dream: to say goodbye to her beloved grandson.

But not going back was the biggest mistake I have ever made in my life. My aunt told me Grandmother's face was angelic, and she had died with a smile. That smile became a permanent feature on her face giving testimony of the peacefulness. She was finally showing a sense of relief.

Seeing Grandmother in this tranquil state helped everyone deal with her death. They realized she wasn't suffering anymore, and the funeral pro-vided an excellent opportunity to say goodbye. That wasn't what I was left with. I was left with the horrifying memories: her swollen face, her purple arms and hands, the images of the intensive care unit. I couldn't tell Grand-mother was indeed resting in peace. I needed to see with my own eyes that she wasn't suffering. That was the only way I could've come to terms with this nightmare.

Because of this, I became very bitter. Everyone else said goodbye. I didn't. For me, there hasn't been any closure, because I skipped that very important step to a normal process of mourning. It's like starting to read a chapter in a book, but you aren't allowed to finish. I didn't close this terrible chapter of my life, the one I knew couldn't have a pleasant ending as I had hoped. However, it could've ended less painfully. But who was to blame? I was the one who decided that saying goodbye wasn't important.

It has taken a lot to erase the painful memories and seek shelter in the nice ones. I still wake up at times thinking Grandmother is still alive. Feel-ings of anger, guilt, and resentment have dissipated for the most part. There wasn't space in Grandma's heart for these sorts of emotions. She wouldn't be able to rest in peace unless I would stop dwelling on this tragedy. She always preached forgiveness, love, and understanding. It was a lesson I needed to apply. I couldn't let Grandmother down. I promised her to try to accept everything as it happened so she could continue her peaceful voyage through eternity.

There are positive memories giving comfort after this ordeal: the family pictures, a dress she used to wear, earrings that once sparkled her appearance, all the birthday cards and grandmother-to-grandson letters she sent me, the memories of dear Grandma in her bedroom reading the Holy Bible before falling asleep, of her watching soap operas in the living room, singing me "Happy Birthday" every April, talking to her flowers in the garden and cooking in her kitchen. These memories have replaced the terrible tragedy and have also helped me move forward in life.

More and more, I realize Grandma is not gone. She is alive! She lives within me. She is present in all the memories I embrace, memories that will never die, but will always be there for me to think of and look at. Sometimes I wonder, if Grandmother is still living in my heart, why did I need to say goodbye? In my heart, she is eternal. Maybe this chapter, although bound to be full of pain and anger at the beginning, marked the start of a spiritual relationship between Grandmother and me where all our hopes and dreams would still be fulfilled. A spiritual relationship in which we could tell each other how much we love each other. A superior relationship in which no disease or human pain would be an obstacle to realize those dreams and hopes.

Perhaps, I don't need to close this chapter in my life. I just have to keep reading it.

Tripwire
by Clinton T. Howard

Unresolved emotions lurk in our subconscious like hidden tripwires attached to explosives. When death takes someone close to us, it often sets off emotional land mines we had forgotten about or thought we had disarmed long ago. I learned the hard way how trauma can trigger old conflicts; unfortunately this is an element of grief that receives too little attention.

I was thirty-four years old and had been married less than a month when my wife, Katherine, was diagnosed with metastasized breast cancer. Neither of us had a glimmering of the horrors we would face before her death two and a half years later. Her forty-one year old body was phenomenally strong except for the cancer, and it served as a support system that kept her breathing, but often little else.

Complications from the cancer and side effects of chemotherapy left her a bald, skeletal figure bereft of one breast, with a swollen, protruding belly. She was frequently hospitalized for weeks at a time, and I would visit her after finishing my day's work, talking with her, reading poetry or playing guitar for her until visiting hours were over or exhaustion forced me to leave. Usually, I received from two to six phone calls a night from friends and family around the country inquiring about Katherine, which required me to recount the hospital scene over and over.

When she was home, Katherine often spent long hours staring holes through the ceiling, wearing ratty night dresses, her hair uncombed, her interest in living apparently already dead. Putting on a cheerful front for visitors drained her energy, so increasingly she discouraged visits. I became her world, and her care became mine. Physically she was capable of doing more than she permitted herself to attempt, and I tried all I could think of to inspire her to do more than lie on the sofa, staring at the ceiling. Reason, pleading, angry confrontations, nothing helped much for long. I became her caretaker, the source of what little laughter and few smiles came to her, and the only available target for her passive-aggressive anger. This certainly wasn't the life together we had imagined, or the ways I had dreamed of showing my love for her, but if this was all that was left to me, I accepted it.

Finding ways to deal with each new crisis—new symptoms, new medical procedures, the strain of meeting even the simplest financial demands on our meager income—became solely my responsibility, to be worked into the schedule of earning our income, running errands, cleaning house, cooking meals, yard work and caring for Katherine's physical and emotional needs. Sometimes her parents or a sister were able to come in from out of state so I could take one of the trips my work occasionally required, and friends asked how they could help. However, I was too immersed in daily demands to think clearly enough to ask anyone to do grocery shopping or lawn mowing. Besides, Katherine didn't want people coming by, requiring her to get dressed and pretend to have strength she no longer felt. A hospice nurse explained to me that my formerly independent wife had been emotionally raped by all that happened, and that was why she plodded lethargically through the days, unable to understand or accept what had happened to her. What no one, including me, realized was the situation had tripped a forgotten land mine in my emotions, and the damage was going to be long lasting.

I had grown up with a mentally ill mother who had been diagnosed with a "split personality" when I was child, although I did not learn of this diagnosis till I was in my forties. Her emotional development stopped at about the age of nine, the time when her own parents died two months apart. She reversed our roles, made me her parent and taught me her happiness was my responsibility. If she was angry, hurt, or ashamed, it was because I had let her down. When she expressed pride in me, it was only in terms of how I reflected on her. I was not permitted an identity of my own apart from her, and my attempts to develop one led to stormy scenes and heavy guilt trips. Once I was out of college, I put fifteen hundred miles between us, sought professional help, and gradually developed a self-image that allowed me to like myself.

Then a few years later, my wife's cancer put me back in a situation where a woman I loved was placing the total burden for her well-being on my shoulders. Trained for this role from childhood, I slipped into it easily without even realizing what was happening. I couldn't defeat my wife's cancer any more than I could cure my mother, but I tried to do more and blamed myself for not doing enough. And, just as in my childhood, only rarely did I receive any acknowledgement of my efforts from the person who mattered most. Withholding praise, as my mother had, was a way for Katherine to express her anger at the situation; unfortunately, I was the only available target for that anger, and my guilt kept building. The trap hidden in my subconscious had been sprung, my efforts at remaking my self-image were blown apart, and I found myself responding to people and events in the familiar frightened, guilty, self-debasing manner I had learned so well as a child.

Eventually, my caretaking ended. Katherine had been confined to the hospital with a broken hip after cancer ate through her bones. Being fed intravenously, and requiring a tube in her nose to keep the fluid building up in her stomach from drowning her, this once fiercely independent woman decided enough was enough and reclaimed her independence by ripping out the tube, letting blood into her lungs. I got to the hospital as quickly as I could and stood holding her hand, telling her I loved her, but it was time for her to go. Inside myself, I was screaming for her to stay, but I had to swallow that as I had swallowed all my other feelings, both with Katherine and with my mother. I subjugated my emotions to their illnesses.

My return to childhood behavior patterns didn't end with my wife's death, however. The pattern dragged on for years, growing worse as I damned myself for not being able to change it, nor to understand why I had fallen back into the pattern. After my father's death two years later, I again became caretaker for my mother's emotions although physical distance allowed me to limit my contact. By now I knew about the diagnosis Mom had received so many years ago, but all it did was confirm what I had long suspected, that my mother had serious mental and emotional problems. Finally, the need to distance myself to keep from being drawn more deeply into her twisted perception of reality ended when she died suddenly, six years after my wife's death.

Three deaths in six years of people I loved kept grief reactions rolling, but I came to recognize the anger, depression, and other patterns of grief and coped with them. What I could not understand was why I had been thrust back into my old, hated self-image and its self-defeating behavior. Why couldn't I break out of it? I found the answer while reading psychological studies to research a magazine article on an unrelated topic. I discovered adult traumas such as rape, injury, financial disaster, or the death of someone close often throw people back into childhood traumas and old learned behavior patterns. Furthermore, the brain will actually reprogram itself to accept and deal with situations it finds threatening; then it resists any attempts to alter that reprogramming once the "threat" is past.

At last I understood! What had happened to me was not unusual, but I had never seen any of this information in the literature on grief, nor could I remember hearing it in counseling sessions. Eventually, with the help of a behavior modification therapist, I was able to break the pattern and start accepting a healthier identity. Certainly, I am influenced by my experiences from my wife's illness and death and by the situation of my childhood, but they no longer control my thinking.

CHAPTER 10

THE IMPORTANCE OF RITUAL AND FAMILY TRADITION

**The deaths of children, parents, mates, and friends are
the basis for poignant stories which reveal
the importance of rituals and traditions for
the living who remain.**

A Light Shines In My Heart
by Karen Gurmankin

On Yom Kippur, I lit a candle for my mother for the first time. In the semi-darkness of dusk, I connected the match with the wick and held it until the flickering flame became a steadfast light, filling the room with a golden glow. I carefully placed the candle into one of my mother's teacups made of bone china with a rose design. I always think of roses when I think of my mother. I placed the cup on a saucer and centered it on the coffee table in my living room. I sat in the stillness of the room, which was filled with the special ambience that comes at the time of the day when the sun descends. I communed with my mother's spirit and the spirit of the holiday about to be observed.

Yom Kippur is my favorite holiday, a time when everyone is equally alone in their own life, with sanction to think, to feel, to connect with the cosmos. I like the introspection and reflection on the time spent and yet to be spent, the contemplation of life, and the remembrance of people and things and their influences on me. I thought of my mother's influence and was thankful at that moment for my privacy so that I could embrace the remembrances without having to share. Enveloped by this glow, I felt her presence in my life and let my tears flow.

I fell in love with the candle, but I did not really know why. I felt protective and nurturing toward it. It tilted in the cup, and I gently set it right, bolstering it so that its short life would remain steady and bright, and the melted wax would not prematurely extinguish the light. I had to leave to attend services, but I didn't want to. I was in conflict—I wanted to hear the cello rendition of Kol Nidre, which I had missed last year, choosing instead to be my mother's surrogate at my father's synagogue while my mother was in the hospital. I doubly looked forward to hearing it this year. But, I wanted to stay with the candle. Why was I so enamored? I resolved the issue by realizing that on each side there was something I loved. There were mother remembrances and rituals in the synagogue, too. There were wonderful thoughts of returning home to the candle's glow. It was just the beginning of the candle's life; it would still have several more hours when I returned.

I did separate. I went to synagogue and contemplated the candle when I meditated and read the prayers of atonement while the cello played. When the choir sang, I heard my mother's voice singing with them, just like when she was alive, her voice always slightly above and apart from the rest. I missed her! I missed her holiday dinners. I longed for her chicken soup and honeycake. I missed the smell of Oil of Olay on her face. I missed the way her hand felt when I held it and the jingle of her charm bracelet against her other jewelry. Through the years of her illness, anticipating her death, I feared that there was not enough of a relationship between us for me to miss her when she died. I cried with joy that I had felt the sadness of my loss. I felt as if the nine months since her death had given birth to a woman she'd like the looks of, someone she might risk getting to know, not just love. I was grateful to the ritual of the candle for guiding me to this feeling.

I rushed home to be with the candle. When I moved to the bedroom, I took it with me. Carefully, I created a new living space for it on my dresser near the jewelry she left for me. I fell asleep in the candle's light, feeling more protected than protective. When I awoke, I watched it like a mother watches the rhythm of her sleeping baby's breath . . . or a daughter watching her mother dying. I realized then that this twenty-four hour candle transported me back to a precious moment in my life: when my father and I were my mother's sentinels as she peacefully lived her last twenty-four hours. We labored over her last breaths together, before she left us. It was the ritual of the candle that illuminated the beauty of that experience and its permanence in my thoughts. It spiritually brought me back to the beautiful sadness of the end of my mother's and my time together. Of all the rituals that comforted me in the nine months since she died, this is the one for which I am most thankful, for in the candle's temporariness was the meaning of life!

written October, 1994
E. Gurmankin, my mother
deceased December 24, 1993

The Earthquake
by Gayle Young

With its porches and wings jutting out in all directions, its yellow aluminum siding gleaming in the sunshine, the house smiled warmly and invited me in. Why was I so afraid to go into the old house?

My footsteps struck the rock walkway, scattering dried, dead leaves and crunching them beneath the soles of my Nikes; my heart pounded, and my stomach churned as I took slow, tentative steps toward the house. The rest of the world seemed to stand still. No breeze. No birds. No children riding their bicycles. No cars zooming down the street. Just me and the house on that cold January day. And I could have sworn I heard it whisper my name, begging me to save it.

We had grown up together, that house and me. When Mom and Dad first bought it, there were only six small rooms and a bath, but after numerous remodeling jobs that stretched out over forty years, it had plumped and fattened to ten rooms, a garage, several storage areas, two bathrooms, and a screened-in porch complete with refrigerator and table and chairs, a great place to sip coffee early in the morning or eat watermelon and barbecue on the fourth of July.

As a young girl I jumped happily from one board to the next while the floors were being refinished, trying, sometimes unsuccessfully, not to put my hands on the freshly painted walls.

Sitting in Mom's favorite lounge chair on the front porch, I reached into my purse and pulled out the latest obituary, but tears clouded my vision and I couldn't see the words I had memorized or the fuzzy newsprint picture of my Dad, so I carefully folded it and slipped it inside the plastic pocket in my wallet. In a few days, when I could bring myself to open the cedar chest, I would place it in there with my mother's and my brother's obituaries.

They were gone forever, all the people who had been with me since my birth, who had comforted me when my dog died, when my boyfriend dated my best friend, when I married, when my children were born, when I divorced, through all the ups and downs that create a life. And now even the old house that had sheltered us through it all would be gone, taken over and demolished by the city and the airport in the name of progress. How could I possibly go through its contents and disperse the memories of a lifetime? It lived and breathed and spoke to me.

Slowly, almost fearfully, I went inside. Every wall and floor, every picture and curtain, every crack and stain that were once so familiar now seemed eerily strange. Except for the creaking of the floor when I walked, the house was still and quiet, and there was a peculiar lack of odor.

I slid my hand across the cool glass of the oak curio cabinet left by my grandmother and through the dust that had never before been allowed to gather on the coffee table. In the center of the table was a flower pot in the shape of a gray elephant wearing a crimson shirt with bright white letters that read "Alabama". It looked out of place there, but because I had given it to her, Mom proudly displayed it.

Gathering some of her photo albums from their perch on top of the long unused Hi-Fi, I went into my bedroom and sat pensively on the same bed I had slept in as a child.

Yes, I did smell something: Chanel No. 5, Mom's favorite perfume. She sprayed me as a teenager while I was dressing for a date, and after adorning me with necklace, bracelet and earrings, stepped back and smiled, "Yes, that's better." I had never liked jewelry or perfume, so the last thing she did every time I went out was to slip jewelry on me and liberally spray me with her favorite fragrance. I coughed, sputtered, and complained when she did this; she always did it anyway, and I always wore them. I still do.

She wanted me to get my ears pierced, but I was one for avoiding at all costs even the slightest pain, so I refused. Refused, that is, until one day in the mall when we stopped at a jewelry counter. "Why don't you sit right here and look at the watches; I might buy one for Dad," she suggested. I did. And before I knew it some woman had come at me with what looked like a dentist's instruments, put holes in my earlobes and sealed them with two tiny earrings. It was over before I could protest.

I lay on the bed; Mom would sit beside me, talking to me as she did during our disagreements, quietly at first and then more loudly. The more I argued, the louder she got. Funny, those arguments seemed so important to me then, but now I can't remember what they were about.

In the kitchen, the aroma of her marvelous pot roast would entice me. I'd lift the top of the electric skillet and for a few minutes watch the meat, covered with potatoes, carrots, and onions, bubble in its juice, and then open the oven door so the aroma of the cornbread mixed with that of the pot roast.

At the kitchen sink Mother would sing, off-key, making up her own lyrics when she forgot the real ones. I remember her singing "How Great Thou Art" as she washed the pots and pans. "If I clean up as I go," she often said, "I don't have as much to clean up after dinner."

She loved to cook for us and we loved to eat her food. After we were grown, she always sent us home with "care packages" of leftovers. How I longed to hug her one more time and tell her how much those dinners and those care packages meant to me.

I remembered how the unmistakable aroma of Old Spice filtered into the kitchen as a plastic spider seemed to jump into the sink. Mother and I would wink at each other and squeal, more to delight Dad, who was standing in the hallway laughing, than out of any real fright.

I saw the four of us—Mom, Dad, my brother, and me—as we came back from one of our grocery shopping trips. We were the only family I knew who made grocery shopping a pleasurable excursion. Suddenly, Dad threw a jar of mayonnaise to my brother, who was standing beside the pantry. "Catch!" Dad called out. My brother, surprised, yet not surprised, never missed a catch.

Who but my father could make a mundane drive to the country fun? With a funny, crooked smile he said, "Let's just turn down this road and see where it takes us." A few minutes later, still smiling, he said, "Wow, we must be lost." And my brother and I would excitedly tell him which turns to take until finally we were "found". Many times in later years I had asked, "Were we really lost?" He never told me. How I longed to hug him one more time and tell him how much his dry wit and sense of humor meant to me.

My brother liked to whistle, though the tune was usually both familiar and unrecognizable. Laughing, he'd chase me through the house with a water gun. I'd shriek as the water trickled down my back, and the wet blouse clung to my skin. He'd chase me out the front door; it slammed with a bang. Moments later we'd come back in, arguing.

"I said do the dishes!" he shouted at me.

"No!" I screamed back.

"While Mom's gone, I'm in charge here and I said do the dishes!"

"No! You're not my mother!"

"But I'm in charge." He hit me on the shoulder.

No pain, but I still managed to conjure up a good cry. "I'm telling on you! Just wait 'til Mom gets home!"

"That didn't hurt." No sympathy from him.

"It did too!"

"It did not!"

"Did too!" Louder crying, more sobs.

"Look," my brother said as he picked up an empty Coke bottle, "if that hurt, you can hit me with this."

Silence. Was he kidding?! That had never happened before. I picked up the bottle and hit him across the ear with all the strength I could muster. He looked stunned, and I was immediately sorry I did it. I don't remember who did the dishes, but I do remember that my brother never again gave me any weapons to use against him.

Outside, towering George ambled down the street. He was at least in the sixth grade, bigger than most of the other kids on the block, and for some reason he liked to pick on me.

"Gimme' that jump rope," he demanded.

I kept on jumping.

"Gimme' the rope!" he screamed.

I kept on jumping. Suddenly he reached out and grabbed it as it swung over my head.

"I told you to gimme' the rope!"

What else to do but cry. "I'm telling my brother on you," I sobbed.

He looked around. No brother in sight. "So what . . . go ahead and tell `im. I ain't afraid of him!" He made some awkward attempts to jump the rope while making fun of me.

I ran toward Suzanne's house, still crying and screaming my brother's name. Sure enough, he was there. For some reason unknown to me, my brother and his friends thought that if they climbed the trees in front of Suzanne's house that she would notice them. They even took turns lying in the street until a car came along—to see who would lie there the longest before he jumped up and got out of the way. I don't recall a car ever getting real close, and I know for a fact that Suzanne thought they were a little strange. But I never told them. It was too much fun to watch.

"Brother, George took my jump rope and won't give it back!"

Ever the protector, he called to his friends, "Be right back," and walked with me toward home. "I'll take care of it," he comforted. But by the time we got home, George was gone and the jump rope was lying on the sidewalk. He patted me on the back and I watched him walk away to join his friends. With each step, the sidewalk and street behind him cracked a little, growing longer and wider and longer and wider.

There had been an earthquake and my childhood was on the other side of the ravine.

Hugging Mom's photo albums close to me, I walked slowly downstairs, sat in the midst of boxes and boxes of memories gathered over several lifetimes, and turned the pages that contained frozen images and bits and pieces of my family's history.

They were all there: the people I loved as babies, children, teenagers, adults, and those who had grown old. They smiled, laughed, frowned, and made faces at the camera; they celebrated birthdays, vacations, graduations, weddings, and Christmases. There were old sepia prints of people I didn't even know. And there were pictures of flowers taken at funerals.

It's been four years since that day. The house no longer stands on top of the hill, but occasionally I drive up there, and an ethereal old house with gleaming yellow aluminum siding appears on the vacant land. I watch two children playing, a brother and a sister, and I hear their Mom calling them inside for dinner and their Dad asking them if they want to go for a ride in the country.

And sometimes when I least expect it, I become my mother, standing at the sink, washing dishes and singing, off-key of course, "How Great Thou Art," while the pot roast cooks.

A Thanksgiving Legacy
by Kristina Chase Strom

Fall 1990

For the past twenty-one years, I have called my mother on "Thanksgiving Eve" for her pumpkin pie recipe. The first few times were justifiable—I was an itinerant soul then, exploring this continent with little more than I could carry. Mother was fairly tolerant when she received a call from a hovel in New Orleans, a hostel in Denver, or a hut on a mountain in British Columbia. However, once I decided to settle down in Cincinnati and my life became more stable, she responded to my pumpkin pie plea with a measure of disappointment and disdain. I am sure she wondered why her daughter was so disorganized that she couldn't keep track of a treasured family tradition.

As time passed, my yearly request became a family joke. Members of our clan who gathered in Georgia would place bets on when Kristina would call and what her excuse would be for having yet again misplaced the famous recipe. Whoever guessed that the phone would ring as soon as Mom started making pie crust was usually right.

Though we lived miles apart, I followed the same pattern for preparing the Feast that my mother did, having of course learned it from her. During the years when I seemed to be interminably pregnant, she would histrionically remind me of the time she was great with her fifth child and slipped while carrying three pumpkin pies to the oven. More tragic than the kitchen being spattered from top to bottom was that, in those days, the blue laws prevented her from running out for more ingredients. Consequently, it was the only Thanksgiving in my memory that the dessert table was not graced by this family specialty. Because of her admonition, I have always stocked "extras" and such a disaster has never visited me.

Long before the theories of Montessori and the like became commonplace, Mother would engage us all with hands-on tasks in preparation for the feast. We all made little pies for ourselves in tiny pans and sculpted designs with leftover crust. Some of us got wretchedly sick from eating too much raw dough. In the last decade, I have invariably found myself surrounded by four flour-dusted daughters who "help" me make pies on the night before

Thanksgiving, as Mom did when all seven of us were little. So history repeats itself, delightfully in this case.

Looking back, I can remember calling my mother in the midst of such
culinary chaos because I actually couldn't find the recipe. Other times, it was
something I did to establish the continuity of a tradition I was trying to build
in my own family, though I didn't realize it at the time. I once called her
holding the recipe in my hand, just to keep her honest! Though Mom and I
talked frequently throughout the year, over time this Thanksgiving interac-
tion became significant for both of us. Our conversations were steeped with
laughter and tears as we reviewed the past year, and years past, all under the
guise of exchanging a recipe.

Thanksgiving has always been an important holiday for my family, since
Mother was a direct descendant of Aquilla Chase, who arrived on the second
Mayflower. Perhaps because of our heritage, she often said it was the most
significant holiday that we celebrate in this country, as it is not mandated by
or based in beliefs espoused by any particular race, nationality, or creed. An
astute student of history, Mom did not have any illusions about our family's
rarified genealogy, and made certain that her offspring did not put on "airs"
about it. When any of us would get pumped up about our privileged background, she would adamantly remind us of the qualities she felt were requi-
site for being a decent human being. Paramount to her way of thinking was
that people not rest on their laurels, particularly ones they had not earned,
but rather carry on with their dreams despite external opposition. As she
tore day old bread for stuffing, she would tell us how many sojourners to the
New World were not exactly the most dignified group. Rubbing sage and salt
into the cavity of the turkey, she regaled us with tales about the nefarious
criminals and heretics who fought among themselves on board the various
Mayflowers. Stuffing the bird, she would lament the ruthless slaughter of
Native Americans that ensued upon the ships' arrivals. According to her,
with the exception of the alleged harvest feast the peoples of the New World
shared so long ago, peace was not the order of the day.

Finally, having aired without a shred of sentimentality her view of our
country's origins, Mom would proceed to tell us that whether or not the first
Thanksgiving dinner was myth or fact, it represented to her an ultimate
dream. When it was time to construct the pumpkin pies, she would revel in
the spectacle of all of the people in the United States gathering together,

albeit for just one day, in groups of myriad designs, giving thanks for the wonders life on this earth has to offer. She always concluded her soliloquy by repeating that Thanksgiving, because of its non-denominational nature, was imbued with the spirit of what a true national holiday should be.

This year Thanksgiving will be different for me and my family, as I am sure it will be for others in our circumstances. For starters, there will be no long distance laughter between me and my mom on "Thanksgiving Eve"; to paraphrase the well known Zen koan, it will be, at best, the sound of one daughter laughing. My mother died last spring. One of her legacies is twenty-one copies of a very special recipe for pumpkin pie that I saved without her knowing. To me, they represent the memory of our relationship far more accurately than an album of photographs could. Some of them are very properly written on file cards, while others are scribbled on the backs of envelopes bearing postmarks from all over the continent. As I turn the "pages" of this most unusual diary and think about all that has transpired in my life, I can almost hear Mom saying that the only true constant in life is change.

Suddenly I know that at some point during the Feast in our home this year, my daughters, whether they want to or not, will hear a time-worn lecture about why this holiday is unlike all others from *their* mother. However, I think I will recount my version in front of all the guests, perhaps when the pumpkin pie is served, so that I can share it with everyone partaking in the meal. And yes, I will probably cry, despite my proper upbringing, for in my heart I will be celebrating and sharing the hope of the holiday that meant so much to my mother. And when all of the festivities are over, when I have washed the last dish, I will be thinking about what I can do to fulfill the dream she infused in me.

The Chase Family Pumpkin Pie Recipe (the 1990s version)

Gather together the people present who will be passing on the tradition. In whatever way that is appropriate to your family dynamic, discuss the importance of Thanksgiving. Pick up the phone and call those who are far away so that they may participate. Remember those who have passed on and know that they, too, are with you since they live forever in your heart. Then get on with the task at hand . . .

- Line two 8" deep dish pie pans with pastry dough (homemade is best, but purchased works too). Flute edges.
- Preheat oven to 450 degrees.
- In a large bowl, whisk four eggs until lemony, then add: two 16 ounce cans of pure pumpkin
- 2 T. flour
- 1 C. white sugar
- 1/2 C. light brown sugar, packed
- 1 tsp. salt
- 1/2 tsp. ginger
- 2 tsp. cinnamon
- 1/8 tsp. nutmeg
- 1 1/3 C. whole milk
- 1 can (13.05 oz.) evaporated milk

Mix at medium speed for a minute and a half, then on high for two minutes. Pour into prepared crusts just to the point of overflowing. Bake for 10 minutes at 450 degrees. Reduce oven temperature to 325 degrees and continue to bake until done (45-50 minutes). Pies are done when a knife inserted in the center comes out clean. Usually it takes a few tries to determine doneness, so be artistic . . . use your knife to slice a star of hope in the center of your creation.

Changes
by Mary Ruddis

Christmas '95 loomed ahead and was destined to be a holiday of distinctive memories. I began Christmas shopping in October, reveling in my early start while others were grumbling about commercialization. Halloween would be simple this year, since my sons, Mike and Matt, had decided to wear the same costumes they had worn last year. After all, we had moved to a new state, a new school, and a new audience for their Grim Reaper costumes. It was ironic that they had both chosen to dress as the bearer of death, yet it was also fitting.

I splurged on Christmas decorations, adding more this year than in any other single year: holiday plates emblazoned with 1995, angelic ornaments and candles, a red and green Victorian Santa throw, and to prove I really had the holiday spirit, a set of battery operated Mr. and Mrs. Claus Bears that lit up and played "Jingle Bells". The boxes stored from previous years would not necessarily need to be touched.

Thanksgiving came and went, and I began planning our Christmas Eve party. For the twelve years my husband and I had been together, we had opened our home on Christmas Eve to friends, neighbors, and relatives. This year would be no different, although Sandy, my best friend, was now fourteen-hundred miles away, the neighbors were all new, and our family had shrunk.

Keeping busy was crucial, but December 1st was a bit too early to begin preparing food for December 24th. The boxes of decorations in the garage screamed to be opened.

Bringing them in, I carefully tore the tape from the lid of the largest box. A stuffed Goofy in a Santa suit was on top, and tears began to well up in my eyes. I blinked hard, and out of sheer determination forced my hands to continue. I took out five sets of window stickers: Santa and his sack at the North Pole, white angels with golden trumpets proclaiming the promise for the Savior, a nativity scene complete with halos, and then, the oversized snowman and the Santa Claus that had adorned the windows of Nikki's hospital room. Gently unwrapping the pieces, I put them on the window, trying to shield them from the tears dripping down my face. Guilt for not allowing Mike and Matt to help was pushed aside. Healing required me to perform this ritual alone, while they were at school.

Then I pulled out the stockings, all five of them. Going to the fireplace, I hung three: mine, Mike's, and Matt's. I hugged Kerry's and Nikki's to me, wanting to hang them and knowing I could not. I reminded myself that they were gone; my husband and daughter both died of cancer in 1994. Kerry on April 3, after battling cancer for two years, and Nikki on August 6, after an eighteen-month fight.

My hands continued digging: three winter-scene snow globes the kids had picked out two years ago, three MERRY CHRISTMAS bags with stuffed animals popping out, three ceramic puppies with Santa hats; there seemed to be three of everything. It felt strange having to remind myself that I now had only two kids. But every time I found things in triplicate I had to stop and force myself to remember. How could it really be true?

Faith was all that remained. Faith that there is "a purpose for everything under the sun." Our lives had changed in every way imaginable and in unimaginable ways. Gently, I laid my husband's and my daughter's stockings back in the box. This year we only needed two of the triplicate decorations displayed. I carefully wrapped the third of each and wiped away the tears.

Christmas Eve arrived on schedule, and people came and went. Kerry was not there to cut the ham. Nikki's giggle was soundless. Sandy's irreverent humor was silent. I could not wait for the night to end.

When at last everyone went home, I tucked my boys into bed with visions of Santa Claus coming in the night and promises of new traditions next year. No matter how hard I tried to make everything the same, it had all changed. I mistakenly thought that if the ritual was the same, then the hollow emptiness would be filled. But the familiar traditions only reinforced the physical absence of my husband and daughter. We could no longer hold on to the traditions of the dead past, but we had to look to the future and partake of life.

That night, as I lay in bed, a stabbing pain pierced my heart, and I turned my face to God, seeking the only comfort great enough to provide a glimmer of understanding. Yesterday is gone. Today is here, making no promises of tomorrow. Life is a series of shifts demanding new headings to survive. Each day that passes will never be back again. Christmas '95 was the time to steer forward, carrying the memories of the past into new traditions in the future. Life will again be good as my boys and I fill it with new adventures. But sometimes it's hard to see that through all of the changes.

My Grief Garden
by Ellen Appleby

My father died five days before this past Christmas. There was a foot of snow on the ground the day he was buried. His grave looked like a raw wound all through a cold wet spring. It may be healed over with grass by now; I wouldn't know. I haven't been there lately. I've been too busy gardening.

When I first heard my father's prognosis, I instinctually turned to nature.

I drove to where our house was being built, walked to the nearby creek, and stood on its banks watching the leaves fall off the trees. Each leaf's whispery flight was a sigh from my heart, a breath from my own life, as if I were dying with my dad. He wasn't gone yet; this was only the beginning of the stages where we would bargain, deny, and hope against hope that his case would be the exception to the rule, the special miracle from God.

But I think I knew even then, as I stood by the creek, that I would soon have a reason to never feel the same about fall, that I would never see a leaf float to the ground without thinking of the day I found out that my father had pancreatic cancer.

I had always been extremely close to my dad. We didn't always talk that much, and I may have assumed more closeness than he really felt, but for almost all of my life I counted him as my closest ally and friend. Besides that, he was a genuinely good and kind man: a rarity. I had always joked to my husband and my children that they didn't want to be around me when he died, since I didn't think I would handle it very well. I say "joked" because I always laughed when I said it, since I didn't really believe that day would ever come. But it did, and my joke had become a nightmare.

To make matters even more complicated, we were in the last stages of building a house, a house my father never even got to see, except for the Polaroids I took to the hospital about two weeks before he died. We moved in the week of Thanksgiving, and all that winter our new home (and sod!) was covered with snow. I spent a lot of time walking through the barren woods and along the frozen creek. While everyone around me complained about the long siege of snow we were undergoing, I felt somewhat comforted by the bleak and frozen conditions that mimicked my heart.

Before my dad's illness I had been looking forward to the day when we would have a brand new "virgin" yard in which to garden. We wouldn't have to put up with anyone else's idea of a garden; everything we put into the ground could be entirely our choice. I devoured gardening books, magazines, and catalogs and even began to keep a gardening journal where I jotted down every idea and dream.

But after my dad's death, I lost my enthusiasm for almost everything: my writing, our new home, my family, my husband, my church, and most of all for my garden. It seemed almost too painful to consider engaging in something that would remind me of our relentless journey from birth to death. I had yet to see the hope in the miracle of growth and rebirth.

Our new house has lots and lots of light, and before my dad went into the hospital, he had offered us some of my parents' large house plants. A few weeks after my father's death, my mother sent me home with two ficus trees and a large palm.

That was the day that my grieving process began. As so often happens with those who are grieving, I found myself engaging in ritualistic behavior, as if the steady repetition would somehow give my life a structure and therefore a meaning. Unfortunately for my family, my rituals did not include cleaning or cooking. What I did become almost obsessive about was my plants.

I watered, rearranged, trimmed, and fussed. I worried when the leaves dropped off, and my heart lifted, just a little, when they stopped. Then they began to grow. Though our sun-lit rooms began to seem alive with life, I felt ambivalent. The growth seemed almost insulting. I had trouble accepting that anything could be alive, let alone thrive, when my father was dead. I hated being reminded that in some forms life continued.

But I was also comforted by the ritual of caring for the plants. Maybe fussing over the plants took the place of the care I could no longer give my father. His days in the hospital had been mercifully few, but I regretted not being able to nurse him there or at home. I had had no desire to see him suffer, but I wanted to minister to him, soothe his pain, smooth his brow. One of the last times I visited him, I stroked his head and he closed his eyes and sighed, "That feels good, honey." Now I had no head to stroke. I had only these plants of his to keep alive. And it seemed inordinately important to me to keep them alive, a feeling I soon transferred to my outdoor gardening efforts.

As soon as the spring rains slowed, I headed outside, puny trowel in hand, and began planting everything I could get my hands on. I ordered flats of marigolds from the Boy Scouts and picked up an odd assortment of perennials at the local garden center. Every time I left the house I came home with a plant. I scoured the local discount store for bargains, or whatever struck my fancy. Not content with just our front garden, I bought window boxes and planted ivy and red salvia and white geraniums and blue lobelia, then fretted when the lobelia succumbed to the sun and the heat, and felt a small but recognizable thrill of excitement when a hummingbird paid daily visits to the salvia.

Meanwhile, most of the marigolds fell victim to the local bunnies and grasshoppers, and the sandwort and English daisy pomponnettes struggled in the unyielding and undrainable clay soil. A few plants shriveled away till I finally gave up and gave them a decent burial. Others clung to life with a tenacity that gave me pause on those days when I wondered what the point of living was.

Because I am middle-aged in a neighborhood of young families, I now know how I must have looked to them, fussing in my garden morning, noon, and night. I know I must have looked like my father did to his young neighbors, and the thought doesn't make me sad.

There were many times when I wondered why I was going to all the effort to create something that would die in a few short weeks. It is only now as I write these words that I think to wonder the same thing about the creation of a human being. Why does God go to all that effort to create, to nurture, to sustain, when we are only going to be here for a few short "weeks"? But I would push that thought away and plunge my hands deep into the soil as if by doing so I could somehow become one with something eternal.

I didn't think of it at the time, but I look back now at all the symbolic burials I performed: digging the hole, leaving mounds of dirt "grave side", then depositing the plant which had only my ministrations to separate it from death. How wonderful to see a plant enter into its glory instead of decaying in the ground! To see evidence of growth and the bloom of life. Even the daily nipping of spent blossoms did not diminish the steady progress of my precious plants' new life.

As the summer's heat bore down on my garden, I was careful to slake its thirst almost daily, then worried that I was drowning it. Our tender young ash tree, which we did not pick or plant but which I was still determined to nurture through its infancy, began to turn yellow and lose its leaves as if it was fall. In my ignorance, I thought I had drowned it, until a friend assured me that, during that summer's drought, I couldn't water it enough. I also worried that it was suffering from still being wrapped tightly in its burlap shroud. It was too late to remove it, but I did the next best thing: I pushed away the dirt, tore off the top layers of burlap, and then gently covered it over again——and watered and watered!

The next day I swore it looked perkier, and I made each member of the family examine it and offer his or her opinion. I'm sure they were humoring me when they agreed, but two more weeks of incessant watering and, despite the drought, our tree looked freshly green while all our neighbors' trees were yellow and shedding. Once more I felt as if I had scored a point on the side of life.

Summer wore on into August, and then suddenly the garden took off. The moonflower vine that had taken two months to look even remotely vine-like began to grow madly. The marigolds mustered their reserves and began to show off both foliage and flowers. The English daisies came back to life and rewarded me with a second blooming. The yarrow divested itself of its desiccated shoots while birthing feathery shootlets. The delicate moss roses offered flowers stunning in their intensity, as if to make up for the brevity of their existence. The eight miniature roses I had rescued, half-dead, from the local grocery's flower shop (for only $1.50 apiece) were developing scores of tiny buds and growing like mad.

But even as the garden was bursting into life, I suddenly lost interest in mine. I withdrew into myself, caring little about anything. My husband faithfully took over the watering, and once reduced me to a stony silence when he accidentally sheared a newly planted azalea off at its base. *One more piece of evidence that things die*, I remember thinking. *What's the use?*

My depression deepened until I finally sought treatment. Weeks later, as I began to climb out of the hole in which I had been entombed, I saw my garden afresh. More beautiful than ever, it beckoned to me. *Don't be afraid,* it said. *Enjoy me while you can; I will be gone soon enough, either dying or sleeping. But I can be reseeded and regrown, and I will emerge again, over and over, until the end of time.*

In my shaky recovery, I fear the coming of winter, but I cling to my garden's promise. I am already making plans for next year's gardens (in the plural, you will note!), and dreaming of a greenhouse someday. I am very busy these days pinching blossoms, ordering bulbs, and lining up large pots for the replanting of my father's ficus trees, which have grown too big for the pots they came in.

As I work, I absorb the silent lessons that my grief garden has taught me: that life is ever-changing, and death is not permanent. I do not know, but can somehow imagine, that my dad's lifeless form was ministered to just as lovingly, until he reemerged in Another's garden, resplendent in His glory, and bursting with new life.

Saying Goodbye To Lisa
by Maryanne Raphael

"Put her underwear on first so we can remove the sheet," the tall middle-aged woman said.

It was my first time dressing a dead body, and I expected it to be cold and hard. Instead, it was room temperature and felt like my childhood doll made of stockings.

My friend Irene is from South Africa, where bathing and dressing the dead is a family ritual. So when her twenty-three year old daughter Lisa died, she invited six women, her closest family and friends, to help her prepare Lisa for her funeral. I was one of those chosen for this strange honor.

As she lay in her living room dying of cancer, Lisa had planned her own memorial service. "I want to be buried in my wedding gown," she said. She had been married six months earlier.

Her mother asked her where she wanted her funeral. "Would you prefer your present parish church or the one you went to as a child?"

"By that time I'll be on to better things, Mom. The funeral is for you. I want it in your church so your friends can be there with you."

When they met at UCLA, Lisa's husband Eric called himself an atheist. Lisa was in love with the Lord but that didn't stop her from falling completely in love with Eric.

Both of them were in love with life, loved to read, to study, to write, to travel, to play. They had their first tentative kiss on Valentine's Day, and five years later, on another Valentine's Day, she died in his arms.

Eric told me that God's presence around Lisa was so strong, especially just before she died, that he could touch God's face and feel God's hand on his shoulder, comforting him with unfathomable promises.

Lisa's body was covered with dark bruises. I slipped her bra on her, then turned to the more difficult job of pulling her bikini panties over her legs.

"My precious little Pooki," Irene said, looking into her daughter's face. "This is the last time I'll dress you, so we must do a good job." We put her beautiful cream-colored lace wedding dress on her. The neck was low and showed some bruises, so we got some scissors and cut the lace from the bottom of the dress to put at the top.

Sun Eagle, Irene's dear friend who is a Cheyenne, said, "Her arms have a lot of bruises, too. She needs some gloves. Give me the scissors and I'll make her some." And so Lisa wore a pair of lovely lace gloves.

"She needs a bouquet," Lupe said. She borrowed the scissors and cut some flowers from the bouquets people had sent. She created a lovely wedding bouquet and put it in Lisa's hands.

Then we began putting make-up on Lisa. "Not much," her mother said. "She never wore much. But she did like lipstick and blush." We found ourselves laughing and joking. It was as though we were helping Lisa prepare for her wedding.

She had lost all her hair from chemotherapy and every time I had seen her she was wearing a wig. I was surprised to see her hair had grown in. It was very thick and very black, a lovely pixie hair cut. She looked darling.

When we finished I felt exhausted, physically and emotionally, much the way I felt after giving birth to my son. And yet Death was no longer a frightening stranger. He was more like an unwanted guest. And I remembered how Mother Teresa called death "the doorway to God".

I don't know if I would advise everyone to try dressing their beloved dead, but I do believe we need rituals where we accept our dead into our families so we can consciously let go of them. When the mortuary people came to put Lisa in her coffin, I thought, *We are her midwives, helping our beloved Lisa journey to Eternity.*

December Thursday
by Rebecca Lincoln

Our small group began the climb to the top of the ridge where the sparse, tenacious pine trees reached into the wind and sky. Our progress was slow, due more to grief than terrain. Not wanting to disturb anything, we wound our way gently through trees and around patches of snow and fresh animal signs. The whispering of the wind through the pine branches beckoned to us as the bright morning sun cast our shadows across the slope. The crisp December air smelled of wild, free things. The sky was near cloudless, the vast blue expanse giving way at the far-distant horizon to the Big Horn mountains. Opposite their snow-capped peaks, to the east, lay our home. As we finally reached the top, the raw beauty surrounded and quieted all of us.

I had carried a bundle to the top with me, wrapped in an old work shirt. I cradled it, careful not to drop it or stumble on my way. It felt so very heavy to me—like lead—but I had carried it gently and now set it down softly on a rocky outcropping beside a small pine tree.

I turned to the others who had climbed with me. What could I say to them at this moment? What did they want to hear from me? I was the youngest of us gathered there. "He" had called me "Little One". I felt love and compassion for them as I looked around at their faces; I, in turn, felt support and approval from them. Quite suddenly I felt like an ancient as I looked into their eyes, somehow wanting to comfort them. Unsure how to, I tried to tell them how I felt. My deep love of one man was the only thing that had carried me through to this moment. This was his wish. And we were honoring it not just for him, but for ourselves as well. A peaceful conclusion was so very necessary for all of us. I reminded them of his need for our part in this and that the beautiful spirit we were liberating would still encircle us.

I opened the bundle, and as I slowly stood, the wind seemed to grow until the ashes poured out into the wind in a pale, swirling cloud. I said:

"We set you free!

We set you free!

We set you free!"

Ash was carried up into the air and fell to the rocks below, dusting a juniper. Ash seemed to blow all around me for a moment, and I stood, unable to see anything through my tears, the empty bag clenched in my fists. I fell to my knees, sobbing on the rocks where the bundle had rested, heartbroken now that I had done as he wished.

Unexpectedly, almost instantly, my sister in the group called out, pointing above us into the impossibly blue sky: "Look! Oh look! It's him!"

What I saw as I frantically looked, almost straight up, made me freeze. I stared directly into the golden eye of an eagle that seemed to hang so low in the sky I could touch it! Breathless, I watched the magnificent bird hover there, and it seemed to return my stare, to gaze into my very soul. It was so close I could count the feathers; I could see each one individually, spread in flight. The intensity of the eagle's gaze struck me deeply, and I lifted my hand to cover my mouth, breathless and in awe. I almost felt as though, at that instant, I could breathe in the spirit of the ashes and feel it fill me.

As the eagle tipped its wings to the group and began to turn away from us, reeling northward, those of us sitting scrambled to our feet, anxious not to loose sight of this winged spirit. We had all noticed some eagles flying along the ridge as we approached that morning. Someone had commented that the eagles were waiting for us to make this journey. Somehow, this one exquisite eagle had touched all of us deeply, and our attention was riveted on it now as it moved slowly and gracefully along the top of the ridge and down the flyway. The only sound was the wind blowing through the pines.

I could not help myself and reached for the eagle in the sky, wishing that I could touch such beauty, that I would be pulled right into the air by it and fly!

Our group then relaxed in the sunlight that poured over us, a relief after the days of turmoil that had led to our ascent. We sat on the rocks or walked along the ridge, each of us keeping an eye on the sky. The smell and smoke of burning sage filled the air with offering and prayer that had no words. I noticed my mother, who sat lost in thought, poking holes in a patch of snow with her finger. My bond with her deepened immensely, knowing she had experienced the same loss, when my father died, so long ago. Each of us grieved in our own way, knowing and caring for the wonderful spirit we had set free: healing begun by the completion of this task, gaining a measure of peace from the beauty around us. We let our anguish be soothed by the sound of his flute song in our hearts. It was good and it was right. It was peaceful and calm. It was freedom and beauty.

After a time, we all made our way back down the steep slope on the east side of the ridge. Even more silent than on our ascent, and even more careful not to disturb this place, we left slowly, in peace.

The magnificent eagle then appeared again and in silent beauty it soared. Soon, it was joined by a second eagle. It seemed as though one of the other eagles we had seen earlier had come to guide this one who was so close to our hearts. *My father?* I wondered.

It seemed the eagle that had so touched our spirits was reluctant to be guided away just yet. It flew along the east slope of the ridge as we made our way home, watching our progress from high above, wheeling in the drafts and thermals of the wind. The eagle finally swooped down and waggled its wings as if to say, "You will be all right now," before spinning away from us.

Written in loving memorial to
Mark Adam McLaughlin
June 5,1961— December 8, 1996
by his wife, whom he named:
Slipwah Two-Socks

All Around Us
by Carolyn Mott Ford

We all have our own ways of remembering our loved ones and those who played an important part in our lives. I find that for me, as for many others, those objects and entities which are around us in our everyday lives resonate more poignantly than monuments or memorials.

I recognized this more fully when I was visiting my daughter and noticed that she used an inexpensive lotion which could be purchased in a supermarket or corner drugstore. It's a fine product which I wouldn't hesitate to use myself, but she is a professional working woman who usually wears designer clothes and uses salon type make-up and beauty products. As she applied the lotion, she held her hands up to her face and said, "I love this smell."

I immediately realized why she liked that particular lotion. Her grandmother had always used it and my daughter was enjoying the comfort that scent brought to her. Her grandmother had passed on several years before and the delicate fragrance still gave a hint of her presence. This helped me to understand the many ways we are surrounded by those things, tangible and intangible, which sometimes help us to feel close to those we loved and remind us of their spirit and grace.

I remembered how, some years back, a good friend and neighbor had given me a clump of mums from her garden shortly before she passed on. I planted the mums in front of my home and, as they took root and spread, they were a growing reminder of my friend. Each year in the early fall, those yellow flowers would bloom and bring back happy memories of our friendship.

And that is why I love those remembrances which frequent our lives— because they often bring back thoughts of the good times. This is especially important during family gatherings when we have reached the point where we are able to look beyond grief and reminisce. It is a way to help children know more about their family members and understand how to cope with life's passages. In fact, don't the young people often bring a smile to our faces as we notice how they remind us of those others we so loved?

I have been reminded of my grandmother when looking at the soft, beautiful eyes of my own grandchild and of my grandfather as I watch the capable hands of my son repair things around the house.

And, oh, how many memories are evoked when cooking or sitting around the table for a big, family dinner! When I think of my mother, I often picture her in the kitchen and never more so than when I make stew. She had developed an unusual recipe and I cannot make that delicious stew without envisioning her standing over the stove.

As we eat and converse, we may laugh about the family member who insisted that his chili had to be hot enough "to cause a sweat to break out on the forehead". He would toss in hot peppers until the chili met that taste test.

When my sisters and I have turkey, we think of the time that Dad insisted on cooking a big turkey while on a camping trip in 98 degree weather. The turkey filled the oven of his trailer, while heat filled the trailer and overflowed out into the screened lean-to, washing over his reluctant guests.

Whenever I use the old-fashioned pie server which once belonged to my grandmother, I am reminded of that very proper lady. She always set a long formal table for our holiday gatherings with fine china and gleaming silver. Yet, as the table was cleared after the main course, Gram would warn us that she was not going to provide additional silver for the pie by calling out, "Lick your forks if you want dessert."

What is so special is that the sad moments, the hurtful times, can be eclipsed by these poignant or funny memories which are evoked by things which are a part of our everyday lives. Sometimes we are unaware of them because they may be so ordinary. They may just give us a happy or contented feeling, the way the lotion did for my daughter. Or they may bring out recollections which help us along the path of healing.

These reminders are truly all around us and, in that sense, they help to keep the essence of loved ones in our hearts and in our minds.

CHAPTER 11

GRANTING TIME TO GRIEVE

These contributors explore the significance of allowing
time to mourn, both in pre-death and post-death
situations, and show how in some cases, many, many
years are required to work through all the stages to reach
acceptance over the death of a loved one.

Healing From Loss
by Christiane Northrup, MD

This piece is adapted from an article in Dr. Christiane Northrup's Health
Wisdom for Women *(Vol.6 No.1,January 1999): 7811 Montrose Rd.,
Potomac MD 20854; 1-800-211-8561.*

When I was in my final year of medical school, my maternal grandmother died. She was only sixty-eight years old and had been perfectly healthy
until the night she died, after shoveling snow from her driveway. Her death
felt like a big deal at the time and was a real loss. Though I missed my
grandmother and, while her death seemed premature, it felt as though it had
a natural order about it.

About nine months after my grandmother's death, I experienced a totally different type of loss from death. My youngest sister, Cindy, was killed
in a car accident at the age of twenty-three. When I heard this news, every
cell in my body went into shock and disbelief. I could barely breathe and I
felt disembodied, as though the whole thing were a dream.

When I returned to Boston after her funeral, my training involved caring for women dying of various types of gynecologic cancers. Some were relatively young with young children. For the first time in my life, I knew deep within me what grief was and what these women and their families were going through. I sat down on their beds and told their families to be sure to say whatever needed to be said, because they still had time. At night I often wept in my husband's arms, grieving for the loss of my sister. And I went to movies with her boyfriend, a longtime friend of my husband's whom my sister had met at our wedding. It helped both of us to get together and talk about the person we had loved and lost.

A short time after my sister died, my father dropped dead at the age of sixty-eight while playing tennis with my mother. When I got that phone call and heard how he had died, I remembered a conversation we had when I was a senior in high school. My dad said, "Someday, a blood vessel is going to burst inside my brain, and I'll float out into the universe." And that's exactly what he did. At the funeral, my dad looked so healthy lying there that a part of me thought, *Why can't you just get up and get on with it?* Then, I cried.

I have gained some wisdom from my personal grieving experiences. I learned that it was important for me to allow myself to feel what author and meditation teacher Stephen Levine calls "the pain that ends the pain". My body knew how to grieve—by making sounds and shedding tears. In other cultures, women often wail together. And even animals grieve their losses through howling and wailing. It helped me to make and release these sounds of grieving. I believe that if I hadn't, the pain would have gotten stored in my body and resulted in illness later.

I gave myself the time to grieve. Depending on the type of loss, it sometimes took at least a full cycle of four seasons to ease the pain. And recovery isn't linear. Sometimes I'd be going along and noticed that I hadn't felt really bad for a day or two. Then suddenly, I'd be overcome with feelings of grief again. I let them wash over me and chose to have compassion for myself when a song or a place triggered a strong memory of a loved one. I just reminded myself that each time I allowed myself to feel fully, the depth and acuteness of my sorrow would be lessened a bit the next time and become more shallow.

Some grief has taken much longer. My mother recently told me, "It's been over twenty years since Cindy died. A part of me will never get over it, and I've decided that that's okay." I couldn't agree more. When I try to talk myself out of the truth of my feelings, it never works. But when I soften and give myself breathing space around them, I always feel better and the pain lessens.

I created an altar and shrine to my loved ones in which I put letters, items they loved, and flowers. I also created an album which I kept in view for as long as it brought me comfort. The process of doing this helped me to work through my loss and also celebrated the individuals' lives and connection with me. I knew intuitively when to move or dismantle them.

If a loved one's place in my life could have been easily filled by another activity, person, place, or thing, I wouldn't have felt the grief. I knew that no one would ever be able to replace those persons fully, so I didn't try. My lost loved ones were not replaceable. Our relationship was unique to both of us.

It's important to talk about losses. I have met people who feel that they can't go to funerals or write to friends who have suffered a loss because they don't know what to say, but having been a grieving person, I know that it feels really good to talk about the loved ones I have lost. Having someone who can share stories or memories about the person who has died really helped me. When my sister died, I cherished the letters I received from my friends who had known her, and even from some who hadn't. Many people shared their own stories of loss with me at that time. I found this to be very comforting and reassuring because, through their sharing, I knew that I was not alone in my grief. It also helped to know that, despite having experienced this pain, these people had managed to go on with the business of living.

Many doctors prescribe drugs, such as Valium to "take the edge off", in what I believe to be a misguided attempt to help people deal with grief. I believe this will only prolong or distort the grieving process. The same is true of using alcohol to numb one's feelings.

Because of their situations, I know of people who were not surrounded by friends and family who knew their loved ones and could share in their grieving process. Especially for them, joining a support group for those experiences allowed them to keep on track with a healthy grieving process so that they were less apt to get isolated or frozen in the process.

I found peace and comfort for my grieving in the writings of Stephen Levine, including *Healing into Life and Death* (Anchor, 1989) and *A Year to*

Live (Three Rivers Press, 1997). Raymond Moody's book, *Life after Life* (Bantam Books, 1988), is also good. And, I highly recommend an incredible and powerful new book on the process of death by Kathleen Dowling Singh entitled *The Grace in Dying* (Harper, San Francisco, 1998).

There came a time during the grieving process when I felt that I had to move on and begin living again; otherwise, my life energy would have become so caught up in the ongoing process of grief that my own life would have stagnated. Generally, a stagnated grief process results from not being able to fully grieve a loss and then let go. I believe one is in trouble when that person's loss is still the major focus of life one year later. An example of a stagnated grief process would be the individual who loses a child and continues to set a place at the table for that child every night. Other indications of stagnated grief are if one can't sleep or eat, finds no enjoyment out of things that used to bring pleasure, or is burdened by guilt and self blame.

As time goes on, I have found myself having a whole new relationship with the individuals I lost. For example, I feel my father around me every day. In some mysterious way, I feel that we have as good a relationship now as we ever did when he was living. He's like a spirit guide for me. I don't feel the same way about my sister, Cindy. Somehow, I don't feel like she's around me at all. But this is not a source of pain for me because I trust that she is where she needs to be.

Special events such as birthdays have opened the wounds. This has not been dangerous, but it has helped to be prepared for it. For example, I have planned to have a moment of prayer to remember my loved ones, but I also plan new activities for those days.

If I am to survive and thrive in coming years, I have to learn how to deal with what life throws my way. That's why I have devoted time to learning practical skills for identifying and dealing with "negative" emotions—fear, anger, sadness, and resentment—in a healthy manner. As with any relationship, I realize that I won't get anywhere unless I am willing to assume 100% responsibility for how I respond and care for myself.

There Is Life After Death—Mine
by Susan Ragland

I have lost both of my parents; one had a long term illness, and the other a short term illness. I lost my husband, very suddenly. There is no good way to lose someone you love.

In the case of the long term illness, there was the grieving process which began when I learned that my mother had inoperable cancer, and a sense of relief when she finally was released from the suffering. But there was still a grieving process when it ended and my role as caretaker came to an end. I was not only deprived of her companionship, but I was also deprived of the role I had been living for the two years of her illness. In addition to the grief and loss of a loved one, I had to adjust to a changing purpose in my life.

In the case of the short term illness, there was another kind of grieving process, which I began when I learned of my father's terminal illness. I felt absolutely no sense of relief because my father did not suffer a lengthy illness, only intense grief. Dad had lived with me for fourteen years after the death of Mother, and even survived my husband. He was the last to leave me.

When my husband of twenty-six years died very suddenly, however, the adjustment was the most difficult of my life. I had no time to get ready, and there was the strong sense of being unprepared for the new life I had to lead. I felt more alone than I had ever felt, weak, and vulnerable. Because his death was so sudden, there were many financial matters which had to be taken care of. To some extent, this was a blessing because it kept me occupied during this most difficult time. When the chaos eventually came to an end, I realized that life would never be the same.

In the beginning, everyone took the time to be sympathetic and concerned for my welfare. I allowed my children to show their love and concern for me, knowing that this helped them with their own grief. It was as necessary for them, as it was for me, and bonded us even closer. I let friends help, since they felt needed, and I admitted that I needed them. But this did not last, nor did I expect it to.

The time came when the children had to get on with their busy lives, as well they should have. They were always there when I needed them, but it was better that I not always show how much I needed them. I tried to get on with the healing. It was imperative that I find a new life that was meaningful to me. I knew, somehow, that friends and relatives would want to spend more time with me if I found something interesting to do and to talk about, rather than losing patience with me if I appeared to be steeped in self pity. It impressed them; they were proud of me, and I was happier. There were many times I did not feel like putting on a happy face, but it was important to me that they thought I was doing so well in my recovery.

At first, I was afraid to go out alone, but I came to understand that if I was unwilling to go alone, I would not go at all. I was forty-eight years old and not ready to give up on life. I took a subscription to a concert series. I went alone, which was very hard but got me out of the house and, as time went on, became easier. I ran into friends who were surprised to see me go out alone, but soon got used to the idea. It was not nearly as bad as I imagined, and it did get easier. I found that as a season ticket holder the same people sat around me. I began to talk to them as time went on, so I was no longer alone.

During this time, I found more in common with people who had been divorced than I did with my lifelong friends, so I tended to gravitate to them.

I found some new hobbies and activities. I learned to use a computer and then went on line where I found many new friends and acquaintances to stay in contact with. I learned to bake bread, and I joined a sourdough conference. I chatted with people all over the world. I didn't tell them of the pain I was experiencing; I wanted this part of my life to be separate and apart from grief.

I discovered that we are many selves, depending not only on which parts we allow to surface during certain times in our lives, but on how we meet life's challenges. At critical times, we are often faced with a fork in the road where, if we had done things another way, we might have become an altogether different person. This was such a time. I had two choices: despair or hope. I looked at my life and decided to take the fork in the road which would lead me to a new and rewarding life, the road of hope. There were times I didn't think that I had the strength to keep pushing forward. I took risks, and I challenged myself to do things that were tough under the circumstances, but when I found that I could do these things, I found a new self respect, a new strength. I think that I like my new, stronger self, even more.

I think this other self has been there all along, but finally has been given that opportunity to flourish in adversity.

I came to understand that out of all bad things good things come. For one thing, I came to realize that those things that used to be so very important were no longer that serious. The little crises that I used to endure paled by comparison to the one I was now going through. I never again got upset over something trivial.

Another good thing that came of it all was my realization that life was short, and that the future is now. I learned to make the most of the present because I did not know how long it would last.

My two sons and I have always been close but the loss of their father brought us even closer, something that has never changed. The sharing of grief can be a strong force in a family. When we, as a family, were able to talk about their father and laugh at some of his foibles, I knew that we were all going to make it.

I tried to look upon this time as a time of opportunity. I was determined to turn the negative aspects of my new life into something positive. I did not like being alone, but I realized that, for the first time in my life, I could do certain things that I could not have done before.

I took a trip to Australia that my husband never wanted to take. I was completely in charge of my life and for the first time, after the initial fear (and there was plenty of that), I liked it! Freedom always comes with a price, but it is, after all, a positive thing.

I sold my home, bought an old house which I renovated and decorated without help from anyone.

I made a list of simple pleasures like being able to turn on the light and read in the middle of the night when I couldn't sleep, without fear of disturbing anyone. I now could listen to any kind of music that I wanted to or watch anything on television without having to consider anyone else's taste.

I enjoyed being totally in control of my money, no longer concerned if I spent it on something foolish.

At first I thought that looking for the good out of the bad might be disrespectful to my husband's memory. Then I looked back and said, "I was a good and devoted wife," "I was a good mother," "I never shrank from responsibilities or commitments." I gave what was expected, and I have no reason to feel any guilt if I find the few positive aspects of my otherwise unhappy existence.

There were times I lapsed back into total despair. I found, though, that it was better to share my feelings at those times with new friends. Old friends and relatives would have worried.

The most surprising and difficult emotion to understand and to come to terms with was the anger. Not anger at my fate, but anger at my dead husband. It wasn't rational, but it was very real. It had a life of its own. Somehow I knew that I had to allow the anger to come, and that it had to be dealt with. Instinctively, I was aware that it would never go away by itself and that I would not get past it, unless I recognized it, faced it, and gave expression to the anger I felt at having been abandoned by him. I once sat on the floor in the middle of my living room, shaking my fist and yelling at my life partner who had the nerve to die. I shook my fist at the ceiling saying, "How could you leave me with such a mess?" "How could you do this to me?" "Why didn't you tell me that it wouldn't be forever?" "Why didn't you take better care of yourself?" I did this alone, out loud, and crying. I felt so ridiculous at one point that I laughed out loud through the tears, but I know it made me feel better.

I have come to learn that hostility is a substitute for fear, and I realized that I was afraid of the future without him. But then I thought of the many times during my life in which a new situation brought some measure of insecurity: a new job, a new baby, or a new neighborhood. In each case the insecurity and fear had passed. I told myself that, in time, I would find security again.

I wondered if my husband's spirit could see me acting out my anger. I knew that he would forgive me, but could I forgive myself?

Before I could forgive myself, I had to look closely at who I was, where I had been, and where I needed to go with my life. I saw that the greater part of my life had been defined by my relationship with my spouse. I understood that many of the things that I found difficult to do were those things that he had taken charge of during our marriage. That was always by agreement with me. It had been a partnership, and as in most partnerships, each assumes responsibility for different tasks.

Even so, I found that I became extremely fatigued when I had to do those things that he had done. They were in addition to my share of the load, and they reminded me that he was not there. Each time I had to take out the garbage or reconcile the checkbook, I resented him all over again. Fortunately, there were not too many of these things that I did not know how to do and which I might have had to learn.

It took a long time before I recognized the resentment. I thought I had lost my competence, competence I had always relied on, and which he had relied on. Weakened from grief, loss, fear, and the adjustments to a new life, these additional burdens had become unbearable. Unconsciously I was telling myself that this burden was thrust upon me. Once I came to recognize that it was my anger that had gotten in the way of my concentration, it suddenly became easier.

I soon realized that the sooner I accepted these new responsibilities, the better off I would be. I said to myself, "Well, I got away with not doing it for all these years, so I guess I better get on with it now." I decided to look upon it as a challenge. When I finally accepted these extra burdens, I knew that I was on the road to independence.

No, I hadn't asked for this independence, but like it or not, it was now me against the world. I knew that if I didn't accept the challenge, it would defeat me. I never ran from a challenge in my life, and this proved to be my salvation.

There are still the sweet memories that I will always treasure: a trip to Europe with the children when they were young and all the funny things that happened, summers in the country, little things that I said and that he said. There are those riches of my life that will still bring a smile to my face and, occasionally, a tear to my eye, for the rest of my life. I have let those memories emerge. I have taken them and held onto them. I have let them live and have shared them with my children, now that, finally, we can laugh. I have told my grandchildren about their grandfather, and they love to listen to the stories, as if they were fairy tales, stories about a man they have never known in life but who has become larger than life to them.

Some memories are still painful, but I will not let them die. They are the meaning of my former life, and they enrich the present in which I now live. In them, I have seen the purpose and meaning of my life.

The healing process is slow and gradual. Many times I wondered why it was taking so long or if there was something wrong with me. Someone told me that it would take about three years to heal to the point where my grief was not always in my thoughts, always an open wound. I scoffed at this, but it turned out to be true. No, I didn't grieve every day for three years, nor did I get over the loss entirely as soon as the three years ended. All of the steps I took to rehabilitate myself brought me closer each day to the day when I could appreciate myself for being strong, be proud of my progress, of the person I had become, still going on, with hope and faith in the future. When I started to look ahead instead of back, I knew that I was well on my way to recovery.

Seven Steps Forward, One Step Back
by Cynthia Kuhn Beischel

"The Great Southern Tour" was supposed to be, in my mind, an *even-ing out* trip. My younger daughter, Lindsay, was invited to go to Bermuda for ten days with the family of one of her best friends. I initially had qualms about letting her go because she had been swimming in the ocean with her father when he drowned six years earlier. I wondered if it was a good idea for her to be so far away from home in a place that might bring back a flood of unhappy feelings, but because she was so excited about the invitation and showed no signs of concern about the things I worried about, I agreed to her going. Having made that decision, I then decided that my older daughter, Merritt, and I would not sit at home during that time. We would also take a vacation. Our route was designed by following the rule of form follows function. We thought of all the friends and relatives we had in the South whom we could visit (and impose upon) and thus our itinerary was born.

The first leg of our jaunt was short. We arrived in Lexington at dinner time and were welcomed by Jill, my sister-in-law, Edwin, her husband, and Jared and Evan, their young sons. The meal and evening were delightful as we caught up on each other's happenings and events.

Just before going to bed, Ed announced that he had something for us. He handed me a video of Jared's first birthday party on which my deceased husband was pulling his usual antics. Ed said that he and Jill had debated about giving this to us, not knowing how we'd feel. They finally decided that they would offer it to us and let us decide whether or not we'd want to watch it. Considering the length of time since Jerry's death, I was amazed at my reaction. I was caught totally off balance by the surge of emotions and anxiety I felt. Though we have lots of photos of Jer, many of which are sitting around the house, the thought of watching a tape and seeing him "alive", walking, talking, telling his dumb jokes brought tears to my eyes and a lump in my throat. I was both grateful for and frightened by the gift.

The next day we headed for Nashville to stay at the house of one of Merritt's good college friends, Rebecca, and her parents, Lonnie and Will. We were welcomed with true Southern hospitality and made to feel right at home.

Within a couple of days, Merritt and I headed for Atlanta. As our Prism climbed the Blue Ridge Mountains in ninety-eight degree weather, the radiator gauge caught my eye. The marker was in the red danger zone. With no good place to pull over, we continued to cross over the top. I was grateful for Jer's help as I remembered something he had once told me about turning on the heater in order to take some of the heat off of the engine. As a result, the marker moved to a slightly cooler edge of the red area. The heat in the car shot up to one hundred twelve degrees before we could stop at the first town on the descent, South Pittsburgh, Tennessee. Merritt and I sat under the shade of a tree with the hood open for a half hour allowing the engine to rest and cool. At 3:30 PM on a Saturday, we attempted to find a mechanic who could flush out our radiator and put in new coolant. At our fourth stop we were successful and continued on our way to Atlanta four hours off schedule.

I had lived in Atlanta twenty some years ago when Jerry and I had both participated in a co-op program through the University of Cincinnati. I looked forward to seeing relatives and old friends and showing Merritt some of her parents' old haunts. We finally arrived in Atlanta around 10:00 PM. With my memory lapses and trying to follow inaccurate directions, it was quite a challenge to find our way in the dark. After a futile forty-five minutes of riding back and forth on a long boulevard trying to find a specific side street, I pulled into a small shopping area, parked at the curb in front of a grocery store, and used the pay phone to call our friend who was expecting us. Merritt, who stayed in the car, talked back and forth with me as I tried to answer Jim's questions about our directions. Finally, after dealing with the noise of traffic and passerbys, I motioned to Merritt to just get out of the car and come over to the phone.

"Do you have the keys?" she called.

"Should I bring the keys?" I heard.

I nodded yes. In a split second we both realized that the keys and both of our purses were locked in the car.

I was on the verge of weeping. Yes, it had been a long, hot, frustrating day, but that is not what sent the flood of sadness and anxiety throughout my being. I was suddenly recalling and reliving the summer six years earlier when Jerry, Merritt, Lindsay, and I had been on a summer vacation in the South. The same scenario of being locked out of our car in front of a grocery store had happened the day before my husband died. I felt a rush of adrenalin as I went in to ask to use the store's phone and then wait for an AAA mechanic to come unlock my car. When he arrived, I held my breath waiting to see which door he would approach and felt a small bit of relief when he headed for the driver's side to unlock the door, because the mechanic who had come to help six years before had gone directly to the passenger's— my—door. I had always wondered about the symbolism of that act afterwards. I felt as if Jer was to be "locked out forever" and my door had been opened because I was to become the new "driving force" of my family.

Panic and concern reemerged as I watched this man give up on the driver's door and move to the passenger's. Again I held my breath. I then decided that I didn't care if he thought I was crazy. I told him that I was superstitious and asked him to please go back to the driver's side. At first he said he had to follow policy rules. However, when Merritt and I protested adamantly, he did us the favor of coming back over. After forty minutes he managed to open the rear door on the driver's side. I didn't know what the symbolism of that was, but it didn't matter—we'd broken the pattern. Perhaps the meaning, if there is any, has something to do with going forward after reentering through the back door or past history.

In fact, over the next few days we spent a great deal of time discussing the past and catching up on our respective lives with both family and friends, reliving the times and events of college days and four generations of relatives. We felt a few pangs of sorrow, but for the most part we laughed a lot, realizing the comfort and enjoyment that comes from sharing.

On our way back north, we followed our route in reverse. It began to dawn on me that this journey had been more than a summer get-away. It was, in fact, an inner journey of retracing the steps and the associations with people from the past which in turn provided an opening to the future.

I'm not sure that I will ever be totally reconciled to Jerry's death, which made an irrevocable impact on my life. Although at times I still feel his empathy, love, and encouragement, I am alone. I make wrong turns, get lost more times than I care to admit, and sometimes feel unprepared for the challenges I meet, but overall I realize I'm okay. I'm making it.

All I Should Have Said
by Crystal Armes Wagner

Dear Steven,

It seems to me that a lifetime is not long enough to say all the things that should be said to someone that you love. Especially when that lifetime is the seventeen years that yours was. In the years that you've been gone I think of the things I should have said, all I should have done, and how much I'm missing you. Although I know it may be seen as "too late" to some, I am writing you this letter for my own sake, to tell you all that's happened since you've been gone.

We received a phone call at 4:00 AM that Saturday morning. The person at the other end said you had been in an accident and that you "hadn't made it". What an odd thing to say. No one wants to say "die" or "dead", especially not to the bereaved person. I must admit it took me a long time to be able to say the words myself. I would say that my brother had been in an accident, but it was years before I could say you'd been killed in an accident.

Anyway, my husband and I left for the hospital where I knew Mom and Dad were waiting. The whole way there I was certain there had been some sort of mix up. A nurse met us at the door, and I grabbed her shoulders crying, "Are you sure it's him?" She assured me that it was, but I still didn't believe her until we entered the little room where Mom and Dad sat crying. Dad was crying; can you believe it? My stomach churned and I felt like I was on a roller coaster with no end in sight. Our sister Sherri was there with her husband. She was crying too. I couldn't cry. Not yet. All I wanted to do was run from the room. Mom was trying to figure out when it had happened. "It had to be after midnight," she was saying. "Because you called when he left your house."

Oh, the guilt. You had been grounded, but were allowed to come to my house. I was supposed to make sure you stayed there. When you left, I was supposed to call Mom so she'd know when to expect you home. As usual, you talked me into letting you go out with your friends and covering for you by calling Mom at a certain time and making her think you had just left. It seemed harmless enough at the time. I had covered for you before. I told you to be careful before you left, just like I always did.

But I didn't tell you I love you.

Why did I do it? Why didn't I make you stay? Maybe if I'd done as I was told you'd have lived to make it home. Now I can't tell you that I love you. That I miss having you around. Or even that I was angry at you for leaving me. I know that sounds ridiculous. After all, I'm sure leaving wasn't your idea. I was so scared and angry and confused that I couldn't think logically. I was trying to make sense of a senseless situation.

The funeral home is a place that no one wants to go to. It smells sickeningly sweet. Everything is supposed to look pretty with the flowers and ribbons that surround the dark case in the middle. It didn't look like you lying there. I kept thinking that maybe there was a chance that a mistake had been made. Maybe it wasn't too late.

It was you. All your friends came. I never realized how many you had. They were crying. Even the boys who tried to act tough could not control the tears that streamed down their faces. The girls were worse. Some were crying hysterically. It almost made me angry because they couldn't be hurting as badly as I was. They couldn't have loved you as much.

The next day at your funeral the sun shone brightly. How could the day be so pretty when you were gone? At the church, the family all walked in together. The people stood and watched us pass. Some cried. The pastor read passages that I had heard before. They didn't make sense anymore. Where was God? Why did He take you away?

I must tell you that of all the places I laid the blame for your death, God received the brunt of it. I blamed Him for taking you. I accused Him of not loving us and I even went to the point where I began doubting His existence. I am happy to tell you that I eventually got over the blame game. I "made up" with God and I think that my faith began to get even stronger.

The next stop in our shocked parade was the cemetery. This was the end. It must be true. But how could it be? Mom was crying, stopping, then crying again. I wondered why I couldn't wake up from the horrible dream I was having.

The next couple of months were a blur. I know my twenty-second birthday was in there somewhere, but I don't remember it. Sometimes when the phone would ring, I'd think for a split second that it was you. Or I'd hear a joke and say to myself, "I've got to remember to tell Steve that one." Then it would hit me all over again that you were gone. How could I have forgotten that, even for a second?

Mom and Dad changed. They went from not caring about anything to worrying too much. In the beginning, they were both so lost in their grief that they could barely function. Mom wanted to talk about you all the time, and Dad couldn't talk about you at all. I think the difficulty Dad had was that he had never felt so helpless. He wanted to be strong for us, but he was aching so badly inside that he couldn't. As time passed they became overly protective. Whenever Sherri or I would leave their house, they would tell us to be sure and call when we got home so they knew we had arrived safely. When I became pregnant with my first child, Mom couldn't get happy about it. I think it was a combination of longing for her own child while fearing that something would happen to her grandchild.

Mom and Dad grieved differently, and sometimes I wondered if their marriage could take it. I had read that bereaved parents often divorced. Fortunately, they found The Compassionate Friends. It's a support group that consists of bereaved parents. I've attended, though I haven't lost a child. The group has helped more than I can express. Mom hated hearing people tell her that they knew how she felt because she said no one knew. These parents did. I think attending the group made things a little easier for me because I met other siblings who felt as I did. While it brought comfort, at the same time it brought uneasiness. I didn't want to know these people because what brought them together was terrible sadness. But what also brought them together was the strength they drew from one another.

While Mom and Dad's marriage has remained strong, mine didn't. I don't know that your death had anything to do with it, but I know I was still grieving a lot when my husband thought I should "get over it". I remember telling Mom that what upset me the most about the divorce was that even if I found someone else, I would never meet someone who knew you. Years later I ran into a friend of yours. We ended up getting married. He knew stories about you that I had never heard. He knew you better than most, and it was almost like getting a piece of you back. We now have two children. Our son is named Steven. As I watch my children grow, I think of how they are like you and how they would have enjoyed your company. They both know who Uncle Steve is. I wish they could have known you.

In the nine years you've been gone, I've come a long way. I used to not be able to mention your name without crying. I felt a great need to understand the grief process and so I took numerous college courses on the subject. I don't know that I understand everything, but at least I know others feel the same way. Some people think I should forget about you and "move on". I know that these people have never suffered a real loss. Others who have walked in my shoes allow me to talk about you if I choose. It was after your death that I found out who my real friends were. The ones that I thought I could lean on were the ones who left me alone to swim in my grief. So many people are afraid to mention your name because they don't want to upset me or make me cry. What they don't realize is that tears aren't a sign of weakness. Tears must flow for healing to begin. I cry when I need to and talking about you isn't what makes me sad, missing you is. Those that understand allow me to cry and talk about you anyway. There is no set time for grief and bereavement. Each individual must wade through it in their own way and in their own time. Others cannot hurry the process, they can only be there to listen. This experience made me realize how terribly insensitive I was to others before I had lost a loved one.

As I've written this letter, the tears have returned. I suppose they will always be there waiting for something to trigger their release. I don't think you ever get over the death of someone you love, you simply learn to live with it. People ask Mom, "How do you do it?" To them she answers, "What else can I do?"

There is nothing else to do except to maybe learn from all of this. I suppose if I've learned anything it's that the time to tell loved ones how I feel is now. Precious moments can never be replaced and lives can be turned upside down in a second. I am more aware that good-bye could be forever and later may never come. I believe you knew that I loved you though those words may not have been spoken. I just wish that they had.

I love you.

A Family Perspective
by Emily Sue Harvey

A portion of these memoirs ("David's Surprise") appeared in Chocolate For A Woman's Spirit *(Simon & Shuster).*

Darkness

On January 31, 1974, six months after we moved to Marion, South Carolina, while our daughters visited another family, our second child, eleven-year-old Angie, was killed by a train.

No "Poor Me"

My husband Lee and I left the accident scene and returned to the parsonage. Friends moved about silently doing what needed to be done. We went directly to Angie's room and closed the door. Already, someone had tidied up. I appreciated their act of kindness, yet I was incredibly saddened to not find things as she'd left them, to experience, for one more moment, her presence. It seemed more than we could bear to lose her so suddenly and completely.

Many bereaved immediately clear away evidence of a deceased loved one to muffle memories. We were the opposite, with our visceral hunger to touch her belongings and clutch her discarded clothing, as if holding her. At least her bed remained unchanged. I put my face in her pillow and inhaled her fragrance. Lee fell to his knees and laid his head on her bed and wept loudly, knotting his fingers in her rumpled bedspread. I wept silently, clutching her pillow to me.

"How am I going to survive this?" Lee asked between sobs. He, the strong, invincible one, looked beseechingly at me for an answer. "Sue . . . how can I go on?"

I'd always wondered how I'd react to tragedy, if I'd find strength, sanity. Now, I knew. There could be no self-pity. With a clarity as clear as a mountain spring, I knew it would destroy me.

In that instant, Angie's love and trust smote me profoundly, and, incredibly, became my primary buttress. Her belief in me sustained me in those first critical days. I knew what her words to me would be: "Mama, it's not your fault. It just happened."

She'd never failed to honor me. Now, I would honor her with a dignity befitting her ideal of me. Lee, still on his knees beside her bed, waited for a word of hope.

I said softly, "We've got two children who need us more than ever. We'll make it with God's help, taking one step at a time. That's all. One at a time, honey."

Saying Goodbye

Funeral preparations and receiving friends consumed the critical forty-eight hours following the accident. This busyness slid us past moments that would otherwise have been agonizing. It also helped me do those "last" things for my daughter. Only later did I realize the healing in them.

I asked only individuals who'd known and loved Angie to participate in her funeral. Her teacher, Mrs. Cartrette, and class formed an honorary escort. I chose for her burial outfit a long white party dress with tiny red Swiss dots. A slender red velvet bow centered the dainty white ruffled collar. And she wore hose, a newly acquired taste of hers.

On the morning of the service, I went early to the funeral home with my Pam, thirteen years old. I spent several hours with Angie, who was so heartbreakingly beautiful in repose. I replaced yesterday's long-stemmed red rose with a fresh one. I combed her blonde, softly waved, newly shag-cut hair, kissed her soft cheek and murmured things I needed to say, asking her forgiveness for allowing this terrible thing to happen. Pam quietly came to stand beside the casket. "Mama," she said in a choked little voice, "I never told her I loved her." She kissed her sister's cheek. "Oh, Angie," she sobbed, "I love you so."

People's care and concern sustained me through those first days. Never was I as bleeding-raw as at that time. And never was I more receptive to love. The grief and remorse of losing a child is mind-boggling. Augmenting mine was my black secret: I'd caused my child's death by suggesting she go on the outing.

For weeks, I carried that crushing knowledge inside me. I began to seek solitude, even before the consolers stopped coming. Finally, desperate, I made an appointment with Dr. Jordan, my psychology professor at Francis Marion. Tearfully, I unloaded my horrible secret.

"Sue," he replied kindly when I'd finished. "What's bothering you is what bothers every parent who loses a child: you do not control circumstances. We have trouble with that, without exception. So many variables played into the accident. Had Angie and Kaye gone to the trestle five minutes earlier or later, they would both still be alive."

"But," I sobbed, "I sent her with them."

He reached across his desk to pat my hand. "You sent her because you wanted her to have a good time, didn't you?"

I nodded, wiping away tears.

"So, you acted in good faith, in her interest. Sue," he added, "had she died from an incurable disease, you would still be experiencing the "if onlys". It's ingrained into parents. How many times do our children go somewhere without us, only to return later safe and sound? Circumstances negate our control sometimes. Sometimes tragically. But the fact remains, no matter how hard we try, we cannot foresee everything. Stop blaming yourself."

We do not control circumstances. That truth freed me from my awful secret. I forgave myself. Only a parent who has walked in my shoes can understand the full impact of that. It was a turning point for me that gradually restored my sense of self and peace.

Stepping Stones

"Stay busy," Lee kept saying. "You need to get back to your classes. You shouldn't sit here all alone."

"I need solitude," I insisted. And I did. More and more.

"Honey, do it for me. Please. I can't stand seeing you alone so much, grieving this way."

To please Lee, I resumed classes.

As a music scholarship worker with the Francis Marion College Choral Group, I was committed to prepare for and sing in the spring concert. Singing, after the accident, was the last thing I wanted to do.

My choral group friends flocked around me, embracing me tearfully and saying how glad they were that I was back and how much they needed me.

I knew they could carry on without me, but hearing that I was vital to them sparked something in me. Need . . . ahh, that magic word. It's life giving.

Our spring concert featured selections from *The Sound of Music*. My sister, Patsy, had taken my children to see the movie just days before the accident. Angie had loved the musical score. Now, I could only manage to sing the first words before choking up. Music moves me in the best of times. Now, I wept even more readily. Dr. Ketchum, our conductor, would continue, averting his gaze until I composed myself. At times, I felt unable to hack it. But Angie's belief in me never failed to stir me. I secretly decided my performance would be for her.

During the following weeks, family and friends came and went, letters and cards arrived daily. People mistakenly worry about what to say to the bereaved. Without some profound utterance, they often pass up the opportunity to console altogether. But foremost in my memory are those who were simply there, the ones who wept with us or silently put their arms around us. It didn't offend. Trust me. I appreciated the affectionate comforting. A simple "I'm sorry" went a long way.

Three months later, I was surprised that I was as enthusiastic as everybody else as we took our places on the stage. I sang from my heart. Baritone Jamie Grimsley sang the last selection, and I realized all the mountains and hurdles I had already cleared.

To Each His Own Way

During those early months of sorrow, while Lee buried himself in pastoring, I isolated myself. I found sustenance in talking with God and journalling. Fortunately, my English professor allowed me this grief-focus in my daily compositions. This process became my emotional salvation and healing. On warm days, I would spread a blanket under an oak tree near Angie's grave and write.

One day, Lee hesitantly broached the subject. "Honey, your dad asked me to talk to you. He . . . he's concerned because you spend so much time at Angie's grave and . . . well, I'm concerned, too."

I turned to stare at him. "Why?"

"We love you, sweetheart."

"I know that. But grief is a private thing—personal." I felt the stirring of anger. How dare they . . . ?

I looked him in the eye. "Lee, have I told you how to grieve?"

"No."

"Then, I expect the same respect from you. I can't turn things off like some—just walk away from it. I'm not equipped for denial. I have to work through this in my own way."

Lee didn't tread that area again. One morning, weeks later, I felt him fall heavily across the bed, cradling his head on my bosom. I quickly realized he was weeping.

"What's wrong?" I asked, instantly awake, embracing him.

"I miss her so-o-o," he wailed and sobbed. "I was playing Carpenter music tapes in the car remembering how she used to sing along."

Lee's grief was sporadic and violent while mine flowed like a deep river. Yet, neither surpassed the other. For weeks, months, in predawn hours, we held each other and wept before facing another day. One thing stands out: our being there for each other. No one else could have filled either place.

Pam, pale and wan, beckoned me to her room one evening. "Mama, I know how much you loved Angie." She gazed at me with teary, fearful eyes. "I wish it had been me instead."

I took her in my arms. Angie had been eulogized for weeks. Sibling insecurities have neither rhyme nor reason and, with less provocation than this, could skyrocket. My preoccupation had taken its toll on the oldest Harvey sibling.

While she wept, I gently consoled her. "Pam, my heart has a compartment for each of you children, equal in size and love. My grief for Angie takes nothing from your compartment or David's. Her space with its memories will always be exactly the same. So will yours. So will David's. Can you understand?"

She nodded, hugging me. After that, I focused more on reassuring her and including her in the grieving process. Again, being needed moved me forward.

David, on the other hand, seemed almost detached from the entire drama except for fleeting pensive expressions on his young face. He began disappearing over a sand hill knoll in our backyard and staying until dusk. He carried shovels, wood, sticks, and buckets of water, refusing to stop even when company came. Young friends were beckoned to join him. He wouldn't let me know what transpired, only that it was a "surprise". I didn't expect a seven-year-old to grieve as I had, but I felt, at times, a bit angry at his enthusiasm as he trudged tirelessly over the hill. It didn't seem right some-how, that he ignored Angie's absence. He never mentioned her. Could he truly forget her so quickly?

One day, he rushed into the house, grabbed my hand and tugged me outside, grinning widely. "Come on, Mama. Wait 'til you see." When we topped the knoll, my mouth dropped open. There, before my eyes, was a miniature pond. A crude split-log ramp carried us to its center, where a white banner, meticulously printed in David's neat script, flapped at the top of a pole. It read: ANGIE SHILOH POND.

"Well, Mom, what do you think about it?" He looked up at me.

I was so shocked, I couldn't say a thing at first. Emotions swamped me. Grief, pride, love . . . and shame. How could I have questioned David's love for his sister? I felt like sinking into the marsh and not coming up.

I swallowed hard, groping for words. "It's a precious gesture. Angie would be proud that you did this for her."

Blue eyes turned up to my face. That's when I saw the sorrow in their depths. "She didn't have much of a life, did she?"

"What do you mean?"

"Eleven years isn't long to live, is it? That's why I couldn't do a dime thing. I wanted to do a . . . a dollar thing." He shoved grubby hands in his pockets, looking suddenly like a wise little old man. "I think she knows, Mom."

I nodded, unable to speak, grasping his second-grade logic. Such was his love for his sister. Grief swamped David several more times in following weeks, manifested by illness, listlessness, melancholy, and a compulsion to talk about Angie. We tried to be there for him during such times.

Some folks think it wise not to talk about Angie in our presence. How mistaken they are! My worst dread was that no one would remember Angie. My warmest memories are of those who were so open and encouraged happy memories to flow. Just as urgent is the need, at certain points, to vent grief.

Vividly, I recall talking with a professor. As I spoke, her face suddenly registered horror. "Please," she stopped me mid-sentence, "You don't have to talk about it. I know it must upset you." Her lack of insight shocked me.

I learned then that to be of comfort to the bereaved, sometimes all we need do is listen.

As David's "do something" phase ebbed, Angie's little pond dried up and he moved on to other healing/acceptance stages. For months I allowed the banner and rough-hewn bridge to remain on our yard's deserted back corner. I couldn't bring myself to part with them. Rain faded the letters and the wood began to crumble, but the message remained alive. It comforted me.

Late one afternoon, I stood on the ramp in silence. Then, a bird song penetrated my haze, sweetly lifting me to a plane of peace. I knew in that moment that this gift of David's surpassed all others. I realized this visit to the pond would be my last. If David could let go, so could I, because I realized what David, with a child's simplicity, already knew. In the Lord, we never truly lose our loved ones. I gazed beyond the tall pines into frothy white clouds. "I love you, Angie," I whispered and walked away.

Acceptance

Sadly, the urgency of personal survival can estrange marriage partners. Lee and I shared the same loss but our reactions often differed. Our frailties were as individual as our fingerprints. Neither of us could fathom the other's frustrations. Even now, twenty-odd years later, we are still surprised by the other's perspectives of those days.

We both agree our marriage survived considerable strain. Soon after the accident, we decided to have another child, not to replace Angie, as some well-meaning friends surmised, but to plant seeds of hope. Neither of us foresaw that I would be terribly ill with this pregnancy. My last months found me mostly bed-ridden.

To divert myself from the sickness, I focused on the baby's arrival. Lee realized, belatedly, that I was not there for him emotionally. Physically, he was not there for me, because during the early pre-pain months, hormonal activity catapulted my libido to unprecedented heights while grief plunged Lee's to virtually zero. Neither of us could meet the other's needs of the moment.

Fortunately, Lee and I were grounded in our commitment. On December 20, 1974, an early Christmas gift arrived: a tiny, pink, squalling bundle named Angela Kaye. Angela's gurgles and coos did magic. We found ourselves laughing a bit more often. The transition was not instantaneous, but slowly, time began to heal the awful shock and keen desolation. The family began lounging on Angie's bed to reminisce, replacing sadness with joyful memories.

I remember that six weeks after the accident, Mrs. Cartrette called me. "I just got back the scores of aptitude tests Angie took the day she died. She was a bright little girl, Mrs. Harvey. She'd be so proud to know." We both wept as she went on to read me a letter written by Angie's classmate, a poor black girl named Joanna whom Angie had befriended and often prayed for. The essay was entitled "The Person I Admire Most". Joanna's subject was Angie. It was a glowing account of a friendship borne of mutual love and respect. I was never more proud of my daughter than in that moment.

Epilogue

I know reaching out to others helped heal our wounds. We knew nobody can console like someone who's "been there".

I never take loved ones for granted. I live each day as my last. I have come to see unspoken needs, read inflections in eyes, learn compassion, and be real.

As a parent, I remind myself that I am not omniscient, nor omnipotent. To think otherwise is egomania. Of course, I do my best to protect my loved ones. Yet, the variables that wrest control from all of us are infinite. I realize this truth comforts those such as myself the most, those standing on the "after" side of tragedy.

I am happy to have made it with God's help, one step at a time. I have found something to smile about again.

Like An Eagle Falling
by Jane Lawliss Murphy

David was dead. The months of anxiety, hope, despair, faith, and fear ended on the sunny slope of a country cemetery with red-winged blackbirds darting restlessly among the cedar branches and swallows scissoring great scallops in the silken, cloudless sky.

It was frightening and sad to stand there in all that beauty realizing that love, the strongest and only weapon we have, just isn't enough sometimes, that the shining blade then turns on us making our wound even deeper.

I do not believe in the victory of death, but rather its sting which feels like sulphur in the eye, like a briar across the face.

He died on Mother's Day, May 14. Pentecost Sunday. Pneumonia, a respirator, convulsions, bleeding in the brain, coma. His great, strong athlete's heart that would have served him for a hundred years the doctor said, leapt and bounded on until the sad realization that it was alone . . . all else had dropped out of the dance.

He should have lived to be old, to see his grandchildren and teach them how to ski and climb mountains, carve wood, shoot rapids. Everything about him had the promise of endurance, of a deep, self-renewing core of strength, dependable as oak.

I have been thinking of the time only months before his diagnosis when our sister Barbara and I visited him and Carol one hot week in August, and he took us for an outing in their new powerboat. We motored out in the late afternoon sun from the marina on Lake St. Francis, just over the Canadian border from their home. We had a calm, sultry passage to Cornwall, Ontario, where we tied up at a dock, walked to a restaurant by the shore and had dinner. When we emerged, only the last sliver of the setting sun could be seen above the horizon and the weather had changed ominously. As we left the shelter of Cornwall harbor and headed out into the Seaway toward home, the clouds joined overhead to form a heavy, dark mass that blocked the moon. The air had the metallic smell of an impending storm, and before many minutes passed, we were sitting underneath the hastily zipped boat cover with rain drumming loudly on the taut canvas. The storm became steadily worse. The surface of the water boiled with whitecaps, the wind drove the rain horizontally against the windows. In the pitch of darkness our only visibility came from the finger of headlight beam on our bow and the flashes of lightning by which David grabbed what bearings he could. Part of our passage was in the shipping lanes of the St. Lawrence Seaway, and several times we shared space with huge, hulking freighters and tankers that loomed abruptly out of the darkness, sometimes so close that we were lifted and rocked in their bow waves.

Before long the windshield wipers could not handle the volume of rain.

As we left the Seaway lanes, all around us in the blackness, small wooded islands dotted the river. The waters around many of the islands were treacherous with shoals and rocky outcroppings. In order to see better, David finally had to unzip the cover just over the wheel and stand with his head outside, exposed to the fury of the storm. Very slowly he eased the boat around rocks and between the islands, their clumps of fir trees printing the eye with jagged silhouettes in the flashbulb brilliance of the lightning.

On and on, he drove, the boat nosing this way and that like a large lost animal sniffing its way home. At long last the lights of the marina appeared; we slid through the channel and up to the dock, safe.

I first knew David when I was seventeen and he was a black-haired twenty-one year old courting my older sister. From that time, I saw him in countless situations, always doing something superbly well, whether skiing or building a house, capsizing and righting a kayak, or just twirling the waxed ends of his handlebar moustache after delivering the punch line of a joke at a family gathering.

Nevertheless, as long as I live, I will carry in my mind's eye the memory of that wild night on the water when he stood with the wind whipping at his head, blinking the rain out of his eyes while thunder rumbled and the lightning cracked, guiding the big boat calmly and safely back to the harbor. If ever there were a story that encapsulated someone's character, I believe this incident is the one for him. He never uttered a sharp word or made a clumsy move. He carried on with a clear grasp of the situation, the perils and the requirements. I never felt a moment's fear, though with almost anyone else at the helm the trip would have been harrowing. The dockmaster at the marina, who had watched smiling and shaking his head as we inched up to the dock, commented, "Lucky for you it was him you were out with."

We who knew him and loved him just accepted as a given that he would endure and prevail, ripen and mellow, and in the fullness of time step firmly over the final threshold, the clump of his big ski boots echoing down the halls of heaven, and always the sound of laughter following in his wake.

To see him instead wasted and waxen amid mountains of flowers, his thick, wild curls reduced to wispy remnants by chemotherapy; to see those powerful hands that built three houses, steered canoes through boiling rapids, and set fractured limbs on icy ski slopes (yet were utterly defeated by the fingering of a six-string guitar); to see these hands resting so docilely, one atop the other was wrenching. And to think all this ruin was accomplished by an enemy he couldn't even see, a disease with a name that should be the name of a flower. Petunia. Gardenia. Lobelia. Leukemia. It seemed wrong and nasty and cruel, and it was.

In our back yard there is a large elm tree that lost a branch in a winter storm, and every spring the oval scar weeps and weeps. How long, I wonder, before our family tree heals from this pruning?

A priest friend, acknowledging the shock of losing someone like David, at the height of his powers said to me, "It is difficult enough when someone of great years sickens and dies, but this, this is like an eagle falling out of the sky."

We thought Dave was something wonderful. We loved him with blood-love and we mourn him, our family's "first fruits of them that sleep". Having him in our lives all those years was a kind of wealth. Remembering him, even in the midst of tears, I feel gratitude. How enriched we were to call him brother, to enjoy his vitality and humor and competence for as long as he was with us. We were lucky, so lucky. And blessed.

With my dear widowed sister I mourn him. I will always miss him. And I am learning that in God's good time, the images of sickness and death fade and are being replaced by all the memories I have of him in the fullness of who he was, brimming with life and always in motion. These will be mine to keep, because I believe that just as love conquers a death, so the loving memories of a life overpower the sad images of its ending. I think it is happening on a deep level, a silent, slow healing that uses the energy of "leftover" love to accomplish its good work. Sometimes, playing with his little granddaughters or coming across his laughing face in a photo album, my eyes still fill with tears, and I ache with a sense of loss and sadness—for what he suffered, for my sister, for her daughter and those tiny granddaughters he would have loved so much, for the sheer pain of being human.

There are also times when I picture David slaloming with his incredible strength and grace down a sparkling slope in heaven's snowy Adirondacks, angels lining both sides of the trail, cheering him on, and I find myself smiling.

A Place
by Margaret Ryan

The front door no longer wears the scabby green paint. Sanded down and stained its original oak, it looks impressive surrounded by the house's new pale cream paint. 98 Bayview Avenue is definitely yuppified—no longer a cheap rental in the working class neighborhood of twenty-five years ago.

My oldest son Mark, a film maker from Boston, and I have returned to the summer rental in Salem, Massachusetts, we thought we'd never want to see again. Curiosity and the softening patina of time have led us back.

The old tree which grew in the oceanside backyard is gone, probably lightening the interior of the upstairs, but I miss it.

Youngsters running along the beach front behind the house are whooping happily. The years fade, merge, and there we all are again—the pretty young family from Vermont. We've come to this beach house because Frank, my husband, had earned a grant to study at Harvard for six weeks. He wanted his family with him, so we'd left our comfortable home in St. Johnsbury and settled in to the cracked linoleum, shabby walls, and hidden dangers of this summer residence.

Today's youngsters become my young sons of a quarter century ago, Mark and Christopher, ages seven and five. Having borrowed my bright red Martex bath towels, they run along the beach playing Superman, the towels streaming behind them. They have been told about Bumby, their little brother, but the reality as yet has not sunk in. Inside, I lie on the worn sofa. Frank sits on the floor, holding my hand. It is the first time I have seen my husband weep.

Four days earlier, our baby son was electrocuted in a freak accident. During those four days our curly haired, blue eyed eighteen-month-old baby fought valiantly for his life in the intensive care unit of Salem Memorial Hospital. Each day Frank and I sat wordlessly in the waiting room, knowing that Dr. Paley would eventually inform us that Bumby had come out of the coma. We were allowed to visit our child only briefly. With each visit I would silently whisper, "Dear God, please don't let them cut into him anymore." Because his veins were so tiny, his pretty little arms and legs were now crisscrossed with black thread. Incisions had to be made for the intravenous feedings and then sewn up again. Oxygen tubes were inserted into the small, retroussé nose. The interns, inured to tragedy, silently went about their work. The nurses, their eyes filled with compassion, exclaimed over Bumby's long, sweeping, dark lashes and the gorgeous curls surrounding his infant head.

On the evening of the third day of our vigil, the nurses greeted us with undisguised excitement.

"Baby Anthony has opened his big blue eyes and actually looked at us."

When we reached his crib, we could scarcely believe what we were seeing. Gone were the tubes from his nostrils, as were the intravenous wires from his veins. For the first time, he had been fed orally and still knew how to swallow.

Smilingly, Dr. Paley stepped forward.

"The signs are all hopeful. It's only a matter of time, now."

We went home and danced in the kitchen with Mark and Christopher. Later we took the little boys out to the Salem Willows Ice Cream Parlour for banana splits. It was the happiest day in all our lives.

Early the next morning came the phone call.

"Mrs. Ryan?"

"Yes."

"This is Dr. Paley. Your son, Anthony David Ryan, expired at 4:04 AM. Please come to the hospital and pick up his belongings."

Bumby, my beautiful boy, was gone and life was changed forever.

The present comes back into focus. My son and I are sitting on the rocks. We are discussing the final phone call on that most terrible of days twenty five years ago. It was the funeral director asking permission for an open coffin wake. He had found white silk knee socks, baby-sized, so that the incisions wouldn't show. Our answer was *No*.

Mark holds my hand just as his deceased father did so many years ago. We are wordless, but in the clarity of that gesture, we both understand. He forgives me for losing my *joie de vivre* and withdrawing into despair. I understand the pain he feels for not ever having been able to live up to the image of his dead brother.

The house does not look threatening. The family within knows nothing of its tragedy.

A seagull rises from the water with timeless grace.

The Mourning's Over
by Bob Ross

As I stood staring at my mother's grave, I was either feeling sorry for myself or a strange emotional disorder possessed me. My life seemed futile and empty; I didn't think I could keep it together. My mother had been dead for thirty-two years, but her spirit had always been with me. Maybe that's what kept me going. Her love, laughter, and joy made her dear to everyone. Her passion for life was so positive that no matter how dismal the situation she remained upbeat. The cancer had spread through her entire body until there was nothing but skin and bones. Yet, her wonderful beaming smile was always there.

Mary Teresa Ross, died on April 21, 1954, at the young age of forty-two. How could God take this lovely lady? I thought for sure the last operation of over ten hours would make her well again. That some miracle would happen.

Why was I pulled to her grave on this warm Sunday morning in 1986? I didn't realize it at the time, but it was my birthday. But that wasn't the reason. I desperately needed someone to talk to, someone who loved me unconditionally. I was deeply upset after leaving my dying Uncle Stan, Mom's brother and confidant. Within three weeks, he too would be dead.

For the past six weeks, I had been visiting with my uncle at his request and trying to somehow comfort him. His condition had not improved, and the prostate cancer was eating away at him. At the age of seventy-seven, he would join his parents, wife, brother, sisters, and nephew at this Catholic cemetery in Cleveland, Ohio. The very last of his generation, and my last link with the only family I knew. This was a tightly knit Polish family that never divulged their many secrets. Today, that family would be called dysfunctional.

On this particular morning, I knew in my heart that I would never see my uncle alive again. I hugged him one last time, kissed his cheek, and drove off. A few miles away, I was shaking so much I had to stop driving. I started to cry and couldn't stop. What would I do without him? Who could I call upon? He was more of a father to me than my real father. Whatever the reason, I felt a deep sense of loss.

After picking up a six-pack of beer, I headed for my old neighborhood.

Instead, I found myself driving directly to Calvary Cemetery. It was very quiet and empty. Everyone was still at church. I opened a can of beer and poured some on the grave for Mom, then opened another for myself. For the next three hours we shared that six-pack, as I kept up a dialog of probably incoherent chatter, being careful not to pour beer where my father's ashes were buried. He lived and died an alcoholic, and I didn't want to encourage him now. Only finding a lost letter of my mother's love for him forced me to insert those ashes in her grave.

When I was a little boy, my mother would take me by street car to this very cemetery. We would visit her mother's grave and, like we were on a picnic, stay for hours. She had great respect for her mother, and I even named my dog in her honor. Babcia, is grandmother in Polish, but as a kid I lisped it as Buzzie.

Buzzie was with me and roaming over the hillside of graves, while I was going through this emotional turmoil. Whether the beer was getting to me or the sadness of losing my uncle triggered this confusing feeling, I didn't know.

I was ranting and raving about the injustice of death, and why I didn't do more to help my mother. Why didn't I make her life easier? Why was I so selfish? My anger against my father took over, and I blamed him for her illness and for being a rotten husband and father. Or maybe it was my fault that he was a drunk. I told her how much I loved her and thought about her everyday. How I wanted her to be proud of me, when I wasn't even proud of myself. I failed her in so many ways, and that guilt made me sick.

Morbid thoughts consumed me. Did I inherit a mental illness from my other uncle who officially was considered incompetent? Were my communication skills so warped that my Aunt Stella (Mom's sister) who helped raise me, disowned me after my mother's death? After years of detective work, I realized she held me responsible for not getting the ownership of the house my parents, myself, and my aunt lived in. I was completely unaware of the actions my father took in obtaining that house. At her funeral, I went through a gut-wrenching grief period.

My non-existent relationship with my father continued long after my mother's death. As little I knew about my mother's family, there was absolutely nothing known about my father's. He lied about his family, his birth, his age, and denied he was an alcoholic. Twenty-six years after my mother's death, he was dead from a lifetime of alcohol abuse. I was deeply saddened that other than my uncle and myself, not one soul attended his funeral.

As I finished my last beer, my self-esteem was so low that if another grave was open I would have crawled in it. With my body trembling and tears in my eyes, I picked up the empty beer cans and placed one at the head of Mom's grave. I asked the beautiful willow tree to watch over her. I kissed and blessed the weathered stone, and Buzzie and I left the cemetery.

Driving across country to California, where I began this trip, didn't soothe my grief or answer any questions. Why was the death of my mother so fresh in my mind after over thirty years? With my uncle, those six weeks were a blessing and I was prepared to make peace and release him. These other deaths were not resolved and kept gnawing at me.

Looking for cures of various disorders, I had gone through private and group therapy, self-esteem and motivational courses. No amount of prayer helped, or maybe I wasn't praying the right way. I studied Science of Mind and learned a new affirmative way to pray, rather than begging, which they call a Spiritual Treatment. This study proved beneficial and brought me closer to God and a calmer inner peace.

It wasn't until early 1990 that I was finally able to understand these feelings. While watching a television interview, I heard the award winning author William Styron discuss at length his new book, *Darkness Visible*. It was about the depressive illness he suffered. I was shocked to hear the exact symptoms of madness I was experiencing. I had experienced what he described as incomplete mourning after the death of my mother. I had never heard or read that phrase before, and going through his book was a spiritual awakening.

Yes, I too was unable to achieve the catharsis of grief, and in my later years carried with me the burden of rage, guilt, and sorrow. The loss of my self-esteem and self-reliance, and dreading the loss of all things, all people, and the fear of abandonment was part of me.

William Styron also used alcohol as a shield against anxiety, as I certainly did in my later years. Which brings me to the day of viewing my mother's body. If my father was handling his anxiety by drinking, it didn't make sense. He always drank, no matter the situation. I know now what a terrible disease he had; I've been there. I also forgive him for not telling me the absolute truth about how serious my mother's illness was.

Above all, finally my mourning is now complete, and I now realize a diseased body can only tolerate so much. At best, if Mom had survived, she may have been an invalid and that would have been the worst situation. My joy is in having known her and how proud I am to be her son. Unfortunately her health did not allow other children.

Although she'll never pass this way again, her joyful spirit remains to those that shared her company.

Just Give It Time
by Pat Goehe

It was late May. My daughter and I were moving from one condo to another within the same complex. My daughter insisted at the last minute that we do it a week earlier. As we hustled back and forth with the help of friends, she told me there was a phone message from my sister-in-law, who only called me when there was a problem with my parents. The message was brief. "Mom is back in the hospital."

Never trusting word-of-mouth information, I hurriedly changed clothes and headed to the hospital which was in my home town some twenty-five miles away. Mom had been in and out of the hospital several times during the year. She had an enlarged heart. My oldest sister, who had been a nurse, told me months earlier that Mom was dying. My sister in Indiana also believed this to be true. She hadn't been home for some time, but she called every Saturday. Dad had said during the last six months that Mom was a sick girl.

When I saw my mother, one of the first things she said to me was that the doctor told her he wouldn't do extraordinary things. I realized she was telling me that she was dying and with dignity. She didn't have a living will, but I had spent enough time with her over the last five years to know she was against machines.

Later, I went to find the doctor at the Nurses' Station. I told him I wanted to be with her during the last hours. I assured him I had training with Elisabeth Kubler-Ross, only to find that some physicians aren't impressed.

Returning home that evening, I made my colleagues aware of the situation. I knew they would be cooperative. My daughter and I worked out how we would visit. My son, some three thousand miles away, wanted to know if he should come home. Grandma wouldn't want him to, I told him, but he should call her. He was very special to her, and to this day, he tells me he should have come.

It wasn't long before the siblings began arriving. While parents say they have no favorites, children usually believe otherwise. Since the numerous generations of children usually visited in early evening, I would try to get there at noon and spend time with her. People were visiting in groups at the same time. I suggested we try to arrange shifts for people so as to have someone there all of the time.

Mom would try to talk, but it was obvious she was having difficulty breathing. Each time, I would tell her just to rest. I just wanted to be there with her. On occasions, probably when they started giving her more morphine, she perspired and I would wipe her forehead. Around 2:00 PM, my oldest sister would bring Dad. He would sit in the chair at the end of the bed. He and Mom would just look at each other. No words were spoken, yet a whole lifetime of words were there between them.

When next I saw the doctor, he told me her kidneys were starting to fail. They were trying an alternative medicine but he wasn't certain if it would work. I reminded him that I wanted to be with her. He told me it was still premature.

The next morning while I was teaching, my sisters decided to look for something for Mom to be buried in. They had selected a deep rose dress she had worn to one of the grandchildren's weddings. I told them I agreed with their choice, but, unless it had been cleaned, there was a spot that would be visible. I called my daughter and told her to make arrangements with the cleaner. I felt time was running out.

My sisters met me at the hospital and told me they had talked with the doctors involved, and they thought it was not necessary for anyone to stay through the night. They were hoping the new medicine would slow down the kidney deterioration.

Wanting to visit, I went into Mom's room briefly. The nurse soon came and asked us to leave so she could adjust the catheter. By the time she came out and told us we could go in, all the children were there. I decided not to go in because there were just so many people.

Sitting in the hallway, I found myself comforting the many nieces.

My sister asked if I'd drive Dad home so that she and her husband could go. Of course I would. It was late.

Later on, I watched Dad and Mom in the room staring at each other to the point I thought I would lose it. Seeing that Mom was exhausted, I told Dad we had better go. He tried to kiss her good night. "I always do that," he told the attending nurse. Mom, filled with morphine, turned away and curled up. I guided Dad out.

When we got home, my sister suggested we go out for some ice cream. On the way back, my car started acting up. I didn't like the sound of it and decided I would stay in Dad's home that night.

I put a pillow and quilt on the couch in the living room. At first I was very restless. Then the day's stress took over and caused me to fall asleep. Shortly before midnight I woke up. Something drew me to the window—a sound, a light, something. Fifteen minutes later there was a knock on the door. I looked out and saw my brother and sister; I knew what had happened. Mom had died shortly before midnight.

We went to the hospital, and what I discovered was that if anyone has never seen a dead body, and especially that of a parent, it's a shock. We, however, set about making the necessary plans.

After the others had left, my sister was even more upset. "You wanted to stay with her, Pat, and I told you it wasn't necessary. How can you ever forgive me?" I tried to reassure her that it was the doctor who said it was not necessary. The truth was, I didn't blame her or the doctor, but I wondered if I could ever forgive myself.

Mom and Dad were very devout Catholics who daily lived the religious life and didn't just "do Sundays". I was always concerned that when they died the current priest, whoever that might be, wouldn't do justice to the eulogy. How could a young new priest, new to the town, know all the things Mom and Dad had done through the years? This was one thing I needn't have worried about. In the few years he had been in the community, Father George obviously saw what kind of woman Mom was.

I tried for months to resolve a feeling of guilt that I hadn't been there when she needed me. I would tell myself that Mom, being who she was, wouldn't want us to have to be with her. Certainly she was headed for heaven. We all knew that. "And there were others to be taken care of," I told myself when I was outside consoling the nieces. I tried everything. Many trips to the grave didn't help. I would just cry and tell her I was so sorry that I hadn't been with her. What kept coming back to me was that all my life I was doing for others—when would I ever do for me? Did my mother have to die alone for this message to finally get through to me? What good did all my training do if I missed the moment? Why did I defer to the grandchildren and great-grandchildren? Why, why, why?

In the months that followed I chastised myself over and over. By this time my brother-in-law was back in the hospital. I spent time there with my sister. She would bring up again that she had told me not to stay when Mom died. I kept reassuring her that I didn't blame her. Matter of fact, I was beginning to forgive myself. Mom had certainly forgiven me. I felt the whole affair had taught me some very valuable lessons. I had learned that taking care of myself was what I needed to do.

I remembered suppressing my anger when my daughter had insisted we move a week early. Now I wondered whether greater forces had been working. Had we waited, there was no way we could have moved. Mom died the day we had to be out of the condo. And why did my car act up that night? What was the sound, the light that made me go to the window shortly before midnight? The puzzle was not solved. Little did I know how all of these things would manifest.

None of us expected Dad would live long after Mom's death. Happily married, still very much in love after so many years, her death as would be expected devastated him. She had been a traditional housewife. Basic things like cooking a meal were foreign to him. For a short time after her death, his children and grandchildren brought meals to him. Later, as they became busy with their own lives, my oldest sister arranged for "Meals on Wheels". He would tell me how good they were, but I knew it wasn't working.

After a year, a widower friend of Dad's started coming in daily to cook and drive him around. Both men needed companionship. With Mom gone there seemed to be little communication in the family. What came to pass was one brother paying the bills and handling house repairs, and such; he was the business end. My sister took over as a combined "get him to the doctor when he needs to go, wash his clothes, get someone in to clean the house" person. I was helping my daughter, a single parent, to raise her children which limited my availability. I was there, however, to help when my sister would need to get away and visit her children. My sister in Indiana had her hands full with her husband and lived in guilt that she couldn't help.

The widower told me something I already knew. Dad's emotional needs were not being met. I had lived with Mom and Dad for almost a year when I was on a sabbatical leave. While I traveled a great deal, I still was present enough to witness their daily rituals.

Mom rose early. She put the coffee on, brought in the morning paper, made herself two pieces of toast, and then sat down with her coffee and paper. Dad, the original Rip Van Winkle, would sleep later. When she heard him stir, she'd prepare his breakfast. Following breakfast, he'd start his list for the day—what Mom referred to as his "bumming" list. Groceries to purchase, friends to visit, fishing, and other errands. Mom would spend the morning chatting with her friends by phone until it was time to begin dinner. Of German descent, the main meal was mid-day which meant anytime from noon to 2:00 PM depending when Dad returned.

After dinner, Dad smoked a cigar and took a nap. Mom wrote letters, sent birthday cards, and at times took a small snooze herself. "Supper" would be at 5:00 PM or so. They would share the days events and news, then it was time for Vanna and "Wheel of Fortune". Dad loved Vanna.

Mealtimes and early evenings were Dad's loneliest times. The widower was there from about 8:00 in the morning to after lunch. I tried, when I could, to join them for lunch which seemed to please Dad and the widower.

During the week, in the winter evenings, Dad was the most lonely. I took it upon myself to spend time with him at least once a week, sometimes more. He expressed a need to engage in what the gerontologists would call "life review". More than once I silently thanked one of my senior colleagues who had dragged me screaming into that area.

In addition to listening to him tell stories from his life as a youth and young man, I found ways to weave things into our little evening talks. I'd tell him things I thought. He'd say, "Is that what you believe?" I'd say, "Sure." I'd remind him how many times he and Mom had to decide what house they'd go to for a holiday dinner, always wanting to be fair. I told him the way I saw it was that in death one could be at all those dinners and other special events. I felt we were making some headway in these discussions. And I knew he appreciated me coming down on those lonely evenings.

In late July he had driven two blocks to the ball field to see the kids play.

He stepped out of the car and fell back. A man drove him to my brother's home. Dad had to stay in his house for a month and received physical therapy three times a week. He hated this. Finally, we agreed that the widower could drive him around a bit.

There was a difference in my Dad. He seemed to be preoccupied. My daughter came down and cleaned his garage. When she realized he was going to go out and weed the rose garden, she did that too. He was pleased, but he was still distant.

My sister was due for another trip to one of her children's homes. I picked up "Dad duty". The first morning I arrived, Dad was distressed because he had mislaid his wallet. I told him I would find it and that he should go "bumming" with his friend. They left.

I found Dad's wallet and put it in the desk drawer where he usually kept it. I began gathering the wash when the phone rang. It was my brother saying the widower had come to his office with Dad. Something was wrong. I should meet him at the local hospital's emergency ward.

Dad had suffered a stroke. The grandchildren and great grandchildren started their visits again. My brother usually checked in the early morning, as did my daughter and some of Dad's friends. I came mid-day and remained late into the evening. The difference between Dad's stay in the hospital and my Mom's was that Mom was articulate to the very end. Dad talked gibberish the second day, then went into a form of coma.

It was obvious Dad would not last long. In the evenings after others left, I would sit with him. Whenever he opened his eyes, I would take his hand, bend as close as I could to his ear and tell him, "It's Pat, Dad. I'm here. You're not alone." He would squeeze my hand.

My son kept calling telling me to tell Grandpa to hold on because he was coming. I tried to explain to him that death didn't quite work that way. I'm certain they would say it was my own paranoia, but I began to feel that one or two of my nieces were uncomfortable with my being there so much. I started making a point to get coffee or a bite to eat when I knew they were visiting. Later, I'd continue my vigil next to his bed.

On what was to be his last night, I decided to stay most of the night. I continued to hold his hand and tell him I was there whenever he opened his eyes. A feeding tube had been placed in his stomach that day, a trauma that I felt was not needed and definitely bothered him. About 3:00 AM he opened his eyes and tried to pull himself up. I rushed over, and before I could say anything, he looked directly at me. With every ounce of effort he could muster to speak, he said, "Mom". I told him, "Yes, Daddy. She's coming for you. Everything will be okay." He smiled and laid back down.

Several hours later, I decided to go home, shower and come back. Once there I took care of some last minute things when the phone rang. It was my brother telling me Dad was close to death. He wouldn't last long. Somehow I knew Dad had already died, but I had been there with him when I needed to be.

My sister from Indiana was going to come to the funeral no matter what, but she didn't want to tell her husband of Dad's death. One of her daughter's had figured out a covering plan. It turned out not to be necessary. Her husband died within twelve hours of Dad's death. It was my opinion that Dad decided to relieve my brother-in-law's intense suffering and take him along on this journey.

There are so many things that I could write about these experiences. I have learned so much. I've chosen to leave out the negativity and dark side of events. Some I continue to deal with. I suspect several of my siblings wrestle with their own demons as well.

My mom had a saying, "Just give it time." She said this about everything. And she was right. Just give it time. At long last, I have found peace. I came to learn "in time" that my not being with Mom her last night gave me additional impetus to be with Dad, and that's what she would have wanted.

Grief Postponed
by Cheri Lynn Hunter

More than eight years have passed since my grandmother died, and up until a very short time ago, I could not let go of her and get on with my life. I have spent the last eight years holding onto her anyway I could, not wanting to live my own life, just reliving my life with my grandmother.

When my grandmother died I was given one week to move out of her house, so right away I had to put aside my grieving to find a new place to live. Next, the institution my grandmother had put her money in went bankrupt, which left me with no inheritance and a lot of medical bills to pay.

Once again, I put off grieving to take care of the problem at hand. To make a long, painful story short, I have spent the last eight years putting off grieving to take care of problem after problem. I think that, unconsciously, I believed that as long as I didn't grieve for my grandmother she was somehow still with me.

It has taken me eight painful years to even begin the path of healing. I have spent these past years holding on to a memory. I have not married. I have not had children. All of my relationships, both intimate and friendships, have been ruined by my inability to accept my grandmother's death. I knew she was gone, but I was unable to get on with my life because in my heart I wanted to be with her—I wanted to be dead too.

I have spent thousands of dollars on medications, have seen a dozen different therapists, counselors, psychologists and psychiatrists, have studied dozens of books, magazine articles and video tapes, all in search of putting a stop to the overwhelming depression which threatened to actually put me in the same place as my grandmother.

In some way I have always known that my self-destructiveness and ever-worsening depression was linked to my grandmother's death, but the key to turning my life around always seemed just out of my reach. That is, until about a month ago. My depression had reached it's strongest point: I saw no reason to go on anymore; no job, no family, no friends, nothing to live for. I began preparing for my own death. I wrote letters instructing others what to do after my death, made sure that all of my legal and financial affairs were in order, then went so far as to prepare everything for when my body would ultimately be found.

Someone was watching over me that night because doing all of that preparation tired me out, so I decided to lay down and rest for just a little while. When I awoke, it was morning and my mood was not as desperate as it had been the night before. I know that I came really close that night to ending my own life. My obsession of not wanting to live without my grandmother almost became a reality.

I scared myself that night, but I began regaining control of my life by finally grieving for my grandmother. I realized I could face all of the hardships in my life and that I had enough strength and courage to believe in myself and not take my life. I can't explain why everything became so clear to me that day, but I do know that my life, at last, had started to come together.

Now I know grieving does not always come naturally. In most cases of loss, there are always things that need to be taken care of such as financial matters and the funeral itself, and, as in my case, the added stress of unforeseen problems.

I can't emphasize enough how important it is to allow the time needed to grieve. The problems and pressures that accompany loss should not take precedence over emotional and physical well-being. I made the mistake of thinking that by putting off grieving that I could hang on to my beloved grandmother. After years of experience and pain, I learned it didn't work. I discovered that when death occurs our loved ones move on and so should we.

CHAPTER 12

REACHING OUT TO GOD AND SPIRITUALITY

The role of faith is shown to be helpful and sustaining during the grieving process.

Death Is Not An Ending
by Neale Donald Walsch

This piece is adapted from a letter previously published in Conversations, *the newsletter of ReCreation:PMB #1150, 1257 Siskiyou Blvd., Ashland, OR 97520*

I am often asked questions by people who are dealing with the loss of loved ones. As they try to find meaning and answers, among their concerns is a wish to know if their departed loved ones are all right. They look for and want signs that the beloved ones are happy and loved wherever they are.

In my desire to comfort these individuals in their sadness, I have shared my understanding that their loved ones could not be in a better place or happier in any way because they are being held and embraced and loved by father/mother God. Their loved ones are blessed beings, as are we all, who came to experience exactly what they experienced and then moved on with their continuing experiences of Life Forever. The souls of those who played significant life roles are linked forever and have been from the beginning of time, seeing each other again and again and again. I suggest that those in mourning be at peace and celebrate knowing that the roles they played with

the departed were perfectly crafted to allow each of them to remember exactly what they needed to know in order to grow and evolve and become
more of Who They Really Are.

Everything is perfect in God's world, and nothing happens without purpose or meaning.

I say softly to them that it is not beneficial to idle away their time
"wanting" a sign from their loved ones that they are all right, wanting some
sort of contact with or from them. By doing so, they may create consterna-
tion on the loved one's side if they see that for some reason the living are
unable to hear what they are already trying to tell them through all manner of
means.

I suggest that they not get caught up in this desire and turn it into a
"need", but rather, "let go and let God". I suggest that they allow God to
work wonders in their lives regarding all of this. Wonders of healing, wonders of wisdom, wonders of love. I suggest that they pray to God not to hear
from the loved ones, but that their loved ones might hear from them of their
love, their everlasting devotion, and of their willingness to let the love ones
go, to release them from the karmic pull of their own desires, that they may
fly high and far, and move on with their next grand adventures, not needing
any more to worry about the ones they left. I urge them to tell the departed
ones that they are all right and that they are going to "make it". This is what
the departed wish to hear. Then they can be fully free. The departed will
come to the living often. In feelings, the living will perceive their lost loved
ones; in their minds and dreams, they will see them; and in their memories,
they will hear their words.

Then, having released any need for the loved ones to "stick around", I
propose that the living move on with their lives in the fullest measure, for
they have others yet to love, others yet to know, and others yet to heal of
their own sorrows. The world awaits their continuing giving of their gift of
themselves. It would be a shame for them to station themselves too deep in
grief that others might not celebrate them.

God's great gift to all of us is This Moment Now. We must use it to
create and to live the grandest version of the greatest vision that we ever had
about ourselves. And, rather than feel ongoing sorrow at our loved one's
departure, we can look to see and choose to experience always the gifts
which our loved ones brought to us and the wonder of their continuing

presence in our lives forever. For their gifts will be present in us every time we give love unconditionally to another. We will do so in their name and in ours. For we are all One.

Dealing With Death
by Kim Harcarik

I've had the unpleasant experience of dealing with death in several different situations. My two-and-a-half year old daughter was killed in 1991, my father died of health problems in 1993, and I had a miscarriage in 1994.

Each of these losses brings out different feelings and different ways of coping.

In dealing with a miscarriage, I grieved what never will be. It is impossible to pretend it never happened. During the time I would have been pregnant, I resented the normal life I was leading. Since I was only three weeks along, not many people knew of the pregnancy.

I wanted to shout to the world, "Hey everybody, I was pregnant and now my child is dead."

The due date came and went with no response from anyone, except in my heart. I knew it would have been difficult handling a newborn, an eighteen-month old daughter, and my older son; however, that didn't matter. I believe, without a shadow of a doubt, that my tiny baby was born healthy in God's heavenly Kingdom.

My father's death brought relief and thankfulness. My father was an active man throughout his life. His hobbies were hunting, fishing, gardening, and auto mechanics. His career was building and moving houses. When he was younger he farmed and drove eighteen-wheelers cross country.

At a young age my dad developed ulcers, and in 1966 he was told he had emphysema. At fifty-six years of age, he was forced to quit smoking. This isn't an easy task at any age, but he struggled through and succeeded. After a few years he needed oxygen several times a day. This increased until he was hooked up to an oxygen machine twenty-four hours a day. He also developed heart problems and his health steadily declined with age. The last two weeks of his life he was bedridden and could digest only baby food.

His mind was clear, and he said to me, "I will miss you, your kids, and your ma, but I am tired. I want to go home."

The last few days of his life in the hospital were spent crying out to God, "Please take me home. Why won't you take me home? Don't you want me?"

God took him home shortly after midnight on March 18, 1993, just five days after my parents had their sixtieth wedding anniversary.

I miss my father, but it would be selfish of me to want him back. He received his wish which was to go home.

Regret is something that always surfaces after someone dies. My dad was not the easiest person to talk to, and I regret not talking openly, sharing my feelings, and having him reveal what was in his heart to me. I desperately wanted to call him those last days and say, "I heard you're dying. Congratulations! You'll soon be in the Kingdom. I'm so happy for you. Would you do your daughter a favor? Please stop in Colorado. I would love to join you."

I've heard it said that when you lose your parents you lose your past; when you lose your spouse you lose your present; and when you lose a child you lose the future. How true that is.

I can't think of anything more painful than death of a child. My daughter was murdered at the age of two-and-a-half. There wasn't any warning—no time for good-byes. No matter what the cause of death is, however, the result is the same.

My initial reaction was shock. I couldn't believe she was dead. Even after seeing her, going through the funeral process, and cleaning out her room. I felt I was in a constant daze, and I kept waiting to wake up from my nightmare. There were several hours of questioning by the police.

My second dose of shock came when the police informed me a close friend of mine confessed to punching her in the stomach, causing her to bleed to death internally. This time my shock came out in screams. I didn't think I could handle any more. For months afterward, I had to constantly remind myself what happened and how it happened.

This, of course, tied in with another strong reaction of denial. I couldn't and didn't want to accept her death or the way it happened. My denial was loud and clear through a reoccurring dream I had approximately three months later. It was the Christmas season, and in my dream she wasn't dead, but kidnapped. I would hear the doorbell, run downstairs, open the door, and there she would be. It was the best Christmas present ever, and then I would wake up. My son and I had to accept the loss of what was, what is, and that what could have been will never be.

I wanted things to get back to normal again. She was an important part of my heart, and part of my heart was missing. I would never be whole again, and I needed to come to the point of acceptance.

I felt as if the very core of my being had been ripped from my body. There was a pit in the bottom of my stomach that wouldn't go away. I cried oceans of tears almost continuously. I would take sleeping pills to sleep, and then I would wake up early from the nightmares. I was taught to persistently pray for the things you really want to receive. My nightly prayer, for months, was death.

God's response was "No."

I drilled the "what if" questions into the ground. What if I hadn't trusted this person? What if I hadn't gone to work that day? What if it had been me, not her? What if I hadn't divorced my husband? What if she hadn't been born? What if I wouldn't have moved to a big city? All the way back to what if I hadn't been born?

Obviously this didn't help, but only brought tormenting guilt. Forgiving oneself for wrong doing can be tougher than forgiving others. I know I loved her greatly and I made a mistake in how I cared for her. Many single parents are forced to let others care for their children when they don't want to. My choice would have been to stay home with my children, but I also wanted to provide them with food and a home in an honorable way. I learned that if I went to God with Godly sorrow, begging Him to forgive me, He would. I know He has and I believe Stephanie has too. I knew that unless I was able to forgive myself, through the power of the Holy Spirit, guilt would eat me alive.

The loneliness drove me crazy at times. Most people look forward to the weekends, but I dreaded them. The weekends when my son was with his dad were the loneliest. Three day weekends were horrible. At one time I treasured space and quiet, but during those weekends the quiet haunted me.

I needed to decide whether I would be a bitter, angry person seeking revenge for the rest of my life, or if I would choose to deal with my feelings effectively. I didn't want to be angry and bitter, as I had observed other people responding to their grief. In dealing with my anger towards the guilty party, I searched the Scriptures. Forgiveness doesn't happen overnight and it does not take away the pain or excuse the act. It did, however, help me to cope, begin to heal, and focus on living again.

Initially, a grief support group was extremely helpful in my realizing that I wasn't alone. It suggested ways in dealing with grief, in finding new ways of spending those empty hours, and it established a network of relationships with people who really did understand because they had been there.

I believe the expression "hell on earth" was written by a bereaved parent. There isn't any other way to describe the pain. Losing children makes people strong or it kills them. Healing is a series of small steps, two forward and one backward. It seems so slow at times.

Living with the loss each day isn't always easy. For me, time doesn't really heal the wounds. It does, however, make the wounds easier to live with. Nor does it mean there aren't days that the pain and nightmares don't come back to haunt me.

Crying out to God, and developing a relationship with Him has been the most helpful of all. He has provided me with answers to most of my questions about Why? What if? How come? He has given me an overall peace in my heart.

The Last Embrace
by Paul Handermann

Four weeks ago today my daughter died. Four weeks ago at this time, 3:00 PM until 5:00 PM, I held in my arms her limp body with more tubes coming out of her than I can even recall now. This little body, that was on the trampoline bouncing and laughing with me just two days prior, now had bruises on her arms from all the needle shots. Her hair had been mostly shaven because they needed to put a probe in her brain to monitor the swelling. She had three needle sticks in each thigh from the failed C line they had tried to put in. The C line was in her chest and stitched to stay in place. It took two nurses five minutes to juggle all the wires just for me to hold her. I was afraid to hold her at first because I knew she was already gone, but I was glad that I did, knowing that this was the last time I was going to hold my very own little girl. I kept thinking how I was her daddy and she looked to me for protection and I failed her. I wanted to go to heaven with her to make sure she wasn't scared on her way there and she knew for certain that every-thing was going to be all right. I trust God. God doesn't make mistakes. But I sure would have appreciated if he would have let me have Kayla for longer. Still, I thank Him for the three years I had the privilege of being her daddy. A single father, I had Kayla Thursday night until Sunday afternoon. It was an incredible feeling to know, while she was with me, I was her sole caretaker.

I could never have imagined in my life what missing someone so desper-ately was like. I am pretty sure I could never put in words how I miss Kayla. When I go sit in her room and see all the teddy bears she used to hold, or the toys that she used to play with, or if I smell her blanket which still has her scent on it, my heart feels like it wants to stop beating so I can go see her again. Something has been taken away from me that I know cannot be re-placed. No one on this earth, including her own mother, knows the love that Kayla and I shared. No one will ever understand. No matter how long I talk about it, no matter what I say. It is a lonely feeling. My chest hurts even writing these words because I miss her with my whole being.

God has blessed me so much. He has taught me so much through the pain in my life. I find great comfort in knowing that I do not have to under-stand why Kayla was taken away from me so early. Because I do not under-stand. I do not understand why so many people are allowed to keep their daughters. I was not allowed to keep my only one. When I look at her picture and realize I won't hold her again in this life I do not understand the purpose it served to end Kayla's life. She was so incredibly special to me, and she gave so much love to everyone she came in contact with.

She affected many people's lives in such a positive way. If a person is judged by how many people love them, then Kayla would be judged one of the greatest. Those of us who were blessed to have spent some time with her know she showed and gave us more love than she ever took. Kayla's heart was so gentle and her favorite thing was to be held while she watched Barney or Pooh Bear. If you left the room, she would follow, usually within minutes.

Kayla was not supposed to have a normal life because of her illness. With few exceptions, however, she did have a normal life. That was Jesus' compassion. She was special from the beginning and not just because of her disease. Many people knew about it and probably thought Kayla must have been a hard child to raise. Nothing could be further from the truth. Kayla was a gift in every aspect of the word and had a warm heart for everyone.

She loved animals and I think she would have worked at a zoo when she grew up. So much love came out of her little body, the same body that had to fight many times to stay in our world, until Jesus called her back.

I thought I knew everything there was to know about love, or that I was going to know, but Kayla taught me more. She taught me love has a depth I didn't know existed. I realize there must be an even deeper love that Jesus has for Kayla, and for all of us as well.

The outpouring of love that I witnessed at the layout, the funeral, and the Memorial Mass was a symbol for me of the love that Kayla and Jesus had provided in my life. How could I ever question God for showing and giving me a love deeper than the one I knew existed. I wish I did not have to "walk through this storm" and I wish I had Kayla back to hold again, to play with again. I wish I could watch her videos with her again and tuck her in at night again. But it is not my plan that is perfect. It is not my wishes that will allow Kayla and me to be in heaven together. It is God's grace that will do that and I must allow His grace into my life, to lead me, even if it is through a storm.

The Gaining Of Faith Through Grief
by PC Denver

Throughout our lifetime together, my uncle, the man who had been both father and mother to me, and I conversed rather often on the eeriness of death. We spent many complacent evenings together, envisioning what horrors the body of a certain person whom we learned recently had expired may or may not feel as it lay in wait overnight, cold and rigid, before heading to its inevitable "six-foot under" destination. We even taxed ourselves over what stage of decomposition the corpse may have reached. We talked about death and dying so much that we agreed that when it did happen to one of us, whoever went first would give the other a sign after "passing over". We'd hoped this would break the mystery of death, because we not only loved and treasured each other, we believed our souls to be inseparable.

I recall, almost vividly, the night his "turn" came. It was the moment I had been dreading my whole life—the moment when he would leave me here. He had been sick for quite some time and had had numerous false alarms. He had, as people often say, "beaten death" many times. And then it happened—the heart-stopping shrill of a 3:00 AM phone call. A death wake-up call. My blood raced and like a stunning reverie, I could hear my brother on the other end of the phone saying what I knew I was about to hear: that the greatest man I'd ever known was gone. He had slipped away. Slipped away? Without me? That wasn't the plan. I was supposed to have been there to kiss the last sweet breath of life from his lips and tell him to wait for me wherever his journey was about to take him. I stood alone in the dark knowing that my life would never, could never, be the same again.

I managed to do the funeral. It was too weird looking at him in the ruffled up casket inscribed "Going Home". All I could think of was how he and I had stood together in front of other people's caskets looking down upon their bodies in ephemeral sympathy. Only this time, it wasn't some other body. It was his, and the pain was unbearably real as I peered down through a veil of tears at the frail remains of the man who'd made me everything that was good. He looked so far away from me. I lost it. I really made a scene. I screamed at him how much I loved him and had to be taken away. My family thought it best that I not be allowed to view him again. I just couldn't believe that I would never experience my uncle, as I knew him, again.

After he was buried, my everyday fears of life dissipated. I had already lost that which was everything to me—him. The way I saw it I had nothing left to lose. And in a strange way, there was strength in knowing this. Yet, all I cared about now was where had he gone and how I could get to him. Was this insane of me? Why couldn't I just release him as others had learned to do? But I already knew the answer—we had shared something only he and I understood. So, no, it couldn't just be over. There was too much that was a part of me buried with this man. How, then, could we share in death, or better yet, as he believed, in everlasting life, together?

My uncle raised me in the church and strongly believed he'd see his mother, father, sister, and all whom he loved on the "other side". He seemed born of that simple faith. I, nonetheless, was a skeptic of religion and wasn't so sure. As I grew older I became almost Agnostic with my belief in the world of metaphysics hindering my ability to accept his simplistic faith. But that aside, I knew, that if he were able to give me a sign the way we had talked about, he would. Strange how I could believe in a sign but not in a God who promised eternal life.

And so I waited, but no sign came. *Where the hell was he now? Could he really be gone?* I began to mentally torture and abuse my own psyche as I wondered: *Was he cold down there in the ground? How many hours, days had it been since we buried him? Had his eyes opened yet? Could he feel the rain on top of him? Did he still have some sort of consciousness?* It was my own morbid interrogation of things I couldn't possibly know. I felt helpless and hopeless. I just wanted to know how to get to where his spirit was as I still could not accept that I would never see him again.

Then, almost as if everything that had happened before was just a practice run, the real torment of grief set in. Everything I experienced, I related back to him. What I ate, the flowers I walked past, the special sounds I heard. I looked for him in corners of the house, on the couch, among the faces in a crowd, anywhere. I thought he would perhaps manifest himself to me. All my conscious and subconscious mind could see for months was him. In mirrors, I could see his face in mine. I began to do things more and more the way he had done them. I was miserable. A friend of mine with whom I had shared my hope for a sign from my uncle said, in an effort to cheer me up, "Maybe giving out signs is against the rules where he's gone!"

I smiled and thought *maybe.* But time has its way with us all and I finally came to terms with the fact that my uncle had graduated from his physical life here on earth to his spiritual life with God—somewhere.

I also became grateful that he visits me in my dreams. Perhaps it is my mind's special way of holding on to him, for there is no way I'll ever be able to fully let go of his memory. I also realize that our outlook on death was not a healthy one. We personalized and intensified what it meant to die far too much. But at the time, it was like an intriguing foreplay between life and death.

Now as the hours, days, and months continue to roll by, I've made the choice to adopt the simple faith that my uncle instilled in me, for I believe it will be my saving grace. How ironic that through his death, I receive my faith. I knew there was no other way out for me except to believe as he had— that God would, in fact, bring us back together again. I have begun to feel better because faith is a powerful thing, much more powerful than grief. I finally "get" what my uncle had been trying to tell me all those years.

Today, whatever stage of grief I find myself in, I know that in order to have a chance at seeing him again, my mission in this life must be to live as well as I can so that, after this life, by grace of the eternal Father, my uncle and I may sit together side by side again. Perhaps it was no coincidence that the choir sang *Soon and Very Soon We Are Going to See the King* when they wheeled his casket away. Because I now hope and believe with all my heart that someday soon, he and I will sit before the King together and ponder not death, but Eternal Life!

Tears Of Healing
by Ginny Stahlman

It has been my desire for some time now to share with others how God has helped me through the trials of my life, especially the death of my husband. On September 26, 1983, my husband took his own life after a long and painful illness. At the time of his death, I found my feelings fluctuating from an agonizing sense of loss to feeling thankful that he was no longer suffering. I was also angry, wondering how could he leave me and our children. I soon discovered that anger was not necessarily a one time process. I would deal with it one day, and just when I thought I had eradicated that emotion, it would raise it's ugly head again a month or perhaps a year later.

Three months after my husband's death, my pain grew worse. By then the numbness had worn off and I was starting to face the reality that he was really gone. At times I would find myself sobbing uncontrollably for no apparent reason. It was as though the sobs were coming from deep within my being. A small thing such as a child's deficiency report could open the floodgates and release a dam of tears. I cannot explain this, but it was the way I experienced grief.

Ultimately I found the many tears of sorrow I shed throughout the next two years to have a healing effect. The tensions that had built up within me somehow eased as the tears flowed. During these times I would go to God for comfort and guidance. My peace would be restored as I meditated on what I perceived to be His promises. I began to see that I could experience peace regardless of my outward circumstances.

Slowly, I began to realize I was faced with a choice. I could choose to accept the circumstances of my life and learn from them, making me a better person, or I could reject them and become bitter. The choice was mine alone.

I chose acceptance and I found God gave me the strength to endure. I believe acceptance of my circumstances was the key to the beginning of my healing. The circumstances had not changed, but I definitely changed in the process. I had become a stronger person through this personal tragedy.

Perhaps the greatest miracle of all is the joy which has replaced the sadness that I felt for so long. The trials were not without meaning or purpose. My darkness has been turned into light. Although I thought my husband's death was the end of my life, I have come to find that it was not the end but rather a new beginning. I have discovered new horizons to explore and challenges to face. I am now filled with excitement as I discover each day, the new person I have become.

Without hesitation I can say that I have journeyed from grief to happiness.

The Falling Star
by Bill Millhollon

Miles from air pollution and the glare of big city lights, the majesty and mighty grandeur of God's starlit West Texas heavens are unequaled.

It was December 14, my first night at a new deer lease. I had just strolled outside in the cool crisp air, saying a prayer, when a falling star streaked in a wide arc across the thousands of miles of black sky, finally dropping out of sight. It's startling beauty quickly gone forever.

I said to myself at the time, "God has called one of his heavenly children back home today."

I walked back towards our deer camp, a comfortable motor home. I noticed car lights approaching as a jeep headed in our direction across the pasture, its lights flashing skyward, then downward and out of sight momentarily as it bounced across the rough terrain.

The rancher who owned our deer lease got out of the jeep with another person I assumed was a game warden, but actually was a state highway patrolman. There was a bit of small talk. Then they told me there was an emergency at home and offered to drive me to the ranch house so I could call my wife.

I was not too upset. My wife's mother was very old and in poor health, and I assumed she had probably passed on. In fact, I had been outside saying a prayer for her when I saw the falling star. I was a brand new Christian after being somewhat of an agnostic for forty nine years. Like a lot of new believers, I couldn't get enough of God fast enough. I was still ecstatic about this new found treasure I had stumbled over for so long.

I called my home, over two hundred miles away. The man who answered was my neighbor's brother who was visiting them at the time; he was a small town preacher and truly "heaven sent" that night.

He said there had been an accident, that I should come home as soon as possible. I asked, "Was it my mother-in-law?" No, it was not her.

"My wife, is she alright?" She was fine but needed me there. "My older sons, Gary or Tommy; have they been in a wreck?"

"No, both are fine. Just get back home as soon as you can, Bill."

"Dubbie, please tell me what it is now; I've got to know. Has something happened to little Dave?" Davy was our youngest, thirteen year old son.

"Yes Bill, Davy had a bad accident, a broken neck."

"Oh no! That high rope swing I put way up in that huge elm tree. He would swing up twenty feet in the air and throw his head back and sweep past the ground with his head inches off the ground, and laugh when he saw the fear in my face. I warned him of the danger, and it tickled him that I was so alarmed about something that was so much fun to him."

Dubbie said, "No Bill, that is not what happened."

"How did it happen, Dubbie? Will he be okay?"

"Bill, Davy is dead."

I will never forget the finality of those words so regretfully spoken. I told Dubbie I would be home as soon as possible, thanked him, and hung up.

Not my little Dave! I sobbed a few minutes in shock. The kind rancher came in and asked if I wanted a stiff drink. I think I said no, and just asked to be taken back to my motor home. They were very kind. I told them I had lost my little boy, but I think they already knew.

Davy was a late child who came long after we gave all our baby things away, long after we expected to have any more children. Our other two boys were in their teens when he was born. He was a special blessing to us because we now had more prime time with him, and we spoiled him more because we were now better off financially.

Davy was a really gifted child. He was a star athlete, a good student, good looking, and a heart breaker with the girls.

That drive back to my home in Odessa was the longest ride I shall ever make. Fortunately I now had God to confide in as I drove down that endless road sobbing and trying to understand it all.

I thought about my wife. They were so very close; she would be all to pieces. What could I say? Her life would be shattered. How could I offer her comfort? What could I say when she asks, "Why?" I cried out to my new God for the answers as tears poured down my face.

"Why God? I know I was pretty bad during my life, but I finally surrendered, asked your forgiveness, and I know I received it. Why now? Now that I have tried so hard to change. Nothing really bad ever happened to me before, and now this . . . what can I tell my wife, Flo? Why God? . . . I just don't understand."

I once thought people who said they talked to God were a little off-base upstairs, especially those who said God talked back to them. But here I was, driving down the darkest, blackest road of my life, tears pouring down my cheeks, sobbing and talking to God . . . and He answered me!

In a quiet, gentle voice I heard him say, "In everything, give thanks." This is what I heard; this is what he said to me. Whether physically, spiritually, vocally, or however, this is what I heard. The answer was shocking and puzzling . . . "In everything, give thanks?"

I questioned Him . . . "What can you possibly mean God? How can I give thanks at a time like this? It seemed so crazy! Yet, His words were softly repeated, and repeated again: "In everything, give thanks."

I started thinking back. How truly blessed I had been these last twenty years, through no merit of my own. Even though I had not known God then, He had blessed me abundantly. I came out to West Texas with everything I owned on top of our old used car; I had a young wife, a six month old baby, a five year old son, and about thirty dollars in my pocket. I didn't even have a billfold, but I did have an unskilled job waiting.

How unbelievable it was. I learned a new trade, soon started my own business, and even acquired a fine home. We had three fine boys and enjoyed good health. I miraculously became financially independent, enjoyed the blessings of many friends, and traveled around most of the world.

We had everything we wanted: a lake home, a motor home, a boat, motorcycles, a ranch with fine cattle, big fancy cars, a Rolex watch and diamonds. I hunted from Texas to Montana and fished from Canada to

Acapulco to Hawaii. Quite a blessing for a poor boy who lived in a tent during his junior high school years.

I thought about my wonderful wife, the world's finest mother and devout Catholic who prayed and lit candles for me for thirty years. She and the boys were always in church on Sunday, regardless of any excuse. I thought about my mother and dad who had adopted me, nursed me through tuberculosis and all other kinds of childhood illnesses, and given me a great home. I was even blessed with a sweet and wonderful mother-in-law whom I truly loved.

God, in his grace, had only recently opened my blind eyes so I could see clearly and spiritually enter into his presence.

So many couples desire children and can't even adopt one. We were blessed with three. Even now, I still had two fine sons. I thought of those who had lost their only child; how tragic that would be. The light was dawning . . .

Davy was a bonus baby, an extra blessing loaned to us for a while. Now he was gone, but what a great life he had. Davy had everything a child could want, materially, physically, and spiritually. He never knew sickness, poverty, or pain. He never had a real worry, a broken heart, an insurmountable problem, or an enemy . . . and he knew God. He never suffered like a sick child who dies slowly. His death was instantaneous.

"In everything, give thanks." I was beginning to understand through the wisdom that comes only from God . . . I was truly blessed.

I drove into the driveway of my home, brokenhearted, but in my grief I had an inner joy. In my helplessness I felt a strength and assurance that I had never known. I knew what to say to comfort and reassure my dear broken-hearted wife. God gave me the right words. I realized that now, with God, in my weakest moment, I was stronger than I had ever been. I was reminded: This too shall pass.

We both agreed that we had to get on with life. Dave was not on loan to us any longer. God had called him back. We thanked God for our thirteen blessed years of good times. We decided his funeral was going to be a happy and joyful farewell; that would have been his desire.

Arriving at the funeral home for the first time, we saw a young girl crying her heart out. Her mother explained that Davy was her boyfriend. She had bought an identification bracelet for Davy's Christmas present. Christmas was only eleven days away. She asked my wife to put the bracelet on Davy's arm. My wife lovingly and compassionately asked her if she would like to do it herself. She was overjoyed, and it was very touching. How sad . . . young love lost.

The church service was more than we planned. The church was packed with hundreds of people: our friends and Davy's friends. The Catholic priest even allowed my Protestant preacher to take part in the funeral service, something unheard of only a few years before. Love, time, and faith change all things.

Near the very end of the sad, yet joyful church service, the priest said, "A star has fallen; God has called back one of his heavenly children back home today." How very supernatural! Those were the exact words I spoke to myself that fateful night at the deer lease when I watched the falling star shoot across the heavens and die.

I had never mentioned this earlier event to anyone else; in fact, I had forgotten about the star until then.

Shortly after leaving the church, we saw a sign on the front porch of a house proudly proclaiming: "It's a boy!" The Lord gives and the Lord takes away.

Driving to the cemetery, we passed a poor fellow standing on the side of the road. In his tattered and weathered clothes, he'd obviously seen better times, but he stood with his head bowed and his cap over his heart. He was giving all he had to offer, and it touched us deeply. Nothing can humble a proud soul more than death.

A young Spanish boy we passed gave "the sign of the cross" as we went by. It is funny how you notice such little things at times like these. How guilty I felt, thinking of the many times I had become impatient waiting for a funeral to pass, selfishly anxious to get on with my worldly duties. I realized I would never be quite the same person again.

The really important little things in life become magnified when our helplessness overwhelms us. Love suddenly is the only thing that matters. My wife and I have experienced a much more understanding and loving relationship in the years following Davy's death. Our life is a better life because of Davy, and I thank God for him. In our deepest sorrow, we acquired a spiritual joy, strength, and compassion we had never known before. Time gradually heals all wounds and life continues, becoming beautiful again.

La Montaña Se Movió—The Mountain Moved
by Roberta Schlerf

It would seem all my life that the men I love would leave me. It began with my dad, whom I adored. He died when I was in high school. Although I grew up in a large extended family, I felt my dad had left me alone.

The boys at school had known of my father's furious possessiveness over me. After his death, they spoke to me at school. In return, my heightened regard for them seemed to chase "Lonely" away. I had a crush on one of the boys, Joe Harp. He was on the basketball team and was tall and handsome. I would lay in bed and fantasize about Joe and me. He and I talked more and more on the way home from school, and eventually talked on the telephone. We even watched the same TV shows together while on the phone with each other. Joe had not lifted a hand to touch me in any way during this period.

One evening, while I was perched on my grandma's bed talking to Joe, he said, "Robbie, do you want to be my girlfriend?" His words floated around my head. Waiting for this question had crippled me, but I must have given an affirmative answer because, at some point, Joe began to list the conditions of becoming his girlfriend. Number one was to make love with him. I decided I would do whatever it took to be his girlfriend.

He took me to a vacant apartment and told me to undress. It must have been funny for Joe to see me shaking like a wet puppy. He laughed and pointed at me. I had gone too far to turn back. The moment he had taken my virginity he got up from the bed and said we should leave quickly. I walked home alone and found the mirror in my bedroom. I looked at myself, but I didn't seem any more like a woman than before.

The next day I found out Joe had bet some other guys that he could be the first person to have sex with me. I never got the chance to confront him. He and his family moved out of town shortly after. I was given a message by one of his friends: "Bye."

After my father died, it was not much of an adjustment for Grandma to assume the role of mother, father, and grandparent. She held her entire family together with effortless grace and energy. Grandma had stood in place of my mother since I was four years old when my father took custody of me because of my mother's drinking. Grandma made me go to church with her, fed me well, screened my friends, picked out my clothes, and took me to the hospital when I broke my arm.

I saw Grandma cry twice in my life. Once, as a small child, when my aunt did not want me at her daughter's birthday party and, the second time, when she and I sat on the bed in my new dorm room at college. We held hands and I looked into her aging eyes. It was wisdom that provoked the tears that slowly rolled down Carrie Lee Miller's ebony face. I was startled to see her cry. Wisdom must have whispered a reminder in her ear of the devilish jokes life plays on a young girl who is alone. I just cried because I loved her and felt the familiar sting of separation. She let me kiss her soft cheek and hug her tightly. Then, she was gone.

I had chosen Grand Canyon College because it sounded like a safe place, but I became influenced by the wayward bunch in the dorm. We snuck out at night and cruised the boulevard with the Lowriders.

Before I was completely engulfed by "La Vida Loca", I received a card from my mother. She and I had begun speaking on the telephone. The card was covered with blooming pink roses. Inside I read: "I love you more than you will ever know, Mother."

After a few weeks I was called to the phone to be told my mother was dead. She had choked on a piece of meat, gone into a coma, and died. Then, a few months later, I was informed my brother, Ernie, whom I had been fond of, had drowned.

My way of coping with the news was to plunge too deeply into the Lowrider lifestyle. Sparkling cars that hopped up from the street with personalities of their own! The brown skinned guys who navigated these creations were equally stunning. Shining black hair that laid back on their heads and big brown eyes which pierced a young girl's heart. These were Cholos and I was captured, lured away from all logical thinking and interest in my future. I quit school to live with some other girls, and we joined the first all-girl car club in Phoenix, called "Las Unicas" (The Only Ones). Life became fast and crazy from that point. Our club was featured in *LowRider Magazine*. These times were a tidal-wave of power that swept me along like a rag doll.

Although I was encircled by close associates and wooed by some of the prettiest men I could stand to be touched by, my dream of marriage and complete acceptance was not possible at the time. Tradition was a large portion of the Mexican heritage. Parents did not accept their son's marriage to a black girl. And these men did not disrespect their mothers!

So I left Phoenix wounded, alone, and pregnant by a beautiful vision of muscles named Oscar. I had wrapped the world around him and was pregnant because he said he wanted a baby. He yelled at me for asking him to help me get an abortion. "You are not gonna kill my kid!"

After I moved back to Yuma, it began to be scary having a baby alone. I drove back to Phoenix to ask Oscar to be involved. As I walked onto his yard he called out to me. "Get out of my yard, nigger!" His family were silent witnesses. They had teased him about having a nigger baby. I thought about driving into the oncoming freeway traffic on the way back to Yuma, but I moved into an apartment next to my Aunt Bessie's. She brought me collard greens and other good food. Grandma gave me a ride to the hospital when it was time for the baby and left shortly after. There was no one there to hold my hand when D'Angelo was born.

During the next few years my large family was assaulted by a black wind that carried death. Grandpa was killed by a car while walking to the store for buttermilk. Cancer sent my favorite aunt, Bessie, into the hospital never to escape alive. Aunt Janice had an identical experience at the hospital. A year later, Uncle Clifford, upset by a phone call, had a heart attack and died. Aunt Betty died after having a stroke.

During this black wind, my grandma's many ailments banded together to take the life from her. For years she had been careful to hide the pain that plagued her. Her death erased the core of strength that was our family. At her funeral I wanted to curl up next to her like I used to do as a child when I was afraid.

As a young girl, basking in the warmth of this grand clan that was my family, I remember wondering and shuddering at the idea of losing them. I had decided back then that I would run to God if such a monstrosity occurred. Now it was really happening. However, instead of running to God to help me with my grieving, I lowered my sights to a tangible man who would love me, protect me, and let me build my world around him. Surprise! I was left with a hand full of feathers and second child.

Her name is Gloria Jeanne Miller, like my mother. She looked like a tiny Indian princess with thick black hair lying close against her tan skin. Her father, Rigo, a tall Latin stud with dark skin, was a ghost that floated in and out of my life for fifteen years. When dust from this sweet illusion settled, I sat alone, again, in a housing project apartment with my two children.

I surrendered to God. My being was encased in everything that was Godly and safe. The members of my church became my strong family that I had missed so much. I woke in the morning excited about what I could do for God on this new day. My joy was in helping the lonely. Women came to me for a place to stay and someone who had time to smile and listen to them. My small apartment was often packed with roommates making homemade tortillas and beans. There was always laughter.

Three years went by and I began to ask God for a husband. The new Christian women, not as devoted to God as I, were even getting married. I couldn't remember what it felt like to have a man's lips on mine. The men in church doted over their children, and I longed for a husband to be a covering over mine.

Bitterness crept up and slid me right from under the protective hand of God. I was ready to toss away the three years I had given my Savior. I would have to do the work of finding a husband myself.

The only place I could think of was a bar. I sat at a corner table and shook, knowing I didn't belong. Quietly, I waited to be swept off my feet. Although I was approached by men and got to know some of them, it was not one of them that swept me from the ground. It was a new friend that turned out to be ever-faithful and unchanging. Cocaine was his name. He introduced me to Crack, and we became pals with Liquor. Now I could make Lonely go away. I didn't have to wear my emotions on my sleeve. Eventually, I didn't have to wear any emotions at all. By this time, my conscience was only a tiny voice in my gut that begged me to consider my children. I learned to ignore it while I was getting high. My son, D'Angelo, disobeyed me and I slapped his face. As I stood looking at blood trickle from his nose, I tried to pretend that it did not startle me.

Living for the high that drugs gave had taken a toll on my appearance. When friends from my past came to see me they began to weep. Cynthia, my best friend from childhood, was one of these. She reminded me that I had beautiful children. As resourceful as I had become to stay intoxicated with this powerful indifference, there were times when I came down. These were trips into the mouth of Hell. I could plainly see the faces of D'Angelo and Gloria riddled with fear and depression, tears in their beautiful brown eyes.

During these clear-minded times, my gut screeched, repeating details of sexual acts that I was asked to do for money. The voice bellowed a throbbing reminder that we had received another eviction notice. No escape was apparent.

Incredibly, there was a man that got himself tangled in my web of malice. Bill thought I was a nice girl. That is the way he thought of most people. Bill, six foot two, with dark hair and pale white skin, was raised by his mother to be gentle and considerate while giving everyone the benefit of the doubt.

Bill came over some nights and sat on the side of my bed until I fell asleep. Then he would lock the door on his way out of my apartment. He came to see me often, and I grew to rest in his kindness. Shortly after he felt he loved me (the good me that showed herself less and less often), we got a positive result on a home pregnancy test. The baby was blonde with blue eyes like my mother's. Her loving father named her Samantha.

Bill struggled like a drowning cat to keep me clean of drugs. He tried pleading tearfully from his knees. He tried choking me and controlling my access to money.

Child Protective Services came and took away all three of my children. I was not relieved on their behalf. It was hard to feel any strong emotion. I knew that if I let myself, it would be devastating. So I was high all of the time.

The CPS case workers had written me off as far as any hope of returning my children to me and began to look for permanent homes for all three children. I was allowed weekly visits with them.

Bill finally ran out of "benefit of the doubt" and was no longer available. When he told me he would get custody of Samantha, he also said I would not be able to see her unless I had enrolled in a residential rehabilitation center.

This time, I believed his ultimatum. The drug treatment center was called "La Casa De Amigas". We were fourteen women confined to a large two story house. I had driven one hundred seventy miles to move in and was told that if I stepped out of the door I could not come back in.

Certainly, this would be a self-made prison sentence. Oddly, these women were not the only ones there when I arrived. I felt the soft caress of God.

He was there waiting for me. Waiting for me to take this step forward. He would carry me the rest of the way.

In the evenings I walked along the back yard enclosure and spoke with God, explaining that I had no desire to stop doing drugs. I let Him know that He needed to give me the desire for the right way of life, acknowledging I had nothing to offer in return but a rotten me. I wanted to understand the pain I made my children feel when I would not hug them. God granted me feelings over these months in Rehab.

Upon completion of the twelve step program, I came home to Yuma, hoping for the strength to stay clean and not run from sorrow.

The director of the CPS was not impressed at my perseverance in the program. She continued the paperwork to sever me from all rights of custody of my children. I enrolled in a local rehab.

This director and I had developed a strong relationship. We were mortal enemies. I hated her for the way she enjoyed her power over me. She hated me for being a child abuser. During our state-required review meetings she kept her distance from me in disgust.

D'Angelo's paternal grandparents had come to take him to Phoenix before I had left Yuma for the first rehab. I remember being called to come and say good-bye. D'Angelo gave me a letter he had written to me at the foster home. In it, he told of how he would leap for joy when he was allowed to come home to me.

When I insisted on knowing if I would ever get to see my son again, the director condescendingly explained. "You are a druggie, Roberta. You must tell D'Angelo you don't want him with you. He is so loyal to you. If you cry, I will end the meeting immediately! You have three minutes in the parking lot to say good-bye to him."

D'Angelo stood facing me and waited for me to speak, tears clinging to his caramel-colored face and years of wisdom shining through his soft brown eyes. He stood straight and brave like a soldier going to war. "D'Angelo, I am so sorry for what I have done to you." This was hard for me to say without tears. "I promise I will get well and learn to be a good mommy. Then, I will find you. I do love you."

After a month, the center was forced to close down due to lack of funds. Again, I was without a place to live. I cried to God for an answer to why my hard work and determination were getting me nowhere. Opening the Bible to look for some explanation, I read: "It is not by might and it is not by power, but by my spirit that this mountain shall be removed." I stopped crying.

Bill, who had been keeping an apprehensive eye on my progress, heard the home was closing and offered me a place in his small trailer home. Among the courtroom fights for custody of my children came the magical question that I had dreamed of since girlhood: "Will you marry me?"

Bill's and my third wedding anniversary has just passed. We now have Gloria and Samantha in our home, along with a large white parrot, a Yorkshire terrier, and a cuddly white Maltese dog named Cotton.

My husband works for Federal Express and I am a Farm Bureau Insurance Agent. That old enemy of mine from the Child Protective Services has become a friend. Cynthia and I unite our families every chance we get. She and I still share our dreams and fears.

The mountain has been moved and my life is filled with a rainbow of glory. During those nights and days of rampant indulgence that I call my past, I wondered what would be the price of it all. It was my son.

My Darkest Hour
by George Ayetin

December 30, 1973 will forever remain indelible in my mind and soul. It was the day that my father suddenly died, and the reality of life—its shortness and unpredictability—was unexpectedly thrust on my shoulders. It was also the day a part of me died and a new part began. Three hours before his death, my father had gathered all of us (my three brothers and three sisters) in the family room to discuss nothing in particular. The discussions were purely general. We talked about my education. He wanted to know what I would like to be in the future. At that time, I was not sure and I told him so. He cleared his throat and began telling us about the family history, his struggles, and his expectations of all of us. He was telling us so many personal stories that my mother became angry with him. According to my mother, we were too young to hear most of what he was telling us. My father replied, "I am just telling them in case I die. I want them to know about me if I die before they grow up."

This made my mother furious. She begged my father to stop scaring us with his "death speech". As far as she was concerned, my father was too young to die and he was going to live for a very long time. After saying this, she walked out of the room and the meeting ended.

Five minutes later my father called me and sent me to the store to buy him some cigarettes. I was about to mount my bike when he called me back. He wanted to go to the store and purchase the cigarettes himself. He told me to go out and play. I requested permission to go to my maternal grandfather's house and possibly sleep there overnight. He looked wearily at me, smiled, and nodded his head in approval. This made me so happy that I rushed out of his presence with lightning speed, unaware that this was going to be my last opportunity to talk to or see my father alive. I was in my grandfather's house for about an hour when one of my uncles came in to take me home. I was confused when I saw my uncle but he told me he had a special Christmas present for me in my father's house and that I should follow him home immediately. Because of this, I did not suspect anything until I was about two blocks from my parents' house and began to hear my mother's cry. I turned to my uncle and asked what was wrong, and he then told me that my father had died. At first, I thought that he was kidding. I told him to repeat what he had told me. He said "Your father is dead." At this, my mind became numb, my body frozen. My heart began to race out of control, as everything else in me came to a complete standstill. Time stopped. I could neither talk nor breathe. I still don't know how I walked the remaining two blocks to my parent's house.

When I got there, it was a mass of relatives and neighbors. I had to struggle and wiggle through before getting to my mother who was sobbing uncontrollably and was now being restrained by two of her relatives. She looked up just in time, saw me, and stretched her hands to me. I ran straight to her. She held me tighter than she had ever done, and the two of us began to cry. After about five minutes, she motioned me to go out and find my two year old sister. When I eventually found her, she was unperturbed, unfazed by the confusion, sadness, and sorrows in our house. She ran to me and demanded to be carried. As I carried her, she began to laugh. Seeing the smile on her face chilled my heart and soul. I forced a smile and took her to my mother.

I then decided to go into my father's room to see his body. Halfway through,

I was sent back because of my age. This hurt me very much and greatly increased my pains and anguish. I still resent their refusal to allow me to see his body that night. A part of me wanted to see and hold him desperately. I wanted to hug him and nurse him back to life. Something in me was convinced that he was not dead. All he needed to be revived was my gentle touch and prayer. At that period of my life, I believed in my strong relationship with God. I thought that there was nothing I could request from God without getting it.

Consequently, I went to the back of the house, cast my eyes on the moon and stars, and began to pray. My prayer was very simple. "Please Lord bring my father back and let the world see your special relationship with me." I kept repeating these words until one of my uncles came out and tapped me on the back. I jumped up thinking that it was my father. He whispered to me that "all will be well."

I nodded back to him and said, "You are right, everything will be fine." In my mind, "all will be well" meant my father was not dead yet. It meant that the Lord was going to bring him back alive and well to us. I spent the next seven days hoping, wishing, and expecting this to happen. Even during his burial, I was expecting him to jump out of his coffin and embrace all of us. But he never did.

His burial was the most exasperating, annoying, depressing, and darkest hour of my life. I hated throwing sand and stone at his six-feet-down coffin. I despised the coffin, grave, everyone, and everything associated with the burial. When they began to cover his grave, a sharp knife passed through my head down to my spine. Darkness fell over me, and everything I had known from my childhood up to that point collapsed into the grave and became buried with my father. I began to hate God very much for letting me down. How could He lead me into believing that we had a special relationship only to disappoint me at my most vulnerable hour? Did He not know what my father meant to me? I paused for a while and resolved never to pray to Him again.

Our house was like a metro station and a ghost town simultaneously. There were people everywhere, but still my family was very lonely and dejected. My mother and older sister continued to cry every minute of the day for about three weeks. My one older brother and I (as the men of the house) were left to control and comfort everyone else. I became transformed from a teenager to an adult in one day. My outlook on life suddenly changed from hope to desperation. From optimist to pessimist, from a happy teenager to a withdrawn and lonely boy.

Three weeks after my father's death and burial, I went back to my Catholic boarding school dejected, upset, and sad. Having nobody to comfort or be comforted by, it was very easy for me to be more depressed, disillusioned, angry, and lost. Tears and sorrow became my constant companion. I spent my days walking around like a zombie and my nights like a scared little cat. I would lay on my bed at night sleepless. It seemed I was being hunted by devilish and wicked nightmares. Slowly, I began to hate school, my teachers, and my classmates. For everyone was having fun except me.

Seven days after I came back to school, I became deeply distraught, so overwhelmed by sadness and heartbreak that I began to cry during the final minute of a math lesson. My math teacher came to my desk and demanded to know why I was crying. I told him, expecting some sympathy from him. I desperately wanted him or someone to hug and console me. I just wanted someone to tell me things would be all right. But instead, he began to curse and scream at me for not acting like a man. Then he accused me of being lazy and disruptive, and ordered me to go to his office and wait for him. At this, my fellow classmates began to laugh. Frustrated and crushed, I ran to his office. I was in the office for about fifteen minutes when he came back, took me outside to the soccer field, gave me a machete, and told me to cut the grasses behind the goal post. This was my punishment for being lazy and disruptive. My mind went blank. I looked up to the heavens in search of a divine intervention but nothing happened. It was then that it finally dawned on me I was alone and my father was no longer coming back. This was also the day I lost my euphoric expectations in the ability or willingness of any human being to make me happy or to help me recover from my grief. I had a choice to make: move forward with my life or wallow and die in self pity. It was the realization of this fact that helped me regain my life. Little by little, I began to accept my father's death.

Christmas of 1973 (five days before my father's death) was the best and most pleasant time of our lives. I received many presents from my parents and relatives. We had an abundance of good food and drinks. There was joy everywhere I turned. I was looking forward to a joyous and fantastic new year until that sad day when my father died. Because of this experience, I am still scared of happiness and Christmas day. My hopes and dreams became completely shattered forever. I still look back to that day with fear and timidity of soul and mind.

But time has been kind to me. Although time has not been able to heal all my pains and sorrows of that day, it has provided me with serenity of soul and peace of mind. With time, I found out most of my fears and nightmares were nothing but a refusal to accept my father's death. None of the terrible things that I imagined ever materialized. Time has given me alternatives to my grief. It has replaced the zeal for life, which I lost, with a firm determination to carry on and enjoy my life. I can now breathe, and I no longer hate God (*though I sometimes wonder about Him*).

I still find myself wondering about so many "ifs". What if my father was alive today? How would my life have been affected? What if I had gone to buy those cigarettes for him? What if I had been patient and attentive to him and everything that he was saying that night? What if I had not gone to my grandfather's house that night? Could all these have prolonged his life? Probably not. Knowing this has also helped me cope with his death. I no longer feel guilty or bear the weight of his death on my shoulders.

My father's death has taught me some valuable lessons. It has taught me about the shortness and unpredictability of life and the need to live life fully in harmony with those that I love. If I love somebody, I must tell and show him or her that. For tomorrow or the next minute is not guaranteed. All we have is now. Therefore, I plan to show love to my family and friends each time I am with them.

I also learned the importance and necessity of believing in a higher power. I could not have been able to overcome the devastating affect of my father's death without my belief in God's kindness and mercies. Praying to him and hoping for his miracles and eventual revitalization has helped me to look beyond my current pains and to hope for a better tomorrow. I still cry sometimes but, during the tears, a soft voice within tells me to be calm for all will be well in due time.

Alone With The Lord
by Patricia Hamaker Shrimpton

Dedicated to all the ones I have great love and hope for. The ones who made my life full of rich rewards along my journey.

***

It is clear to me why some choose the single life. As a single person it is possible to spend more time with the Lord.

When I had a mate and my children, there were so many distractions. Meeting the responsibilities of my chosen married state took all my time. I have no regrets about my choices. It is only now as a widow that I savor my single existence. There are no restrictions. I do not have to meet expectations or wonder if my spouse wishes I do things in another fashion.

Yet, after living for so many years in a double harness, it does seem strange at times. Total freedom takes some getting used to. For instance, I miss talking with my man. We had long chats about many topics. We seldom agreed on major issues. We did have a perfect understanding of the love we shared. For fifty-three years I never doubted my husband's faithfulness. Even during long absences, Tom, my dearest friend, was a proper man. He was trustworthy. It was easy to trust in the knowledge that our commitment was forever. When we said, "'til death us do part," we meant it. All of the years were not spent in total happiness. For thirty years I always thought we had an enviable marriage. Then, as we entered the late forties and early fifties, we were not as happy as we had been. I imagine menopause was a factor and Tom's job status was more wearing on him. Retirement was less fulfilling than I expected.

After traveling and a life of so-called leisure grew tiresome, we spent too little quality time together. I am not a sports person; I am a music person. Tom wanted me to play golf. I was not adverse to playing, but I had poor scores and would rather not deal with the summer heat on the golf course. In addition, I didn't do well in meeting social commitments. I thrive on spontaneity. Tom belonged to a group which met certain days a week for golf. Also, there was a luncheon group that consisted of his men friends from his school days. They were his friends, but were my acquaintances. We had many discussions on the subject of my less than enthusiastic attitude toward meeting with these men friends and their wives. I did not dislike them, but had no special interest in spending time with them, which embarrassed my husband. He had to tell them I would not attend some of these gatherings. I felt put upon and didn't like having to defend my position.

Today I have none of these hassles. If I want to attend an affair, I go. If I choose to stay home, I am not uncomfortable in refusing the invitation. There are other freedoms which present themselves as I adjust to my widowhood. I buy or sell items. I exercise my prerogative to change my mind and not have to explain why. If I sound off, no one need stay in my company. A husband is caught in the trap of his spouse's moods, just as a wife is. I don't profess to be an easy person to live with.

However my life goes now, I acknowledge God has blessed me with so many unforeseen days of excitement and unusual experiences that I look forward to each new day with great eagerness and expectation. Each day I say upon rising, "Let it be done unto me according to thy will, Lord." He takes it from there. I feel more calm and experience little anxiety, no matter what the day brings.

My good night prayer is one of thankfulness for the many benefits God has bestowed on me. Sometimes I pinch myself to be sure all of this good stuff is really happening!

I can only say, "Thank you, thank you, dear Lord." Amen.

CHAPTER 13

JOURNALING

Journaling proves to be a useful tool for coping with the stress and difficult emotions that follow the death of loved ones.

The First Month
by Cynthia Kuhn Beischel

Jer,

It's been ten days since you've died. I'm feeling sorrow and loneliness. The hustle and bustle of funeral plans is over; the void is becoming bigger. I miss you rolling over to hold me in the morning and your comforting me when I'm upset. As I fixed the kids' breakfasts this morning, I missed hearing you tease them in the bathroom and Lindsay running out with a squeal because you "threatened" her with shaving cream. God, I wish you were here. There's so much more I wanted to share with you—including a sexy week on our vacation.

Jer, please come talk to me sometimes.

I was so scared when I first realized you guys were in trouble, and I'm not too thrilled with how I acted. I knew I couldn't help in the water. Isn't it odd how over the years I kept warning the family never to count on me to help save anyone from drowning? I think a neighbor called for help before I got outside. I kept misreading things. I think it's because you were so full of life. I couldn't believe that you wouldn't survive. You always found ways out of problems.

When the four men were dragging you in, I pictured Lindsay riding in on your stomach—like a game. Then Lindsay ran to me from another direction and I realized I'd been wrong. Did you watch all this? She broke down and said it was all her fault. I didn't understand. I hugged her and told her to go to Merritt. When Merritt came running in and said you and Lindsay needed help, I didn't ever imagine you in that much trouble. I'm sorry I didn't run out sooner, but part of me knows it wouldn't have changed anything.

Jer, I wish I could bring you back. I wonder what people on the beach thought when I kept telling you to get back into your body. When I saw you with foam coming out of your nose and mouth, I knew we were in big trouble. A medic held me back when he heard me yell, "Oh, my God!" But do you know what? I still believed you could make it. I got so excited when somebody said, "We've got a pulse!" I went over to one of the men who had gone out to save you and thanked him. His body language told me that he didn't think you were going to make it, but I knew it would be okay because I knew you—a survivor. People were pumping on you and giving you electric jolts all the way to the hospital. The ambulance driver said, "I know it looks pretty grim now, but he's fighting real hard." That gave me some encouragement. When we arrived, the doctor met me and walked me to a room. I pictured you coming back with a fantastic story to share with me. But then it seemed to be taking too long.

When the doctor came into the room I asked how it was going. He looked at me and said, "He's dead."

"Dead?!" I shouted.

He said, "Yes."

Your dad said, "Oh, my lord," and then asked the doctor if he could give me something for anxiety. I snapped back that I didn't want anything. I was angry at the facts.

Honey, you must have felt so scared. I want to hold you. I wish you had gotten into the jacuzzi with me the night before. I wish we'd made love before you left.

I guess I'm still denying it. Sometimes I think you're on a business trip. I wait for night-time calls. I miss your coming home for lunch or hearing the garage door at dinner time, and your talking to the dog when you thought no one would see you. I miss your sense of humor. I'm afraid I won't be able to offer a balanced upbringing for the girls. They're remembering lots of good funny stuff. I'm going to work hard to keep that part alive. It's painful, but it's also good.

I included your mom and dad in all the arrangements. I knew right away I wanted to see you in your good charcoal-colored suit with the subtle stripes, your pale pink shirt, and the Escher lizard tie we gave you for Christmas. You wouldn't have liked how they trimmed your mustache and dyed the gray parts brown—without asking. I would have told them you didn't like it that way.

Your mom offered a burial plot next to Gram. I didn't think it mattered that we wouldn't be buried next to each other, and I knew you were close to Gram. I'm thinking she was probably one of the people who met you on the other side, so it all seemed appropriate. Do you remember my telling you about a dream I had several months ago in which she came and hugged me?

Your parents had a beautiful "spray" made for the top of the casket. It had wonderful colors of yellow, pink, salmon, rose, lavender . . .

The kids had recently bought you a little trophy: "Father of the Year". They both had ideas for it. Merritt wanted to put it with your body. Lindsay wanted to put it on a tall block of wood so it would stand taller than anyone else's. To make both girls happy, we bought a second one; so now we have one on the mantle and the other one's in the casket.

The girls and I are going to miss so much without you here. I know I can follow through on some of the plans we had, but even those won't be the same. What made stuff really fun was doing them with you.

The funeral services were nice. TJ gave the eulogy both days. I liked the first, more personal one best. He talked of your enthusiasm about life and your sports car and how much noise it made. He called it a Triumph, though, instead of a Healey!

I just saw a maroon-colored Trooper go by. For a second, I thought you were coming home. It's happened before. When Bob brought your car back, since we all flew back home, I pulled into the driveway and said to myself, "Oh good, Jer's home." I would love it if that could be true, but I know you're at home somewhere else now.

***

I've been really busy with all the paperwork. I wish you had been a little more anal and left stuff more organized.

I had a thought today. You were so vital, and loved life and wanted to get so much out of it. I wonder if that's characteristic of people who die young.

Yesterday was tough. Father's Day.

By the time we got back to town, Jean had already organized everything. There was a "crew" to clean the house and yard because everyone came back here after the funeral. They brought wonderful food for the gathering, and people signed up to bring us dinner for weeks to come. It truly is a blessing; I have no desire to cook.

We girls, including Mom and Carolyn, went for a walk after dinner. I looked at architecture and wanted to share a conversation about it. I looked in apartments and houses and thought of you. I envied couples starting out, and older ones that were still together. I miss you so much.

Tonight, when Lindsay got into the tub, the water was deeper than usual. I helped her wash, then left her alone as it drained. Within a few minutes, she was standing next to me crying. She looked so young and scared. I told her that I wasn't sure if it would help now or not, but to let me know if she wanted swimming lessons. It might make her feel safer. She asked if I'd tell the teacher about what had happened, and I said, "Of course." She also told me some kids made fun of her for not going in the deep end. I told her to tell me if it happened again. I would talk to them or to their parents, or back her up if she told them off. She also told me that she doesn't ever want to wear the bathing suit again that she had on when you died. Practical me is hoping that it's the smaller one! She added that your death is beginning to hit her more now. I know what she means. I held her and we cried together for about a half hour. I'm so sad for her to have experienced the fear of drowning, plus watching her dad die and having him be gone. Why? Was there no way to avoid it?

I've got to get some sleep.

***

Every once in awhile, I fall back into an "if only" mode, and can then find comfort from the fact that there were so many signs, with hindsight, that this ending was inevitable and that you had had forewarning: your distancing from me and your work partner, your uncharacteristic cleaning up of your office, your trying so hard to finish the bathroom project, your asking me for a priority list of what I'd like to get done, and my "Twilight Zone" feeling thirty-six hours before. Sometimes I wish I'd known as much as some of my friends did about your feeling at the last minute that you didn't want to go. What I remember is your thanking me for wanting to go months before.

Looking back, I remember watching myself on the beach as they worked on your body. There were moments I felt empty, with no energy to encourage you to come back. Maybe I knew it was over. I read somewhere one time that some people believe we have three possible "exit" dates from this life. If that's true, I wonder which exit you used—the first, second, or third?

I was thinking earlier of how we walked along the beach the night before and I told you how I felt like Jackie Kennedy at Hyannis Port—sort of separate. I felt like her again riding in the ambulance. I also remembered how we held hands as we took a walk the night before you died and that I knew you cared about me.

If I could just *know* that it was going to happen no matter what, I could remove the "what ifs". I'm torturing myself.

Cynthia, it was meant to happen. The circumstances were just the vehicle for it to occur.

Jer, why did you have to leave us?

I've asked people to meditate for both girls. Merritt's emotions are playing havoc with her blood readings and her face broke out with acne like it never has before. She's had some tough days. She doesn't like to talk about it much or cry in front of anyone. I've decided we're going to try the support group for grieving children. I think we need it.

I wish you'd come talk to me. I've had two dreams where your representation played a part, but it wasn't really you. I was just trying to work things out.

Friends and relatives have called to see how we are. They're concerned about us. I know that some of them have called each other about us, too.

If I'm going to look for positives in all this, I see Merritt learning to be more demonstrative. When I tell her I love her, she says it back to me now. We've all learned a valuable lesson in saying it while the person is still here. In the little bit of talking I managed to do while your body lay on the beach, I never said, "I love you." I'm sorry. It was just understood.

***

It's been two weeks since I started writing this. Tonight is my first night alone. The girls are both babysitting.

I'm throwing out the awful black bean soup that was in the freezer since you were the only one who would eat it. That made me smile. Whenever there was food the girls and I didn't want, we'd say, "Does Dad want it, or should we give it to the dog?" This would have been our time together.

Jer, why didn't you tell me about your premonition? I know you probably thought that you were protecting me from pain, or maybe you didn't want to acknowledge it to me because it might not come true, but you also cheated me out of some precious time with you. We could have loved each other like we never had before. Yes, I know, we should have been loving each other as if each day was our last all along, but human nature isn't like that. We could have told each other how much we loved each other. We could have connected on such a deep level. There have been moments when I let my false self talk and play mind tricks. Then I interpret your distancing in your last few weeks to mean that you didn't care. I know better. I think it was too painful for you to address. You had grown so much. I still wish you had shared your thoughts and fears with me. We could have held each other and said goodbye more thoroughly.

Do you remember on the beach when Merritt was asking you not to leave us, that we needed you? We all felt that way. I guess we're going to learn that it's not so much need as want. We're finding out what we can do by ourselves and also how to reach out to others for help. You were so talented and could do so many things. It's taking about ten people to fill your shoes! I'm so sorry you're going to miss big events, like the girls' first dates, their proms, awards, graduations, weddings, and so on. I told Merritt you'd be with her on her first date, so she'd better behave! She smiled. See if you can be there.

***

I walked the dog out to the back of the yard the other night and thought about how the two of you would go out together at night and "talk to the stars". I came in crying. Lindsay asked what was the matter. I told her I missed you. She hugged me and said God must have needed you and He knew we'd be okay without you. She's good, isn't she? I told her I knew we'd be okay, too, but I still miss you. There are moments I feel good about myself and how I am doing.

***

I've switched to an angry mode today. I feel cheated. I feel like I've had a big chunk of my life taken away from me. I want to go to movies with you, go dancing with you, have you help me with the raising of the girls, help me deal with Merritt's diabetes. I want you here to comfort me and so that I can comfort you, and share in the excitement of new projects, and travel with you, and stretch each other, and grow old together. I'm so upset that you're gone.

Why haven't you come to visit me in my dreams? My false self keeps popping up saying it's because you don't care enough. That's not true, is it? There must be another reason.

We went to Riverbend last night with *our* friends for a picnic dinner, the symphony, and fireworks. I care a great deal for them, but it was so hard. Sometimes, the "mirroring" is too painful. Brian tells your kind of dumb jokes, and I pine for you. I watch their family and am happy for them, and at the same time, I'm jealous.

At times I get the feeling of wanting to jump out of my skin, to escape. That feeling was so strong the first night you were dead. I was ricocheting around in my body, wanting to *get out*. I wanted to run, but there was no place to go.

I've had a couple of dreams about another man coming into my life after I am finished mourning. Part of me wants that to be over quickly because it's so unpleasant. There's another part of me that doesn't want anybody else, or to have to deal with the dating scene at all. I made a commitment to you, loved you, and wanted to be with you and share with you as we grew old together.

I think one of the things that hurts so much or troubles me is that I feel I could have loved you better. I didn't always appreciate your gifts as I could have. I now know I sometimes had fear block my total acceptance. I didn't want to get hurt again. I wish now that I could have totally accepted the beauty of you and your giving. I wish you could come back so we could have more time together, more chances to express the love in our relationship. At least we ended up further along than where we started. Thank you for what you taught me.

***

You've been gone a month now. You have caused, by leaving, an environment in which I am becoming more empowered. There are moments I can feel the early stages of what might be called excitement. Then I go back to sadness, anger, and love—the whole cycle. Sometimes I start to cry, like just now, and I feel a tingling sensation around my temples or on the top of my head, and I think you might be here trying to comfort me. I guess I'll hold onto that idea. If it's not you, it's some other kind of energy trying to help me. I miss you. I look forward to hearing from or seeing you.

Random Thoughts And Fleeting Images
by Barbara Murdock

My husband Don had a shunt put down his throat the first night he was in the hospital. The haunting wonder is about how much he knew, what he would have said if he could. That will never go away and is probably one of the saddest feelings I have.

April 1995: *Everyone asks, "How are you doing?" They all want the reply of "fine", but, of course, I'm mostly not doing fine. Small frustrations bring on tears. My chest is heavy, and the sense of anxiety is all around me. It is difficult to concentrate for more than a few minutes at a time. Trying to read is impossible. The act of cooking does not appeal to me. What I would like to do is be by myself, I think. But, that's not an option right now. If I were by myself, I'm not sure I'd want to be.*

Music is one of the things that can trigger a sudden remembrance. My husband was a wonderful dancer. Now, it is hard for me to attend wedding receptions. The music at the reception, along with the significance of the ceremony, is just very difficult to deal with.

July 1995: *I finally had a few days in Michigan by myself. I came to terms with where I am right now and feel better.*

The night my husband died, my youngest son was on the porch alone. When I came out to join him he said, "Dad was just here." I asked him how he knew and he said, "I just felt him come, he stayed a minute, and then left. But while he was here, I told him I was okay but he needed to help Lori (our daughter)."

Also on the night he died, my son and I were putting my granddaughter to bed. She entered her room and immediately became agitated and said, "Tell him to get off." When we asked her what she meant, she replied, "Tell Grandpa Don and his mom and dad to get off my bed." Both of my husband's parents were deceased, and as we spoke to him in the hospital, we had continually said, "Don't be afraid, you will get to see Mom and Dad again." My granddaughter was never at the hospital.

December 1995: *I was looking at a magazine and saw some things I liked. I thought of telling Lori to tell Dad to get them and realized we can't do that anymore. Christmas will be sparse for me from now on, I guess. At least I have family and am not alone.*

Don knew I loved jewelry and he was generous to me. Over time he bought many lovely pieces including two emerald rings. The second ring was at Christmas right before he died. It was beautiful, and I couldn't believe he had picked it out by himself. I thought we should return it because I already had one. He insisted that I keep it and now, of course, it is very special and I am very glad I did.

Money and I have a new relationship. I was always the frugal partner in the marriage. If I didn't save regularly, I would get very concerned and work harder until I was caught up to the goal I had set. We had fun, but I wasn't frivolous. Now it is different and I feel better. I still try to save something each month, but as soon as I do, something usually happens to eat it up. Now, I just don't worry about it. I just feel lucky if I was able to save anything since the last catastrophe.

It seems like we are definitely a target for bad luck since Don died. My son and I just look at each other, laugh, and say, "Oh, well, here's another one." I can now find some good in what happens.

When my son's brand new, one month old car was hit by a truck, I was thankful he wasn't hurt, it wasn't his fault, and the man who hit him had insurance. Before my husband's death, I would have just focused on the car wreck and the inconvenience. I have totally accepted the fact that I cannot change many things that happen, so I just go on. I cannot say how much I wish I had learned this years ago.

April 3, 1996: *It is one year today. I have been thinking of this day for a couple of months now. I had chest pains and went to the doctor. My EKG was okay which is good. I believe some of it was the anxiety of waiting for this day to come and going through another "first". My daughter called at 6:40 AM and we cried. Thank God she is so loving. I feel so lonely because I think no one is aware that it was a year ago this week and I am so aware. That day was exactly the same kind of day as it is today. It is cool in the morning and will go into the 70s this afternoon with some wind. When we came home from the hospital a year ago, it was 1:00 in the afternoon; a breeze was blowing, but it was sunny and warm. That day my daughter said, "Mom, come out here." And in the front yard hundreds of white cherry blossoms were blowing across the yard. We felt Don was passing by us and it was comforting. Today will be the same kind of day. I am going to walk past the old house to see if the cherry tree is blooming.*

Excerpts From My Journal
by Carol Fortiere

It started with a pain in his hip. We thought it was muscle strain from skiing. In August 1986, a Sports Injury Specialist could find nothing on the x-rays. Lee was referred to a chiropractor for six months.

In March 1987, Lee was given a bone scan. The scan found cancer had invaded his every organ by then, and on March 12th Lee called me at work and gave me the news: he had six months to live.

I didn't cry when he told me. I just wouldn't accept it. Instead I started keeping a journal to record the upcoming months.

4/87:
Lee started radiation treatments.

Ordered information packet from Oregon Health Sciences University for both of us to become body donors. There was a clause informing us that they have the right to refuse the body when the time comes, if they have a surplus of cadavers. Lee turned to me and said, "Now that really would be the ultimate rejection!"

Had a dream on April 1 that seemed so real. I felt I was wide awake and three monks in black robes with hoods came into the bedroom. They stopped at the foot of the bed and raised forefingers to lips as if to tell me to be silent. I couldn't see their faces, the hoods covered them. In single file, they went around to Lee's side of the bed and, standing side by side, they each bent over and peered down at him. I was terrified! I couldn't scream and kept wondering if I was dreaming. With their hands behind their backs, they stood there, looking down at Lee.

I woke up.

5/87:

Lee is having very vivid dreams about ascending grand staircases.

6/87:

Lee has graduated from using a cane to crutches. He still refuses to take any medication and has gone to his office every day. He claims that if he doesn't go, he'll feel that he's already given up. He's still alive, so he wants to act like it. Most of us still are in great denial over this, even though we can see him deteriorating before our eyes.

7/87:

Lee is still going to radiation treatments. They've burned his skin so badly he can barely get dressed.

On July 5th he was propped up on the sofa reading a book. His eyes suddenly went very blurry. If he closed one eye or the other, he could see just fine out of whichever eye he left open. We bought a black eye patch. At work, if he has appointments, he will switch the patch to the other eye if the person leaves the room for a moment. He said that he could almost hear them thinking *Wasn't that patch over the other eye just a few minutes ago?* He loves doing that.

8/87:

Lee and I drove over to the coast one weekend. He wasn't able to walk on the beach, but we had a lovely room and he sat and watched as I strolled along and did some thinking. It felt good.

We've really talked a lot about this dying thing. I still cannot believe this is happening.

9/87:

On the first day of September, I finally broke down and cried. I feel he'll be going soon, and I have to learn to accept it.

September 2nd, We sat up late and talked. Told him I could release him now.

September 3rd, Lee informed me that when he can no longer drive himself to the office, or the day he cannot get up out of bed, he is going to "check out". He will simply give in and pass on.

Lee called my office to tell me that he'd fallen down. Stayed home with him for the rest of the day.

September 4th, Lee and I stayed home together today. Anything and everything is setting me off now. I went from denial to outrage.

September 5th, Though he hasn't been eating well, Lee wanted me to fix him lots of pancakes and syrup. He ate four of them and promptly lost them. "But," he said, "I got to enjoy the taste when they were going down."

September 6th, More people are coming to visit now.

September 7th, Lee is down to 98 pounds. Had to buy him some teen-sized clothes in order for him to be able to go to the office.

September 8th, Lee has refused any more radiation. He's made a doctor's appointment for Friday, September 11th, to get a general idea of what's going on with him.

September 9th, He came home really early from work today. It hurts to look at how shrunken he's become. I cannot remember him complaining or appearing without his smile.

September 10th, One of our friends will stay the night and take Lee to his doctor's appointment. The three of us stayed up and talked until quite late.

September 11th, Lee slept in. I waited for him to get up. When he swiveled out of bed, he fell down and couldn't move.

Our friend and I got him to the sofa and I called the ambulance. On the stretcher, Lee said he loved me and goodbye. I was at the hospital within the hour and at 3:15 PM, Lee "checked out".

He was only forty-nine. I am forty-three.

4:00 PM: Went to Lee's office to break the news. I broke down and sobbed.

5:30 PM: Two friends accompanied me home. It started to rain. We got drunk. They spent the night.

September 12th, My friends and I started making the necessary telephone calls. Several friends dropped by this afternoon with all kinds of prepared foods. I'm not very hungry.

September 13th, More people came by the house. I want to be alone right now.

September 14th, Sent even more people away today. Where were some of them when Lee was alive, for heaven's sake!

Early evening: Got a call from our friends down in Eugene. We hadn't told them Lee was ill. I explained all that had transpired over the last six months. There was a pause on the line, then John said, "Boy! Some people will do anything to keep from turning fifty." I laughed and it felt very good.

Later in the evening: My aunt from Grants Pass called. My uncle just passed away after a long illness.

Evening: The friend who stayed here on Lee's last night called. Her brother passed away unexpectedly. Isn't there a saying that deaths come in threes?

September 15th, I feel badly that I can't be there for my aunt and friend right now. Am feeling guilty about a lot of things. I'm crying a lot and taking this week off from work.

September 22nd, went into the office today. Spent a lot of time walking along the river last week and sitting on a large boulder in the middle of the river.

10/87:

October 10th, Very interesting dream last night. It started with a truly dilapidated house. Nothing worked. The toilets didn't flush and were filled with waste. I turned to Lee and said, "We have to move from here. No one can live in a house like this."

He smiled and said, "That's the way my body had become. No one can live in a *house* like that."

October 20th, got a letter from the Lions' Eye bank today. They informed me that now two people can see as a result of donating Lee's eyes.

11/87:

I wanted to be alone for Thanksgiving. Lee and I always skied on that day because there were very few people on the slopes. Then we'd go to dinner at a restaurant afterwards. I wanted to cook a turkey with all the trimmings for myself. So I did.

Kitso, my cat, still isn't eating normally. She's mourning, too.

12/87:

December 11th, Lee would have been 50 today.

December 25, Fixed myself a complete ham dinner for Christmas. Lee and I always skied on Christmas Day, too, then went out to dinner.

December 28, Lee and I would have been married five years today.

December 31st, I wanted to be alone on New Year's Eve. I went to bed early.

1/88:

I hope 1988 will be a restful year for me. I have a lot to work on within myself.

Kitso still isn't eating much, and getting very thin. The vet told me it's cruel to watch her starve herself to death. C'mon Kitso. You can do it. Don't you leave me, too.

2/88:

February 2nd, While visiting some friends, I listened as they complained about their AKC registered Giant Schnauzer having gotten out some months ago and going out on a "date" with a AKC registered Black Lab across the street. The result two months ago was the arrival of thirteen puppies. Three died within a few days and all but three have now found homes. Would I like to see them? Sure, but don't think I'm taking one.

Evening: Brought my new puppy, Keeta, home. No reaction from Kitso to this bounding black ball of energy.

3/88:

Kitso is now eating well. She's starting to stalk the pup.

4/88:

Kitso has been going to the forest with Keeta and me each evening after I come home from work. I still have an ache and a large hole in my life and need to spend time alone.

7/88:

My best friend Jeanie came up from Medford to spend the fourth with me. We went to dinner and drove over to the golf course to watch the fireworks. She informed me that her colon cancer has gotten worse. She was diagnosed with it almost a year before Lee was diagnosed.

8/88:

Turned forty-four on the 19th. I feel like I've lived twice that, though I'm not looking or feeling as tired as I have been.

9/88:

September 11th, Lee passed on a year ago today.

10/88:

Was burglarized this month. They only took jewelry and two guns.

6/89:

Have been thinking of selling the house. Lee is still in every room I enter. I made him a promise that I'd wait three years before selling, if I was going to, so as not to make an emotional decision.

8/89:

Jeanie was able to come up for my forty-fifth birthday and took me to lunch. She was able to only stay a couple of days. She really needed to talk.

9/89:

Jeanie underwent surgery. They removed seven inches of colon.

September 11th, Lee has been gone two years now. It still hurts tremendously.

10/89:

Received Lee's remains in the mail from Oregon Health Sciences University.

8/90:

Turned forty-six on the 19th. Put the house on the market on the 20th. Had a signed earnest money agreement by nightfall, cash offer, 30-day escrow.

On the 21st, I found a "for-sale-by-owner" four miles from this one and across the river. And it's vacant! We can close in 30 days. The way this deal has come together tells me I'm doing the right thing.

On the 22nd, I started packing.

9/90:

Moved into my new home on the 24th.

Lee has been gone for three years. I haven't skied since he died. I still can't bring myself to go up to the lodge.

9/91:

Lee has been gone four years now.

11/91:

I know I should scatter Lee's ashes this winter. He had asked me to take them up to the lodge, but I just haven't been able to do it. I figure I'll wait for a really good snow and scatter them into the wind and snow here at the house.

5/92:

Jeanie was able to come up from Medford with her son and stay the night with me. She's on morphine now. We sat up and talked about dying. I told her some of the conversations Lee and I had together. We sat up most of the night.

1993:

My friend Joan was diagnosed with a brain tumor and melanoma. A group of us took turns staying at her home with her so she wouldn't have to die in a hospital. She passed away in July at age forty-three.

My friend Judy lost her husband to cancer this year. She asked me how long it will take for the pain to stop. I told her no two people experience things in quite the same way. Some people snap out of it in a year or two and some of us don't. We take as long as we need to heal. No one can tell us when the mourning period should end. I bought her the book, *A Time To Heal.*

1/94:

My stepfather passed away this month.

5/94:

Jeanie passed away the morning of the 20th down in Medford.

8/94:

Had a great fiftieth birthday party.

10/94:

The association I've worked with since February of 1984 lost its funding this month, and we closed our doors.

I'm going to take the winter off. I'm tired.

11/94:

Snowing outside. I walked up to the road to get the newspaper. When I got back, there was a bird hopping around on my deck. I went inside and broke up a rice cake and scattered it around in the snow. The bird wasn't interested. When I went back inside, the bird hopped up on the railing so it could keep me in its sights. When I'd go to another room, the bird would too, and just perch where I could see it. This was on the 12th of the month. The bird was still there when I went to bed.

On the 13th, the scenario repeated itself, and again on the 14th. On the 14th, however, I was reading the newspaper, looked up, saw the bird, and thought *I can scatter Lee's ashes now. It doesn't get any more blustery than this.* In the far part of the property, I had a private little ritual. The wind mixed the ashes with the snow and they headed up the mountain. I felt a calm I hadn't felt in a long time, and all I could think was *It's done!* I got back to the house and there was no sign of the bird.

On Thanksgiving, I fixed myself a turkey with all of the trimmings and called some single friends to join me. No one wanted to go out in this storm. I dished up plates and delivered them.

12/94:

I fixed another turkey and took plates to friends on Christmas Day. It was still snowing outside.

1/96:

Listed the house, and it sold in one week. I called Jeanie's daughter, Kelly, down in Medford, and asked if she knew of any rentals. I handled everything by telephone. United Van Lines brought me the boxes and I started packing.

6/96:

Haven't been to lunch with my mom in fourteen years. Am using this time to catch up on things with her.

I have no idea where I'm going from here, career-wise or with my life. After fourteen years, I'm glad to be back in Medford.

I've seen a lot of my friends pass on during the last nine years and, with those deaths, I have seen my own growth. By losing Lee, I was able to talk with them and empathize rather than just sympathize. I could feel their pain, not just guess at it. I have to be honest and say that I would repeat all of this over again, knowing what the outcome will be, in order to be where I am spiritually today.

I'll be fifty-two on August 19th, and I feel my life has begun once again.

The Touching Wall
by Jean McElroy Miller

11 June 1970 *"I got lucky,"* he wrote from Vietnam, *"and was put in a mechanized group, so I ride more often than I walk."*

His obituary stated " . . . was killed while serving as a gunner on a military vehicle brought under enemy fire." He was twenty-two years old. He had been in Vietnam for three months. I was left with only memories and letters.

Having suffocated all thoughts that he might be killed, I was not prepared for his death, and my emotions shutdown. Grieving consisted of thinking over and over, *Just one more time. If I could touch him just one more time.*

29 June 1970 I'd written him that I didn't like snow. He wrote back: *"Well, I miss it bad. When I see snow again, I'll know that for me 'Nam doesn't exist anymore."*

In late March, seven months after his death, I returned to the northern town where he and I grew up and dated. I'd come to visit his grave.

In the cemetery, his headstone sat large, rigid, and immovable. I tried praying the prayers taught to me in childhood, but they seemed not enough.

Kneeling, sliding my fingers through the snow, touching the hard-packed dirt covering his casket, bowing my head, I whispered over and over, "I'm so sorry you died. I'm so sorry. I'm so sorry."

11 June 1970 *"We have our missions in the morning . . . You don't know whether your next step will be on a mine or if a sniper's bullet will come at you. I've been shot at seven times."*

Somewhere in the miles of flat land west of Houston, five years after his death, I stopped at a fast-food restaurant. The place was deserted except for a young Vietnamese woman standing behind the counter. Other than on television, she was the first Vietnamese person I had ever seen.

Holding her order pad at attention, her whole being was focused on serving me. "May . . . I . . . help . . . you?" she said in hesitant, accented English. Her smile beamed across the counter brightly.

Looking into her guilt-free eyes, careful to avoid touching her hand offering a menu, I thought, *You're not worth his death.*

29 July 1970 *"I sometimes wonder if I'm really dead and in Hell. For every redeeming feature of this desolate country, I can think of ten things to curse. We have no damn business being here!"*

Watching World War II movies on television throughout my childhood, I decided war was exciting. My father had been a Marine Corps captain in the Pacific and his few war stories were wrapped like a package in silver paper. He'd talk about Rest & Recreation in New Zealand and the exotic food and the warm people. But when asked if he had killed anyone, my father ducked his head, hid his eyes, and mumbled, "Oh, I shot my gun. God knows if I ever hit anyone."

Ten years after the Vietnam War ended, my father, near his own death, for a reason I will never know, ripped off the silver war wrapping and released the sadness inside. He told of fighting on corpse-strewn beaches, of eating C-rations while squatting next to stinking, bloated bodies and feeling no repulsion because of his intense hunger and fatigue.

No longer a child, I cried, saying, "Don't tell me. Don't tell me. Don't tell me."

17 September 1970 Letter from the Department of the Army: *" . . . I regret to inform you that Private . . . died on 31 August 1970. Please accept my deepest sympathy . . . "*

Helping others cope with losses caused by sudden death seemed a way of releasing my own pain over my mother's unexpected death. Training as a Grief Counselor involved telling the volunteer group about the feelings we'd had when someone we loved passed away. Planning to speak about my mother, I was startled when the grief over my boyfriend's death, buried for thirteen years, screamed up from my heart.

A woman reached over and patted my knee. I was grateful for her touch.

8 August 1970 *"Miss me? You know I miss you."*

On a warm, March Palm Sunday, sixteen years after his death, I walked toward the Vietnam Veterans Memorial, where a middle-aged woman in a red business suit faced the tribute, tears carving through her makeup. Where three men in combat fatigues saluted a silent name. Where a grey-haired couple held each other tightly.

Emotions fighting my resolve against crying, I walked across the green grass, located his name on the wall, and put my hand flat against it, his name forever and forever to stay on that black wall . . . and touched him again.

Entries From Eternity
by Janice Porter Hayes

This piece was previously published in Daily Meditation, *August 1996.*

July 29, 1980: *Well , today is definitely the worst day of my life . . .*

So begins the first line of the first entry in my sister's journal. Today is the first time I have read the twenty-seven pages. When Terri sent me her journal to type, the years of my life dropped away. Again, I heard the news that Terri's husband, Walt, had been in an accident. And, I remembered my sister's journey through grief to acceptance and finally to joy.

At 8:00 PM Gary Rosalind came running to our mountain cabin and said there had been a terrible accident. I turned off the stove where I was cooking dinner, grabbed my first aid kit, and ran. I remember saying to myself, "Oh, no, this couldn't ever happen to me."

But it could happen to her. Terri had been married eighteen days and her husband lay critically injured in a mine shaft located in a remote western mountain range. Walt had been working the mine with his brother, John, and his father, earning money for college. The three of them were placing dynamite in the mine shaft when lightning struck the dynamite's blasting caps, setting them off.

The resulting blast hurled Walt's brother from the mine shaft, piercing his neck with a rock. He lived long enough to die in his father's arms. After John died, Walt's father managed to dig Walt from the rubble, and then ran for help. When Terri arrived at the scene of the accident, her training as a nurse served her well.

When I first saw Walt after the accident, I thought I would die. All this time, I'd been calm, so I forced myself to check John, but he was dead. I then checked Walt. His breathing was rapid and labored. He had blood and dirt all over and his eye sockets were swollen four times their normal size. His jaw looked dislocated and he had blood from his nose. His head was the worst because his brain was showing. He didn't have any chest or neck or back injuries—thank God. We met the Lifeflight helicopter at 9:45 PM.

Terri began her journal on the day of the accident, in the hospital waiting room. As she wrote, accurately documenting this difficult time in her life by recording her thoughts, fears, and observations, those simple sheets of paper became her confidants and her friends, gratefully fulfilling both purposes.

July 30, 1980: *Walt's brain surgery lasted from 3:00 AM to 7:30 AM. They irrigated the damaged brain tissue of skull fragments. The doctor said Walt had severe brain damage to his left side which meant he could have paralysis on the right side and be unable to talk. Later, they will have to reconstruct his whole skull. They said he might be blind but he doesn't have as much eye damage now as was thought. Walt has not regained consciousness.*

July 30, 1980: *It is now 2:00 PM and all the relatives have left. Janice and I are here waiting. We get tons of phone calls and people stop by. People really care, and the faith and prayers of many are with us. Walt's doctor said a normal kid couldn't have made it this far. Walt has a will to live and the Lord is with us. I have a peaceful feeling and I know that no matter what happens, we can handle it.*

Much of Terri's peaceful feeling came from the support of those around her. Carefully, she recorded how everyone, from Walt's wrestling coach to her distant cousins, gathered around her like a protective wall. These entries in Terri's journal are rays of light in her tunnel of darkness. She writes:

In times of crisis, it's good to be reminded that people do make a difference.

But around these rays of sunshine, Terri's struggle continues:

July 30, 1980: *It's 7:00 PM and we've gone in and out visiting Walt. He seems more alert than usual and when I talked to him, he moved. I asked him to squeeze my finger and he did it with great difficulty. We asked him to move his right big toe and it took him thirty seconds, but he did it. I don't think I've ever been so happy.*

July 31, 1980: *Walt remains the same. The doctors gave him paralyzing drugs to prevent him from moving too much because the movement ups his blood pressure and his intracranial pressure. The doctor said he could remain unconscious from weeks to months. I broke down when he told me that, but I went in and stayed by Walt until the spirit of prayer comforted me. I sit by Walt and touch him; I love to feel his skin because he seems more real to me when I do.*

The family comes in and out. I gave Walt a special talking to. I told him I know he is concerned for me but, if he dies, I'll be taken care of and will feel his presence daily.

Dad, Mom, Janice, and I slept the night in the waiting room.

For three more days the waiting continued. From August 1st through August 3rd, Terri held vigil by Walt's bedside and despite her turmoil, or because of it, Terri continued to write in her journal. When Walt's vital signs became erratic and he worsened, she wrote fiercely, as if the words couldn't come fast enough to describe the agony. On August 2nd, the doctors could no longer control Walt's blood pressure and further tests revealed an absence of brain activity. The doctors decided they would gradually remove all life support.

From Terri's journal, one now feels a new pain: the pain of waiting for death. On August 2nd at 9:45 AM she relates:

Walt looks dead to me and he does not respond at all. I sit close and tell him I love him. Walt's brother John had his funeral today.

August 3, 1980: *We went to eat breakfast this morning in the hospital cafeteria. I actually slept last night, from about midnight until seven this morning. I stayed with Walt a few minutes and really felt numb; I don't know how long he can hold on. I took his hand and told him how much I*

loved him. Walt looked dead but his face is less swollen and he looks beauti-
ful and sweet to me.

Walt died at 9:40 AM. I was alone with him so I grabbed him and gave
him a big hug and kiss and assured him I would be all right. We drove straight
home.

There Terri's journal ends: *We drove straight home.* But the benefits of
her writing the journal did not end. The twenty-seven pages became known
as Terri's "entries from eternity", and time and time again after Walt's death,
she returned to those pages. Somehow, reading of the strength she had shown
in her past helped Terri find the strength needed for her present.

A Symphony Of Mourning In Four Movements
by Marguerite Hughes Phelps

Movement I— The Bear Trap

My first thought was that the voices I heard coming from my aunt's
garage were not human. My family had gathered at Aunt Kay's after my
grandmother's funeral, and I'd slipped outside for a breath of fresh air. As I
listened closely, I realized that the sounds were of a man sobbing loudly in
incredible pain.

Years later, when I'd recall this scene, an image came to mind of a
wounded animal caught in a trap gnawing away at its own flesh in an attempt
to free itself from the cruel device.

I never told anyone about hearing my father so overwhelmed with grief.
I was only fourteen years old. Although I didn't know it at the time, it was the
last moment of grief my father would allow himself for over thirty years.

It's not often that we're able to pinpoint the exact moment when everything goes awry, but for my family it was my grandmother's death.

Never close to his own father, my dad's siblings took on the responsibility of liquidating my grandfather's assets and making arrangements for his
comfortable retirement. My father felt left out of these proceedings. My
mother seized this opportunity to further drive a wedge between Dad and his
family.

Although she loved me, my mother had never quite forgiven me for

having been born. On some unconscious level, she somehow held me responsible for the love and acceptance she felt my father's family withheld
from her after my arrival at an indiscreet distance from their wedding day.
She was never able to reconcile the differences.

As a result, she spent years silently sowing the seeds of unrest. My earliest recollection was when I was seven years old. She took me aside as I was
preparing to spend the weekend with my cousin at my grandmother's house.

"Come here," she'd said, kneeling down in front of me. She peered
directly into my eyes and I listened as her words pierced my insides. "I don't
want you to go to Nana's house this weekend."

"But why?"

"You're just a little girl; you're too young to understand how grown-ups
are. You think that because they talk to you that they're interested in what
you have to say. Well, they're not. Nana and the rest of them are just looking
to trick you into saying something that will make Daddy leave us. You don't
want that to happen, do you?"

"Oh, no, Mommy!"

I never stayed overnight at Nana's again. I carefully censored myself. I
never knew what inadvertent slip of the tongue might disintegrate our little
family, so I erred on the side of silence. No doubt, it fostered the perception
that I was either aloof, sullen, or simply a boring child.

My mother honestly believed that my father's perception of her and us
children was heavily influenced by his family's impression of us. Following
this logic, we would be forever diminished in his sight until she was able to
hold up a new mirror.

Nana's death had slammed the door on my father's relationship with his
family. I think I was the only one who ever recognized what that estrangement meant to him. Mom, having satisfied herself that we'd all joined her in
achieving black sheep status, felt nothing but relief.

Slowly I realized that I'd be growing up with a father who'd never get
over his mother's death and a mother who couldn't accept her first child's
birth.

The thing about bear traps is that frequently small woodland animals get
caught in these traps. My siblings and I had become helplessly ensnared by
circumstances far beyond our control.

Movement II— The Banshee's Wail

No Banshee's wail
Nor morbid keening
Marks your passing
From this realm.

And I will grieve
In a deafening silence
For a muted life
Whose ending has an eloquence
Never voiced in a lifetime.

The above is an excerpt from a poem I wrote shortly after my estranged husband's suicide. My husband had been a sweet and gentle man, given to great tenderness and moments of joy. He was also subject to deep bouts of depression which had become increasingly painful to stand by and power-lessly observe. Our separation was really more of a desperate challenge for him to seek professional help before it was too late.

That poem was the only available vessel I had at the time in which to pour out my grief. I deeply mourned his passing as I cursed the crippling anxieties and the despair that had led him to end his life before he was thirty years old.

The awful ambiguity of my marital status meant that I wasn't even en-titled to the grief which enveloped me. No one, least of all my parents, understood that my hopes for a reconciliation with the father of my six year old child and the man with whom I'd promised to spend a lifetime were being buried with his remains in a premature grave. I wanted to at least own my personal grief. I'd chosen the images of banshees and keeners for my poetry because they offered me at least a metaphorical means of shattering my silence.

I dealt with my sadness by refusing to let him go. I guarded my memo-ries like precious gems. "His favorite (fill in the blank) was . . . your father would always . . . when Frank and I . . . " So I kept him alive by remember-ing him fondly and speaking about him often.

Because I wasn't openly despondent or visibly non-functional, it never occurred to anyone, least of all me, that there was anything strange in how I was coping with my loss. During the years when I missed him terribly, I consulted his daily horoscope, refused to discard his shaving equipment and treated invitations to date as somewhat obscene gestures.

Death by suicide doubly isolates those of us who are left behind. For years after Frank died, I poured over my journal entries searching for clues and insight. I reread what I'd written about his having confided in me that he didn't know what to do with all the fears bottled up inside of him and that there were other things he couldn't tell anyone, not even me. It was all there! How could I have missed the signs? I should have been able to prevent this tragedy from occurring.

Those of us who've lost someone to suicide form something of a secret society. We learn to recognize others sharing our private hell from that slightest hesitation when we disclose that a brother, a husband, a daughter is deceased. There's always an awkward pause afterwards. *We* never ask how someone died. *We* know by the silence that the speaker is begging us not to inquire. Each time we speak of it and provide details is like exposing an open wound to the air. There's never a gracious way out.

What I've never been clear about is which aspect is ultimately the most unnerving. I'm always painfully conscious that if I mention suicide that the listener will be shocked. Is it shame or embarrassment that makes me want to immediately amend my statement by saying that it wasn't my fault, or, "no, he wasn't insane; he just got too close to the emotional edge"? And is it really politeness or consideration for an unsuspecting soul which causes me to edit my reply to stating it was an accident? After all, accidents, by definition, are things which were never meant to happen.

In these politically correct times, I hear the listener saying that I should feel free to divulge my grief without fear of recrimination. Yet at my grandfather's funeral several years after Frank's death, my father took me aside and whispered that his side of the family hadn't been told of Frank's death and asked that I please not embarrass him by bringing it up.

During that mourning period, I'd developed an uncanny sort of euphoria. Before my loss, I'd been a very shy and self-conscious individual, obsessing about whether people would approve of and accept me. Frank's death had freed me of all those fears, anxieties, and inhibitions. Suddenly, I was blissfully unconcerned about approval and acceptance. What could possibly happen to me that could ever wound me the way his death had?

Like the Buddhist tenet which holds that the world is the error of the finite mind, I saw myself existing outside life. My world had turned upside down and I was in no great hurry to correct a reality I simply couldn't accept. I stood with one foot planted solidly in the past and the other only tentatively in the present. Like a grieving Wovoka dancing my own private Ghost Dance, on some level I felt what I was experiencing was a nightmare which would somehow be straightened out. When I woke up, I would find everything back to normal.

I did, of course, realize that I couldn't resurrect the past and that I would eventually need to recreate a viable present for myself. Until then, I was determined to remain in a holding pattern until I saw a sign that it was safe for me to move on.

I'd expected, or at least hoped, that the rumblings of great happiness would eventually displace my unhappiness. As it happened, the opposite occurred. Without warning, I became very ill and needed an operation. Serious thought about my own mortality convinced me that I actually cared a good deal more about life than I had been willing to admit while I was wallowing in self-pity.

The mere thought I might not continue to be part of my daughter's life was a terrifying wake-up call for me. I was surprised at how much I did want to live. Soon after I recovered from the surgery, I discovered that I'd stopped looking for external signs that my torment was over.

If my husband had had one abiding joy in his life, it was his motorcycles. It was an unconscious movement but, for years after he died, I'd turn my head each time I heard a cycle approach. The day I realized that the roar of a motorcycle's engine didn't affect me was when I knew that I had finally completed the deep mourning period and was ready to get on with my life.

Ride swiftly and well, my darling
In that journey transcending time and space
Get beyond the shadows and the sorrows
Look back without regrets on life
Watch for the shadows as they dissipate
And see me, a being of substance
In the softest shadow of all.

Movement III— The Money Tree

"My sister's not well, you know," he said in a scarcely audible tone.

"I know, Dad," I'd say gently, and so began each conversation I had with him during that painful period when his sister was terminally ill.

Sometimes, he'd tell me about the kind of night she'd had, whether she'd gotten any sleep or had been able to hold down some food. He spoke about the weight loss caused by the cancer which was ravaging her formerly robust body. I worried that her reduced weight made her skin vulnerable to debilitating bedsores.

Mostly, the conversation centered around fond childhood memories . . . like what it had been like growing up with three sisters. I'd heard the stories many times before, of course, but I listened because I knew it made it easier for him to dwell on happier times.

Invariably, he'd get around to the money tree anecdote. He and his sisters had been given candy money. He had promptly disappeared while they were making their confectionery selections. When he resurfaced, he approached Kay, asking her to share with him. "What happened to your money?" she'd asked.

He'd hesitated, wondering whether to confide in her about the money tree he'd planted. Apparently, he'd overhead their parents talking with other adults about making money grow. He had taken that to mean it might be a smart thing to bury his coins and wait to harvest his cash crop. He always knew Kay would come to his rescue because she was the one who was most like his mother, whom he absolutely adored.

The death of a sibling is always sad, but especially so when unresolved issues are involved. He was her only brother and they hadn't spoken in years. His vigilance during her final days had been done surreptitiously through a friend on the hospital staff who'd been furnishing him with daily status reports.

Ostensibly, their falling out had occurred when their mother's estate was settled. He told himself that it was essentially an integrity issue, that the distribution of the assets hadn't been equitable. However, their estrangement had never been about money, but his perception that his sisters had shut him out. The most crippling blow of all was this meant that Kay was no longer his protector and confidante. Although he longed for a reconciliation, he was too stubborn to initiate a visit. Instead, he waited to be summoned.

"We've had our differences," he said. "But, of course, I'd never refuse a deathbed request." Whether or not she was simply being as stubborn as he was, as I suspect, was a secret she took with her to the grave.

The man who hadn't been able to express his feelings to his beloved sister during her lifetime now had no appropriate vehicle with which to mourn her passing. As I observed my father standing beside her casket, I didn't see an elderly gentleman at a relative's funeral. Strangely, he seemed less like my father and more like that little boy who'd planted the money tree so many years before.

When that child recognized he would never be able to harvest his cash crop, he revised his thinking and retrieved his buried treasure. Sadly, it never occurred to the man he'd become that he only needed to do the same thing with his hurts and resentments. Bringing them to the surface would have freed them. Instead, the bitterness had taken root, burrowing so deep into his soul that excavation was no longer possible.

Movement IV— The Phoenix

A mighty fire ignites
shooting flames flickering
as sparks fly, then die.

Yet still the embers glow
where sorrow and hope
are forged together.

Out of the ashes
the phoenix takes flight,
reborn on the wings
Transformation.

In less than two years, I lost both my parents to cancer. In the aftermath of their deaths, I've attempted to make some sense out of their lives and deaths.

No one ever thought that my mother, eight years my father's junior, would die before him, but she did. Although we were saddened by the loss, her death began some serious healing in our family. Strained relations had existed among some immediate family members along with the unresolved differences between my father and his sisters. Just days before her death, my mother's eyes welled up with tears as she expressed the hope we'd be able to come together as a family once again.

Apparently in answer to her last wishes, our family united as we never had before. Some bridges were mended in our immediate family. For the first time in decades, my father reconnected with his last surviving sister. All of his relatives turned out for his funeral, to restore him into the bosom of the family.

I've always thought death is probably God's ultimate practical joke. Perhaps if we understood it a little more, we'd fear it a whole lot less. Crossing over to the next life may well be an indescribably joyful state of being where we are reunited with loved ones and freed from the sorrows, pain, anxieties, and insecurities which held us captive during our mortal lives. In any event, this is how I hope it was for my parents.

Mourning is for those of us who are left behind. Losing both parents, even as an adult, made me feel a little bit like an orphan. A friend said when it happened to her, she found herself thinking she wasn't anyone's daughter anymore.

As for myself, I know that I'm still very much my parents' daughter and the progeny of all my ancestors before me. I see their traits in many aspects of my life and personality. Where else could I attribute the source of the psychic power I possess to interpret dreams if not from my paternal grandmother? My mother's incredible ability in forming close bonds with women wasn't lost on me, nor was my father's business management style. In my lifetime it's been a pleasure to observe charming, talented, and gentle people on both sides of my family. Collectively, their lives have enriched and ennobled my own existence, yet it's always saddened me that the lack of opportunity or the failure to recognize them diminished some potential for love and success along the way. Maybe we're all a bit like those mythological birds of paradise, in that each one of us is able to choose whether to extrapolate the very best or the very worst of those who've come before us. And perhaps, like the phoenix, we are always able to breathe new life out of the pain of the ashes of what's come before.

From The Eyes Of A Child
by Jane L. Remillard

For reasons unknown to me, I began writing this story of the loss of my brother as the young child I was at the time and then of the loss of my son in a series of flashbacks.

When my brother died, I had just turned seven years old. February 17, 1950 was a day of incredible pain and sorrow for me. Denis, just eighteen months old, had swallowed a little gold safety pin. He was rushed to the hospital. The doctors operated on him, but they never found the pin during the operation. Mom and Dad brought him home from the hospital thinking he would be okay. I held him for a little while, but he was throwing up his bottle of milk. He felt just like a rag doll in my arms. I was so scared for him. Mom and Dad decided to take him back to the hospital. They had a baby sitter come over to take care of me and my two older sisters. I began crying and could not stop. I knew Denis would die and I would never see him again. I cried all night. No one could console me.

***

Dad says they are going to lay Denis out in a coffin at Grandma's house. I wonder what that will be like?

***

Dad, Mom, all my aunts, uncles, and cousins were at Grandma's. I saw Denis in the coffin. He looked so still. I stepped up to the kneeler so I could be close to him. Roses were all around him, one even in his hand. As I stood there looking at him, the rose in his hand moved. I heard my aunt, who was standing behind me, say with surprise, "Did you see how the rose just moved by itself as Jane was standing there?" I thought it was because Denis was trying to tell me he was still with me.

***

How precious you were, Denis, with your bubbly laughter. You made me squeal with laughter when we played together. I never felt alone with you around. Now everything is empty inside me. I just cannot laugh any more. Mom told me today I am never to mention your name again because it will hurt Dad too much. I must be a good girl and do what she wants, but it does not seem right that I cannot talk about you. I'll just keep you inside me and talk to you myself.

***

February 20, 1950: This morning I was bundled up along with my sisters to go to the cemetery. It was very cold outside. Dad told me I had to stay in the car while everyone else went to the grave. I pushed my face against the window of the car to try to see what was going on. I wanted so much to be there with Denis. I was very angry that I had to stay in that stupid old car.

Then everyone returned. I wondered what they did there?

***

October, 1951: We have moved from the big old house I love to a new one Dad has built for us. Outside, walking around the new house, I feel so empty and lost inside. I want God to take me to be with Denis. I do not want to live without him anymore. It is just too lonely and sad to not have Denis here.

***

Winter, 1960: I am seventeen now. It has been ten years since Denis died but I still miss him so much. Sometimes I talk about Denis to my friends if they ask me if I have any brothers. It is odd, but my eyes always water and tears flow down my face every time I talk about him, but I do not feel like crying. I do not get a lump in my throat or pain in my heart. It is very odd. My friends notice it too. Why does this happens to me? I wonder . . .

***

March, 1966: The years have passed swiftly. I am expecting my second child having lost my first child to a miscarriage. Determined my brother's name will be spoken once again among our family, I have promised myself the first male child I bring into the world will be named Denis. The silence has been too long and I love Denis too much to pretend he never existed.

***

On November 18, 1966: My son, Dennis, is born. I am elated at his birth for the precious child that he is and that his presence breaks the silence imposed upon me long ago. When Dad asks me how I came to choose the name Dennis, I tell him how long I have waited to break the silence Mom imposed on me as a child. Dad is surprised: he never knew we were all under such an injunction. He speaks of Denis with emotion in his voice and tears in his eyes, still missing the only son he had.

***

Mother's Day, 1969: I lay on a stretcher outside the delivery room, recovering from the birth of my third child, Dean. The doctor who has helped deliver my child tells me my baby has a very serious deformity called spina bifida. He believes my child does not have long to live. I am left alone to absorb this terrible nightmare. I shiver uncontrollably and begin to cry, not understanding how I could carry a child for nine months only to lose him.

As the days pass, I am kept sedated and in a room devoid of new mothers because it is thought best to keep me isolated from the rest of the maternity floor. I keep asking the question "Why?" Why did this have to happen to me? Why did God send us a handicapped child? My husband, Carl, and I are also faced with the dilemma of leaving Dean in his present condition, which means almost certain death within a few days, or electing surgery, which might give Dean a chance to live for a number of years; but there is also the possibility he will develop water on his brain, enlarging his head to the size of a watermelon. This would lead to further complications in his care. In my own struggle with this life and death issue, I cannot bring myself to abandon

Dean in his own struggle for life. He must be given a chance to live. Carl and I decide on the surgery and pray.

***

Unlike my brother, who died from surgery, Dean has survived his. However, within days of our taking him home from the hospital, he shows signs his head is enlarging. There is not much doubt that water is accumulating on his brain. I find myself crying softly in the night, hiding from Carl the constant terror that I will find my precious child dead in his crib. My emotions are so locked within me. As I struggle to deal alone with all these devastating feelings, I begin to fear the onset of a nervous breakdown.

***

Dean was home with me for only a week when he developed a rash on his body which became so severe that within days his precious soft skin crusted and cracked open. This took me beyond my endurance. Panic stricken, I called my doctor and insisted that Dean be hospitalized. In the short drive to the hospital, I knew without a doubt I would not ever have Dean home again. I could not handle the strain of death hovering over my head. Yet, as I gazed upon my child in the small crib, his eyes fixed on me. I so very much wanted to hold him close and assure him I would never leave him. Those precious eyes would haunt me for the next twenty-nine years.

***

With the help of our pastor, we have found a nursing home for children. It is three hours from our home and we will only be allowed to visit Dean once a month. My heart is torn in two. To continue to care for Dean feels beyond my coping ability; yet, to give him up to a home, to another woman to care for him, tears at the heart of my maternal instincts. How can I possibly give up my child to another woman? He won't even know me as his mother. How can I abandon him like this? The sacrifice of giving him up is excruciating. "God," I scream within, "this sacrifice is too great! It's killing me to think of placing my precious child in a strange home."

***

Released from the hospital, Carl and I take Dean to the nursing home. The drive north is far too short as I savor the feel of my son in my arms. Leaving him behind at the nursing home, I feel the intense pain of separation and the welling up of guilt and shame at not being capable enough to care for him. I hold myself totally accountable.

***

As the months pass, our visits confirm that Dean is being cared for with love and gentleness. Knowing this, Carl and I decide to have another child. I am due to deliver the end of November, 1970.

***

October, 1970: Dean is eighteen months old, though physically the size of a six-month-old child. He does, however, appear happy and plays with some new toys I bring him. His blond hair has grown quite long so I give him a hair cut. It is a good visit and, happily, Carl has taken movie pictures of our visit.

***

November 4, 1970: Yesterday we received a call from the nursing home that Dean had a very high fever—107 degrees. The doctor had seen him and was not very hopeful that Dean would survive. Today we are notified that Dean has died. I know in my heart he is now free of the crippled body in which he was living and is in heaven with God, yet I feel a part of me has died with him.

***

All I want to do is to be able to see Dean one last time, to say goodbye, and to touch him again. However, Carl insists the casket be closed at the funeral home. I dare not challenge him. I deeply resent Carl for not allowing me to see my child for the last time, but I seem unable to let him know how I feel.

***

Following the birth of our daughter on November 30, 1970, I suppress the resentment toward Carl from conscious memory.

***

My family has grown, having given birth to four more children between 1972 and 1980. My happiest years have been when I was holding an infant in my arms.

In my mid-forties now, I am experiencing immense turmoil within. Once again, I feel as if I am nearing a nervous breakdown. I feel so numb, yet in deep emotional pain. My life seems to be falling apart. It feels hopeless and despairing. Only sleep relieves the unrelenting pain of living each day in darkness. I think of taking my life; it would be so much easier if I could just die. I know I need help but the thought of entering counseling is simply too fearful to contemplate. I am choosing instead to see a spiritual director.

***

My fourth child begins to "act out", and, as a result, our family enters family counseling. This exposure to counseling enables me to enter much needed individual counseling.

***

I have begun to get in touch with my feelings for the first time in my life. The journey, at times, is overwhelming when forty plus years of feelings surface and demand my attention. I know I must find myself or I will die inside, and yet, I cannot accomplish this task under Carl's authority. My marriage is ending in divorce.

***

July, 1995: After many years of psychotherapy, I have come to a new understanding of the deaths of my brother and my son. These two babies brought me love and conveyed to me that I am a lovable person, a belief that eluded me for most of my life. I have been holding on to these two precious souls all these years, unable to let them go. It is now time to do that.

I go to the cemetery where Dean is buried, carrying balloons and roses. I place the roses on the ground in honor of Denis and Dean as a symbol of my love for them. I let the balloons go into the evening sky as a symbol of my own letting go, a symbol of the healing of guilt and shame I felt for many years. Though releasing the balloons tugs at my heart and it is difficult to let them go, peace follows.

In one respect, healing of the self-condemnation and the ability to forgive myself and Carl in the life and death struggle of our child has occurred. The pain of separation remains, however. I believe this pain will only be healed in the next life when I am once again reunited with my beloved brother and son.

CHAPTER 14

THE GIFT OF SUPPORT

The comfort received from support of family, friends, and groups plays a significant role in the healing process of the bereaved.

A Faithful Friend Brings Healing Hands
by Georgeanne Gaulden-Falstrom

It has been said that a friend is a person who walks in when everyone else walks out. I found this especially true when I lost my son.

The death of a child is one of the most devastating losses a person can experience and one from which a parent never completely recovers. After all, a child represents ones's hopes for the future and, sometimes, an understanding of the past.

In addition to the loss of our child and the portion of life he represented, we had to deal with the loss of people associated with this relationship. At the time we most needed the support of friends, they were often not available. They, too, were trying to understand the loss. Yet God somehow sent us those persons who offered comfort and reassurance into our lives just when we felt all was lost.

When my son Steve was killed, my life and my relationships with friends turned upside down. My healing began with the people who came into our lives immediately after Steve was shot. There was the stranger who stopped, when others passed us by, and drove us to a nearby hospital. The hospital was minutes away from the home of my high school friends, Karen and Jack. These special friends came right over, bringing their pastor so we would have God's representative beside us. Other long time friends, Martha and David, came to drive us home.

The next person who helped was the police detective who usually worked theft, but fortunately was assigned to homicide on that fateful night. We felt his compassion as well as his concern. We spoke with him more about how important our children were to us individually than how angry we were toward the shooter. The detective treated us with respect and humility as he helped us make the initial arrangements for the beginning of a new phase in our lives.

Immediately after the news story of the shooting broke, my home was filled with people. Some of them were old friends whom I had not seen in years. Some were casual acquaintances, and some came just because their hearts told them to respond. I can only offer sincere thankfulness to the random acts of kindness and compassion offered by friends and strangers.

My friend Carol almost apologetically gave me a book by Edith Shafter, *Affliction.* Carol wanted me to know that God was with me and not to blame Him for this. At that time I was struggling with my faith and with God's hand in my life. I am grateful for her stepping beyond herself to offer me reassurance when I had more questions than answers. I was also grateful for the photos she gave me of Steve's party which helped remind me of happier times and how he was respected and loved by his friends.

Ladies from my church served as angels tending to our physical needs. They took over the kitchen as well as the transportation of family and friends from the airport. I never knew who was doing what, but it was all getting done. For the first time in my life, I allowed strangers to make my arrangements for me and trusted completely in their direction. While they took charge of the daily details, they let me be free to begin my grieving and my healing.

A co-worker, Rosie, arrived and asked what she could do. I had recently learned a former college friend, Dick, was a priest living in the Dallas area and I asked her to find him. He not only helped conduct a service I never thought I would be attending, but had just started a bereaved parents' group at his church. I felt God's hand in this reunion, putting the right people in the right place for us.

Another friend, Marian, knew that, although the house was filled with delicious food contributed by friends who had a gift for cooking, food would not pass down my esophagus. Each morning a hot pot filled with delicious chicken soup was placed on my doorstep. It was my sustenance until my appetite returned several days later. How did she know this was the perfect offering at the time?

My other son had a band concert scheduled the day before the funeral. In his usual way, he announced he needed to have his dress shirt ironed so he could leave the house within the hour. I was shocked back into reality, recognizing the living had obligations while I was so focused on the dead. Instead of attending the band concert, my priority was to spend my evening beside my dead son's coffin. My response of shock was a signal to a friend who was standing by wanting to help. She jumped up, ironed the shirt, and whisked him off to his concert.

Steve was killed during the holiday season. A casket and a cemetery plot was not exactly what I had in mind to purchase for him on his twelfth Christmas. It was during this time that my husband and I discovered there was tension between us. It seemed as though we were making decisions individually and not considering the needs of the other.

For instance, I wanted a plot close by so that I could visit it every day. My husband wanted one in the country cemetery where all of his family was buried. I finally gave in, deciding Steve would like to be near everyone else. This decision challenged our relationship.

I was fortunate to have known the funeral director prior to this crisis and respected Ted's advocacy for letting people do what is necessary to support their healing. Having become familiar with Elisabeth Kubler-Ross, I knew what I had to do to begin the letting go process, and Ted supported me.

Because of the head wound the sniper had inflicted, we decided on a closed casket funeral. Ted first opened the casket so that I could spend private time with Steve, touching him and telling him all the things I had not taken the time to say. For me, this was healing and brought a sense of reality. I needed one more opportunity, and Ted accommodated me with another private visit on the morning of the funeral. This special time was extremely important to me.

My husband refused to view Steve or attend the private session. Our style of bereavement was as individual as we were. I believed that each of us should be allowed to respond in ways which seemed right to us. I was later to discover the death of a child is a strain on a marriage because, on any given day, we could each be in a totally different stage of the grieving process. With both of us grieving, there was little left we could give to each other.

For weeks, cards came from friends and family offering their sympathy. I looked forward to mail call because the thoughts were uplifting. Some folks continued sending special thoughts throughout the year. My friend Ruth left cards on my windshield to encourage me on days that could be rough.

Each note reminded me there were still people in the world who cared and could show unconditional love. This was a sharp contrast to the person who murdered my son. Receiving the cards helped restore my faith that there was still good in the world.

I found a note attached to some paper goods which an anonymous woman had dropped off. She had lost a child and wanted me to know that my son was not alone in heaven. I never dreamed how comforting it would be to know that parents who have lost a child still survive.

My boss sent two co-workers to house-sit during the funeral. At the time I could have cared less about my material possessions, but the thoughtfulness of these friends protected my home and family.

Our tragedy made front-page news. Reporters from all of the media arrived to get their story. Our bereaved faces and story were featured on TV and in the papers. Basically very private people, we felt we needed to allow coverage in order to cooperate with the police in finding the murderer.

The newspaper reporters interviewed family and friends more often than they did us. I appreciated their respect for our grief. They had a shocking incident to report and most of them handled us very sensitively. Their goal was also to find the murderer, and we were totally supportive of their efforts.

My co-workers were also helpful and patient. At first tears were unpredictable. I would have to excuse myself and grab for the tissues. I learned not to be embarrassed by my loss of control and that people understood my difficulty.

I had a supervisor, Winnie, who had experienced a life of hardship, family illness, and crises. When I would call in saying I didn't think I could make it that day, she would tell me to get up, take a shower, and then call her back. Once I hit the floor, I could usually make it. Had she not been somewhat hard-nosed, I would have quit my job and spent my days in bed with my head covered up. Some days I resented her pushing me, but I knew it was her love and encouragement that helped with healing.

Staying through a church service became a real challenge. The tears would start without warning. At first the ushers were very concerned and tried to offer condolences and help. Finally they agreed to let me go unattended to the cry room with my tissues. In time the tears came less frequently, and I was able to stay through most services. I almost gave up on worship, but God did not give up on me. He sent a pastor by the name of Bill who guided us through our toughest times.

Often I would be driving down a street and see a figure that looked like Steve in the back of a car full of children. I would find myself in hot pursuit of the car, almost obsessed with retrieving my child from the vehicle. Once through a light fog, I thought I saw Steve walking in a park. I stopped the car in the middle of the street and ran into the park only to find myself alone. I was beginning to think I was going crazy.

We started attending the bereaved parents' groups on Saturday mornings. A co-worker I had known years earlier learned about our experience through the news media. She had lost her oldest daughter in a car accident just a few weeks before our loss. Our friendship was restored in the group.

Meeting with others who were going through the experience of grief was what kept us going for several months. We found out our emotional changes were not ours alone. By openly sharing what was working and what was not, we began to develop a greater sense of reality. What I had thought was me going crazy was quite "normal". We healed as we gave and received support and encouragement through the common bond of loss.

One of my thoughts was I must have been a terrible parent or person for something this horrible to happen to me. My self-esteem and sense of worth was challenged. I discovered that other parents had similar concerns. Our children had inspired us for a greater good through their untimely deaths and had brought us together.

Through our sharing, I also discovered comfort from the Bible. At that time, I was walking in weariness and I latched on to the Bible's powerful messages of hope.

We learned that Mary LaTour was bringing the Compassionate Friends organization to the Dallas-Ft.Worth area. This group provided information on such issues as surviving holidays and other special family occasions and understanding the need of siblings. From them we gained self-confidence to allow ourselves the opportunity to grow from grief.

Most of the time, though, I seemed to still be taking one step forward and two steps backward. I was on a roller coaster of emotions.

I was sitting in the cafeteria about two months after the funeral. My principal was telling jokes. I was half listening but managed to laugh at one of them, my first laugh in many weeks. A co-worker came up to me and said, "Well, it looks like you've gotten over it." My thought was *Gotten over it? I'll never get over it. How insensitive.*

I managed a thank-you and thought how American people expect you to get back to life as usual as quickly as possible. I wondered if this was to support their denial of pain being part of life. Yet, I had to commend this person for noticing a change and responding to me in the only way she knew.

My living son suffered from the loss of his brother and essentially the loss of his parents to grief. A friend asked me what I was doing for the living. I understood what she meant and realized it was time to join the band concerts and other activities important in his life. I could still schedule grief time but had to balance it with real time. This is when I discovered journaling as a helping hand. I scheduled an hour here and there to write down my thoughts and emotions. I no longer needed to burden friends with my pain. I wrote letters to Steve. I dealt with my anger before I spewed it on the first person who crossed my path. I was far from "healed", but in control. I even began to schedule "tear time" and made it all the way to Friday afternoon until I was driving home from work before I broke down. Once home, the tears stopped and I could attend to the events important to the family.

About three months into grief recovery, we discovered my husband, Joe, had metastatic cancer. Grief for Steve was interrupted by our battle with a terminal disease. We were in and out of hospitals in Dallas and Houston for one and one-half years.

The bereaved parents' group, church, and both old and new friends stood beside us. Surgery was a frequent option and on those days, the family room at Presbyterian Hospital was filled with people who came to cheer us and give us support.

Following a trip to Houston when we had been given the option of four to six months or a liver resection, I was so troubled I called several friends in the medical profession to get a referral to a local doctor. One of my faithful co-workers called to see how she could help and within twenty-four hours had arranged an appointment for us with the greatest earthly physician I have ever met, Dr. Zack Lieberman. When complications set in, Dr. Lieberman took over the case locally.

We worked as a team. Dr. Lieberman kept us informed of every change and option and even helped me face the difficulty of preparing a last will at the hospital. With his guidance, we planned the funeral well in advance and Joe participated. Through the doctor's support, the transitions were made much easier.

The death of someone who has been terminally ill and experiencing pain and loss of quality of life is accepted differently from the sudden loss of a healthy and vibrant child. The grieving began with the diagnosis, and the blessing was in God's mercy and restoration of my sense of reality, hope, faith, courage, and strength. Again, I received comfort from the Bible and believed that my healing hands were sent to me by God.

At the young age of thirty-nine, I was a widow and a single parent of a sixteen year old son who had, during his last two years of life, grown up with me hardly being there. In some ways we were almost strangers. Friends had taken over when I was with my husband but this, too, was a loss I had to grieve.

Being a good parent had been a primary goal of mine. My own parents had divorced when I was twelve. I wanted to spare my own children that pain. At this stage, I felt a lot like I had when my parents went their separate ways. Regardless of how much I wanted to wipe clean the slate, my son and I had to go from where we were and not from where I wanted to be.

Where did I really fit in? What was my next step? I had a lot more questions than answers. In two years I had missed out on a lot and wanted to run away, leave, vanish, and start over. That was impossible. Through the guidance of friends, I was able to stay put and regroup while Scott finished high school and then college. Stability seemed important. As one friend reminded me often, "You have to sit still and feel the pain. The only way out of it is through it."

Although I wanted so much to reconnect my life, with each relationship, I found I still had a lot of healing to go through before I could trust myself to risk those deeper intimate feelings to another. I'd already given up a husband and one son. My surviving son was on his way out into the world to build his independent life. To be honest, I was just plain scared to take a risk.

More healing hands arrived with direct guidance from now Best Friend

Jesus and Creator. It was time to seek the new purpose for my existence. God opened a lot of windows. Some let in lots of fresh air and sunshine, while others I had to close myself because at the time I wasn't ready to let the new in. Both God and my friends were very patient with me as I took the journey from eulogy to new life.

Help With Healing
by B.J. Gardner

July 8, September 5, December 25, January 22, March 13, May 11. Significant dates. My birthday, wedding anniversary, Christmas. The day my husband had his first seizure, the day of his surgery, the day of his death. I don't need to try to remember these dates. They are deep in my memory. The sad ones are as indelible as the happy ones. People don't understand this. Someone said to me, "You really keep track of all this don't you?" No, my subconscious does that for me.

I am often reminded by my body that an important date is approaching. I feel anxious and apprehensive. Once I realize what is happening, I am able to deal with the feelings. I remember the first spring after he died. I was working a new job. It is in the same part of town where the hospital and the hospice are located. I was alarmed because every day on my way to work, the closer I got to work the worse I felt. My heart was pounding and I would feel very nervous. I finally realized that for the previous two springs I had been driving this same route every day for very sad reasons. Once I understood that, I wasn't nearly so anxious.

Without a doubt, the best thing I have done for myself since my husband died is to participate in a support group. The group is comprised of women who are all approximately the same age and who all lost their husbands within the same year. It is hard for me to believe that three years ago I didn't even know them. The feelings I described before, feelings that are inside whether I am acknowledging them or not, would elicit a round of nodding heads in my group. It was no stretch for them to understand what I said.

Another huge benefit of the group is that it takes a burden from my family. I have another outlet for my grief, and I am not asking my children or sister to help as often. They have their own grief to work on. Some of that work we do together, but they cannot understand what losing a spouse means.

There are days now, three and a half years into this work, that I feel as if I have made no progress at all. Days that seem endless. Then I look back to what I wrote at that time and realize that I am moving forward. Sometimes I feel overwhelmed by the everyday problems that occur but I seldom have the feeling I am unable to handle them. I may not want to, but I know I can. This is the hardest work I have ever done but I want to see it through. I think it is the only way to be healed.

Living Through Suicide
by Teresa G. Donley

"Now stay calm. They aren't sure, but the police think your dad may have shot himself."

With those words, my father's life was over and my life had changed forever. Suicide. That awful, forbidden word, had entered my family. The questions started immediately.

Why did he do this?

Why didn't he tell me (or anyone) how sad he was?

Why didn't I see what was happening?

Why didn't I do something?

Why, Daddy, *why*?

The questions just kept coming. But they all started with one unanswerable word: why? There were no answers to that word then, and there are still no answers to that word today.

What followed were several weeks of shock. The pain was just too deep to be felt completely. The human body has an amazing ability to protect itself. Just as a burn victim goes into shock and experiences great pain while beginning to heal, the mind shuts down when tremendous emotional pain hits it. Then later, as the healing begins, the true pain hits—and hits hard. Healing hurts.

I was forced to face things that I had never even contemplated. There was the tremendous loneliness. I missed my dad so much, it was a physical ache.

Then there was the disbelief. How on earth does one accept that a person they loved with all their heart has chosen to end his own life?

Besides the loneliness and disbelief, the anger was nearly all-consuming. My anger was directed toward anything or anyone other than my father. I certainly couldn't be angry with a dead man. Could I? I was angry at anyone who had ever thought he was less than perfect. I was angry at the doctors for not seeing how seriously ill my father had really been. I was angry at the people in the church because they couldn't understand my pain. I was angry at God for allowing this awful thing to happen. I was even angry that heaven existed because my dad had chosen to be there rather than on earth with me. If heaven weren't so wonderful, he wouldn't have made that choice. Or so I told myself.

But I believe that the hardest thing I had to face was the fact that my dad wasn't perfect. When someone commits suicide, the survivors are forced to look at that person as they really were—not as a perfect person. I didn't find out anything terrible or shocking about my dad, but I had to accept how very, very sad he had been, and how he had tried to hide it most of his life. I really saw him as *human* for the first time. He didn't have a good self-image, even though I thought he was the greatest man who ever lived. He hid his pain and his loneliness behind a smile for nearly everyone. He made mistakes—one very big one when he pulled that trigger.

I trudged along through the pain and depression for several months. Eventually, I even became angry at my dad. How could he be so selfish as to think only of himself and *his* pain when he shot himself? Didn't he think about *my* pain or the pain of my mother, sister, and daughter? What about all the things he had wanted to do—was he just throwing them away? Didn't he know that we needed him? The anger at my dad was healthy—but it didn't last long. It was eventually replaced by profound sadness.

I was convinced that my pain and the pain of my family was unique. No one had ever suffered such devastation—or so I thought. I just knew that if my dad had died in any other way—any natural way—I would have been able to accept his death and move on with my life. But with suicide, so many things were unanswered and so many wounds went too deep for me to believe that anyone had ever suffered like this.

Then I took my daughter to Fernside, a Center for Grieving Children. There was a parents group there as well. For the first time since my dad died,

I listened to people who had lost their loved one in a "natural" way. I was amazed to find out that they had the *same* feelings as me. They were lonely. They couldn't believe what had happened. They were angry—just like me. And they, too, were being forced to look at their loved ones as they really were. I found that the pain of death is universal no matter how the person died. For the first time, I realized that what I was experiencing was not unique. Others really did know what I was feeling—because they were feeling it too!

All my life I have heard that good things come from anything bad that happens to us. I didn't want to see anything good come from my father's death. But, with time, it did. I became a stronger person. I looked at my father in a more healthy, realistic way. I became more empathetic with other people who were hurting. I have been able to share my story with other people who have lost a loved one through suicide. The good that has come from it is in helping other people.

Time Heals All
by Marlynne Harrison

"Aunt Marlynne, you have to let him go." These were the words that came from my niece's mouth, as we walked down the hall toward an empty, lonely waiting room. I was slowly going into shock. I could hear her talking, but her words were bouncing off me.

How could I give up someone who had been my husband for thirty-five-and-a-half years? This couldn't really be happening! *There must be something someone can do! This can't be the end!* My mind was rolling over and over.

When they were notified of their dad's condition, my five children immediately left their jobs and daily routines. For the past three days, we had watched and waited, as my husband was being transferred back and forth from a private room to the intensive care unit. The doctors and nurses had been doing everything they could to win the fight for his life as he remained in a semi-coma condition.

While he was in the intensive care unit, we were only allowed to be with him for short periods of time. To pass time otherwise, in the large medical center of Houston, Texas, we would walk through the underground tunnels leading from one hospital to the other. We went to the gift shops of each hospital and while we were in one of these shops, my oldest daughter said, "Mom, let's buy Dad a balloon." So we chose a metallic, helium filled balloon with the words "Some Bunny Loves You" written on it.

When we returned to the room where we were staying, I tied the balloon to the knob of the closest door. I was going to take it to him the next morning, but in our haste to leave, it was forgotten.

His condition worsened, and somewhere around noon, he passed away. We returned to the room to gather our belongings and start our journey home. My youngest son, who was seventeen, was sitting on the couch as if in a daze of disbelief. I handed him the balloon and told him to do whatever he wanted with it. He hung his head, and started jerking the rising balloon down toward the floor.

After I had put the last suitcase in the trunk of the car, I noticed my son standing in the middle of the parking lot, still holding the balloon. As I walked past him, the streamer tied to the balloon released its hold. While the balloon rose higher in the sky, I looked at the face of my oldest son. He was glancing at me with an amazed look on his face. Our thoughts crossed, and I stepped toward my youngest son and pulled his arm down, away from his reaching attempt to retrieve it. We stood and watched the balloon ascend into the clouds as if it had a determined destination. This incident seemed so strange to me, like something you might see at the end of a movie.

This is where one struggle in my life—trying to live with an alcoholic husband—ended in a horrible nightmare and a new life began.

I can't remember much about the first three weeks after my husband's death, except getting up in the morning, sitting in the recliner in front of the television, and going to bed at dark. Nights seemed a week long. I woke up about fifteen times each night, hearing every little noise, and feeling so alone. The fear of someone breaking in kept entering my mind.

Then, after three weeks, I started crying and asking myself, "What am I doing here?" I realized I had been sitting as if waiting for my husband to come home, and the horrible truth finally dawned on me: he isn't coming home!

I had been in shock, walking around in a daze. I can't remember eating, but I know I must have eaten something. I stepped on the scale and found I had lost fifteen pounds. I was glad to see the weight loss, but I knew fifteen pounds was a lot to lose in just three weeks. I decided while my body was in a losing mode to change my eating habits so I would slowly continue to lose my unwanted extra pounds.

Finally I got to the point where I told myself I had to sleep. If the sweet little widow in my neighborhood could survive being alone, so could I. I suppose my body was exhausted for I started sleeping all night. I slept so soundly I realized I didn't have a single dream. I was thankful I wasn't dreaming. I remembered when my dad died I had horrible dreams about him for at least a year. I knew I didn't want that to happen again.

Depression and anger were causing me to stare at the walls. The walls seemed to be closing in on me. I kept asking myself questions. "Why did he do this? Why did he leave me alone like this? It was so uncalled for. Our life didn't have to be like this! We could have been so happy if he wouldn't have let alcohol control him!"

I was a member of a small church in our community, but I started drifting away. I felt like a bump on a stump and came to the conclusion most married people treat you differently when you become single.

My mom saw what was happening to me and came to my rescue. Someone had told her about a singles group in the area. She said, "Marlynne, I am single and now you are, too. We are going to attend this singles group meeting and see what it is about." I was apprehensive. This was all too new for me. Married at fifteen and widowed at fifty, I had never been single before! My mom insisted we go, so I finally gave in.

There were many people at the singles group meeting. We all had something in common: everyone had experienced the feeling of being alone. Understanding and acceptance existed here. I finally found a place where I felt like I fit in. I was starting to adjust to being single.

I couldn't find the full-time job I so desperately needed. I was holding three and four part time jobs at one time, grasping every little chance to make ends meet. Two years later, I was offered a janitor's job, paying minimum wages. There were no benefits, but it offered forty hours a week I could depend on.

Nine months later, I decided I had to get out of the rut I was in, so I left that job and returned to school. This was made possible by someone dear to me.

Today I am married and live quietly by a lake, located on the Texas and

Louisiana border. As my mind rolls over my life and my experiences, I realize how God has taken care of me.

Many people think they understand what someone is going through when they lose a loved one. I now know the only people who can really understand, and give the best advice, are the ones who have experienced it. We must go on with our lives more intelligently and with understanding from the experiences we have survived.

Time heals all.

Angel In Our Family
by Gail Schroer

Yesterday she would have been five years old. Yesterday I placed a tiny pink rosebud on her grave. My granddaughter, Samantha, lived to be three days old. For some reason, we will never know, Samantha's heart was fatally flawed.

It is always heartbreaking to lose someone you love; when that someone is a newborn baby, people sometimes say things like, "It's good that no real attachment was formed"; "They'll get over it soon"; and "It's all for the best." While, of course, these insensitive statements are not true, people who lose a newborn do tend to have private ceremonies and burials, thinking it better to get it quietly over with, not involving family and friends, and get back to their normal routine. Eric and Judy taught us a better way. They wanted the whole family to know Samantha. They wanted friends and family present. They wanted to acknowledge Samantha as their beloved baby daughter before God, their families, and the world.

Samantha's story really began one crisp autumn evening. My daughter, Judy, and Eric, the young man she had been seeing for several months, came to our house. During the course of that visit, Judy announced, "Mom, we're going to have a baby!" Astounded, I stammered something inane like, "Why did you do that?" She laughed and replied, "I didn't *try* to get pregnant, Mom, but we're very happy about it and want you to be happy, too."

They weren't married. Judy had recently been through a divorce and I assumed she wasn't yet ready for another marriage. Even in the nineties, parents agonize over such things.

Shortly thereafter, Judy told me, "Eric got plane tickets to Las Vegas. He wants us to get married there. We're going next week."

Ever the devil's advocate, I said, "Eric wants to get married? Don't you?"

A few days later Judy phoned to tell me that they would fly to Vegas, because the tickets were noncancellable, but she guessed she really wasn't ready for another marriage. "I'm just not sure," she said. "I guess I just thought it was the appropriate thing to do."

They went to Las Vegas, but had a miserable time, both of them unhappy with the way their relationship was headed. The only bright spot was their mutual feeling of joy about the baby.

The due date for the baby happened to be the date of my mother's birthday, April 21. When I visited Mom in the nursing home and told her that Judy had a very special birthday present for her this year, she retorted, "She didn't have to do *that*; she could have just bought me a card." We laughed, but except for Judy and Eric, no one was exactly overjoyed about the impending birth.

Judy decided that Eric would not be her coach for childbirth classes because of the stress it might cause them both. She asked me to do it and I said, "Okay, but I might need help when it comes right down to the wire." My daughter-in-law, Laura, had given birth twice in the last two years and promised she would be at the hospital when the time came. Judy and I attended classes and when the due date neared, Judy came to stay with us.

Since I had recently retired, I agreed to take over Judy's job for a few weeks while she recovered from childbirth and spent some time at home with the new baby.

Labor began the morning after my mother's birthday, April 22, at 5:30 AM; Judy's water broke and I drove her to the hospital in the early morning light. Everything progressed normally until mid-afternoon. I asked Laura to take over, because I was having difficulty seeing my little girl going through so much pain, apparently unable to make further progress.

Finally the doctor interceded. He announced that Judy would have to undergo a C-Section because the baby's head was too large for normal vaginal delivery. Judy was disappointed, but exhausted, and agreed to the operation. Everything went smoothly and soon we had an eight-pound, one ounce baby girl. Eric, who had been in the waiting room all day, was overcome with joy at the sight of his beautiful daughter. She was so perfect.

By 8:00 PM, all three were settled in Judy's room. Laura and I left, congratulating them on their daughter, and later congratulating ourselves on what a good job we had done. We stopped to eat and even had a glass of wine to toast the event.

About 8:30 PM, Judy and Eric gave Samantha her first bath and they had a perfect evening together as a family.

The next morning I was making a second pot of coffee before going to the office when the phone rang. It was Judy asking me to come right away. "They're taking her to Children's Hospital, Mom. She's not breathing right."

I left for the hospital immediately and when I got there one of the nurses said to me, "You probably want her baptized—just in case." We sent for the hospital chaplain and he baptized her just before they took her, intubated, in an ambulance to Children's Hospital. I'll never forget that sound—the siren—as the ambulance left Mercy Hospital. Judy couldn't go with Samantha and waited, alone. I had to go to Judy's office to work since the manager was out of town that day. I waited, alone. Eric went with Samantha, and while tests were conducted, he waited, alone.

He called me late in the afternoon and asked, his voice breaking, "Can someone be with her when I call?"

I asked, "How bad is it, Eric?"

"The worst." He was sobbing. "She has only two chambers in her heart. She can't live long."

We rushed to Judy's hospital room, but it was too late. Someone else had called, and Judy had been all alone when she learned of Samantha's condition.

Somehow, through all her physical, mental, and emotional pain, the next day Judy notified all the relatives that she would like them to come to the hospital to say hello, and goodbye, to Samantha. She even talked to the Monsignor at St. Paul's Cathedral, asking if Samantha could receive the last rites of the Church. Monsignor, of course, explained to her that it wouldn't be necessary; Samantha was totally innocent and would surely go to heaven.

Everybody who could—aunts, uncles, great-aunts and uncles, cousins, even her great grandfather—came that evening to hold, love, and talk to Samantha.

The next afternoon, the immediate family on both sides gathered. We took turns holding Samantha as her music box played and her baby mobile turned with the music. We made a videotape of the gifts she had received and of her as she was held and talked to by each of us and as she slipped away from us, breathing her last breath in her daddy's arms.

Funeral arrangements had to be made. Although an infection had developed in the incision, Judy insisted on leaving the hospital to help Eric pick out the tiny white coffin. She made telephone inquiries and discovered there was a baby section in the cemetery at Epiphany Church in Coon Rapids, Minnesota.

Judy and I went to see Father Reiser to ask if Samantha could be buried in Epiphany's baby cemetery, even though we weren't parish members, and also, if we could have the ceremony in Epiphany's chapel. Both requests were granted. At one point while we were talking with him through our tears, Father Reiser gently said, "I know it's hard, but try to think of Samantha as your family's own special angel." That thought sustained us through those tough days and still gives us comfort.

All the friends and family of both Eric and Judy joined in the funeral ceremony. It was raining as the procession headed toward the cemetery. Eric carried the small casket from the chapel to the grave side. Our own parish priest, Father Grile, came to the cemetery to preside over the grave side service. Two great-grandparents were present, their grief tripled, as mine was doubled, as we grieved for our children and grandchildren, as well as ourselves.

I can't imagine how Eric and Judy would have weathered this tragedy had they suffered in silence with no family, no friends, no public outpouring of sympathy, and no sharing of grief. They would not have the memories of their families coming together at the hospital to meet and talk to Samantha, Judy's grandfather holding her tiny daughter as tears slid down his cheeks, Eric's sister, Gail, tenderly holding his daughter while her music box played softly in the background, and Samantha's grandparents cradling their precious grandchild, knowing she had to leave us.

As I laid the tiny rosebud on Samantha's grave yesterday, I remembered Father Reiser's words, and thought of our angel—a baby forever in my heart. I said a little prayer and thanked God for giving Samantha to our family for those few days to love and hold close, and for helping us learn all over again, through her, what life, love, and family are really all about. She truly is our family's special angel.

The Hope Group
by Molly H. Jenkins

My friend Marcia was leaving for Wright-Patterson AFB, Ohio, and this was her final Hope Group meeting. I had brought a cake inscribed with, "So Long, Marsha." She took one look and commented, "Molly, you still can't spell my name!" With that comment almost four years of a close and special friendship that began in tears and grief ended with a laugh.

I met Marcia in December, 1971, on T3North, Wilford Hall USAF Medical Center, the seriously ill Pediatric Ward. Our youngest son David had just recently been diagnosed with Ewing's Sarcoma, a particularly vicious and fast-growing form of bone cancer. Because of the cancer's location, the only recourse was an intense regime of powerful chemotherapy and radiation. He had just started on his first of many, painful chemo treatments. On the ward, Marcia introduced herself and began quietly talking to me. I tried to act polite, but at that point, I really didn't want to talk to anyone.

Over the next five months, Marcia would become one of the most influential friends of my life, gently, yet slowly, bringing me to terms with our son's illness and approaching death. Dr. K, the Pediatric Oncologist (one of the top in the country), was our son's doctor and kept in close contact with not only David, but all of us. He firmly believed in treating the whole family and included us in all decisions concerning David's care. He relied heavily on Marcia to coordinate the families of his Pediatric Oncology patients. All I saw was this petite, beautiful woman scurrying around in her Red Cross volunteer uniform and clutching her 3X5 cards, quietly offering help to all of us in so many ways. Only after two or three months, did I learn she had lost her six year old son to leukemia in August, 1971. I could only marvel at how she could submerge her own grief and be of such comfort to me and other parents and their sick children.

Out of a joint effort on the part of Dr. K., Marcia, the Red Cross Case Work Supervisor, Ward Case Worker, and the Pediatric head nurse, the HOPE group began. The first meeting was held April, 1972. By this time, my husband, my son Bruce, and I were practically living at the hospital as David's condition continued to deteriorate.

The HOPE Group held its first meeting the same week David celebrated his thirteenth birthday. Though our son was slowly and very painfully dying, he wanted desperately to make it until April 21st so he "could see what it was like to be a teenager." I wondered why there were so many parents on the ward at 7:30 at night, but was so numb I paid them no attention. By this time Ralph was coming to the hospital around 5:00 PM and we three visited with Dave in the increasingly few moments between morphine injections. Bruce and I would go home to TV dinners and hopefully rest, while Ralph slept in David's room. In the morning, Ralph would visit as long as he could before going on duty.

The day after David's birthday, Marcia told me about the first HOPE Group and what it planned to accomplish. She said maybe I might be interested in attending. At this stage, we were just trying to help David get through the day and night as comfortably as possible and I wasn't interested in going anywhere. I did learn how the name of the group came about. It was an acronym for"Hematology-Oncology-Parents-Endeavor". Initially the group met with some resistance from the parents, especially the fathers. Like us, so many were hesitant to open up and "spill their guts" as one father put it. It was a very divergent group, with rank varying from young airmen and their equally young wives up to senior officers and wives from bases throughout the U.S. and overseas. All of us had been uprooted and forced to move into a very scary medical environment and all had been forced to make urgent life threatening medical decisions about our sick children's diagnoses and treatment. At the same time, everyone had to find living quarters and assure that other children in the family were enrolled in school. Overwhelming life, career, and economic decisions had to be made very quickly.

HOPE had on call pediatric M.D.'s, nurses, the full resources of the hospital Red Cross Office (both social actions and recreation), as well as key T3North hospital personnel. Marcia and Dr. K. chaired and coordinated everything. Dr. K. was a small, intense man, forever walking at a fast pace down the hall with a group of residents and interns running to keep up. It appeared he could dart into a child's room, size up the situation, say a few kind words to the patient and family, and be gone. We quickly noticed the dedication and devotion of the whole staff. One resident told me, "Dr. K. leads and we follow, ALWAYS." Many times this kind doctor would see us in the hallway and stop to talk quietly. He always seemed to be sharing the burden of our child's illness with us. His compassion for "his kids" was unlimited and so many times after he'd talk and joke with his patients, we'd notice tears in his eyes and how he'd quickly bolt for his office to recover his composure. Like most of the patients and parents, we learned to quickly love and respect him and trust his judgment.

Between April and May, our son's condition rapidly deteriorated and he died May 12, 1972. During all this time, Marcia was there for me, either knocking on the front door at home with cupcakes for Bruce or to just stop and talk. She was never intrusive, respecting our need for privacy or, in my case, the need to get out and let go. She often stopped to talk to David, and he truly loved her. After each time, she would go off quietly somewhere to shed her own tears.

For some months following David's death, we were in a state of numbness and grief beyond words. In June, my husband resumed his AF duties full-time and found a measure of solace in long hours of hard work. Like so many parents who have lost a child, we grew together as a family, yet still apart, each trying to deal with grief in our own way. Bruce often stayed in his room, reading or listening to his music. Slowly, as other teenagers started stopping by, he began to come out of his room. I never resented having a home full of loud teenagers; rather, I was grateful that Bruce had found friends who helped him come out of his shell. I loved them all and miss them to this day. Again, Marcia helped by pointing out to me that maybe Bruce was afraid of hurting us further by trying to talk to us. Teenagers often deal with their grief and loss on a quieter basis than adults. Whatever the case, Bruce began to be more like his old self and smile and hug us more. How wonderful to be able to talk to him on a normal basis again!

So, Ralph had his job to keep him busy, and Bruce had new friends to help keep him busy and make the transition to senior high school. And what did I have? A beat up old rocker-recliner, a mangy robe I seemed to live in night and day, and the struggle to deal with my own grief and RAGE, RAGE, RAGE at the horror and agony my beautiful son endured for an entire year.

In August, Marcia stopped by to, discreetly as possible, check on my mental state and lack of response. She took one look at me and bluntly said, "Get out of that beat-up rocker, get out of that ratty robe, get dressed—we're going out!" She then added, "Molly, you can sit there forever, or you can try and get back to life. It is painful as hell and it will hurt even worse, but Ralph and Bruce need you and you need to start healing yourself."

Heal myself? How does a mother do that? How do I go out, meet people, and react to them, or worse, see their reaction to me? How? "Easy", she said, "we go to the Wilford Hall Medical Center. We go to the ward and we introduce ourselves to a young airman and his equally scared wife whose little baby has been diagnosed with a malignancy and ask if we can help. We find out if they want to talk or not; if they'd like a cup of coffee or something to eat; if they need help getting quarters or finding an apartment; if they need help with finances. We help them do all the things that have to be done to ease the way for the entire family."

My first trip back to WHMC was terrifying. We headed for the Red Cross Social Actions on the 4th floor and met with the supervisor, a no-nonsense but very kind lady who hugged me and told me I was "very brave".

I remarked, " . . . or very stupid." My flip remark was a coverup for my fear, but she understood. Dr. K. walked in and hugged me. He showed concern for my emotional and physical state, as well as that of Ralph and Bruce. I wanted to work with the Pediatric parents and do secretarial work in the Social Actions office. It was what I knew and I felt, for the present, I could do more good there. I also began attending the monthly HOPE Group meetings with Marcia. Hard as it was to be on that ward, I made it through the first and succeeding meetings and gradually began to come out of my shell.

Very slowly, HOPE had begun to coalesce into productive sessions, electing a slate of officers, formulating goals for the group, suggestions and plans for future speakers, programs, and general meetings for parents to air grievances and problems and to relieve the constant state of stress we were experiencing. No matter what the situation, we tried to find a common ground: to help our children and ourselves cope with the myriad problems. There were times when stress caused a few of us to blow up, but most of the time we were a friendly group who shared goals of helping our children and surviving. The few who came and had lost children tried as best as possible to let the parents know they could cope, painful as it was. The message was that each person had to find their own way of handling these situations. I noticed that so many of the husbands present did not speak out or offer comments but seemed to sit back and let others do the talking. It seemed they often had much more difficulty expressing their feelings. The wear and tear on marriages is enormous and separations and divorces were not uncommon. There were also related problems with other children in the family, often neglected by parents. These children, regardless of their age, felt left out of decisions, and while trying to handle their sense of cancer, they still needed time and guidance themselves. By talking and discussing these concerns, we were able to help each other. At various times, child and adult psychiatrists, pediatric dentists, marriage counselors, the pastoral chaplaincy department, and the pediatric residents themselves gave informal talks.

Slowly, we began to have a sense of belonging and understanding that others could reach out and help one another. We even had parties and other social get-togethers two or three times a year where the object was just to have a good time! I found my niche in HOPE by taking the minutes of the meetings and publishing a monthly newsletter. Speaking in public is not my nature. I can, however, talk one-on-one and, in my own fumbling way, found I also could contribute. I began to sleep through the night for the first time in many months. The nightmares didn't stop, but at least they went away at times. My family very slowly began to resume something approaching a normal life. At least as normal as could be expected, I guess. I wondered then, as now, what the hell is normal, anyway?

During this time, Marcia and I became even more involved with the HOPE Group and the hospital. I also proceeded slowly back into Air Force wives affairs. The Air Force wives are a very special sorority of friends. We help each other. Though most were strangers, the Wing Hq. wives were wonderful to me. Like most of the parents with sick children, we had arrived under unusual circumstances and our lives were centered around the hospital and our child's wellbeing. I had met very few of the wives and husbands in the wing until several months after David died. When we finally got back into the social life of the Wing, we were met with open arms. Thank God for family and friends. They stick with you through the really bad things life throws at you.

I stayed very active in the HOPE Group and the Red Cross Volunteer program with Marcia and began helping out on the ward with parents.

There were many times when I felt I couldn't take it but kept at it with Marcia's gentle encouragement. I remember one occasion when I went by the Nursery and saw a nurse rocking a sick baby in the rocker I had given to them. She smiled at me and waved. I thought, *Oh, Lord, help me. I can't do this by myself.* Then, Dr. K. was there with a hug. Once again, I plowed through, smiled, and kept on going.

Gradually, other people in the Group became more active and involved in functions and took over some of our duties. Marcia and I still continued our Red Cross Volunteer work but began to let others take over some of the many duties. Around this time, Marcia's husband, Jim, received new orders, and my husband was notified he would be leaving in a few months for yet another one year tour in SE Asia. So we knew we would probably be moving once he returned. I began slowly withdrawing from the HOPE Group. I had so many mixed emotions.

On one hand, I had enjoyed the friendship of this special group of people, but also felt Marcia and I had done what we could to help. It was now a cohesive group of parents helping each other through the denial, fear, pain, anger, and finally the acceptance.

Over twenty-eight years have passed since David died, and I still have questions. I guess time does heal all wounds, but I'm still trying to understand why David had to suffer like that and I still rage at its iniquity. I want to know why and I never will. I wanted so much to see David grow and have his own life—the good times and the bad—making his own decisions. I guess that's why I still carry the anger. But, I also remember the love he gave, his generosity, his sweet and beautiful little boy gifts, and our wonderful Christmases. I remember the arguing and the mischief he and his brother got into and his yelling, "Curses! Here comes the wicked witch; let's get out of here!" I remember, "Hi, mom, love you, I'm hungry."

So, with misspelled cake, I said a very emotional and painful goodbye to my buddy, Marcia. I'll miss her always. I continue to thank God for bringing her into my life at a time when I needed all the help I could get.

In addition to Marcia's helping me survive day to day, the HOPE Group helped me, and we all prevailed. We got through it. By helping others as I had been helped, I found a measure of peace. There is still plenty of scar tissue but we survived with the help of friends and our families. Could I have made it without the support of family and friends, my sweet, gentle husband and son, who carry their hurt inside? Yes, I could have, but how cold and lonely the journey would have been and how much longer it would have taken.

CHAPTER 15

THE ROLE OF CAREGIVERS

Professionals discuss the impact of helping others who are dying or who have lost a loved one.

Time On The Cross
by Michael Ortiz Hill

Journalist Anrei Codrescu once wrote of a friend of his who got a job on an assembly line nailing little wooden Jesuses to crosses for forty hours a week. Eventually he had to quit because it was driving him crazy. Sometimes it seems to me that my work as a medical-surgical nurse at a large urban hospital bears a strange resemblance to that of Codrescu's friend—night after night, I'm mindlessly nailing people to the cross.

A couple of stories: two dying patients, one week.

The first was Ruben, a twenty-seven-year-old Mexican man with brain cancer. His family had come from Mexico to be with him during his last days alive. They gathered around the bed weeping and praying, but clearly accepting with grace the inevitability of the final moment. As I watched Ruben's blood pressure drop on the cardiac monitor, I could see that the oxygen in his blood was thinning out, and the peaks and valleys of his heartbeat were leveling towards the moment of silence and death. Because the doctor had had the kindness and good sense to write an order that Ruben simply be kept comfortable (one of only three such orders I had seen in a year and a half at this facility), my work was to protect the profundity of this situation. Ruben also, thank God, had an order not to be resuscitated if his heart should fail.

Roughly twenty minutes before he died, the nursing supervisor and charge nurse insisted that Ruben be moved to another room so that a difficult patient across the hall could change roommates. I registered my outrage at this crude decision, but to no avail. Ruben was hurriedly disentangled from his monitors, his oxygen, the apparatus to suction his lungs, and wheeled into the hallway, where he died. I tried to explain to his family in Spanish the logic of all this as they wept. My Spanish is good enough, but there are things that don't translate between cultures, and probably things that cannot be said in any known language.

Three days later I was with another young Mexican, a woman named Maria with end-stage AIDS, acquired from her recently deceased husband. She was in and out of a coma, all of the systems of her body failing. Her heart was beating irregularly at over twice the normal rate. The oxygen in her blood hovered at about 70% which meant she was suffocating even though she was receiving five liters of oxygen a minute through a face mask. Nonetheless, after days of struggle, she looked quite tranquil as long as she wasn't moved too much, in which case she cried out in agony. Her mother sat at her bedside around the clock, also quite tranquil. Since Maria, too, had an order not to be resuscitated, she had all the makings of a good death in the company of one who clearly loved her deeply.

But Maria had a very high potassium level in her blood, and a young intern insisted that I give her a liquid medication by mouth that would lower it. I refrained from mentioning to the doctor that it could also be given as an enema. I left work at sunrise, kissing Maria on the forehead and offering my blessings for her passage to the other side.

The next evening I met her doctor in the hall, who with great enthusiasm told me that the drug she ordered could be given as an enema, which, of course, it was. "We are doing everything we can for her," she said. My heart sank as I smiled, trying to pretend I shared her delight. My pathetic effort to spare my patient had failed. She lived several more days; her enema was one of the lesser of the evils visited upon her.

It's always easy to wax self-righteous in these situations. Sometimes it seems to me that most eight-year-olds have more complex ethical self-reflection than many of us in the "healing professions". I question the sanity of medical "standard operating procedure" that makes the patient's body and mind the battlefield where we fight death with our full arsenal, even when death is attempting to come gently and can only be briefly postponed at best.

But self-righteousness is always beside the point. Because I've participated in such dramas, I am aware how easily such violence is enacted while pretending it is healing. Thinking with the heart in such situations is an extraordinary challenge, and much more compelling than self-righteousness are a few simple questions: What happens to us in these institutions that we disconnect and forget the simple fact that any given patient could easily be our grandmother, our child, our best friend, a childhood buddy, or for that matter, ourselves? Would we treat our kin this way?

Why is it that doctors often fail to recognize or fail to act on the recognition that making a patient comfortable is often the best, the kindest, and the most appropriate treatment? Why is it that even the most reputable hospitals in the world seem to rarely address practical issues of healing, death, and dying that have been discussed in the public forum for over twenty years? "Dying with dignity" is a commonplace idea in the Sunday editorials in any newspaper in America, so much so that it has been transformed into a cliché. How can medical professionals participate in a culture of obliviousness to the extent that we enact "medicine" with less depth of thought than mainstream America?

What is the etiquette of skillfully and compassionately addressing the issues surrounding "Do Not Resuscitate" orders? Ruben and Maria were amazingly among the more fortunate: the situation was explained, options offered, and choices made. Why does this routinely not happen even when death beckons? Why do we allow people to be violated on their deathbeds when it's clear that with a little courage it could be avoided?

How can we quietly be better allies for those who are most helpless? Immigrants and non-English speaking people are the most likely to be martyred by hospital "business as usual", alongside those who are senile or deranged. Some are dazzled by the technology and have unreasonable expectations of it. Others are engulfed by a world they can't begin to understand as they stand helpless before the stark realities of disease and mortality. This is a dire situation, one alien to most of us, and one where basic concerns such as patient rights and informed consent rarely penetrate. How can we change this?

Finally, how can we support each other in the real work of thinking and acting from the heart, in trusting the heart's intelligence in the midst of the cynicism that allows many to accept what is so patently unacceptable? In what ways do we suffer when we don't think and act according to what we know is right and true?

These are just a few questions. There are many more. Some I know, many I don't. I lay them on the table with bluntness and with a great deal of both joy and sadness, having wrestled with them all of my adult life, aware of both how much I've learned and how little I understand.

The twin mysteries of death and grief have made me who I am. When I close a patient's eyes with my two fingers, I congratulate him or her for one journey finished, and another just begun. When I prepare the flesh to be returned to the earth, I think inevitably of that day when, God willing, the end of my life will be sheltered by such kindness. In truth the way is clear; it's just that what we know in our hearts is so often muddied by circumstance and fear that even in the most precious of moments we forget: "Do unto others as you would have them do unto you."

The Nature Of Death
by Gloria McAndrews

I began working in Critical Care as soon as I graduated from nursing school in 1981. I've seen a lot of people die. For some, it is tragic: a young mother who came to the hospital for diagnosis of a nagging cough. She died of lung cancer before she could make it back home to make arrangements for her young children, one of whom she believed her ex-husband sexually abused. It was never proven, and she died terrified that he, the father of the children, was going to get custody of them. I still wonder what happened to those children.

Other times, death seems less like a tragedy and more like a natural part of life. For many dying of painful or debilitating diseases, death is an old foe who becomes a friend. Many talk about spouses who died before them, and say that they can't wait to see their long lost loves.

When I was about six months post-graduation, I took care of a man who had had a heart attack. His heart stopped several days later. We worked on him and brought him back, but when he woke up a few minutes later, he was angry. It turned out that he had married his high school sweetheart; their children said that they were like two parts of the same soul and incredibly happy. Unfortunately, she had died of cancer several years before. During the time his heart stopped, he had a near death experience and saw his wife waiting for him, but was jerked back to this earth by our efforts. By this time, his children had arrived. He made the decision, supported by his children, that if he died again, we weren't to bring him back. He died several hours later, with his children and grandchildren at his bedside.

A few times elderly patients have outlived everyone, are dying alone, and don't want us to bring them back. This always seems to happen on a quiet night, and the nurses taking care of these patients are able to quietly sit with them and hold their hands. I can cry then.

Death is rarely pretty and is frequently quite ugly. But we were designed to be born and later to die. I don't believe death is a bad thing. This isn't to say that I celebrate when someone dies. I almost always cry a bit, right along with the family. Sometimes it is because I've gotten to know the patient through numerous admissions. Sometimes it is in sympathy for or empathy with the family. No matter what the reason, I am deeply affected. A common myth about my profession is that those of us who have been around for a while develop an immunity to death. My experience clearly speaks otherwise. Each death, like birth, is unique and profound, making me realize on a daily basis how fragile and precious life is.

Reaching Out
by Steven Mayfield, MD

This story was written in 1994 a few days after the death of one of my patients, an infant who had been on ECMO (extracorporeal membrane oxygenation), a form of heart-lung by-pass for babies with severe lung disorders. After his death, I found myself, as always, haunted by images. I wrote the story as a sort of therapy, I guess. I think I wanted to convince myself that I'd not really forgotten any of the children and families I'd cared for over the years. Of course, we do forget names, even faces, but we don't forget the feeling of loss. And, in particular, we never forget the sense of utter failure, of having somehow been to blame even when, as is virtually always the case, no blame can be assessed. Moreover, there is a peculiar vacuum created by the loss of a child in the intensive care unit. The incredible activity is replaced by an empty bed—as if none of it had ever happened.

I won't presume to say or even think that the loss a doctor feels is in any way like the loss the family feels. But, with this story, I wanted to say that all of these patients and their families matter to us, and are mourned, and are not forgotten. They have left an indelible imprint every bit as permanent and inescapable as the ink that splatters on the wall in "Reaching Out".

***

The baby lies on its back, not looking like a baby at all; more like a whitish heap of suet splattered on the mattress of the radiant warmer, fatty lumps haphazardly shoved here and there as if some amateur sculptor had begun to fashion arms and legs, giving up when the medium, resisting any attempt to create life from it, proved unworkable. Wires and tubes run in and out on all sides, and the baby's face is partially hidden by a phantom's mask of tape. The breathing machine chugs beside the bed, sounding like a muffled lawn mower engine. Simon prefers the whoosh of the older, more elegant ventilators; those that push in a breath of air and then wait politely for it to be properly exhaled. These newer ventilators, the oscillators, are sleeker, with chiseled, fastidiously machined lines. They work better but do their jobs dispassionately, without regard for their patients; chugging along with utter precision in defiance of the very physiology they are attempting to vibrate back to normal.

Normal.

Simon almost laughs aloud. There is nothing normal about an intensive care unit, only what is typical.

The baby's mother stands beside the radiant warmer, her husband behind her. They are young, and the father has struck the pose he thinks should be struck at such a time: protective, strong. The scar along his jaw betrays him, changing its hues like a mood ring. Right now, it is pale against dusky cheeks. In another minute, it might turn red, then fade to gray. Simon has seen several shades so far.

The mother's arms are against her chest, hands clasped tightly, knuckles as ashen as the scar on her husband's jaw. It's very bad, Simon tells her, and something in his face makes her believe it this time. She'd heard it earlier but believed in God and television instead, thinking that one might save her using the magic she'd seen played out on the other. She looks at Simon with watery, reddened eyes, searching for something behind the words that will tell a different story. Tears brim and spill over. Her hands unclasp and instinctively she reaches out for the baby she's never held, knowing her touch is potential death. Her arms hang in the air, fingers aching, empty. She sighs, gives up, embraces herself, shivers. And then a guttural sound escapes her lips, and she reaches out again.

***

It is the mother's arms reaching out that Simon can't forget, even later, after the baby is gone. The memory makes him hesitate for a moment before stilling the throb of the oscillator with the press of the button. A shrill alarm instantly sounds, quickly gone when Simon stabs at another button. He watches the monitor as the already slow heart rate falls. The nurses watch the baby. And Simon, too. They watch him utterly, scarcely moving or even breathing until he nods. Only then do they begin to pull away the wires and tubes, one by one. It is done gently, as if the baby were still alive and, indeed, it suddenly seems to Simon that he might be. A nurse plugs a stethoscope into her ears and listens to the still chest. She shakes her head, then hands over the stethoscope without a word. Simon listens for a full minute before speaking.

"Eleven-twenty," he says finally, looking up at the clock. One of the nurses writes down the time. The baby is dead—has been gone for hours—but now it's official.

They pull tape from around the mouth, peeling it back slowly, wetting the skin beneath to preserve it. Tape removed, the breathing tube dangles freely and Simon extracts it in a single, quick motion. The still face remains twisted, pulled to one side, and a nurse reaches over, gently massaging the lips until they form a proper mouth. She wipes the face with a warm, wet cloth, removing dried secretions and just a trace of blood, afterward pursing the lips again. They stop and study the baby's face. It was a boy. A baby boy.

***

Later, Simon gives up on sleep and draws a bath, sitting in the steaming water, reading until he nods off. When he awakens with a jerk, his book is floating just beneath the surface of the water, its pages saturated and heavy. He curses and retrieves it, pressing it between his hands as if squeezing a sponge. Black ink leaks out and spills over his fingers. When he tries to open the book, its pages fall apart. He curses again and tosses it onto the floor next to the tub. It lands, flat and loud, ink erupting, tattooing the wall. Simon studies the pattern of the ink, then closes his eyes and sees the mother's arms reaching out for her baby boy, stopping in mid-air, jerking convulsively. He sees the face emerging from beneath the tape, the tiny, perfect hands and feet. He sees the nurses bathing the dead baby, an ancient ritual reclaimed amidst the cabalistic horror of modern technology. Of all the things done, only the bathing seems normal, carried out with gentleness and love. He hears the nurses talking about the baby as if he is still alive. How much he looks like his mother, they say. How sweet he is. How fat. How perfect.

Simon remembers the baby boy dressed in a soft, white gown, toes peeking out at the bottom, his fine, silky hair brushed straight. A nurse had taken pictures for the mother, and afterward, another had swaddled him in a cotton blanket. Simon covered the face with a corner of the blanket before carrying the baby away, a nurse alongside as an escort. They had walked down the corridor reluctantly, taking turns leading, passing the nursery where people were crowded around the windows. A few had turned, looked at Simon, eyes drawn to his arms. They had smiled, not knowing.

Simon feels the baby's warmth against his chest, sees himself lifting the edge of the blanket; relives the hope and disappointment. He remembers the first day when the baby boy had been so sick and yet still retrievable, the long night that followed, and all of the next day. He sees again the frustrated faces of the nurses and respiratory therapists, of the other doctors. He hears the pounding of the now dormant oscillator and the whistle of its alarms. He sees the grandmother, angry at first, then embarrassing him with under-standing and gratitude. He tries to remember the last baby like this one and can't. He hates himself for forgetting. He sees the father's mood ring scar. He sees the mother beside the bed, reaching out.

He sees a dark corner, too soon reached, then another corridor, this one shorter, and the last few steps to the mother's room. And now, his memory brutally clear, he sees himself pause before entering, taking a moment to mold his face, to form the proper expression. The grandmother opens the door before he is ready, her own carefully prepared mask dissolving into tears. She steps aside and Simon can see the baby's mother. She sits on the edge of a chair, her eyes not on his well-practiced face but on the still warm bundle held against his chest.

Her arms reach out.

Roma's Purpose
by Stephen Baggs

I knew from the look on the ultrasound technician's face that something was wrong. I'm a funeral director and very tuned in to people's body language; my job requires me to be constantly looking for cues as to how people are feeling, so I can look after them as best I can and meet their needs.

Two days later, we were in Melbourne, and the specialist told us it was bad, very bad: our baby wouldn't survive. I remember collapsing in a wash of tears and disbelief. My world was turned upside down.

Though we never had with our other children, we asked to know the sex of the baby, and named her Roma—just one precious name. My wife Violeta and I set out to make Roma's life as significant as possible for us and our children.

I'm also a grief counselor, and was, at the time, about to receive my qualifications; I hadn't imagined I would be my own first client. Some people would consider it a disadvantage living, as we do, about three hours from Melbourne, our state capital. Those hours were precious, however, as we drove back to our home town of Bairnsdale, piecing together what we had been told by the specialists, gaining clarity, and spending some close intimate time. We had us to ourselves for that time, with no outside interference.

As a funeral director, I spend my working life caring for and supporting the needs of others. But this didn't make me immune to the same trials and tribulations that befall others. I remember, in those first few days, coming to an absolutely rock-solid decision that the short time we had to share with our new daughter was going to be something special for us, and that it would help us to build a better and stronger marriage. I also resolved that, amid all the pain and suffering I knew I would go through, I would look carefully for every bit of good that there was to find and hunt down those silver linings.

It was interesting to witness close friends and family with strong religious and anti-abortion feelings grapple with this situation. They immediately began to feel the pressure and to understand that these situations are never black-and-white. The pregnancy was slightly more than half way over, and they saw that this was going to be a long and drawn out scenario. They started to say to us, "We don't necessarily believe in abortion, but we'd understand if you wanted to ease the pain." For me, the hardest thing wasn't waiting for Roma's birth, but simply making the decision to carry her to term. The decision was easy to live with once we had made it. While I found Violeta's idea of wanting to give Roma as much life as she possibly could comforting, I particularly wanted our other children, Sarah and Jeremy, to have an opportunity to see Roma and hold her if they wanted to. For them, I was happy to let the pregnancy continue. In my work I'm very aware of the fact that it's only been in the last century, as we've become better at extending people's lives, that death has been removed from the home to the sanitized hospital environment.

People honestly thought that if death was taken away from the immediate environment, it would be in some way easier to deal with. My experience has been that there is no moving on with life until we face up to death. It may be too painful today or tomorrow or the day after that, but eventually we have to experience it by ourselves, whether it's our own mortality or the death of someone special to us. When there was no hope of changing the inevitable, it became important to me that nature take its course. It's only when we stand up and look death straight in the eye that we can fully appreciate the beauty and wonder of life and creation and death. I didn't want to miss a bit of it.

Several months before Roma was born I started to trim a coffin for her. I had a few false starts. Once, I started, then had to put the coffin aside because I felt I hadn't been doing it well enough, and actually started on a new coffin. The coffins we use are plain wood coffins, only tiny, as you would imagine, for a baby, but carefully and lovingly covered with beautiful embossed white cloth. I found it very hard to trim that coffin. I've trimmed dozens for other people, but this was for my baby, and only I could do it. I finished the coffin, wrapped it up carefully so it wouldn't get dirty, and set it aside.

As Roma's birth approached we made many preparations to get things just right for her arrival. Violeta had set aside some special baby clothes: white booties and a beautiful little embroidered linen smock. I lined the coffin with the shawl that Violeta's mother had crocheted.

When Roma was born at 2:30 PM on January 8, 1993, it was very quiet. I remember saying to the doctor, "Is she dead?", though I knew from her color and stillness that she was. Also, there was no one rushing about, trying to look after her. She was given to me, and my heart ripped, and I cried. A little while later my mum and dad brought Sarah and Jeremy in.

To make it as easy as possible for our family to gather from all the points they had to travel from, we made a carefully considered decision to set Roma's funeral for the following Saturday, eight days away. This was really terrific. I have found that most people seem to wait only three or four days to have the funeral, and I have often heard people express their regret at not having taken a little longer to fully consider their options. Having eight days was a luxury. We were free to plan the service we wanted, without the stress of a restrictive time frame.

After the autopsy, I began the process of getting my child ready to be buried. I waited until five o'clock in the afternoon, when everyone else had knocked off from work, and I patiently washed her, dressed her, and readied her over the next six hours. There were other family members who would want to see her.

When I had finished getting Roma ready and placed her in the coffin, she looked like a tiny angel. It was eleven o'clock at night. Far from being in pain, I felt such peace at that moment. I'd done everything I could have done as a father or funeral director. It was a wonderful, wonderful experience. I felt such love for my daughter.

Emotionally, this was a difficult time, but it passed quickly. In fact, the eight days between her death and burial seemed like a flash. I can vividly remember things that happened in that time, but they seemed so quick, because we had Roma with us such a short time.

The funeral service was beautiful. I spoke at the service but found it very difficult. I simply wanted to tell people what a beautiful baby daughter we had and what an impact she had had on our lives.

In the years since Roma's death and burial, her life and death—her life, really—has given new purpose to my work. We now have many family members, mums and dads and others, come to dress their loved ones. I learned from my experience with Roma that postmortem scars (or "imperfections") are almost invisible to a loving parent. I have been truly privileged to share in some moments with families as, in their own special ways, they have said goodbye to their sons or daughters, husbands or wives. And each time I am privy to one of these special moments, it seems to me that Roma's life takes on an added dimension and purpose. I've come to realize over these years the quality of her life; she came into the world so briefly and lived only the nine months in her mother's womb, but left great changes in our lives. I guess the thing that most struck me was the amount of love a father can feel for a child he essentially doesn't know. The mother has a special link with the child in her womb, and the father can place his hand on the mother's belly and feel it move, and even talk to the baby, but he has no sense of carrying that child. Yet I felt so tied to Roma: she was mine, and I was brought to life by the strength of this love. The other side to this coin was the degree of pain I felt at the loss: I've always said that we grieve in direct proportion to how we love. She was part of me, and I know I'll always love her and regret not experiencing more of her life than I did. The extent of what I was to miss was driven home to me a few weeks before Roma was born, at our church's Christmas pageant. I sat and watched my five-and three-year old children sing in the program, and as I saw them sing, and laugh, and enjoy the moment with their friends, it struck me that I'd never get to hear Roma's voice, that I'd never get to hear her laugh; and the pain of that was like a knife that slipped between my ribs and stabbed me in the heart. I sat and cried. The saying "You don't know what you've got until you've lost it" isn't true, because I had appreciated what I'd lost before I ever had it.

I tell my friends I've had a wonderful experience with Roma, and I've learned many things, but I paid a terrible price. The loss of a child is not something I would wish on anybody, but with all of the wonderful things that Roma has taught me, I certainly can't feel cheated. She's as real, and as much a part of me, as the three children we now raise. Roma helps me every day to try to make the world a better and friendlier place in which to live.

Living With The Grief Of Alzheimer's Disease
by Bonnie M. Haley, LSW

They call it "the long good-bye" for good reason. The average life expectancy for an Alzheimer's patient is about eight years from the time of diagnosis and some have lasted as long as twenty years, which is a long time to live with a death sentence. A very long time.

Alzheimer's disease slowly, insidiously destroys brain cells, affecting a person's memory of his past, of people, places, and words. A person will gradually forget how to dress himself, bathe himself, and go to the bathroom by himself. As brain cells continue to be destroyed, he will lose his ability to walk and perform all purposeful movements. Eventually, he may forget how to swallow. Alzheimer's can also cause disinhibition and changes in personality that are often shocking to loved ones. The patient may develop psychotic symptoms and become paranoid or combative toward his caregivers.

Most of us can only speculate as to what it feels like to have Alzheimer's disease. We can try our best to offer care, patience, and emotional support. However, what we have to offer the patient is naturally affected by our own emotional state as we grieve for the gradual loss of the loved one that we knew.

As a Geriatric social worker, I have spent many years working with patients and their families as they progress through the various phases of the disease. I have heard their stories, let them yell and scream in anger, and held them while they cried. I have led support groups and watched and listened as family members reached out for help and found other family members there to give it. I have listened to the frustrations of staff members who were struggling with feelings of loss or trying to cope with irrational and combative patients.

Some might think that all of these experiences have made me an "expert" in the field of Alzheimer's disease. Not so. Professional experience gave me a strong foundation, but I was not a real "expert" on Alzheimer's disease until it touched me personally.

My father-in-law went from mail clerk to vice president of a bank with only a high school education. I knew he must be very bright to have accomplished that, but to me he was always just my lovable, goofy father-in-law.

I mean no disrespect when I say goofy, but that's honestly how I saw him for the first twenty years I knew him. After all, I never saw him at work. At home, he was a rather quiet, gentle man with a goofy sense of humor. He told the dumbest jokes, and he'd repeat them over and over. Luckily he never took himself too seriously; he often joked about himself and his bad jokes. When he wasn't joking, he lived to play tennis and loved reading books about history. He was a caring father who enjoyed long talks with his children and grandchildren about what was happening in their lives.

It's hard to say when "goofy" turned to real confusion and forgetfulness because he tried hard to cover it up. Alzheimer's patients do that. Eventually his condition could no longer be denied and he went to his doctor for some testing. My husband Dave had the difficult job of telling him that what he was experiencing were symptoms of Alzheimer's disease. He explained what that meant and a little about what he might expect. Papa was a devoutly religious man and his response still moves me. He said, "I don't like this, and I don't want this to be happening to me, but I will accept whatever hand God deals me. I just don't want anyone to make fun of me."

Papa's reaction was unusual, I think, and it was a reflection of his deep religious faith and his easy going, accepting personality. Most people cling vehemently to denial, at least for awhile, and when their deficits cannot be completely ignored, they minimize or justify them irrationally.

Family members also try to deny that something serious may be wrong. After all, we all can be forgetful at times, or perhaps the symptoms are a side effect of medication. Although Alzheimer's disease can only be diagnosed definitively upon autopsy, the diagnosis is usually made when other possible causes of confusion have been eliminated. The process usually involves a full battery of tests and evaluations. When the diagnosis is finally given, some patients continue to run away from it by going from doctor to doctor seeking other opinions, hoping that someone will finally tell them what they want to hear.

Some families choose not to tell the patients that they have Alzheimer's disease for fear of the devastating effect this will have on them. That's an individual decision and there are pros and cons to be considered. I know that telling Papa was the right thing to do because he knew that something was seriously wrong with his mind. Many people who are aware of their confusion are frightened and worry that they may be going insane. When they learn that they have a physical illness that is affecting their memory, they can begin to deal with it.

After that initial discussion with my husband, we tried to help Papa to live as normally as possible. Most of us did what we thought was the kindest thing: we didn't talk about it. We overlooked his increasing confusion and tried to be patient when he did things like putting the car keys into the freezer. The more we tried to ignore it, the harder he tried to cover it up.

Then Papa came to stay with us for a week so that my mother-in-law could get away. The change of environment caused an increase in confusion. A few days into the visit he joined me while I did my usual mommy car-pooling, and he said to me, "Did you know that David used to play in a band?"

I said, "Yes, Papa, I know that."

He said, "Well, did you know that he used to work in a prison?"

I said, "Yes, Papa, I know."

He said, "How do you know that?"

I said, "Because I'm married to him."

He said, "You are?"

I said, "Yes, I've been married to him for almost twenty-three years."

He then clenched his fist and said angrily, "Then why don't I know that?!"

That moment was the beginning of a brief but positive experience for him and an incredible learning experience for me.

I said, "Do you remember going to the doctor a few years ago and talking about your confusion and forgetfulness?"

He said, "Yes, I remember. He said it would get worse, and it has."

I said, "That's right. You're confused because you have Alzheimer's disease. But it's okay. We understand."

We then had an hour-long talk that will stay with me for the rest of my life. Walking along the beach, we talked about our lives and learned that in the ways that count, we were very much alike. I took the opportunity to tell him how much I admired him for his faith and his courage and the way that he was handling such a devastating disease.

We also talked about how frightening it is to be so confused and disoriented, and how difficult it must be to always try to cover it up, to keep up with conversations that you don't understand, and to pretend that nothing is wrong.

After we got home, he called me aside, sat on the couch and held my hand saying, "You have no idea how good it's been for me to be able to talk about this."

Later that week he became extremely disoriented and distraught. I said, "Papa, remember the talk we had the other day about your confusion and what the doctor said?"

"No," he said. "What talk?"

It was gone. In his mind the talk had never happened. Does that mean it was not important? No. That talk helped him to get through a difficult moment. With Alzheimer's patients, sometimes that's the best thing we can hope for. The moment lives on, however, in my work, as I have learned the importance of acknowledging what is happening to dementia patients and developing relationships in which they feel safe talking about their fears and frustrations.

I find that most Alzheimer's victims and their family members go through a series of stages that closely resemble the stages of grief described by Dr. Elisabeth Kubler-Ross in her book, *On Death and Dying*. For many family members, much of the grieving is done before death occurs. Of course, the process is different for each person. Some people skip a stage or get stuck in another for a long time. The patients themselves are often unable to complete the process because of their increasing confusion. They also tend to get stuck in stages because of obsessive behaviors and their inability to work through their thoughts and feelings. The general patterns are clear, though, and family members are often surprised to find that what they are feeling is a normal and healthy response to a horrifying situation.

Once a family gets past the denial and accepts the diagnosis, they focus their energies on tasks such as providing care and planning for the future. They busy themselves with practical matters, though the full emotional impact of what is happening to their family has not yet hit.

After a time, my mother-in-law was burned out. She had gone without rest and Papa's continual, repetitive questions were trying her patience. When he became incontinent and started to fall frequently, we knew it was time for nursing home placement. At least we knew it in our heads. Our heads and our hearts, however, were not always in sync.

When we arrived at my in-laws' home one Friday night, Papa had had another fall requiring a call to 911. When Dave's mom greeted us at the door, she told us what had happened and said, "There's good news. A bed has become available at the nursing home and he's being admitted in the morning."

I had such an ominous feeling as we visited with Papa that night, trying to pretend that this night was no different from any other. After we tucked him in bed, we tried to watch TV for a while, but I was much too distracted by a gnawing feeling in the pit of my stomach. *He has lived with the woman he loves for the past 47 years,* I thought. *And he has lived in this house for the past 25 years. This is the last night that he will ever sleep in his bed, and probably the last time he'll ever be in his house, and he doesn't even know it.* These thoughts troubled me deeply but I didn't share them with anyone until much later. I knew that I needed to be strong so that others could find the strength to do what needed to be done.

On the morning of admission, Dave got Papa cleaned and dressed. Caring for an incontinent parent is an act of true love and a difficult emotional experience for both the parent and the child. When the time came to go downstairs, we saw how profoundly Papa's spatial awareness was affected by the disease; he was frightened and unable to manage even one stair. Without hesitation, Dave put his father on his back and carried him down the stairs. He then led his father to the car by walking backwards while holding both of his father's hands. Papa good-naturedly followed him, taking baby steps and chatting incoherently the whole way. When we arrived at the nursing home, Dave led him to his new room the same way.

Papa never asked where we were going, nor did he show any reaction to his new environment, almost as if he knew something had to be done and he wanted to make it as easy on his family as he could. I'm not sure that he had the reasoning powers to really think about it that way, but that's the way he acted, and it's what I would expect from him.

Having been in the business for a long time, I knew that it was as smooth and "easy" an admission as I had ever witnessed. Still, it was not an easy admission to *experience.* That horrible feeling still lay in the pit of my stomach, and turning away to leave the nursing home without Papa took courage for all of us. We supported each other and said all the right things. We knew that it was necessary and that he would receive the care that he needed, so why did it hurt so much?

Later, when my husband and I were alone, this devoted son finally gave in and wept for his father. His body wracked with sobs, he kept saying, "He trusted me. He just followed me with complete trust and then I left him there." The guilt. Ever present, ever painful.

Papa was in the nursing home for two years. He stopped walking shortly after his admission and eventually had to be transferred from bed to chair with a mechanical device known as a hoyer lift. When we visited, we fed him like we had once fed our infants, because he was no longer able to feed himself. He no longer knew who we were. His speech was usually garbled, but he tried ever so hard to participate in our conversations and to be appropriate. It was also clear at times from his mannerisms and affect that he was trying to tell a joke.

Some people with Alzheimer's disease experience profound personality changes, but Papa never did. He endured his illness with spiritual acceptance. He faced each day with courage, clung to his dignity with tireless effort, and his sense of humor, goofy as it was, never failed him.

Dave and I were privileged to be with Papa when he took his last breath, and I will be forever grateful that we were. In the five years since his diagnosis, he had touched my heart and soul and taught me more about Alzheimer's disease than any textbook or workshop could have. Although saying goodbye was difficult, his family had finally reached the point of acceptance and welcomed the end of his suffering.

As I look back, I realize that it was only through Papa's tragic suffering that I came to know his strengths. Once upon a time I just had a goofy father-in-law. Now I have a hero.

A Job Of Love
by Kelly Beischel

I had an identity; I was Paul's nurse. Paul, or as I called him Dad, was my father-in-law. The relationship between Dad and I changed drastically when I became his nurse the last three years of his life. I spent at least one night a week caring for him during that period. Our relationship was unlike any other I have ever had with anyone. I was assisting him with medical help and he was giving back tenfold, teaching me through his actions and words. He helped me to understand my husband's work, guided me in the how to's of raising loving and well-rounded children, and helped strengthen my relationship with God. I was a better person just for having spent time with him. Blessed am I for having had the opportunity to care for him. When my youngest child was in kindergarten, he began going with me to Grandpa's on Sunday nights. He looked forward to those evenings. My other children were jealous and, as a result, in the summer took turns. The first few Sunday nights after Dad died, I cried. I missed our special time together. Even today there are times my heart becomes heavy when I think about what I am missing without his being here.

I remember the day he died as if it was yesterday. Although the pain that accompanies it has lessened considerably, his death is still vivid in my memory. Guilt, or maybe it is embarrassment, is a big factor in my memory. I was shopping, spending a ridiculous amount of money on a pair of jeans for my daughter, while Dad was dying and my sister-in-law was attempting to find me. I remember feeling guilty afterward that I was doing something as trivial as shopping and spending his son's money when Paul was dying. I never thought it would end this way. I'd always imagined I would be there with him when he died.

Upon arriving at the hospital, I looked into the eyes of the people I love so much and I knew. I had an outburst of denial, and my mother-in-law held and comforted me. My immediate reaction was one of embarrassment. What was it that overcame me and made me break down like that in front of his own children, people who had more rights to his love than I did? Furthermore, there was his wife, the very person he lived for, comforting me. How could I have cried so in front of her? I remember thinking that I had lost my identity. I was no longer Paul's nurse. I felt as though I was free floating, lost. I did not even get to say goodbye.

Telling my husband about his dad when he arrived at the hospital, watching the pain in his face, and feeling his fierce hug made my heart ache worse. Watching my husband bottle up his emotions was maybe harder to deal with than if he had released his anguish and cried. I was relieved when he did finally cry out loud the next morning.

The drive home from the hospital is still etched in my memory. It was a sunny and unseasonably warm day so there were people out walking, enjoying the reprieve from the cold. I remember wondering how the world could still be moving as if nothing had happened when I hurt so much.

Just when I thought I could not hurt worse, we told our children that their grandpa died. Within the days that followed, I saw things and felt emotions that were heart wrenching enough to bring me to my knees. After my daughter stoically attempted to hold in her feelings, my husband and I held her late one night as she cried, suddenly afraid of her own father's mortality and her helplessness in comforting her dad in his loss. I caught a glimpse of the man my ten-year-old son will one day be as he stood by his grandma greeting the mourners at the wake and walked by her side at the Mass of Christian burial. And finally, we also comforted our youngest child as he realized the grandpa he visited every Sunday night, the one who challenged him with weekly quizzes, would no longer be there. We told them they were blessed in the fact that they were able to know their grandpa and love him as much as they did. When I was alone and contemplative, I many times questioned if it was worth loving someone this much knowing what the pain was going to be when they were gone.

The family gatherings in the ensuing days were comforting. I felt a need to be in Paul's home, around family who were grieving as I was, helping plan the Mass, visitation, and funeral. I was unjustly irritated with anything that kept me away from that. I wanted and needed to talk about Dad and felt an almost obsessive need to keep his memory alive. I still feel the need to talk about him and often bottle this up so as not to sadden others.

I found that there were many times I would reach for the phone to tell him something funny that had happened, or to ask his advice only to realize that he was not there to answer the phone. My husband and sister-in-law confided to me that they were doing the same.

There were times I felt angry that my husband went to work for the two days before the funeral as I prepared for the seventy people we expected after the funeral service, but at the same time I understood that he needed to be where he felt closest to his dad. I was actually jealous of the fact that he was surrounded by people who were grieving too and understood what he was feeling. I, on the other hand, was stuck with just myself, weeping while I cleaned. And clean I did. I even finished wallpapering and painting my bathroom the day after Dad died. I suppose I had an urge to put things right.

It is the week following Dad's death that still evokes feelings of guilt and frustration. My parents were in town that week from Florida for Thanksgiving. They were due to stay at my home during that time. Because they are wiser than I am, they volunteered to stay with my brother in order to give my husband and me time to digest all that had happened. I didn't take their advice because I was afraid that I would hurt their feelings and also would later regret that I did not see them. So they came and I spent my time trying to hide the hurt I was feeling inside at losing this wonderful person in my life. I tried to hide it for two reasons. First, they told me to keep my "chin up" for Joe and that I was to be there for him while he grieved, so of course I was afraid to let them see my feelings of grief. I was insulted that they did not believe in me enough to know that I would put my husband first and hurt when they implied I should grieve silently because it was my father-in-law, whereas it was my husband's own father. Second, I was afraid that they would be hurt if they realized how much Paul meant to me. Would they understand that my love for my father-in-law took nothing away from my relationship with them? The time spent with my family that week was strained to say the least. I was screaming on the inside and trying to hide it and instead ended up being an irritable wreck, snapping at everyone.

For the first few days following Dad's death, as long as I had a job to do, a way to keep my hands from being idle, I did okay. I couldn't sit still. I had an energy that was endless. I crashed soon after, though, and had a hard time wanting to participate in daily activities, especially if they did not concern my family. I quit an aerobic instructor position I had because it was taking time away from my family that I no longer wanted to give. I less readily volunteered for jobs at church or school that I felt were too time consuming. I remember feeling overwhelmed when I saw extensive Christmas decorations outside and felt pity for the person who was going to have to clean it up. It seemed like a daunting task.

This changed yet again in the months that followed. I cleaned out our house, throwing away anything that was not nailed down. It became a family joke: If you want it, you had better hold onto it or sit on it because it was going. I craved a simpler life. Material things just cluttered that up. I threw things away that I had sworn just weeks before were essential to living. Just last week, my youngest asked me where something was and a guilty look my husband has come to recognize was instantly plastered on my face. My husband's frequent phrase about the loss of things in our house has become "It didn't make the cut."

Lastly, I treasure the fact that Dad's grave site is within walking distance from our house. I go there frequently and bring him flowers or just sit to visit, which brings me comfort. My mother-in-law told me recently that she said to her sister, "I know Kelly will care for Paul's grave site." I was relieved when I heard that as it gave me a job to do. With each day there are things that get easier about Dad's death. When I least expect it, I think of him and smile. And during the times that memories of him make me sad and I wish I had more time with him, I walk to where his body is resting and talk to him and care for him there.

CHAPTER 16

ALTERNATIVE ORIENTATIONS TOWARD DEATH

The benefit of metaphysical approaches to healing when
the death of a beloved one is presented.

Between Two Worlds
by Cynthia Keyes

This piece previously appeared in Earth Changes Report *(issue #78/April 1998), a publication of the Matrix Institute, PO Box 336, West Chesterfield, NH 03443; 1 603-363-4164.*

We live in two worlds. The physical world is the most real to us because it is solid and we can experience it through our senses. While we may acknowledge the existence of a spiritual realm, the physical world is so all encompassing that we sometimes find it hard to allow anything else in. It often takes a life-shattering event to force us to accept that there is something beyond that which we can see and touch. Sometimes that event can be global in nature, experienced by a whole group of people, like some of the major Earth changes going on currently. At other times it is more personal, like the seemingly "untimely" death of a loved one. Our family is experiencing just such an event right now.

When I began to write this my brother, Ted, was in a coma waiting to take his last breath. He had suffered with brain cancer for over a year and a half. Surgery removed the initial tumor, but before he fully recovered from that, his body was simultaneously subjected to massive radiation and chemotherapy treatments. Helplessly, we watched in horror as his body slowly deteriorated from the effects of the treatments. Alternative therapies were also tried, but to no avail.

Little by little his life force grew weaker and weaker. Yet, throughout it all, his inner strength and faith never wavered. His concern was always more for his family and what this terrible disease was doing to them than for what it was doing to him.

For five days my brother lay in a coma, caught somewhere between this world and the next. During this time, his home took on a kind of surreal atmosphere as his dying increasingly became the central focus of the family life that continued to swirl around him. He was never alone. Friends would stop by to see him for a few moments; different family members would sit with him; his little grandson, not yet two, would pat him saying "pa pa" and then go about his business, sometimes looking puzzled, wondering why people were crying.

If the measure of a person can be determined by the quality of people he has touched, then my brother is a great man. He leaves behind friends who weren't afraid to cry and tell him that they loved him, and parents—themselves in their eighties—who couldn't believe they could be losing their beloved son, yet were with him, in spite of their pain, at every possible opportunity. My mother would sing to him as he lay hovering between this world and the next, the same lullabies she sang to each of us when we were infants. His younger sister was there for him, even as she was forced to relive the suffering of losing her own husband not that long ago, also to cancer. His sons demonstrated their love and loyalty time and time again, and his wife and daughter put aside their own fear and grief, lovingly and patiently caring for him to the very end.

As for me, I felt such overwhelming helplessness and grief as I watched him slowly being taken from us. On the night he fell into a coma, I could not fall asleep, feeling as though I was abandoning him if I slept when he was perhaps taking his last few breaths.

When I finally dozed off, I began to dream, a dream that seemed to go on all night. In it, I saw my brother's body as he lay on the couch in his home. Then, out of his dying body, my real brother emerged, young, vibrant, smiling with that kind of twinkle in his eyes that he had. We began to talk to each other about what was going on, about his life, his death, and what was in store for him. He assured me that he was fine, at peace, and that this was an event that we all had to get through, but that we and he would be fine.

There was so much more, but I can't remember the words, just the feeling—how happy I was to see him looking like himself, and how at peace he was with what was happening. Somehow, in that dream state, it all made sense. It was as if Ted and I were discussing a play we were watching, but weren't personally involved in.

Throughout his illness, we couldn't understand how this could have happened to him, so suddenly, so unexpected. Why? This was the question we constantly asked ourselves and each other; all the time hoping that somehow we could lick this thing and he would be fine again. But it wasn't to be. It wasn't to be for him, and it wasn't to be for so many others who have been unfairly taken from us. I don't pretend to know why these things happen. I know it's part of the cycle of life and death, but it seems that more people are leaving us in an untimely fashion than ever before. As I struggle to understand the why of it, I can only think that we must need an emotionally-charged event of this magnitude to shake us out of our complacency and force us to look beyond the world we see around us. Perhaps it is the special ones who are chosen to be our teachers and our emissaries to worlds beyond our understanding. Through them we are able to look past the physical reality that we are so attached to and begin to understand that there is so much more.

When my brother's spirit finally withdrew from the body he no longer needed, [my husband] Gordon—through his clairvoyant vision—was able to see Ted appearing as his young self of nineteen or twenty years of age. Another young man had come for him—maybe his guide or guardian angel? We don't know. We are sure, though, that this being came to help him find his way into the new world he had just entered, that he is not alone, and that he is no longer suffering.

We, his family and friends, have sent him on his way with love in our hearts, and we are grateful to him for teaching us that there is more to life than what we see around us. But we can't help missing him, and hoping that he will stop by now and then in our dreams or quiet moments, just to say hello.

Journey
by Francesca A. Jackson, DC

She dreamed me. Lying in her bed, flesh melting away from her bones while the expansion within her belly pulled tight at her skin, her mind drifted heavenward, asked what road her feet should take on this earth, and she dreamed me.

***

The voice on the machine was faint. It held none of the strength I was used to. What could this mean? "Yo, Ernestine, what's up?" I said.

"Well, I've been a little ill, nothing serious, just that my abdomen is swollen and I was wondering if you could come out and have a look at me."

Brushing aside her protests that there really wasn't any hurry, I began to hypothesize as to why this woman, taller and stronger than myself, sounded so weak and wondered if I would be able to do anything about it.

By the time I got on it, the road to Richmond was clear. Ernestine's instructions were impeccable; I was drawn there like a homing pigeon. Why then was the house dark and I could hear no answer from the door? I went around the house, tried all the sliding doors and called out her name. After about fifteen minutes, I heard her, with a faint voice straining to say it was open and to push harder. Everything was dark as I entered. Then down the hall, I saw a room with an eerie blue light. I made my way there and I walked in; I looked into the face of Death.

Death openly returned my gaze and then quietly receded. Training is a welcome crutch when faced with horror. I approached the skeleton with the distended belly with my warmest smile. The eyes, large and ever beautiful, reflected the shadow of a woman resigned to her circumstances, the warrior in stance weary from battle, a child swollen with fear. Death waited quietly in the background, her Spirit seemed ready for release.

I couldn't take it all in so I pulled out my "nurse" personality and went to work. I said, firmly, "The first thing we need to do is get you out of this wet bed and into something warm and dry." There was a flurry of changing sheets and a warm water sponge bath, lighting candles and incense, finding soothing music to complete the atmosphere.

That done, the "doctor" personality entered the room. "Okay, tell me from the beginning, what happened? When did it start, what has changed along the way, how long have you been unable to walk?"

Even being propped up, her tale unfolded amidst deep gasps for air and every word was labored. It had become apparent in August that she was to be laid off from her job. Being the woman that she was, she accepted that and trusted that God would present the next plan when it was time for it. Not one to be idle, she continued to go inside herself to see what she felt was the next best step.

In September, the pain came—sharp, wrenching, bringing her to her knees. She was a woman with no job, no health insurance, and the county hospital was not an option she considered. In her mind she rationalized that it was just a pain and would eventually go away. She'd had a reading recently and wondered if this pain was like a psychic attack because the two seemed to be somewhat coincidental. The women from the group she'd become involved with suggested castor oil packs. The packs seemed to work, and in about three weeks time, the pain moved on and the swelling moved in. As if pregnant with a child in a hurry to get here, her belly swelled rapidly and began to affect her ability to breathe. The swelling pulled the flesh from her bones and sapped her strength. By mid-December she was unable to walk. A neighbor took on the task of bringing her orange juice and milk when she could no longer leave her bed.

I spoke to her in the best mild-mannered professional voice. "Orange juice and milk? That's what you've been living on? And what was the reason for that?" She replied that after being unable to walk and getting weaker and unable to even make it to the bathroom, the juice seemed to bring nourishment while the milk created a constipation of sorts so that the need to eliminate was less frequent.

"Okay, well let's take a look at that abdomen now and see what we've got here." Like a frightened child she exposed her belly. Denial fled from the room and reality came sweeping down as my hand touched the flesh. From the umbilicus down there was a hard, immobile mass; above it there was fluid retention. The skin was stretched tight trying to restrain the mass that fought to burst through. There was no flesh on the bones, bedsores open and oozing, grey pallor and cachexia. I couldn't miss this diagnosis even if I tried.

I stepped back and looked around the room now under glow of candle-light. The walls were covered with Realized Beings: Jesus, Muktananda, Sai Baba, Gurumayi, Satchinanda, angels. "Have you talked to any of these people? Have you asked them for help? What do *you* think is going on here?"

"Well," she explained, "it's surely a spiritual test of some kind. All the great beings have had to go through that at some point before they reached enlightenment.

As she spoke, I remembered walks together in Muir woods, talking about Spirit and Truth and what enlightenment was anyway. Anger popped through my voice, "What do you think you're doing here by yourself? When Muktananda had his heart attack, do you think he stayed in some dark room alone? He had every saint and person on the path come to be with him, if not in person, at least in Spirit. Give me the names and phone numbers of ten of your friends and let's set up a hot line and we'll . . . "

The strong Taurus I'd always known looked me straight in the eye. "I have to be quite firm on this. I called you because I was told to but I really don't want other people involved in this. As you know I'm a very private person, always have been, and it's just not necessary to have others in on this."

It wasn't worth the fight. Then I came back to say, "All right, listen to me. I'm setting up this table here with some of the veggie broth that I made. I want you to continually sip it, as much as you can, and it'll help to get your strength back. I'm going to let you stay here tonight, and tomorrow I'm coming back and we're going to the hospital."

I quickly went on, "No, this is not a choice you get to make. You've called me—I'm on your team—in fact, I'm the captain and I get to make this decision. I will walk this journey with you. I will not abandon you and I will not let you do this alone. And you see all these people on the walls? Well, they're going to go with us, so talk to them tonight and tell them what you want done."

Indeed it seemed as though the people on the walls paved the way. We arrived on a quiet night in the ER—unheard of! There was nobody there except all the staff and us, so we got the royal treatment. As the nurses went through their usual protocol they would look at me with that look in their eyes—asking me if I was aware of what was going on. I would signal back and we became partners in a conspiracy.

By 2:00 AM, as she was finally settled into her bed, I set up a little altar for her and lit a candle. Her eyes, ever large and beautiful looked into mine. "You know," she said, "in my heart of hearts I just feel that it can't be a tumor. You've been talking to them . . . what do they think it is?"

My heart shattered, my knees gave way, and I lied. "Well, there are still some more tests to take so nothing is really definite. In the morning your doctor will come in and finish the tests and talk to you about what he thinks is going on. I just want you to rest now. There are people here to take care of you and you no longer have to worry."

Her journey was long. Somehow she didn't hear or comprehend when the MD told her it was cancer and the nurses couldn't understand why she didn't know what was wrong with her. I called in my Guides because I was too afraid that I'd blow it if I did it alone, and the Guides and I talked about it for a long time. The doctors and I wondered how this could be happening since she had been vegetarian for so many years, didn't drink, never smoked or did drugs, and had been on a spiritual path for so long. What would the plan of action be?

Well, she wanted to try the medical protocol first, since she was there, and told me we could maybe try herbs or homeopathy later. If it came down to a final stage, she wanted no long, drawn out painful process, no life support or any such thing.

I read her articles of women who had overcome cancer in its severe stages and gone on to live full and productive lives. She told me of the astrological reading she'd had years ago where it was predicted that she would die at age ninety-four and that meant she had some forty odd years left. We clung to those visions. On a daily basis I asked if there weren't people who were wondering where she was and how she was doing and did she want me to call them? She ignored me, so I sat, crocheted lace while she slept, held her hand while they drew fluid out of her belly and her lungs and interpreted the medspeak into language she could understand to help her decide what she wanted to do. The tumor was as stubborn as she was—it continued to grow.

In a relicensing seminar one weekend and not really listening to what was being said there, I was reading Stephen Levine's book on working with people who are dying. He pointed out that *you* might want the angels to sound their trumpets and herald you into your last breath but the person who's actually dying *might not want that*. I left early and drove to the hospital. She was sitting up with her feet over the edge, leaning onto the nightstand to facilitate her breathing. She looked up and the eyes of a frightened child met mine. I told her I was really sorry that I'd been pushing her to give me phone numbers and to do all these other things. Now I knew she was doing the hard part and I hope I hadn't imposed too much of what I would want onto her.

She said, "You always said things that I needed to hear." We held each other and cried together for the first time. Then I left the hospital to go to her house and clean it up in preparation for her coming home. That was her great desire, to be at home and die there, if that was what was going to happen. I fervently promised her that I'd see that it happened that way. In the hours while I scrubbed, washed, and disinfected, the truth settled over me. I was preparing a death bed but she would not be coming there to lie in it.

Though still in the background, Death moved in closer and would show her face more frequently. I arranged for my close friend, CAE the channel, to come and do a reading. It was late afternoon, the warmth of the sun filled the room. CAE went into trance and the Teachers came forth. Ernestine wanted to know why it was that she had called me, from among all the people she knew. They spoke of another time and place, when she had been the strength for me in a similar circumstance and, as such, calling me was really the return of a favor.

She asked what was next. They took us to the other side, where the door of the Christ Light was open wide, where only love and radiance was available and waiting. The energy in the room was thick and the pull from Spirit was very strong, very appealing. She sighed, thanked them, laid back and began the dance.

The dance between the Vital Force, the Will, and the Soul is intriguing. The Soul looks toward sweet release shedding the body and merging with Spirit. The Vital Force is fierce in its determination to maintain life. The Will might refuse to let go, refuse to give up. Morphine robbed her of lucidity. Two friends who had come to be with me left after several hours, and I continued to sit and wait. She woke up clear and asked where her favorite nurse was. I went to get her; they spoke for awhile. She lapsed back into a morphine fog and the nurse and I sat in the next room, held each other, and cried.

At 3:00 AM she woke up and looked directly at me. "You look tired."

"Well, I've been sitting here all night, so I guess I am. How are you?"

"I really want to be able to let go but I seem to be having a hard time. I think the only way it's going to work is if I'm alone."

"Are you saying you want me to leave?"

"Well, I think you'd talk about it but I don't think you'd really be able to do it."

"Listen, for these past two months, I have been here, I have done what you asked, and have, in the best way I knew how, done it the way you wanted it done. If that's what you need, I'll be on my way."

"You know that I'll see you on the other side. I want to really thank you for everything you did for me. No one could've done it better, you know that, don't you?"

"I know that. I'm honored that you allowed me to walk this part of the journey with you. I leave you with my love. I'll see you on the other side." She'd sent me away from her bedside and I drove home, my heart heavy.

When I called the nurse's station at 6:00 AM there had been no change. I gave them the number where I'd be in seminar all day and continued to call throughout the day. At one call the nurses told me she had awakened and asked where I was. I told them to tell her I'd be there before the sun went down. I walked in, sat at her bedside and began to read *Healing Into Life and Death* out loud. She opened her eyes, looked at me and said, "I didn't think I'd see you again. What do I have to do? Why can't I let go? What do I need to do?"

"That's why I'm here. You don't have to "do" anything, you just have to "be". These words are magical and powerful and they'll help carry your Spirit across. Just listen, drift off . . . let go . . . "

I read for four hours; she drifted in and out. The next morning she had drifted into a coma and they moved her up to the terminal ward. At the end of the day, I came to say good-bye. She was in the room alone, her breaths were deep and spaced far apart. I talked to her for a long time and apologized for not getting her home.

I continued for an hour to read *Healing Into Death*. It was near midnight when I kissed her and said goodbye. When the phone rang, the nurse told me she had expired at 1:15 AM. I called a friend on the phone and wept.

When I had calmed down, I put on Voicestra to sing the 23rd Psalm to me: "Even though I walk through a dark and dreary land, there is nothing that can shake me, She has said, She won't forsake me, I'm in Her hand . . . ". I lit my candles and pulled out my power cards to read for her. The deck brought forth *Harmony—Release—Transformation*. I went out on my back landing and looked up into the clear sky. The big dipper was pouring down onto my head. I heard a train pass in the distance and then a mockingbird began to sing. She is gone. The journey has ended.

Big Picture Premonitions
by Adele DelSavio

This piece was originally published in the Oswego, NY Palladium-Times.

It's early 1978. My son Mike is about four months old, sleeping in my arms. *Dust in the Wind*, a haunting, despairing song about life and death, comes on the radio.

I look down at Mike and a train of thought runs through my mind. I see images of him growing up. They stop in late adolescence.

Summer 1985: Mike is seven, going on eight. He's watching his favorite movie, *The Never Ending Story*, and the theme song begins to play. *What a pretty song*, I think absently. *Mike likes it a lot. If I'm ever planning his funeral, I'll have to remember to have it played.* Reason kicks in. *This is nuts*, I say to myself. *Why in the world am I thinking of Mike in terms of a funeral?*

1989: Mike is now twelve. I have a dream that still seems real after I'm awake, unusual for me. In the dream, I am standing on a pier looking down into the ocean at Mike, who floats face down. His friends crowd around me. They tell me he fell and hit his head and drowned.

Summer 1994: Mike's almost seventeen, working, dating, driving, partying, weight lifting, taking senior pictures, living life with an energy I remember for myself at that age. I'd never told him about my strange experiences or seen much of a connection among them myself.

Now, for the first time in a long time, I remember my dream. *No, I* convince myself, *too much time has passed. He's not twelve anymore. It didn't mean anything.*

November 19, 1994: I'm standing on the road above Honolii Beach Park on the Big Island of Hawaii, looking down at the water. Mike's friends had lost sight of him while they were body boarding that morning. A search is under way; he has almost certainly drowned. I'm numb. I'm living my nightmare.

Since Mike's death, I've puzzled over all of this. Nothing in my background predisposed me to worry about losing a child. Although I had four children, these premonitions of death only concerned Mike, a healthy child, who had never even broken a bone until the broken neck that took his life.

I've also found that I'm not alone. I've heard and read stories about the dreams, fears, premonitions, and uneasy feelings of other bereaved people before an unexpected death.

Do they mean anything? Does the spirit, or soul, somehow sense what is going to happen? Are we given these experiences to prepare us for our loss?

These premonitions, or whatever they are, do seem to affirm the idea of the "big picture". But, as with so much else about death and life, we'll get no definite answers now, although we'll probably gain some spiritual maturity as we try to figure them out.

What Do We Know?
by Cynthia Kuhn Beischel

A lot of planning had gone into the family reunion. My husband's mother had conceived the idea as a Christmas gift. In June his parents would be treating their four children and seven grandchildren to a week in Sea Pines, South Carolina. We all saw it as a lovely idea.

"I can guarantee you that this will be the last time we will all be together," remarked Jerry as we packed for the trip. I thought he was simply concerned about his aging parents.

My responsibilities for the trip had been to get all the foodstuffs we would need, make sure all our clothes were clean and packed, and get the dog to the kennel.

It seems no matter how many lists and outlines I make, I still run out of time. This trip was no exception. I had, in the flurry of activities that morning, decided to give Moochka a prescription drug to kill fleas, a problem that might come from being with so many other dogs. On the long ride home, I had a thought that greatly upset me. I suddenly remembered having read not to give that pill if the area in which the dog was confined was sprayed with other flea poisons. It could be fatal.

As I pulled into the driveway, I was confronted by my husband who was upset. Actually, he had been anxious and irritable for a few weeks, but I took his agitation to be from having left work early and then having to wait for me. I got out of the car and apologized, and then I broke into tears. I explained what I'd done, and he dismissed it as not being a big deal. "Jerry, we're talking about death!" I said loudly. "About death," I repeated. He shifted his concerns some, gave me a stiff, distant hug, and suggested I call to tell the kennel about the situation. The line was busy. Because everyone else was ready to leave, I called a friend and asked her to telephone the kennel and explain it all. Jean promised she would, and we left uncomfortably.

By nightfall, we were about halfway there and decided to call it a day. We had a late dinner and then rode a little farther to a motel. My husband went into the lobby, while my daughters and I remained in the car. "Something feels really strange," I remarked. "It feels like we're in the Twilight Zone." It was a very distinct feeling to me.

We got in our room, had the usual family horsing around, and got to sleep. The next morning I awoke to the sound of my husband in the shower. It was no surprise; he was always an early riser. I suddenly felt sadness and fear come over me. For months, maybe years, I had asked him if he'd consider removing his mustache. It made him look very handsome, and I knew he loved it, but I really wanted to experience a clean shaven face again. I wanted to kiss without getting pricked for a change. I had suggested that this trip might be a good time to take it off. He'd said he would think about it. As I laid in bed that morning and heard him spray shaving cream from the can and turn the water on and off to rinse his razor, I began to feel something like panic. I was suddenly frightened that he'd removed it. I wanted to call in and tell him not to, but I worried that if he had already done it, or had it halfway off, he'd be very upset with me. I started crying. What was going on? I was the one who had asked him to do it, and now I was feeling sick. I wanted to shout, "Don't change!" As he dried his face and walked into the bedroom to wake the rest of us up, I held my eyes tightly shut. I was afraid to look. As he sat down on the bed beside me and touched me, I knew I had to open them. I looked through tiny slits and saw the mustache! He hadn't changed. I felt great relief. If he questioned the hug that followed, he didn't let on.

We made the rest of the journey in good time. When we got to the town, we stopped at a grocery store. As we walked down the aisles, we ran into Jerry's sister, her husband, and son. Upon leaving the store, it became apparent that Jer had left the keys in the car. Ed offered to help by using his auto card to call for someone who could open the lock. When the mechanic arrived, I found it odd that he chose to work on the passenger side, my side, versus the driver's door. Within less then an hour, we were on our way to the beach houses.

Everyone volunteered to chip in for the first meal, but before the kitchen work began Jerry went down to the beach to take a walk. He told me, "I want to prove to myself that I really made it." I assumed he was responding to all the driving. He had seemed stressed much of the time.

After dinner, Jer and some of the family members played a version of football on the beach; I went for a walk along the water's edge. I remember wondering as I watched the clan play if what I was feeling was anything like what Jackie Kennedy had felt. I dismissed it as being part of my strange imagination. Later, Jer joined me, and we walked hand in hand along the beach.

During our stroll, he asked me a question that seemed to come from out of the blue. He asked me to make him a promise. When I asked what it was, he responded that he wanted me to promise him that I'd finish the book I was writing. I said I would with a thoughtful smile, and we walked on. He commented on the water; he liked the ocean. I responded that I was in awe of it, but found its power frightening.

When we went back in, I said I thought I'd go soak in the jacuzzi and asked him if he'd like to join me. He declined, saying that it had been a long day and he just wanted to go to bed. He was asleep when I got there.

The next morning was a Sunday. I heard people moving around. Most of them were going to church, but this was going to be my day to sleep in. Some time later, Jer appeared with a glass of freshly squeezed juice and told me it was time to get up. I told him to leave me alone; I wanted to rest. "Fine, it's the last time I'll try to do something nice for you," he said as he set the glass down before leaving the room. "Oh, come on," I yelled after him. "This is my vacation!"

My husband drowned that morning—about an hour after he left the room.

In the days that followed, I kept replaying events that had led up to his death. Upon notifying his office, I found out that Jer had uncharacteristically left his desk in order, with notes telling his partner what steps he had taken on various projects, who should be contacted for follow-ups and what still needed to be done. That made me think about the project at home. On one ambitious weekend, Jer had torn out our second bathroom to redo it. Following that, we had lived with one bathroom for almost two years. Suddenly, approximately three weeks before our trip, he had tackled this long-neglected work as if he was driven to get it accomplished before we left town. During that time, I overheard him tell our youngest daughter in an angry tone that I had blown getting the counter finished because I hadn't immediately ordered the formica the day he mentioned it. I didn't understand the vehemence of his statement. After all, what was the big rush all of a sudden?

I thought of conversations I had had with friends following his death. Two friends told me that he had expressed a desire not to go right before we left. Based on the answering machine's statement of time, another friend had called us just minutes after we had pulled out of the driveway. Diane told me later that she didn't know why she had felt so anxious, but it was almost as if she had been hoping she could stop us from leaving. Something didn't feel right.

My sister said that the day before and the morning of Jer's death, she had observed a single, female Mallard out on her lake. Knowing that they mate for life and stay close together, Carolyn remarked to her husband that she felt sorry for the duck.

My mother reported that for the two days prior to Jerry's death, my father had walked around and around the back yard and seemed very anxious and irritable, and had no clue as to why he was so disturbed.

I began to see that when I had awakened in the motel fearful and crying, supposedly over the possibility of Jerry's changing himself by removing his mustache, I was probably afraid because of an awareness on some level that he was going to "change" by leaving this world. The loss would be his essence, symbolically represented by the physical statement of his personality, his beloved mustache.

I found myself thinking of the last three books I'd read before Jer died. I remembered how I felt *Scarlet* had such a strong message for me. I saw her mature and take care of herself. Then, *Woman of the Wyrrd*. I'd been disappointed with it and hadn't liked the fact that the couple couldn't be together because they were on different planes of reality. It had depressed me. And the last book, that I was reading at the time of his death, *Soul Sounds, Mourning The Tears Of Truth*. How appropriate! Does all of life reflect itself over and over around us? It took my breath away more recently when I read in *On The Death Of My Son* that we never die unwillingly or unknowingly.

I also reflected on the locked car incident and began to think it was a foreshadowing event. I enjoy dream interpretation, and in such analysis a car is often representative of one's body and its condition, one's freedom to come and go, one's course of action. I began to see it as being also symbolic of our family's course of action. Ed had come to the rescue by getting a mechanic to help with the car. When my husband drowned, Ed was one of the men who swam out to help pull in his body. He also gave mouth to mouth resuscitation. My husband's soul was no longer to be in his body, his vehicle on Earth. The mechanic had opened up our car, our way of moving ahead through my door. It was now my place to open up the way for my family to proceed. However I drove would direct our path.

I have pondered over all these things for the past few years. I am not implying that every time someone feels agitated, gets suddenly organized, or says it's the last time he'll do something for someone else, that death is imminent. But, I did and continue to have a sense that we operate on many levels of consciousness and that sometimes the events and objects around us reflect and symbolize another level of reality. I believe that on some unconscious level my husband and I, and others, knew that he was going to make his transition to death.

Cloud Dream
by Lindsay Piper Beischel

Before I ever had the dream—the dream that relieved my pain, comforted my mind, and reassured me of my dad's love—I went through a very rough time.

***

The day began like a normal one. We were on a trip in South Carolina, and it was our second day there. I woke up with the sun shining down on me. I got out of bed and looked out to see the ocean. It looked so calm and peaceful. When I went downstairs to get breakfast, I was in a very good mood because in a few days I would be celebrating my birthday.

Soon everybody else was up and I asked if someone wanted to go out to the ocean with me. My sister and dad offered to go. By the time we finally got there it was about 11:30. At first we played around on the beach, then went out into the ocean. I was a little bit hesitant about going out too far, but I thought it would be okay since I was with my sister and dad. We were pretty far out when Dad began yelling to my sister and me to swim in and get help. I didn't understand what was the matter. I asked him what was going on. He just told me to go into shore. I asked him again, but he yelled at me again to go into shore.

The water began to change. It might have been that the current was coming in faster, but it seemed to get very rough, and I couldn't swim with it, so I just stayed out there with him. Suddenly he was holding me above him to rescue me; he was under me. The whole time I was screaming for help, yelling, "9-1-1".

Some men who had gathered on the shore attempted to come out but couldn't seem to go beyond a certain point. I finally swam in to safety with the help of a board that one of them had thrown to me.

Unfortunately my dad was still out in the ocean. Soon the people helping brought him up on the shore. He wasn't breathing and didn't have a heartbeat either. My uncle, who had been a lifeguard, tried to give him first aid. Soon the rescue squad got there.

I felt sure he was going to die, but I tried to stay positive. The squad took him to the hospital. Soon afterwards my uncle took my sister and me to the hospital to meet my mom. When we got there, my sister and I were told that Dad was dead. I didn't want to believe them.

***

About ten days after this frightening experience, when I was still feeling very sad and guilty about his death, I had the most wonderful dream. I was surrounded by a light blue cloud with hundreds of rays of sun coming through. I was standing there on the right side of a table. It was such a light and free feeling. I felt so comfortable and loved. Once I was aware of my surroundings, my dad came in. His appearance was misty. It was as if he was molded out of the clouds. I could see all of his features very clearly, but he didn't have a real body. He was on the left side of the table which was a very light white color, and he seemed weightless.

I continued to feel very comfortable, but felt even more loved when he walked in. We started out just talking about things that had happened. One of us brought up his death. I was still feeling very guilty, but he told me it wasn't my fault and that it was just his time to go. We kept on talking about these things until I resolved most of my feelings and the guilt of his death. The dream ended with us being very happy about the way we had talked things out.

That morning when I woke up, I remembered the dream, and I felt great about it. I felt very loved.

Letting Go Of My Dad
by Judy Goodman

This was one of those rare weekends when all of the children were at home for a visit. We were raised in the South and had become accustomed to the wonderful meals we enjoyed when we went home. Daddy always enjoyed good cookin'. Even now, when we were not able to carry on a conversation with our dad, even when we had not heard him speak a word in a couple of years, he still loved to sit down to a good meal.

It was sad to see such a strong man in a state of limbo. His body was still reasonably healthy but he was lost somewhere in the shadows of his own mind. They told us it was Alzheimer's Disease. Whatever it was, we had already lost our daddy and we would have to stand by and watch his body die.

After our meal, I was the one elected to sit with Daddy and keep him company. The rest of the children stayed in the kitchen and did the dishes and put everything away. Daddy was settled in his usual place. While he sat in his oversized chair, still "master of his own castle", I sat on the foot stool right by his knees.

In my own way, I had continued to communicate with Daddy in a way that the other children couldn't. I had been born with a gift of seeing and knowing about spirit and things of "the other side". I had always been able to see angels and spirits of other people. Because I had such a deep understanding of these things, I communicated with Daddy on an entirely different level. I talked to his soul, the very core of his existence.

One of my earliest memories from childhood was the idea that one day I would help my daddy die. As a child that had no particular meaning to me because I didn't understand how or why this would come about. Even after I became grown and had children of my own, the understanding of this evaded me.

Without warning, my daddy began to speak to me. I was so excited to hear him talking I tried to get the attention of my brothers and sister. They were so involved in their own conversation that they didn't hear me calling them. Later, I realized that the communication was meant to be between me and my dad. This was one of those rare moments in time when the mystery of how and why just couldn't be answered. Once he started talking, I had complete understanding of what was happening. Even now, it makes me cry to think of this.

"You know, I haven't always been a good man" he said. "I know Daddy, but that's okay," was my answer. My words were spoken softly and with a gentle sound that I have learned means something extraordinary is taking place, and I am part of it.

"I didn't always listen to that Jesus stuff."

"I know Daddy, but that's okay."

"Do you really think it is okay?"

"Yes."

He looked me straight in the eyes and said, "Why do you think it is okay?"

I patted his knee, looked him straight in the eyes and replied, "Because when you weren't listening to Him, He was always listening to you."

He looked away from me but not before I saw a tear slip out of the corner of his eye. I had never seen my daddy cry.

"You know, I am going to see my mama soon, but I don't rightly know how to get there." His mother had been dead for over fifteen years.

"I know Daddy, don't worry. When it is time, the way will be very clear to you and you will know exactly how to get there."

As quickly as the conversation had begun, it was now ended. In just a few moments Daddy had reached beyond the darkest parts of the shadows in his mind, he had heard that everything would be okay and he would find his way home. That was the very last conversation I had with my daddy but it was not the last time I would help him find his way.

About one-and-a-half years later, just before Easter Sunday of 1996, I had an appointment with destiny. I had already made plans to go home for the weekend. Daddy had gone through many situations that let us know that he was almost out of time. On Thursday, my ability to see and know told me that I had to go home immediately.

When I got there, Daddy was on oxygen. I never did get used to seeing him so gaunt, just a shadow of the man he had been all his life. His eyes were wide open, they were fixed in a stare and he never blinked his eyes once. The clear blue eyes that had sometimes been full of mischief were now beginning to cloud up and grow dim.

I sent everybody else home so they could rest. The last night that my daddy spent here, we spent together. I sat up all night and talked to him, sang songs, patted his hands, rubbed his frail body with powder and just tried to comfort him and give him a special message. Even though he could not acknowledge me in any way, I knew that he could hear everything I said to him.

Many years earlier I had gone through a near death experience myself. Because of my gift, because of my own experience, and my deep understanding of the spirit part of each of us, I knew the mind was the last part of our body to separate. I kept talking to Daddy most of the night. I knew he not only heard me, but that he understood.

"Daddy, I can help you with this if you will only let me. I promise that it will not hurt me in any way. Your time to cross over is almost here and I can take your pain and any fear that you have. All you have to do is make a conscious thought to let me have it. I promise it won't hurt me in any way. When the time comes, just let me help you. It will all be okay and over very quickly." I really did understand what I was saying and knew that I would be able to do this for him.

Friday morning, Good Friday, as I sat holding my daddy's hand, two spirits walked into the corner of the room. It was the spirits of my grandmother and grandfather, his mother and father. They smiled at me but never did say anything. They had come to help Daddy at his time of crossing. I knew the time was drawing very close and started calling the other family members. Within a short time, they were there with me.

It was mid-afternoon, I was sitting on the side of the bed holding my daddy's hand. Suddenly I felt a jolt of electricity shoot up my left arm. Just as I felt the current go through me, Daddy blinked his eyes once, moved his head slightly, and looked into my eyes. All at once I felt my daddy's spirit go straight through my body. The sensation was so overwhelming that I let out a slight yell. In that brief instant I experienced all of the emotions of my daddy. I felt his pain, his fear and sadness, the relief, the wonder of what was happening, and the joy of being free. My words will never truly explain all that happened between me and Daddy as I let him go.

A Final Gift
by Isabel Meisler

This piece is adapted from an article in Voices *(1991), a publication of Perelandra, the nature resource center: 1-703-937-2153*

The year 1991 was a year of confrontation, struggle, and finally, partnership with death. In late January, my sister, and closest friend, committed suicide. My mother and I were stricken with grief and guilt. We were the only ones left in what had always been a tiny nuclear family without relatives. It was during the weeks that followed this loss that I discovered the full power and depth of flower essence aid. I actually began to feel a personal relationship with each healing plant, and in my growing gratitude would begin to visualize each flower as I used its essence. My mother, whose pain was enormous in regard to her loss, allowed me on occasion to offer her essences. In early April, while staying with me, she suffered a massive stroke.

The two weeks that followed were at times a nightmare of solitary and lonely decision making. Suggestions were made by my supportive physician husband and other kind attending physicians. But as next of kin, I had to give the final yes or no on life support decisions ranging from nutrition to antibiotics. Many a morning I would rise feeling absolutely "in extremis", and always I found that after testing and taking essences for myself I would experience whatever calm and strength was needed for that day.

During the early stages of my mother's illness I tested her for flower essences on a daily basis, but did not keep the suggested chart in the beginning. For one thing it was a hectic process. Lacking confidence in my muscle testing, a form of kinesiology using the fingers, I used the security of a pendulum for surrogate testing mother, and the entire procedure had to be absolutely surreptitious. Pittsburgh, in the throes of a medical "overdose" scandal, legally required all bodies to be tested for insulin surplus after death. This was one reason I could not ask any night nurse I might engage to administer flower essences. It would jeopardize them even should they agree. In addition, with my twirling wooden pendulum and boxes of little bottles, I really did appear weird, if not downright suspect. Actually this aspect of things provided me with some much needed comic relief. With apologies to her friendly roommates, I would pull the bed curtain as pendulum swinging time approached, hoping they would think I was taking some private prayer time. In a way that's what it was. There was also the frequent attendance of solicitous nurses who would swing in, once catching me with essence bottles spread over the bed.

"You in the fragrance business?" asked one, picking up White Lightnin'.

"Kind of," I replied. Muscle testing with my fingers would have been faster and saved a lot of heart pounding. It was hard enough to focus, without fear of being caught, but I finally worked out a method where, through a crack in the curtain, I could see the doorway reflected in the roommate's TV set. If someone entered I had ample time to clear the decks.

The process began as follows. Unable to communicate directly, due to her semi-comatose state, I used pendulum kinesiology and connected with mother's higher self. I believed that even in a state of coma, a person is present and able to hear. Every experienced nurse I questioned on this assured me this was so. Speaking out loud, I told mother about the help available for stabilization on all levels: physical, emotional, mental, and spiritual. I asked permission to use essences.

Arriving early in the morning, I would test my mother and administer drops to her forehead, taking care that nothing ran into her eyes. Her throat was paralyzed and she could take nothing by mouth. Just before the private nurse came on duty at 6:00 PM, I would test her once again for essences. This was the best I could do and it was an important lesson in letting go of "should" and "oughts", for part of me feared that those late evening dosages might be necessary. Yet even with the hassle of hiding my actions, the probable lack of focus on many occasions due to interruption, the lack of more than two dosage periods any given day, and my own often rampant doubts and insecurities, this whole thing worked, as became evident in the final death stabilization period. It has become clear to me that intention, when fraught with love, overcomes most things.

Five days before her death, the doctors assured me that nothing short of a miracle would keep my mother here more than a few days. At this point, I felt an inner shift. My whole focus strengthened. I could not rescue my mother from death, but with her permission, I could give her a final gift of love, as she, in thus allowing, could "gift" me immeasurably. It was not without a certain amount of awe and deep reverence for this journey with my mother, that on Wednesday, April 17th, with permission from her higher self, we began the death process.

I first made up a four column chart with four categories: (1) Basic, (2) Heart, (3) Brain, and (4) Death Process. The Basic was for essences to balance and stabilize her complete body environment; the Heart and Brain columns for essences that would address and move her through the necessary issues and transition involved in the major and specific physical aspects of her illness; and finally the Death Process column for those essences that would in the most sacred sense, assist the final transition. After testing and clearing myself (essential in order to remain balanced and not cause projection), I would test mother for overall physical, mental, emotional, and spiritual balance, listing the essences in the Basic column. I would then test for the heart, listing what was needed, then the brain where an infarction had

occurred, listing those. Finally, I tested for those needed for the death transition or process itself. After each test, I put the necessary number of essence
drops on her forehead.

As mentioned, I did this twice a day, beginning anew each time. Over
the next few days I could see patterns evolving. She required all the Rose
Essences in the beginning, sometimes in two categories on the same day. I
drew deep comfort from administering these wonderful flower gifts. There
was "Peace", the rose that offers courage and opens the individual to the
inner dynamic of courage that is aligned to universal courage, "Eclipse" for
acceptance and insight, "Orange Ruffles" for receptivity, and "Gruss an
AAchen" that offers balance and stability for the body/soul unit on all physical, emotional, mental, and spiritual levels as it moves forward in its evolu-
tionary process. I felt enormously supported as I offered each of the required
Rose Essences and the variety of Garden Essences that were called for.

The brain area required more Garden Essences than Rose, and as infection increased, Tomato for cleansing became a constant, which assists the
body in shattering and throwing off that which is causing infection or disease. The miracle was that I could begin to see clearing occur. By Saturday
morning, the day before her death, her heart was clear, no essences required
and the brain needed only Tomato and Yellow Yarrow; this in contrast to as
many as twelve essences required in different categories just three days earlier. By Saturday at 4:30 PM, after a Basic test which required Rose Essences, all three other categories were clear. I couldn't believe this was really
happening. I felt my own spirit begin to soar. On Sunday morning she still
needed all Roses for Basic, but Heart and Death Process were clear. With
fever now high, Brain continued to test for Tomato and four Rose essences.

At 5:20 PM, I tested her for the last time before she died. Again, all
Rose Essences for the Basic column. Brain no longer tested for Garden Essences, only two Rose essences, Eclipse and Royal Highness. My heart gave
a little leap when the latter appeared, for Royal Highness offers final stabilization. I felt sure this was occurring on all levels. Death Process required
Eclipse and Orange Ruffles. But the Heart column was still gloriously empty.
Nothing needed. Her heart was clear. I felt deep within myself that her
broken heart had been healed on this side of things and she wouldn't have to
deal at all with that after death. By this time in the process I was feeling
stable, strong, confident, and astounded by the gift I was receiving.

Through working in partnership with the essences and my mother's spirit, I was watching her heal on a spiritual level right before my eyes. And I could feel my own anguished heart begin to heal.

On Wednesday I had begun requesting a private room in order to have three hours of complete, undisturbed quiet to spend with my mother after her death. I had learned that this would allow time for her to detach from her body and move through the transition as peacefully as possible. I was extremely fortunate in being in a compassionate Catholic setting where such requests were not unusual. I also found out that without such a request, the body would be removed within the hour, placed immediately in a body bag, and left for the coroner to do the insulin test mentioned earlier. I really only needed the private room for the day of death and in the flow of things, one opened up Sunday morning, just in time.

In the evening that Sunday, I received a call that she was going, and before I returned she had died. I did not feel great regret over missing the moment of death, for we were so bonded one of us might have held her here. As it was, a priest was passing exactly as she was dying and read the beautiful 23rd Psalm that was her favorite. When I returned and found her gone, I still felt completely calm and full of my own inner peace. The nurse said that she felt there was something special about my mother; that she had seen so many deaths and hers was unusually peaceful. Shortly afterwards, the priest returned because he particularly wanted to tell me the same thing; that somehow it was a remarkably peaceful passing.

Within fifteen minutes after my mother's death, I had arranged to be alone with her and undisturbed for the three-hour period of requested quiet. Alone, I tested myself first, cleared, and then tested her. She needed all eight Rose essences now to move through what Machaelle Wright calls the "birth" stage of the process. I put them as usual upon her forehead, telling her I would be with her as long as needed. By now it was 8:30 PM. Turning off all lights but one, I sat quietly, in a state of total inner peace. At approximately 9:50 PM, I was so startled by a change in the room that I sat up straight. I believe that was the moment of her soul's departure. Going to her, I bent over, wished her a safe journey, and offered my gratitude for the gifts we had exchanged. A final good-bye. One final test. All clear.

Allan's Words
channeled by Linda Stein-Luthke

2/23/97

Starting a real dialogue with the newly dearly departed Allan. Trying to trust him to come through at the highest vibrations only. Invoking the Archangels to be with me. Especially Michael, to cut all negative Karmic ties that may still exist between us because I had been angry with him for helping to create the circumstances that brought Sandy to us to help her gain a bit of healing.

But Allan transitioned so beautifully and seemed to sense that it was time to live in the moment that I have assumed that he is clear about all of that, but am I? He certainly has been a great source of Love and Light for all of us during the trying times following his disembodiment.

So, talk to me, Allan. What's going on? What do you want to tell me now? I know you have many things to share, so okay, go ahead, now I'm ready to turn this over.

***

(quoted verbatim during session; edited for clarity)

Thanks, Linda, yes, I do want to talk through you. I appreciate how open all you sisters have been to me since I've died in sharing a very clear vision of what's going on now. I have changed very rapidly, and because you all are open to it, you've come along with me, in a sense. It is more complicated than that, but for the time, that will suffice. It is too difficult to explain everything that I see now. Just as you used to say, there really are no words for what I've experienced.

Wasn't it neat that there was an earthquake when I left for good? I don't think I caused it, I just think it was another sign of the times. People are dying all over the place now. It gets pretty crowded with confused new spirits, and since it was so easy for me, I'm helping them understand the program so that it is easier for them and those they've left behind.

That was pretty nifty that you figured it out so quickly, but then I've been feeding all of you information when you've let me come through.

That was very good today when you told Sandy that I won't leave her, but that she can feel that I have if she closes off to me. You guys hold all the cards, and if you don't want me, then I'm gone. And I don't want to be gone. Not just yet.

There is too much going on there now, as you are well aware, and I can still be part of it in many ways, not just in helping people when they cross over. Although that is pretty important work, too, because it does lessen the confusion there when people here get the picture and can help the ones they've left behind.

I thank you for telling Susan, Fred, and Gary to consider these possibilities, but compared to you, they are neophytes, and I'm still impatient to do as much as I can. So, I thank you for letting me come through you tonight when I see that you are so tired. I know you've been running around a lot to just get some of the pain and fear out of your system that my departure generated for you, but I'm glad you finally decided to sit still. I know this isn't easy for you, so I do thank you. I know that you're also afraid that no one else will believe you about all of this, but because it is so real to you, you simply have to talk about what is happening. And that's okay. In time, as you learn more things about what I am doing now, you'll see what is true for yourself. And that is all that matters anyway. Yes, go ahead and tell Sandy. She will believe it. Martin gets it also, and he knows it will be good for both of you.

Linda, just trust that there is really nothing to fear now. For any of you. You know that people are moving off the Earth faster than ever, but that isn't your decision, nor Martin's, nor your sister's. You will be fine if you just keep opening to this program. Now you ask, who runs this program? As far as I can tell, you do. When you give your power away, as we were taught in Landmark, then you lose it, become a victim, and life is terrible. When you stay with the program and understand your own divinity, your own divine grace, then the program works. Each one is a contributor and in so much as you contribute, that is what you get back. As long as you keep opening to do the work, then you are taken care of by whatever you are reaching whenever you do the work. This sounds strange, I know, but you do understand me, don't you? I know you do. That is what always fascinated me about you. You seemed so sure of the answers and I wasn't. Your conviction drove me crazy at times, but then I see that you pretty much do have the facts. It is still a little romantic for you and filled with some legends that are based on half-truths as I see it now but, over all, you got the stuff pretty straight. And that is amazing because that is a rare commodity from my perspective.

It is amazing, for instance, that my own mother and my own brother are so afraid of the "dead me" when I try to make contact with them. If they don't get that straightened out soon, the road can get pretty tough for them in time. That is why I am so very happy that you were there with Sandy right away to help her see the picture so clearly and verify her experience of me. What a blessing you are to each other now. It is really very wonderful to see that much love between you and to feel it coming to me from both of you.

I know there is a lot of stuff we are not talking about, such as family, and what I see in the future, because you know I do. And you know I can't talk about that in great detail because so much of it is only set in stone as you put it there. Besides, you get information from all kinds of sources, so you pretty much know the score already. But I will tell you this, the more you insist on investing in dramas with family or anyone else, and the more you put your emotions in the wrong envelopes, the harder this will all be for you. That is a promise, and you already know that. So let it go, kiddo. Don't hold onto it. It simply isn't worth it. All these people simply have to do their little dances the way they have to do them, and your input doesn't help a bit if it is only to condemn or criticize.

You got quite a bit of good advice today for the umpteenth time. (*Note from Linda: We channeled in the Sunday meditation group.*) I advise you to listen well. Give it over to a higher cause for everyone's sake, including your own. Do the work, Linda. Holding on to any of that crap does not serve you well. Not now, not ever. I should know, because I couldn't let go of my anger until after I died when I saw how useless and futile all the emotion really was. I can't come to you in my anger. I couldn't have been as effective as I was with any of you right away if I was still wallowing in my stuff.

Death was a great way of getting me off it. I don't recommend it for everyone, but it sure worked for me. Now, I just have to love everything and everyone as they are in order to be at all effective in the work I do. If I'm holding anything negative, it blocks everything from flowing through as I need positive energy to stay in communication with all these beings of Light. They fade away when I go dark.

The same is true for you, kid. It just doesn't pay. You can count on me for this one. So, just pretend you're dead already. As you told Sandy, life is preparing yourself for death. She was a little stunned when you said that to her. You were stunned, too, when you said it. I helped you. So just pretend you're dead, and you can't afford any longer to carry any of that stuff around. Give it up and be free, freer than I ever could be. You can do it while you're still alive. Wouldn't that be worth it to see what a stuff-free life is all about? I know you can do it. That's where you're headed now. Don't stop and get stuck in family, or whatever. Go away from it, and stick to the Light which I now understand holds all the power for change and being healed.

That's what I am now, a healed being. But you, and Sandy, and Martin can all do that while you're still alive. And I can help you figure out how. That's one of my jobs now. Do it—not for my sake because I'll be okay no matter what now—but for all that's still human. Do it for that. Because you're all part of the same thing, and any part of you that gets well affects all of you. You know that even my wellness after I transitioned affected all of you, so you see how powerful the program can be. Love one another and forgive. Say it and mean it. I love you—all of you. Wheeeeeeeeeeee!

2/24/97

(Note from Linda: I'm asking him what it's like for him there.)

Where I am, it's not as pretty as you might imagine. As I understand it, if I were to go to other areas, I would see some incredible beauty, but I'm not ready to do that because I am afraid of losing touch with you, and I don't want to do that yet. Probably once Sandy dies, we'll both go together. It will be the most incredible trip together that we'll ever take, from what I understand. But I feel totally supported here in staying where I am for now, because it suits my needs and my purpose to still be very active in taking care of you guys, insofar as you will let me until we are all in this higher place of awareness. I know you like to talk about vibrational frequencies, Linda, but not everyone understands what that means. That is why I like to use these other words to describe what I am seeing here. Certainly, everything is filled with what you might call a refined form of electricity. Even you. Yes, I do see you differently now. And you do stand out because you have done so much work to clean yourself out and get whole. But you are one of many who have done this now and there are more that just need a little push to get themselves going too. I understand now that that is the work that you and Martin do. You help others to get whole and as complete with this electricity as possible—what you call the Light. And the more it flows through you unencumbered, the more beautiful you are to me from where I sit. I can see right through you, and that is pretty nifty. I can also see when people come around you who are carrying more than an average load of stuff, and this does not frighten me because there are things you can do when that happens. When your only response is Love to no matter what crosses your path, it immediately changes the effect these people can have on you.

I know this sounds pretty simple, but that's the whole program. Keeping your heart open and not being afraid of anything is all that it takes to change everything around you and create a stronger flow of this electricity into the world around you. It's simple. When I go into spaces where more of that electricity or Light is flowing, that is a most beautiful place to be. That is why I loved the Mount so much. On some level, I instinctively knew that the flow was more powerful there. From here, it becomes iridescent and filled with the most wondrous colors. When you said to Sandy that the grapefruit tree would become gorgeous someday for her, that is what you were talking about. You knew that. If she would open herself to see what I see now, then this would happen for her. It would happen for you all. Just align your energy, your electricity with mine, and the world will begin to glow. That is what I see.

I also see the pockets where the darkness is as well. This doesn't frighten me because I am literally above it all now. But it did frighten me when I was alive, and it did make me angry. I'm not ashamed to say that now. But I knew better when I was alive, and I still couldn't help myself. But I see now that if your response to that darkness is to keep the love flowing within you, then it does change what is happening around you.

The goodness in your heart is all the safety you need while you are alive. But it has to be sincere goodness, not just goodness in order to be safe. That doesn't work. It's the kind of goodness that comes from letting go and trusting.

Now, I know you want me to address this subject called God, or what you call Infinite Source, and the Devil, and good and evil and all of that.

This has never been anything I've easily ascribed to, so I'm not attracted to that stuff here. Although I do see a lot of disembodied ones who are attaching themselves to either Jesus, God, Allah, Buddha, or the Devil, and many other things as well. It is fascinating to watch. That stuff really works for them, just as it did when they were alive, and that's great. It just doesn't work for me. It's part of what I call your romantic stuff, and you are still attached to. But I still see these things just as concepts that are crutches that help these people get with this higher-powered electricity that will ultimately help them. They kind of go through those concepts to get there. I just don't feel a need to do that. It works okay for me to just accept that electricity directly.

Now you're asking about the Archangels. I will tell you that there are many beings of great Light all around. Some of them have never been on the Earth, others have, such as your Ascended Master guys. These beings all have a lot to contribute to what is happening to you. And you have taken advantage of them. The one you're most attached to, Michael, is a pretty powerful character, and I do step aside when he comes through to you because I don't have that much electricity yet, and he would take me out if I tried to blend with him just yet. I'm more interested in staying closer to the human realm, so I just catch his rays, so to speak, and enjoy the show without getting directly connected and involved.

You are saying there is nothing to be afraid of. Ha Ha Ha. Very funny. I'm not. I just don't want to try to go where he is yet. In fact, I guess until I've finished my work with you, I won't. But I guess the possibility of checking all that out sometime is there. It just isn't my focus.

Now you're saying that is how I might ultimately find my God Source. I think that God Source is in me and you and everyone already. Michael's just part of the show we have created in order to literally make life more interesting.

All these beings of Light, as far as I can tell, are our creation. We are all beings of Light and have it within our power to invest each other with this Light. When you give that much Light to a Jesus, Buddha, Allah, whatever, then it does become more powerful and invested with ways to help us in our human drama. But each of us is the center of it all. That's the Get Smart program—just realize that and the rest follows.

History repeats itself, but not necessarily with the same cast of characters in the same roles. It's all in the choosing. Now, you're choosing what is happening in your life as it is. If you begin to worry that these other things could happen to you or the ones you care about, then you can bring that into your life. You know this. Worry and fear make things happen just the way

Love makes things happen. It's all in the focus. If you want a drama, you get a drama. If you don't want a drama, then you don't get a drama. Understand?

Now I know you have to get back to the Earth things. But please come back again to me. I love you. Wheeeeeeee again!

==

Messages From Michael
by Sherwin Kaufman, MD

This piece was reprinted by permission of New Age: The Journal For Holistic Living. *For subscriptions, call 1-800-755-1178, $23.90 a year.*
www.newage.com

During my many years of medical practice as a fertility specialist, if anyone had mentioned contacting the dead, I would have scoffed. The concept of an afterlife is discussed in nearly all religions, including my own. But to me, it was all speculative. I had never known anyone whose experiences would lead me to think otherwise—no friends or relatives who had any experiences with communicating with the dead. It just never came up.

But then, eleven years ago, tragedy struck. My son Michael had struggled with depression for years. My wife, Claire, and I tried to help him—with psychiatrists, medications, and finally hospitalization for his own safety. But in 1988, during the summer, he slipped away from the hospital. For weeks he had been pretending to take his medications. In fact he was stockpiling them. On July 24, he fled to a motel room in Easthampton, New York, and took a fatal overdose. We found a note addressed "to my dearest father and mother" in which he promised us "love forever". Almost as an afterthought, he scribbled a small smiley face at the end. He was twenty-one years old.

Nothing in life prepares one for the loss of a child. And this was *our* child—our intelligent, witty, artistic and fragile boy. A great-grandson of the noted humorist Sholom Aleichem, Michael was sensitive, tender, and gentle. But he was not yet ready to exist peacefully in this world. We were crying for a young life unlived, an enormous potential not realized, a future that had vanished.

Claire and I were broken in mind and spirit. To deal with the shock and loss, we saw grief counselors and became involved in survivors' support groups, which were particularly helpful because everyone in them had similar losses. One group we joined became particularly close, like a little family. We referred to it as "the club no one wants to belong to". We also became board members of the American Foundation for Suicide Prevention.

This work helped us greatly in dealing with Michael's death—we felt we were making some good out of tragedy. But at the end of that first year, we were not ready to face the bustle of the holidays, especially since Michael's birthday was Christmas Eve. So we took a trip with friends to Morocco—as far as we could get from Christmas and New Year's celebrations—and distracted ourselves by photographing Moroccan street scenes. We brought along a snapshot of Michael to have with us in our hotel room.

When we had our film developed, the first photograph stopped us cold. It was a blurry picture of Michael! The hair stood up on the back of my neck. Recovering slowly, we realized that it was a picture of the snapshot we had brought with us and placed next to the hotel telephone. But neither of us recalled taking any photos in our room. Did the camera go off by accident without our noticing it?

I didn't know the significance of this strange event, but I wrote it down. It was soon followed by others.

* A book spontaneously fell off the shelf in our apartment. Its title was *Fathers and Sons.*

* A record fell off our music shelf. It was Beethoven's 7th symphony. I had always loved classical music, but Michael was a pop fan. He played electronic keyboards, and he wrote and recorded pop songs in the style of his idol, Billy Joel. But the second movement of Beethoven's symphony caught his ear, and it became common ground for us. A pianist myself, I played transcriptions of Beethoven's symphonies, and Michael would always stop and listen when I played that movement.

* We had never turned off the telephone in Michael's room. It was a number he had given only to his friends, but now it began to ring occasionally. When we picked up the receiver, there would be no sounds—no voice, no click.

* There were strange electrical disturbances. On two occasions, when Claire and I were discussing whether to see a medium, the lights flickered off and on—only in the room we were in.

* The dove was my mother's special spiritual symbol, which she had

shared with me during her lifetime. I recall making her a wooden dove when I was ten years old, and she cherished this gift. Michael knew about the significance of the dove to me. And now I seemed to encounter doves and dove symbols everywhere.

The eeriest encounter with a dove was at the Montammy Golf Club in New Jersey, of all places. I was on the fairway when a white dove suddenly appeared next to my ball. I had not seen such a dove anywhere at our country club in my twenty-plus years of playing there, nor had I seen this one alight. I felt chilled as I met the bird's gaze. When I looked away for a moment, it disappeared. I didn't see it fly.

About an hour later, I was on the last fairway. My ball had landed in some bushes, and as I looked for it, I saw the dove again. I was mesmerized by its gaze, and I heard myself asking, "Michael?" My golfing partner called from a distance, and I turned to look. When I looked back, the dove was gone.

* In 1992 I retired from medicine. I often played Michael's keyboards, and I eventually developed an interest in pop songwriting that has blossomed into a second career. For a time, I tried collaborating with another songwriter on country tunes. He told me that he had lost a brother, and I told him about my son. He happened to have a keen interest in psychic phenomena, but that never came up in our work. Then one day he called me, very agitated. He said that during the night, Michael had spoken to him! Michael had said he wanted his parents to know that he was well, that he loved them, and was around them. The songwriter had asked him, "But how will they know its you?" "Just mention the plaid shirt," replied Michael.

I went numb. Only Claire and I knew that Michael had worn a red and black plaid shirt almost daily during the last months of his life. It was one of the few items of his clothing we had preserved and cherished.

* One day I checked the phone messages on the answering machine. The first message had to do with Claire's real-estate business. The second began in silence, and then a male voice said, "Dad, I . . . " and cut off. Shaken, I replayed the message several times. I pressed the save button, but when I tried to play the message for Claire, it was no longer there.

These are but a few examples of the many strange and eerie incidents that I kept recording in my diary. The accumulated evidence in this diary— now twenty-four pages long—challenged my skepticism. Perhaps Michael *was* trying to communicate. Claire had occasionally brought up the idea of seeing a medium, but I had resisted. It was not until 1993, five years after Michael's death, that I gave in.

We chose Suzane Northrop, who had a good reputation and lived nearby on the West Side of Manhattan. On the appointed day, when we arrived, she asked us to wait in her backyard while she finished with another client. The sun was shining, a gentle breeze was blowing and from the porch of the second-floor apartment we heard wind chimes tinkling softly. Months earlier, Claire and I had visited Mexico, and while we were there we had bought some wind chimes shaped like doves. We had never seen anything like them in the States. Now, tinkling from a Manhattan building, were the same wind chimes.

"Well, at least we know we're in the right place," laughed Claire.

Northrop is a simple, down-to-earth person who ushered us into a modest living room and excused herself for wearing house slippers—it had been a busy morning for her. As we sat down, she said, "So, you must be the couple. There was a young man around me telling me his parents were coming. He asked me to buy white roses for his mother, but I didn't have time."

What amazed me was that she came right out with this, with no hesitation. She knew nothing about us but our first names. How did she know about a young man?

"Is his name J. Michael?" she asked. It was Michael Jay. Why didn't she say "Tom" or "Joe" or any of a thousand other possible names?

During the session, she would listen, as though Michael was standing behind her, talking. Then she would relate to us what she heard. "He was upset that you weren't with him when he passed on, but he didn't want you to see him in the state he was in. He says he died away from home. The weather was warm, and he was near water."

This was all accurate.

Northrop asked, "Who had a recent leg injury?"

"I did," said Claire.

"Your right leg?"

"Yes."

"He says it could have been worse, but—and this is really strange—he says he helped you with it. Does that mean anything to you?"

"My God," Claire blurted out. "Only Michael could have known that!

We were in Mexico when I fell and thought I broke my leg. It was terrifying. The ambulance looked like a hearse, and they brought me to a shack they called a hospital. I looked up at the heavens and asked Michael to help me. Thankfully, there was no fracture."

The meeting, which we taped, went on for an hour and was filled with more and more specific information. We left stunned, speechless. All my skepticism was shattered—I knew our son had communicated with us. Claire and I had been given a glimpse of a world beyond this one, and the pleasant spring day in Manhattan suddenly seemed unreal—a dream. Somehow we found our way to a small coffee shop where we held each other's hands and wept.

Determined to make contact again, we began making appointments with various recommended mediums. The next one we saw was James Van Praagh. We met him in Manhattan at the apartment of a friend of his, which he used as an office when he was in town.

Van Praagh is a gentle, unassuming man who makes contact with the other side as casually as if he were talking on the telephone. We saw him twice at what he calls "demonstrations", before large audiences. Through Van Praagh, Michael accurately described details of our house, and he talked about what he was doing now. Significantly, Michael referred to himself as alive. Van Praagh describes the other world as a realm of energy that vibrates at a higher frequency than our own. He says it is a peaceful place, without suffering. Michael said, "Dad, you'd be proud of me. I've been working with little kids, teaching piano." He even mentioned our shared love of Beethoven's 7th symphony but added, laughing, "Beethoven himself isn't here right now."

We saw several other highly regarded mediums, including George Anderson, Shelley Peck, and John Edward. We were no longer surprised when they came up with Michael's name, how he died, or intimate details of his life that only we and Michael knew. We taped all the readings—each had new information to relate, and each was both amazing and comforting.

Two readings with Van Praagh stand out. In 1994, we attended a demonstration he gave for about eighty people. He had not seen us in the audience and gave several readings for others before saying, "Someone is coming through strongly, a young man. I don't know why, but he's showing me fallen leaves. This is summer, but he's showing me leaves." Claire gasped, for she was holding a photo of Michael surrounded by autumn leaves.

In 1995, Van Praagh gave a demonstration at the Roosevelt Hotel in New York City. Claire and I brought several family members and friends who were eager to witness a medium. Van Praagh, who didn't know we were there, said, "There's a Michael coming through." Claire and I thought a dozen hands would go up for such a common name, but none did, so we cautiously raised ours. Van Praagh recognized us and said, "Oh, Claire and Sherwin, I know you. I never do public readings for people I know—it looks suspect. But Michael is coming through so strongly." Then with eyes closed, he said, "Yes, I hear you, Michael. He's saying to both of you: Break open the champagne. Is this a birthday or anniversary?" We replied that it was a very private anniversary, one that few people, Michael among them, would know. It was the date Claire and I met. Van Praagh continued, "Michael says he was with you, Sherwin, when you went through one of his drawers." "No!" Claire said—she knew this had to be wrong. "Sherwin and I agreed we would only go through his things together." I had to sheepishly confess that I had gone through some of his things the night before, without telling her.

"Well, Michael knew!" laughed Van Praagh.

Then he said, "Michael is leaving now, but you will receive something in writing from him. I don't know what it is, but that's what he's telling me." Our relatives and friends were as puzzled as we were.

About a week later, I opened the *Sunday New York Times* Magazine (March 5, 1995) and saw an article called "The Hush of Suicide". As I read the first paragraph, my heart almost stopped. The first line read, "It was the smiley face that did it." The writer, whom I didn't know, went on to describe Michael's suicide note in detail. As soon as I showed the article to Claire, she smiled and said, "James told us there would be a message in writing."

I contacted the writer, Jennifer Farbar, whose article was actually about her father. She explained that some four years before, she had attended a suicide survivor group at which Claire and I were present, and she vividly remembered Claire's description of the contents of Michael's last note.

It was clear to us that Michael was able to communicate even without the help of mediums, by making his presence known in unexpected ways. In 1997, on Christmas Eve, Michael's birthday, my eldest son from a previous marriage was Christmas shopping with his wife at Barneys on Madison Avenue in New York. Although the store was packed with holiday crowds, a young salesman went straight to them and said, "My name is Michael. May I help you?" He attended to them the entire time they were shopping and showed them a Hermes tie with a dove and harp design.

They bought it for me and told me the story, both visibly shaken. A few days later, Claire and I went to the same store—we wanted to buy the same tie in different colors. We asked for a salesman named Michael and were directed around a corner where a young man was finishing with another customer.

"Are you Michael?" we asked.

He turned to face us. "No, I'm Angel."

Claire and I just squeezed each other's hands.

We have traveled a long path these past eleven years. It began with a tragic death but led to an understanding that death does not extinguish one's spirit. We know our experiences don't constitute scientific proof of an afterlife. But we have found comfort and serenity from them. Knowing that Michael's spirit is alive, and that his love for us is still present in the universe, has made our lives extraordinary. I believe that death is actually a new beginning for those who have passed on. It can also be a beginning for the survivors because knowledge of the world beyond assures us that we are, in a sense, immortal.

We feel that Michael may wish to communicate with us, so we still see mediums occasionally. The last time was in 1998, with Hans Christian King. At that meeting King said, "Michael tells me he had a special relationship with his father, and that he took part of Sherwin's heart with him. And Michael says, `Don't worry, I'll put the piece back when you come over.'"

As we left the session, King handed us a piece of paper on which he'd jotted things as we talked. Although we had not mentioned Michael's last note, on the paper was a drawing of a happy face.

"He's all around you," said King.

And we said, "Yes, we know . . . we know."

CHAPTER 17

MEMORIALS

**Touching stories explain how donor gifts helped soothe
the pain from loss.**

Christian's Legacy
by Alfredo J. Herrera, MD

This piece is reprinted with permission from For Those Who Give and
Grieve, *Volume 6, Number 1, ©1997, a quarterly newsletter published by the
National Donor Family Council of the National Kidney Foundation*

On December 8, 1994, at 8:30 PM, my phone rang. When I picked it
up, a deep male voice on the other end of the line said, "Are you Dr. Herrera?"
I answered, "Yes."

"This is Maryland Shock Trauma. We have your son, Christian, here."

My body froze, my hands shook so that I dropped the phone. I realized
the call was from a medical surgical unit reserved for severely traumatized
patients. When I picked the phone up again, I asked, "What happened to my
son?" The line went dead for a few seconds. I knew then something was
terribly wrong.

The voice on the other end of the phone added, "He was flown here
from Howard County and you must come immediately."

I don't remember how, but I drove to the hospital in about fifteen minutes. I rushed into the emergency room area and when I saw my son, I
couldn't do anything but cry, hug him, and kiss him. He was surrounded by
physicians, nurses, respiratory therapists, and many others. He was connected to a respirator and lines were coming from every extremity to monitor

his condition and give him life support. His face was bruised, swollen, and difficult to recognize. Then I saw that his pupils were fixed and dilated, a sign of severe brain damage. As a physician, I knew my first-born, my companion, was already in heaven, but as a father, I couldn't let him go without trying to do whatever I could to keep him alive and with me.

My son Christian was sixteen years old, one month shy of his seventeenth birthday. A very popular, good-looking young man, he got his driver's license in September of 1994. Like any other sixteen-and-a-half year old young man, Christian was eager to have his own car and taste freedom. I bought him a Ford Explorer, and he and I had an agreement, which we both signed, that under no circumstances was he to drink or drive recklessly. I realize now that I was naive to believe that he was going to abide by our agreement. When the accident occurred, he had been speeding, passed cars on the shoulder, hit a ditch, and rolled over four times. In addition, he had not been wearing a seat belt and had been drinking some. Christian was ejected from the car through the passenger window and landed twenty-five feet away.

Over 700 people attended his funeral. No one could remember a funeral in which there were more people in attendance. This was a tribute to how in life and in death he touched so many. Cars were lined up for miles following him to Crestlawn Gardens where he now rests.

I am a divorced, single father, and the parent of four beautiful children. Christian was my oldest child and the only one living with me. His brother and sisters live with their mother. He had been my support, my comfort, my best friend through extremely difficult times. He had encouraged me with his words and his actions at times when I thought I was not going to make it. I needed him more than he needed me.

During the extreme pain and anguish that I felt, I recalled that Christian had mentioned to me when he got his driver's license that he wanted to be an organ donor, so it was time for me to honor his wish. Thus, in death he gave life to six people: he donated his heart to a forty-eight year old married man who had two children and who is now doing well; a left lung to a sixty-three year old man, also married with nine children; a liver to a fifty-seven year old man; a kidney to a young woman; and the other kidney to a thirty-four year old man. In addition, Christian donated his pancreas, and two corneas, giving sight to two more people.

After Christian's death, I was stunned when I learned that approximately 6,500 teenagers are killed every year on America's roads. This is the most common cause of death for young people between fifteen and twenty-one years of age. Automobile accidents kill more young Americans than handguns, alcohol, drugs, AIDS, and cancer, according to the statistics. Of those killed, no more than 10% have any alcohol in their bloodstream, but 90% die because of reckless driving. These young people drive too fast, do not obey traffic signs, pass where they are not supposed to, and do not wear seat belts.

It occurred to me that through Christian's death, I as a father have an obligation to make parents and teenagers aware of the tragic consequences of reckless driving. I started a campaign in Howard County, Maryland, to create awareness among our citizens and their children of these horrendous, tragic, and needless statistics. Toward this effort, I am using all means available to me to spread the word in the broadest way possible. I have developed a pilot program at my son's high school with the cooperation of the County Board of Education, the Fire and Rescue Department, and the Police Department. This program is designed to teach teenagers safe and proper driving practices. Hopefully in the near future this program will be implemented in every high school in the county. In addition, I am campaigning for state legislature that will protect our children, such as mandatory seat belt laws, graduated driver's training, and a mandatory safe-driving course as a requirement for teens. I am also trying to establish through the County Council a Task Force to look into teenage mortality rates in automobile accidents because I believe we can make some of our roads safer for teenagers. We only have to work a lot harder, but that is our job as parents.

I feel we must not allow our young people to die so senselessly. My son Christian's death must not happen to others. Prevention is part of the legacy of Christian's life. Not only did he save six lives by donating his organs and give sight to two other people, but he will continue to save countless lives forever.

The Gift Of Blood
by Adele DelSavio

This piece was originally published in the Oswego, NY Palladium-Times.

Believing that death is easier to accept when some good comes out of it, my husband and I signed Uniform Donor cards early in our marriage. We became potential organ donors. With this taken care of, we turned our attention back to raising our young family.

Our children grew and were healthy, full of life and energy. By 1994 our family included three teenagers and an eight-year-old, all thriving. I realized how lucky we were.

Then our son Mike died. I still believed strongly in organ donation, but it was out of the question for him because his body wasn't immediately recovered. Along with the shock and overwhelming grief, I felt some regret over this lost opportunity to bring good from Mike's tragedy.

Although it was only a small part of grief, this regret remained. Mike had been a healthy child and he died in a full bloom of adolescence. His sparkling eyes, keen hearing, strength, and stamina made it obvious that he would have brought second chances at life to many people.

Three months after Mike died, his autopsy report confirmed what had seemed obvious. His arteries were clear, his heart was perfect, his lungs had been fine until the sea water rushed in. The time that it took to find him took what he could have given to others away from them too. What a waste.

I was still following this line of thought as the six-month anniversary of Mike's death approached. I was edgy, wanting to find a meaningful way to pay tribute to him.

One afternoon, a notice in the newspaper caught my attention. A Red Cross blood drive was being scheduled and the date was, coincidentally, Mike's anniversary.

That was it—I knew immediately what I was going to do in Mike's memory on his anniversary. Maybe Mike wasn't able to be an organ donor, but I was his mother and we were genetically related. Giving part of myself was as close as he and I could get to giving part of him. The logic was unusual but it felt right. I called and made an appointment.

I had never donated blood before. As with so many things in life that we should do, I'd considered it but had never gotten around to actually doing it. But this time I had an appointment and was doing it for Mike, so I followed through.

As a first-time donor, I had the procedure explained to me as it was being done, and in my mind I dedicated it to Mike. It turned out to be an interesting, not unpleasant, experience. A classic rock station played softly, providing distraction. Afterwards I was offered juice and snacks. I left feeling comfortable and happy that I had found a truly meaningful way to honor Mike's memory.

Since then I have become a regular donor, and each time I donate I still privately dedicate it to Mike.

Joe's Story
by Nanette Lang

Friday, September 29, 1995 was like any other Friday night. Josh and Joe were going to a birthday party, and Darrell and I had decided since we were alone for the evening that we would go out to eat. Joe came in, gave me a kiss and said, "See you later, Mom."

Later that evening, after our return, the phone rang. When I answered it, I heard Julie, one of Joe's friends from school, say, "Mrs. Lang, Joe has been in a really bad accident at the corner of Highway 177 and 45th Street; you need to come right away."

I said all right and hung the phone up very calmly, giving what she said a few seconds to soak in. Then I screamed at Darrell, "Hurry up! Joe's been hurt. We need to go!"

When we arrived at the accident, we saw Josh standing in the road screaming at Joe. As we got out of our van and walked closer, we saw the paramedics were giving Joe CPR. Josh kept screaming at him to live. A highway patrolman advised us to go to the hospital and wait.

The waiting room at the hospital was full of children and parents. In the confusion a doctor finally said, "Lang family." Darrell and I learned that Joe was in critical condition. He had a collapsed lung, a few broken ribs, and a massive brain injury. The doctor kept saying how sorry he was and, at that point, I couldn't figure out what he was sorry for. Joe was sent by Mediflight to University Hospital in Oklahoma City.

We rushed to the hospital from our home in Shawnee. After sitting in the waiting room for a couple of hours we were told that Joe was being moved to the Critical Care Unit and a doctor would be in to talk to us. By now it was after 1:00 AM, and after sitting in a dark waiting room, we waited even longer before the doctor came in to talk to us. When the doctor entered the room, he never turned the light on. He mumbled a lot of medical talk, and Darrell asked him to speak to us in English. The doctor replied, "Your son is brain dead. He has the equivalent of shaken baby syndrome and there is nothing we can do for him."

We asked for and got a second opinion which led us to three choices: Let him die naturally, while on the machine. Unhook the equipment and let him die. Make a decision about donating his organs.

I remembered the time Joe was with me at the tag office when I was renewing my driver's license. When he saw me check the organ donor box, he said, "Why did you do that?"

I asked, "Joe, why would you take something to your grave that someone on earth could use to live? Your body will turn to dust anyway and you don't need the organs in heaven."

He gave me one of his looks and said, "That sounds so gross." But a few days later he came to me, said he had thought about the organ donor thing and that when he got his permit, he was going to check that box too.

So when they asked if we wanted to donate Joe's organs, we knew what he wanted. Someone from our local agency came to talk to us and told us the harvest teams would be in around 4:00 PM to get started. We spent as much time as they would allow us with Joe that day because we knew these were our last moments with him. Friends were notified and they drove in from all over Oklahoma. The Red Cross notified Joe's brother, Jared, in the Navy in California.

When it was time to leave Joe, it was one of the hardest things we ever had to do. We just couldn't believe Joe was going to die. He didn't look hurt; he just looked like he was asleep. Our friends and family took us home. God took Joe home.

A couple of months went by and we received a letter from the Organ Sharing Network and learned Joe's donation had helped four people to live.

They had transplanted the heart, liver, and both kidneys. I wrote, anonymously, to each of them to see how they were doing, knowing I couldn't tell them anything about Joe. Easter Sunday our local newspaper ran a full-page story about Joe and how he had helped the lives of four people, plus helped to better the lives of twenty-two more through tissue donation. What an array of miracles for these people.

My question was, "Where was our miracle?"

Two weeks after the newspaper story came out, we received a letter from a nurse at St. Anthony's Hospital. It said that if we would call her she would give us the name of one of the kidney recipients. After learning the name, Darrell called me at the bank where I work. When he told me the name was Charles Oldham, it rang a bell. I had waited on him in the drive-by when I was a teller. Later we were told it is pretty rare for the donor and the recipient to be from the same town. I invited Charles to come to our house so we could meet one another. He is such a good man. Charles and his wife, Christi, now have a beautiful baby girl who is so precious. I was so proud of Joe and his legacy.

Our son, Joe Don Lang, brother of John, Jason, Jared, and Josh, will be forever fifteen.

We still miss him.

My Wife's Wishes
by Paul R. Rupright

My wife Shirley passed away on March 11, 1996. Following that event, because she had expressed a desire to donate organs and tissue, I received literature provided by the National Donor Family Council. I am thankful to this organization for the wonderful work they are doing, and I have been helped a great deal by reading the stories and poems provided by the families and relatives of other donors. These stories which have been so thoughtful and loving share what their writers want others to find—a better existence in their journey through life.

I was told one of my wife's kidneys provided a better life for a lady who resides in North Carolina. I know my wonderful wife is just as happy as she can be to know through her love for her fellow man that she has made whatever time the recipient has in this world a little more tolerable. I always liked to say that Shirley was a big woman, but she had to be because they couldn't get a heart as big as hers into a small space!

Sometimes I get the feeling from some of the correspondence I read that some families are unhappy that they aren't in touch with the recipients. I have given some thought to that myself and I can understand it. But for me, just knowing that Shirley's desire of wanting to make someone else's life a little better was accomplished is all the thanks I need.

My dear Shirley taught me so many things in the years we had together. And with her generosity at passing, she has taught me another thing: that giving the love to your fellow-man speaks volumes about the kind of person you are.

Although I was not in favor of her being a donor, I came to the realization she was indeed following the right course. I have now altered my own choice so that I will arrive at the same destination.

CHAPTER 18

TRANSITION TO JOY

With time and humor, things do get better.

Press On
by Kathleen Moore Joiner

Of slings and arrows hurled, I've caught my share;
I've known the scream of pain, the crippling leach
Of pulsing lifeblood draining from my heart.
I've paid my dues in pacing moonlit floors,
And strained for comfort, always out of reach.

I've wept until my well of tears ran dry,
Then turned my face, like Job, in numb despair.
Yet, even when the road is hard and steep,
And darkness hides each rocky precipice,
Somehow I'll find the inner strength to bear

This trial, too, and keep my footsteps aimed
Toward the goal I'll reach at journey's end.
Some days, it seems, the best I can achieve
Is but a shuffle from my starting place,
And no one has a kind hand to extend.

On other days, the sun is warm and bright,
Enticing me to wander from my course
With silky Siren songs that beckon me,

Disguising evil schemes with sweet allure,
While leaving me encumbered with remorse.

Today I'll take whatever steps I can
Until the curtains of the night are drawn.
Eternal hope, the star that guides my path,
Illuminates a joyous final home;
And, trusting in that promise, I press on.

The Gift Of Significance
by Sue Gallehugh, PhD

I laughed at my husband's memorial service. My doing so was not a sign of disrespect or any lack of love, but a tribute to how he had lived his life. Our many friends who gathered to show their respects all shared one common quality—a sense of humor. Clyde had cultivated his friendships carefully and weeded out any one who could not see the lighter side of life. I had expected the service to be dark, with a parade of people fumbling for words of condolence over Clyde's heart attack. Instead, each person gave me a gift—a story of how Clyde was significant to their lives.

As they told their stories, I noticed a change in their faces. A look of sorrow transformed to joy as they shared some mischief that Clyde had talked them into, or a bad joke that he had told.

My husband was a professor of Medical Ethics, so it was particularly rewarding to see the number of young medical students who found time during their exams to attend the service. One student told of how his class decided to wear Halloween masks one day to my husband's class. In true form, Clyde pretended that nothing was out of the ordinary throughout the lecture. Each story seemed to have a grounding affect on me.

Since laughter helped cut through the numbness, I decided to use humor to begin the healing process. I rented comedy movies, and went to upbeat plays and musicals with my friends. I spent time with my children and grandchildren who always bring me joy. I know that it is not healthy to take a permanent vacation from your feelings, but a few side trips sure do make it a lot easier.

I dreaded the emotions involved with cleaning out my husband's belongings, but my children and I were able to lighten up the task by laughing at the strange things my husband had collected through the years. He had an eye for truly terrible Western art and had accumulated a mountain of hotel shampoo bottles. My kids were pleased to see that he had saved all their old school art projects and handmade Father's Day gifts from when they were young.

On a more serious level, I joined a widows and widowers club. I had support from my established friends, but I felt awkward sometimes at gatherings designed for couples, such as our regular bridge club. The widows and widowers club was great because there I did not feel like anyone was feeling sorry for me. Showing up for the first club dinner seemed overwhelming, so I broke it down into smaller pieces. I talked my son into going with me to the restaurant where the group was meeting, and we spied on them from afar. Everyone was laughing and seemed to be having a good time, so I was less scared to go to the next activity by myself.

If there is a key to surviving the loss of a loved one, I found it to be the examination of the significance the person had on my life and those around me, the seeking out of laughter and support of friends, and breaking up any overwhelming tasks into manageable pieces. It was not and perhaps never will be easy, but I found that I am tougher than I thought.

Crying, Too, Shall End
by Wendell G. Hubbard

Grief is a universal phenomenon but we must deal with it on an individual basis. Why? Each of us is a unique being. The lines of separation between us and our fellow men are as distinct as our fingerprints. We walk alone, each of us bound for the same destination. At our journey's end we share the same experience. How we deal with that experience is an individual undertaking, whether it is our own journey's end or that of a loved one.

We live in a counseling-crazed culture. Counseling is seen as an ameliorate for all of the problems that trouble mankind. Who are the counselors? Have they undergone similar experiences? Has the rape counselor been a victim of spousal abuse? In short, has the counselor walked the bitter road of experience? Does the counselor have "territorial knowledge" of the area of his expertise or is he limited to "map knowledge"? If the answer is "map knowledge", then I may have to find my own way. In such a case, any advice coming from the counselor is at best superficial. The biblical proverb, "physician heal thyself", comes to mind. I know better than anyone else how much I hurt. I know where I hurt and how I need to be stroked. If you cannot provide the help I need, then help me to find what I need. The role of facilitator extends beyond the funeral director. If it becomes your lot, then what I require of you is assistance.

After my father died, I felt as if there would never be an end to my grieving. The man died in my arms. I closed his eyes. The night he died I couldn't shed a tear, but when I could, the tears kept flowing. Between the time that the mortuary had his body prepared and the funeral, I made numerous trips to the mortuary. At each visit I allowed the tears to flow unchecked. After the funeral, my grief persisted. I began to wonder if there would ever be an end to my sorrow.

Time after time, I visited the cemetery and at each visit I cried. After repeated visits and many tears, the night came when I would weep no more. It began with my usual cry but on this night I extended it. Three times I did this, wailing loudly, not holding anything back. That was ten years ago and to this day I have not felt the need to cry anymore. Pleasant memories of my father continue but there are no tears. Even when I dream of him, which I do more often than when he was alive, there is no sadness.

Whereas my father died in my arms, my mother's death was different. She died in a hospital sixty miles away. I received word of her death about 11:30 on a Saturday night. I had already committed myself to deliver the morning message at a church the following day. I could have begged off, the brothers would have understood, but I didn't want to inconvenience them. I put my feelings on hold. I had a calling to fulfill.

I slept peacefully that night and arrived at church the next morning without any difficulty. However, when one of the brothers asked me how my mother was feeling, I couldn't tell him. I told him I would let him know when the service was over. Having made it through the sermon, I managed to relate to my friend that my mother had died during the night.

God had given me strength to stand and the power to proclaim His word and return home. I was able to get inside my house before I could no longer contain my grief. I cried and cried. I talked to my mother of how life would be for me now that she and Dad were gone. That one long session of talking and crying relieved me of the pain I suffered from my mother's death. Since that day, alone in my room with the pain of my mother's death, I have not felt the need to weep over her again.

At my father's funeral, my two brothers, cousins, and I served as pall-bearers. At my mother's funeral we repeated this procedure. As I look back, I can see that this involvement with the funeral served as a type of balm for the pain of bereavement. This last act of service for them was an expression of our love, a final act of kindness. We had accepted their deaths. We knew they were gone forever. We carried their bodies to the tomb. It was a final goodbye.

We often fail to finalize death by our choice of words, by carefully avoiding the unpleasant aspects of the experience. We bury reality in the soil of euphemisms and entrust the activities of the occasion into the hands of strangers. The typical American funeral is denial of reality. Much of the pain of mourning could be absorbed in a ritual that is raw and real, but we resort to desensitizing practices. We have elaborate funerals with expensive caskets, artificial grass to hide the dirt, and the family is dismissed from the grave site before the casket is lowered into the grave. We hear much about the closure in the literature that deals with death, but we shy away from it. The lowering of the casket and closing the grave provide excellent symbols of closure. Whisking the family away robs them of this benefit. There was a time when death was raw and real, seen in its natural, mean state. The raw earth was exposed. The gaping hole in the ground was not shielded by a vault hovering over it. After the casket was lowered into the grave and the lid placed on the wooden box containing it, the attendants went about their task of closing the grave. The first shovel of dirt sounded a note of finality when it fell. It was a doleful sound, hollow and mournful, one that came to be associated with death. Today we go to great extremes to take the pain out of the moment and by doing so may be extending the days of grief. I met the grief of final separation from my parents head-on. I did not try to bury sorrow. I gave full vent to my agony allowing the storm to pass over in a short period of time. I assisted in the parting rites.

After the death of my father in 1986 and five years later the death of my mother, I have on many occasions reflected on the years between then and now. I can understand now what Paul Tillich meant when he wrote about our aloneness, our uniqueness, and the capability of walking with our loved ones to the hills of eternity. Numerous times during the years since the death of my parents we have been together beyond the shores of time. They were so close to each other in life that I cannot dream of one without the other. Time after time we walk together to the hills of eternity.

Grief is a part of the human experience. It is as sure to come as the setting of the sun. We must learn to accept the inevitable. Let us not allow euphemisms to rob us of the richness of any of life's experiences. Let us learn that ecstasy comes after agony. We cannot know true joy without sorrow. Finally, let us learn from the psalm which reminds us that "weeping may endure for a night, but joy comes in the morning."

Window of Life
by Donna L. DeMagistris

On the far end of town, there is an old, abandoned house. The wood is splintered, the paint is peeling, the roof is caving in. The bushes around the house possess weeds growing through them and they bear patches of dried up leaves and dead branches. From neglect, the grass runs amuck. From the house one can see a beautiful, lush, green park where all of the children love to play.

We all know the stories about that one fateful night that transformed a happy inhabitant of the town into a skittish woman, afraid of her own shadow, too scared to even go outside to tend her once garden-like grounds. After the unspoken tragedy, she shut down and began to rot away like her house. No one has seen or heard from her since.

As I walk past the house, I notice that one of the windows is partly open. The right side of the window is filthy. It is coated with dirt and spider webs. I can't see in and no one can see out. On the other side of the window, I can see a black curtain blowing in and out of the window with the breeze. Looking more closely at the window, I catch a glimpse of a figure watching the children play. I quietly creep closer to get a better look at the figure. I can clearly see the pale, ghost-like face of a woman about my age. There is extreme sadness and pain in her eyes as she gazes at the exuberant children romping in the park. She has a look of longing, as though she wants to join them, but there is something blocking her. As I attempt to sneak closer, I step on a lifeless branch which crunches under my feet, and I am spotted. The woman is frightened by me. She slams the window shut and it shatters. Pieces of glass fly towards me. I'm cut, but the wounds will heal. I brush myself off and carefully step over the jagged pieces of glass. I stop when I get directly in front of the window.

The woman tries to hide her face with her hands, but I already know who she is. I extend my hand out to her. She hesitantly accepts it. Warily, she slowly climbs out the window, being careful not to cut herself on the broken glass, and begins to walk towards me. Her eyes are wide with fright, but she continues forward, overcoming her fear with every small step.

Behind her, the house and window that sheltered her from life fade away. At last we are united. I am now finally whole and able to face the world. Ahead of me stands a brand new window, a fresh, clean window that glistens in the sunlight and is fully open and inviting. On the other side of it is the delightful park. Before I enter through the new window, I look back over my shoulder, but I don't see the decrepit structure. I see the magnificent beauty it once was with its manicured lawn and yellow and white flower beds. What a beauty to behold! I can even hear laughter emanating from inside the house. I freely pass through this new window, bringing with me the good memories, and join the children at play.

Reflections Of A Typical Day In August
by Jessica Kuzmier

August is just past. I had begun writing this in August, and it has carried over to September. I have always disliked August, even before all that occurred. Summer romances that soared fizzling into a slow death, the stores proudly displaying back-to-school sales like it was some great holiday. The end of freedom, the stifling of creativity. The nights, little by little, slowly getting colder, a harbinger of things to come. August was always a time when all good things came to an end.

August is a month that, as an adult, I sit in bafflement at the family I lost. I am now twenty-nine years old, and I am bereft of a biological family.

There are those who say that I am not entitled to feel the loss I do because I did not not act the way a daughter should act when her father is dying. If I had come to be the nurse they wanted me to be, or tolerated their verbal abuse, perhaps then I would be entitled to an iota of sadness. I have discovered many people of all ages that believe mourning does not belong to the young. There are those of an older generation that believe the young are the destroyers of the good they knew, and thus believe that pain visited upon us is justified punishment from their raging God. There are those who say that one should not feel so much pain with so much of life ahead. There are the middle-aged ones who wonder where they went wrong that their children are so distorted. There are the young who do not want to see their own peer in anguish, for it means that they too are vulnerable. Only children have such acceptance of pain. It is not something they are suppose to understand. But they do understand. They understand the heart.

Sometimes my friends tell me about a fight they have had with their parents. I am jealous. They have the luxury that I don't have. My husband has two parents, and a grandmother as well. These people all have something I don't. They have parents to hate. When they yell, someone yells back. They have family parties that can be destroyed by squabbling or alcoholic insults, or, conversely, can actually be an experience filled with joy and trust. These realities were robbed from me. When I yell, at best, a concrete slab with engraved dates will give me its unchanging gaze.

My relationship with my family wasn't all that charming. I came from what is now labeled a dysfunctional family, punctuated by addictions of various sorts, including some of my own. There were many times I avoided going to family functions because of the abusive behavior these things usually brought out. Regardless of the opinion of those who think me evil for doing such a vile thing, I do not regret those decisions. My accusers believe that duty comes before sanity, and that the young should live in servitude to those older just because they had the "luck" of being chosen by God to be born at a later date. Choosing to avoid these encounters was necessary to my sanity. But I will never know if one day I would have been accepted by my parents. I am just left to question.

August is a time of anniversaries, not of life, but of death. Mom's on the fourth. Grandma's anniversary on the fifth. Dad's on the sixteenth. Like a list of casualties of war. I am glad to have survived the onslaught for one more year.

Football season has started. I remember the first year after my father died, I kept wanting to call him to complain about the Giants, and every time, I had to stop myself. Many things have happened, and my father has not been there to see them.

Life still happens during grief. When death was still fresh, it irritated me that life dared to go on without me, and that it sometimes forced me to participate despite my pain. It has changed color over the years. Once an ugly gray, it has gradually dissolved into a colorful mosaic with some colors bright, some dark, but it has many colors. Time has perhaps healed some things. I do not sit paralyzed from trauma. I can move more freely, and sometimes the air seems fresh and clean. I notice these things more now that I have lost so much. I wonder why that has to be.

I remember how the passage of time meant nothing to me when I was younger. My sense of immortality had already been tempered by the death of my mother, and there were some times that I actually wanted to die. Perhaps I had not sat and thought of what death really meant. Like many who have tried to take their lives, I wanted the pain to go away. I wanted to hurry up time. Now, I have so much that I want to do, I panic when I see the seconds of the day slipping by, so little accomplished. I want time to go slower.

Now, five years later, I have decided that my life is my most precious gift. I do not want to waste it on things that people think I should be doing, or what a young person should be doing, a woman should be doing, or what a married woman should be. What I want out of my life has become quite clear to me. I believe that this life is what my dreams should consist of, hopefully fruitfully fulfilled. Knowing how precious each day is, I want to fill it with things done that will make me satisfied if my Creator called me tonight. I look not to satisfy others' needs. I look to satisfy my own, whether it is writing a book, or choosing to forgive instead of wasting time on vengeance, or loving instead of hating. Life is filled with enough destruction. I would like to create positive experiences as much as I can.

Things are sharper, more in focus. While I feel more pain, I see more beauty. While I feel older than my years, I also feel my life has been richer for it. Perhaps I will never be fully healed. But perhaps what I have experienced the most is that each day is a rich treasure not to be wasted. I believe that my depth of loss has taught me to have greater joy in the life that remains before me.

The First Laugh
by Cynthia Kuhn Beischel

Death and humor. My guess is that most people don't see these two subjects connected, unless in a black humor piece such as *The Loved One* by Evelyn Waugh. I generally didn't associate the two either, until I awakened to the healing effect of laughter.

Several months ago, I saw Joan Rivers speaking about how many people had misunderstood her style of mourning. Because humor is an integral part of who she is, she had naturally used it to help in dealing with the loss of her husband. As I recall her story, she and her daughter, Melissa, went out to dinner after the customary eight days of mourning that is observed in the Jewish tradition. While looking at the menu, Joan commented on the high prices by saying it was a good thing Edgar was already dead because he would have died at the sight of them. Melissa laughed with her, enjoying the joke. Apparently, others around them found it inappropriate and distasteful.

I laughed at hearing the story; I wondered what that said about me?

My assessment and conclusion came quickly: as in life, so with death. For a person who enjoys using wit and humor in the course of everyday life, it makes perfect sense to use it as a coping mechanism when dealing with the grieving process. In reflecting about how humor can be used to soothe, connect, and buffer, I remembered the moment I first laughed after my husband's death.

After the funeral, I was faced with not only the loss of my mate and the task of raising our two daughters, but I was also immediately engulfed in the duty of preparing our extended taxes. Because that had always been one of my husband's responsibilities, I felt unprepared to handle the task and enlisted the help of his mother among others. One day, about three weeks after his death, she and I were sitting at the dining room table which was covered with all the confusing paperwork. The phone rang. It was a friend of mine, checking to see how I was. In the conversation, my friend said something that made me laugh out loud, so hard that I had tears running down my face. I looked in the direction of my mother-in-law and saw her looking at me. I remember feeling concerned about her reaction. Did she think that it was inappropriate for me to be laughing so soon after her son's death?

As I hung up the phone, I stated what I was thinking: that it was the first time I had laughed since his death, and that it had really felt good. She said she understood. I became aware of starting a new phase.

I was once told by my friend Kristina Strom that laughter is the highest form of prayer. That idea had pleased me and made me happy because I love to laugh, and I found comfort in it. I was first attracted to my husband because of his humor and actually fell in love with him through laughter. Humor had been an integral and vital part of our relationship. In some circumstances it had been the glue that held our marriage together and carried me through some of our most difficult times. In our family, humor had also been established as a high form praise.

When I lost my husband, I also lost my sense of humor for a time. But when I could laugh again I knew that laughter did not show a lack of love, disrespect, or a forgetting of my loved one. To the contrary, I immediately knew that my husband would want me to laugh and have fun in the course of my healing process. His greatest wish for me and his daughters was that we embrace life, savor it, and live in a home full of warm memories and lots of love. As one of his dear friends had said in a sympathy letter, "If he could speak to us now, he would joke about our grief and tell us to 'get on with it!'" That's what we're doing.

CHAPTER 19

JOY

And, finally, an upbeat note allowing those in the early stages of grieving to see that, in fact, there can be good times ahead.

Excerpts From *Samurai Widow* by Judith Jacklin Belushi

Samurai Widow was published in 1990 by Carroll & Graf Publishers, Inc.

On March 5, 1982, a friend came to Judy Belushi with the devastating news that her husband had died. In 1990, she wrote a book titled Samurai Widow, *which details the moving and inspirational process of how she coped with his death and how she, over time, courageously created a new life for herself.*

People often talk about the "overnight fame" which came to John after *Animal House*. It didn't feel all that fast. By the time he graduated from high school, John was committed to his dream to be a movie actor and worked in the business for ten years before his first movie role. This transition was a period of growth, filled with struggles, disappointments, and successes. During the fifteen years we shared our lives, I helped John pursue his dream, letting it become our dream. I wanted to be an artist, and I pursued that as well, but John's work quickly became the first priority. His struggles, his disappointments, his successes—these too became mine.

I didn't realize how intertwined our lives had grown until long after John's death. I was a teen of the sixties and thought I had maintained an independence that my mother's generation had not. John and I lived together for five years before we were married, I used my maiden name professionally, I made certain my name was on credit cards and contracts. But these external acts did not stop the internal integration. Maybe this happened because we were so young when we became involved that we didn't have a full sense of ourselves as individuals before we merged our lives, and therefore developed a common ego of sorts, an intense interdependency. I suppose this happens to some extent in any long relationship. At any rate, John's death meant not only the loss of my loved one, but also the death of a part of me. The grieving that followed, although perhaps more complicated due to our history, I believe is basically universal; or at least it was that notion which inspired me to write about this overwhelming transition.

What I've attempted to capture on these pages is my emotional progression and subsequent evolution during the first seven years after my husband's death. I wrote in stages, sometimes setting the book aside for up to a year to allow more time to pass. I would like to stress that my stories are based on my memory and my viewpoint and interpretation of incidents. I have tried to stay in the time frame of which I write and not allow hindsight to interfere with what I'm describing. Sometimes this was difficult to do, as there are many issues I see differently now than when they occurred. But that progression, that chronicling of events and reactions, is the heart of my story.

After John's death I began keeping extensive journals, accumulating twenty-four in as many months. The excerpts in the book are about eighty-five percent as originally written. There were times when something was in such shorthand as to be unclear to anyone but me, and so I rewrote it. And occasionally I rewrote something to make it less awkward, or to fill a gap. There are also a few inclusions which are actually from an audio tape. My objective, however, was to remain as true to the original diaries as I could.

I began this process because I felt it would be helpful to me and I hoped that, ultimately, it would be helpful to others. The result is a memoir of my journey through a troubled time, toward . . . well, toward now. It was a journey I didn't want to take, down a road I didn't want to travel, with a destination I could not have imagined.

March 6

I awoke in a void, as if I were rushing through deep, black water toward the surface for air. I expected a rush of relief as I broke through, but instead found large block letters floating before me: JOHN IS DEAD. There was no refreshing breath of life, only this startling image. These three-dimensional letters, surrounded by darkness, bobbed up and down like boats anchored at sea, and took up all the space in my mind. I was overcome by the enormity of this reality; it was suffocating.

March 19—Early April

Days were easier than evenings; it was hard to stay home alone at night. TV was impossible. I'd turn the set on and within minutes I'd be hysterical over a commercial about phoning home, or because a game show contestant won his dream vacation. Then there were the constant news flashes and reports. Anything from a fire sweeping a building to a boy losing his dog left me shattered.

My perspective on life had changed drastically in one month. I was in pain and had this odd feeling that death was the only way to stop it. Odder still, the idea of dying didn't scare me. It was as if I were perched on the edge of a dark abyss, knowing I should hang on but not caring to. I was just standing there, looking down, unafraid, thinking how easy it would be to just fall forward and end it all.

I wished I had John to help me through my mourning.

April

Everything made me think of John. An old Volvo: that was his car. A man with a beard: he was so huggable with a beard. The Chicago Bears won? He loved the Bears. Seeing a couple walking hand-in-hand made me jealous. Something as inconsequential as a pocket flap accidentally pushed inside the pocket of a man's suit jacket nearly sent me into hysterics. I would flash on an image of John, all dressed up and smiling, standing with his hands in his suit jacket pockets, unknowingly stuffing the flaps inside. It was one of those unimportant things I could fix. I'd reach for his pockets and he'd grab me and give me a kiss and a hug. Damn it, how could he be dead and be so alive in my mind? It was as if he did live in my mind! Like a genie in a bottle, he was trapped there until I could find the secret to letting him out.

June

Occasionally there were moments when I felt good, but feeling good made me uncomfortable. I'd find myself laughing at something, sense my mood lifting, then crash! I'd have recognized the change in my feelings and remembered why it was I suddenly felt odd. How can I feel okay when John is dead? My body ached.

September (diary entry)

When I think of how I've structured the next few years (video tribute, documentary, book, etc.) around these things connected with John, I feel that it's something I do as a sort of unspoken promise . . . almost a tying-up of loose ends. At any rate, it's a way to go on. And when that's done, if I find there are enough other reasons to go on, I will. If not, I'll probably die of a broken heart. Not to sound dramatic, but I believe one can.

Life is really strange. I still wish John would come back.

For the first time, I thought, I really don't want to go to the grave. I drove home a longer route to avoid passing the cemetery. I'm not going to let myself feel guilty for this, I thought. But I did. It worries me. Am I going to get resentful of giving too much now that he's dead?

November (diary entry)

A few days after returning from Chicago I had a disturbing dream. John was in his casket, his hair wrong, and he was too big for the box. The image faded and for a moment there was only darkness. Then suddenly John appeared as a ghost, but not the ethereal, spiritual type I'd fantasized in the past, this was a frightening decaying version . . . It startled me awake . . . I imagined John said I was holding him back from his next world and I had to release him.

December (diary entry)

How unusual it is to be unafraid of death, and the freedom it gives you to live. I'm sometimes a little afraid of losing that feeling . . .

Xmas Season, walking New York, uptown. Great stores, crisp feeling, not too cold. Can't stop image of John saying to me, "You'll see, it will be easier when I'm dead." I think he had said something like "I'm not going to live as long as you" first. I don't think he was high. I know

I was crying, and I told him that was not true, that was all I could say, and now I hope he understood that my inability to say more was because the idea was so upsetting.

As Christmas draws nearer, panic decreases. That's not what I thought I'd write, but it's basically true.

Xmas is funny. I want to enjoy it, but it's hard. Had a nice time to-night . . . It was fun. I can't explain my mood shifts. When I was running around today, shopping, I started to cry in the back of the cab. I have that feeling again of vulnerability.

January 29, 1983

. . . I realized I hadn't cried for at least one week, which made it the longest time I was aware of during which I hadn't. It was a funny accomplishment to note, but it gave me a sense of improvement. I also had a curious "daydream". I saw an image of myself as an old woman, sort of a fantasy jump to the future. A kid asked what my life with John had been like and I sort of scrunched up my wrinkled face as if trying to remember, and said, "That was a long time ago." My imaginary reaction startled me and I wondered if it could be possible that someday I would be so blasé about that time of my life.

March 5

. . . [I] had passed into the dreaded day. My heart sped up and I began to feel anxious. I found myself thinking about three things at once . . . It's just another day, but it's crazy to think it isn't different. It's the day that changed everything.

. . . in the afternoon I went to the grave alone and took Polaroids of the flowers, which looked very nice. Then I sat there and cried. I spoke aloud, because I wanted to speak out to John. I said I missed him and was working on getting over being mad at him. "Of course, I guess you counted on that. You know I always do." I said I loved him and would forever, and then cried again, wishing none of this were true. I don't know how to feel any less sad, and I guess I shouldn't worry. It will just take time. But time is so unreliable. I remember a year ago as if it were yesterday. And yet the time between seems like forever.

June (diary entry)

There is something about the ocean and fresh air which makes you wake up and see things more clearly. I've been making a rock garden with beach stones, which is also soothing. I think I'm accepting John's death better. I thought, okay, J. is dead and that is sad. But I go on, and I'm going to make it, I'll be happy again. I can still enjoy things. I can still create. And maybe I'll even fall in love. I have a lot of things to be thankful for. Dr. Cyborn is right about putting myself first, but I don't think he realizes that a lot of things people think of as things I do "for John" are ultimately for myself.

Saw a shooting star when I came home and made a wish—to find happiness and someone to share it with.

November (diary entry)

Weepy tonight. Found a note from J. to me. It was a short note, just to tell me how much I meant to him and that he loved me. I broke down. Later I fantasized getting married again. As we stood to say our vows, I said to my new husband, "I never thought I'd be this happy again." But he's a faceless man, it seems like a hopeless fantasy.

I had a thought that John is like an echo, an endless echo that keeps coming back, slightly softer each time.

February 1984

Friends began to comment on my changed behavior . . . [Anne] said that of all the women in our crowd, I was the only one who was "trying to make it on my own", that most of our friends continued to rely emotionally on men. "I don't mean to sound weird," she said, "but I really think you've grown a lot since John's death." I felt bolstered by her support.

March 5, 1984 (diary entry)

Well, here it is, the second anniversary of J.'s death. I'm certainly doing better than I was last year . . . I'm on a plane to M.V. [Martha's Vineyard] right now, making my pilgrimage. I had serious hesitations this morning when I woke to find it snowing . . . I thought about what I'd do if I didn't go and realized I needed to do something in connection with J. today. So I decided at least to try. After all, what kind of a pilgrim would I be if I stayed home just because the weather was bad?

March 5, 1985

It's the third anniversary of John's death. Even last year, I could not have imagined I would have come so far, be feeling as—I hesitate to say "good" and consider saying "okay". But I'm feeling pretty good in general. At least I see a decent and worthwhile life in front of me. The lack of love in my life makes a dramatic difference. But these past ten months or so have been a remarkable change from the previous two years. And I feel more, and better, changes coming within the next few months, the next year.

The nightmare is over, but the pain is still with me. The loss is still frustrating . . . To think of John as reborn into another life requires faith—which I partially have. Sometimes I feel a tremendous sense of everything being interrelated. That "all is one". But that consciousness is hard to hold on to.

In a way, I think of John's passing as a new adventure for him, one we all are part of, and he's just begun ahead of me. He is like an astronaut whose destination is so far away that he will not return in my lifetime. I want to be happy for him, and I'm pissed off at the same time. But I will take the voyage one day, and he will have made my trip less frightening by his pioneering. I don't put much on the idea that I will ever figure it out, but I do have moments of feeling it is true. Trusting in those feelings is where the faith comes in. The universe is so magnificent, why not just have faith in it?

March 6, 1988 (diary entry)

I decided to look for some documents I need . . . Before I knew it, I was shuffling through copies of police and coroner's reports, searching for a form an officer filled out the day John died . . . It was odd that I would be doing that on this date, I knew, and yet it was interesting. I didn't get hung up reading details, I simply flipped through the papers looking only at forms.

Perhaps it was some kind of test of how far I've come since those papers first entered my life. Going through them didn't get me down. Some are familiar to me now, like pages from a book that I remember, not only the contents, but the emotional turmoil they caused. Looking at these papers I remembered, but did not react, did not relive the emotions.

. . . the energy is good in my life now. I will not live in fear, but in the Light . . . Day by day I can only try to enjoy all that has been given me, to share what I can, and to be who I am.

The Gift
by Sandra Hein

At first, and for a long time afterwards, the only connection I thought I had left with Dad when he died in 1980 was that a part of me died with him. He was the light in any darkness, a God on a pedestal that had crumbled before my eyes, leaving me empty and incomplete. I had lived as my dad's daughter and always feared being less than what I thought he expected of me. When he died, I thought I had no identity. I found out years later his death was a gift to me, and that the pain was the first conscious step towards my recognition of that gift.

I am familiar with pain. All my life I had been absorbing others' pain, starting when as a small child I took in my grandfather's emotional pain during his last years. The pain continued through years of experiencing abuse which enabled date rape at age seventeen.

My coping methods to deal with this pain included eating compulsively and later, as a teenager, drinking the pain away, denial, and isolation from others. Even at the time of Dad's death, I showed very little emotion, denying my feelings which resulted in the end of my marriage of seventeen years in 1994.

Years after Dad's death, and after the death of my marriage, I found I needed to let go of the pain I had held all my life. I found that, unlike the quick fixes I had tried to use throughout my existence, this was a slow process in which the pain would not go away quickly. My pain consisted of layers that had to be peeled away requiring patience, trust in myself and others, and love. I discovered that along with my children, I was growing, although from within. I was starting over, for the first time facing all types of feelings and experiences as I was willing to let go layer by layer.

My first step toward recovery happened shortly after Dad died and my daughters were less than two years old. I released the pain through rage, which I expressed to them and their father. I knew I needed help. I contacted Parents Anonymous. At meetings I started to express my feelings in healthier ways and learned coping skills for facing life's stresses with children. But a lot of pain was still deep inside and it wasn't lifting fast enough for me. The more I let go of, the more came up to the surface. I thought this pattern would never end. As I continued to use food as a coping tool, it escalated into full blown bulimic behavior about eight years ago. When I realized I needed help again, I attended Overeaters Anonymous, but after years of attending meetings at various locations I realized I needed to get more focused help concerning the reasons why I compulsively ate. I then found C.O.D.A.(Co-Dependents Anonymous) and individual therapy which allowed me to really face myself and start letting go of absorbing other people's pain. I discovered what part I had been playing in all relationships, especially intimate relationships, and learned skills to create healthier, functional relationships. I finally was aware I was in the right place, on the right road. That was about five years ago.

As the deeper layers lifted, I discovered a new confidence in myself and a wish to know my whole self. I continued for the next three and a half years searching almost obsessively for the missing part, still believing it to be in the form of a male. I kept myself in emotional limbo with many males, waiting and believing that someday someone would make me whole. I feared letting go, which resulted in feeling used and frustrated. I thought I had gone backwards, but soon found self love and awareness of a oneness from within as the result of giving myself permission to let go of a dependency on males, to take care of myself, and to affirm myself as a whole being.

I am discovering more of who I am and as a result, am allowing myself healthier intimacy in all relationships, but especially with males. I am expressing my feelings in healthier ways too, including effective verbal communication and journaling, as well as a new found creative expression through art, dance, singing, and writing.

What started out as a tragedy almost seventeen years ago on Christmas Day has transformed into a present in the form of my true self. Like the phoenix, I believe old life gives way to new life, accepting that only through the grieving process could I have attained joy.

The gift is now in my hands to pass on to my own children, although the joy is that I am alive to witness their transformation by encouraging and allowing them to find their true selves now.

Tears, Wonder, And Joy
Upon The Transition Of My Father
by Jan R. Faust

Seizing the gift of joy in death may seem like an illogical sentiment. Nonetheless, the feeling of joy is within reach. The ability to seize the gift of joy in the death of a loved one exists in a belief in life after death and the existence of a forgiving God. There is no hard evidence of a God who is compassionate and caring, nor one who is malicious and unkind. However, many people believe that there is a God and some people feel this God is a power with which we have to deal. Of those people who believe in a God, some presume God will send us to hell if we act in a way that could be interpreted as reprehensible.

My belief system does not support a God who will castigate and punish us by casting us out of eternal joy. On the other hand, I don't believe in a God who will create a blissful eternity. I believe we have immense input into our own essence and eventual death.

I believe we are watched over and guided. I also believe that I am a compilation of the experiences, both painful and joyous. Mine have enriched and made me wiser. They are the result of choices I have made, some good, some bad. Nonetheless, I am a compilation of my experiences and what I have learned from them. Some think that death is to be feared but, because I believe it to be just another phase of life, it is not something I fear.

I have been fortunate. The only person I dearly love who has transformed into the next stage of existence is my father. I don't know about anyone else, but stretching is what love does to me. Stretching is what it takes to grow in love and life. I find it painful to experience separation, not just a death, but any separation from a person I love. However, from that painful experience, given a little time, come the joyful musings, release from pain, as well as being more pliant for God.

Daddy died about ten years ago. His transformation was caused by a malicious cancer in his brain. The time of year my father chose (I do believe this is a choice we make) to make the transition into the next stage of life was the Christmas season. We were fortunate to be able to care for Daddy at home.

Mother began the task, and she was near exhaustion caring for him alone. But, my dad wanted to die at home.

God began orchestrating Daddy's joyous evolution here. This would be the only semester during my seven years of college in which I would have no final exams. I had six weeks to be at home and to help care for my father. My ability to care for him would be a source of both satisfaction and pain.

He rarely complained. But when he was uncomfortable he would yell, "Jan." It gave me so much pleasure to be able to help comfort him as he had helped me so much during my life.

As is natural for a person who is making the transition into the next stage of life, Daddy slowly stopped eating and drinking. I could not watch my father, the man who had given me life, die of dehydration. After consulting with my family and the doctor, I decided we would hydrate him with water through a tube which I inserted into his stomach through his nose. No food mind you, just water.

On Christmas Day, before the family meal, I broke my own rule to only give him water and fed him a liquid food supplement. My mother and brother were wishing Daddy could participate in the feast. When I told them what I had done, it seemed to ease our pain to some degree.

Our care included daily bathing, giving him water and medication through the tube, and repositioning him every two hours. This meant a lot of work; it was work my mother and I took on joyously, but work nonetheless. As my father's cancer progressed, he never seemed to be in pain. However, his lungs began to fill with fluid and it was essential that he go to the hospital. It was essential not for his purposes but for mine, it seemed. I could not stand by and allow him to die in this manner. So, my dad was not to get his wish to die at home, but it turned out that this was a good thing.

I could not see it then, but in the passing time I have watched a family keep a person who obviously needs to die alive primarily through their presence. Often I have seen a person who is ready to die hang on just because the family cannot seem to allow the transition.

In retrospect, I made a good decision when I said, "We can't take care of Daddy here any longer. He needs to be in a hospital." My dad was taken to the hospital where he was able to make the transition into the next life in three days. His death was attended by a friend of the family who had a feeling that he needed her. She was holding his hand when he died. Both of these events were part of the beautiful music that God and my father orchestrated for his movement into the next life.

My father was a person who lived life to the fullest. When he was younger, he jokingly said, "I want 'I Did It My Way' to be sung at my memorial service." My father contributed to my happiness in many ways that I can't articulate. However, I do remember two things that he said that have helped me over the years. As I struggled in high school, he always said, "Jan, you are smart and pretty." He may have been biased, but those two positive tangible assets that he asserted were mine really encouraged me to keep going.

I am sure that if not for those comments I would have never gone to college, which has been a great help to me. I will always remember his constant cheerful whistle drifting through our home; he seemed always happy. He continues to help me in many ways simply because he existed. Because of his example I am a risk taker, which has held me in good stead throughout my life. Daddy had a very strong belief in God which was an additional gift to me. Without his powerful example I would not have my strong belief in God.

I was not able to attend the community memorial service held for him because I had to start school and I would have just cried. I did attend the ash sprinkling held at the family summer home.

The cabin is in a beautiful part of the northern Minnesota woods overlooking Lake Leander, where there is the subtle aroma of pine. We were awaiting the perfect sunset on an August evening to row out on the lake and sprinkle the ashes. That is what Daddy wanted, to be sprinkled on the lake. We had gathered wild flowers, pie plates, and candles, all to be a part of the memorial service.

One evening my brother came running up from the lake saying, "This is it. This is the night. The sunset is beautiful."

We collected all of the wild flowers we had gathered earlier and took our candles stuck on aluminum pie plates—except for my brother who did not want to pollute the environment, so his candle was on a flat piece of wood. Then we headed for the boats.

The idea was to strew wild flowers behind the boats which would be pulling the lit candles on pie plates. Mother had written a beautiful eulogy which she intended to read before we scattered the ashes. We were all set to be morose and cry at this beautiful ceremony. What really happened was much better.

It was a beautiful sunset evening. Not a cloud in the sky. We got into a row boat and a canoe, connected the boats to the strings, pie plates, and piece of wood, lit the candles and rowed out into the lake casting wilted wild flowers behind the boats. I can still see the clumps of wilted flowers. Just about the time Mother got to the part in the eulogy about Daddy's sense of humor and I started to cry, from nowhere came a cloud which dumped buckets of rain on us. I sat there for about a minute getting soaked before I said, "I'm getting the hell out of here. Dump the ashes."

Mother, who had not opened the ash box until now, dumped Daddy's remains into the lake. How were we supposed to know the ashes would be in a plastic bag? The bag floated until someone grabbed it and opened it, spilling the ashes into the lake. I started rowing for all I was worth; it was pouring down rain. In my furious rowing, all of the strings that we were trailing got tangled up in the oars. By the time we got back to the dock, the cloud was gone, just a sunset and wet laughing people. It was as if Daddy was saying, "Be joyous, not sad, I'm better now." The ash sprinkling ceremony was robust and joyful just as my dad had lived.

Is there joy in death? There is at least some. I would not want to minimize the pain involved in death because it is there and very real. Still there was a familial bonding among all of the people attending the memorial service that took place in the Minnesota woods that could never have happened had the memorial service not been such a hilarious affair. Furthermore, I enjoyed caring for my father in such a wonderful way.

Missing Ben
by Andrea Warren

"Missing Ben" first appeared in Ladies' Home Journal *(Volume 114, #12), December 1997.*

Jay was always aware of the telltale signs before I was. Shortly after Thanksgiving, I would become distracted, my normally easygoing outlook tinged with gloom, tears ever closer to the surface.

"You get like this every year," my husband said in exasperation last November, sitting on the bed where I lay teary-eyed. "I do everything I can think of to make you feel better, but nothing works. It's no fun for either of us anymore. Is it always going to be this way?" When I didn't reply he left the room.

In my misery, I thought that he simply didn't understand—though if anyone understood, it was Jay. But he couldn't make Christmas okay for me. No one could.

In 1986, Brendon (Ben), my ten-year-old son and the stepson Jay had loved deeply for seven years, was hit by a car and killed. I had hated the holidays ever since. While I missed Ben every day, his loss was keenest at this time of year, with its emphasis on celebration, joy, and family togetherness. For years after Ben's death, I went through the motions of a happy Christmas for the sake of our other three children—my daughter and Jay's daughter, and his son who didn't live with us. I kept my spirits up for them while grieving in private for their younger brother. But now that our daughters were in their twenties and lived away from home, my holiday depression had resurfaced with a vengeance. I wanted to turn back time. I wanted my little boy back so we could experience the wonder and joy of Christmas again, the way it was before our family was plunged into anguish by a tragic moment on a busy street.

As I wrestled with my feelings, I realized that I didn't want to ruin another holiday season for Jay. I owed him more than that. But did I even have it within me to feel the spirit of Christmas once again?

One evening several days later, I was talking to one of my daughters over the phone when I mentioned how much Ben had been on my mind. For a moment, there was silence. Then she spoke, her voice breaking with emotion: "I've been thinking about him, too. Ever since he died, I've just wanted to get Christmas over with."

Her words jolted me. All those years, I thought the girls had still had a good time celebrating the holidays. Had they just been putting on an act for my sake? Had they, too, become incapable of enjoying what I knew deep in my heart could be the happiest, best time of year?

I had thought that somehow, as the years passed, I would naturally begin to anticipate the holiday season again. As I hung up the phone, I realized that time couldn't make this happen; Ben would always be missing from our lives, and we would always feel his loss most acutely at this time of year. But if I could acknowledge my grief instead of stifling it, and honor my son's memory at the same time, perhaps I could find joy in the holidays again—which meant Jay could, too. Then we might be able to help our daughters rekindle their own Christmas spirit.

After much thought, I told Jay I wanted this year to be different, that I didn't want to spend December under a cloud of gloom. I could see the relief in his eyes as he offered to do whatever he could to help me. We came up with a plan that we hoped would work for both of us.

First, we would work at finding pleasure in all that was magical and wonderful about the holidays. Second, we would speak of Ben whenever he came to mind—no holding back for fear of depressing ourselves or others. Finally, we would do one special thing to commemorate how much we missed our son. All three, it turned out, were important.

Starting with the first goal, I concentrated on engaging my senses to the fullest. For the past ten years, I realized, I had shut them down, numbing myself to the twinkle of lights, the sound of carols, the smell of evergreen, the tastes of mint, almond, and ginger. Now, I embraced them. I also gave more thought to each holiday task—from wrapping presents to mailing cards—appreciating them as time-honored rituals instead of dreary chores to be gotten out of the way.

I unpacked several paper-and-paste ornaments Ben had made in grade school, including a primitive little yarn frame with his school picture in it. Closing my eyes, I ran my fingers over the aging wool and the small image of Ben with his happy, gap-toothed grin, a child who loved the Chicago Cubs, books, cats and dogs, silly sayings. After the accident, I had stored these precious creations away, unable to bear looking at them. But our son had made them for us, to be displayed and admired. We hung them on the tree. From now on, we would bring them out, touch them, and allow them to touch us.

Several weeks before Christmas, I had lunch with a friend I had not seen for many months. She dwelled at length on how much she hated the holidays—too much rich food, too many expectations. Then she lamented feeling "deserted" because her newly married son would be spending the holidays with his wife's family.

The old me would have nodded while inwardly screaming, "At least you *have* your son. Look at me—your pain is *nothing* compared to mine!" But I had vowed not to keep quiet when Ben was on my mind. I took a deep breath and forced myself to sympathize with her. Then, measuring my words carefully, I told her that I was trying hard to enjoy the holidays in spite of how much I still missed Ben.

My friend looked startled, and for a moment I regretted saying anything. Then she put her hand on my arm. Her eyes were moist. "I think that is is the first time since Ben's death that you've mentioned him to me," she said. "Whenever I started to say something about him, I could tell you didn't want to talk about it, so I assumed you must be over your grief. But now I know . . . " Her words caught in her throat. "You've just given me a special gift. I'm going to be grateful for what I have and stop complaining."

I would have given anything to be able to commiserate with her about our adult sons, but at least I had finally spoken. And in breaking my silence at long last, I let my friend draw me close.

A few days later while out shopping, Jay and I stopped in a busy cafe for espresso. I was suddenly reminded of one Christmas we had spent nursing Ben through the flu. As I recalled this to Jay, tears welled in his eyes, then in mine. "I miss him so much," he whispered. There, amid the bustle of holiday shoppers, we held hands under the table, let our tears fall and managed to smile at each other, enriched by our shared remembrance and our love.

We were discussing how best to accomplish our third goal of honoring Ben's memory—a special holiday concert, perhaps?—when we saw a notice in the local newspaper about "A Service of Remembrance: In Memory of Those We Miss the Most at Christmas." Jay and I didn't belong to that church's denomination, but no matter. We gathered with a hundred other bereaved souls, and in a lovely, quiet candlelight service, we listened to comforting words and beautiful music, including the haunting song "I Miss You Most at Christmastime." Then we put the names of the people we had loved and lost into a special basket on the altar.

My tears felt especially healing that night, and I entered the busy final week before Christmas with a sense of peace that had eluded me in years past. Over the phone, we shared our feeling with our daughters and offered heartfelt support as they expressed their own sadness about Ben. When we wished them Merry Christmas, I felt we all could truly have one at last.

On December 25, Jay and I toasted our families and the memory of Ben at a family gathering in my brother's home in Nashville. When January 2 arrived, I realized that for the first time in ten years, I had actually *enjoyed* Christmas. It would never be what it was, but it could still be good. I felt that Ben would be pleased.

This year, with the holidays approaching, I am aware once again of my sadness for what cannot be, but I am focusing on what I still have and what is worth celebrating. For the bereaved, whether our losses be new or old, our challenge is to be happy in the moment, to see the star, to celebrate the magic of the season, and to cherish the memory of our departed loved ones.

"'The Time Has Come,' the Walrus said . . . " by Cynthia Kuhn Beischel

I'm not actually sure when it started. If I look back over recent weeks, I guess there had been lots of signs pointing towards it. I had given myself a birthday present: a psychic reading . . . in the year ahead men would be in pursuit of me (not all of them necessarily to my liking). Then Dad asked me one night whether I was having any fun these days, going out on dates, that sort of thing. When I said not really, he suggested I go to places and events where I might meet new people and make new friends. The innuendo was that they be male, preferably marriage material.

I knew his suggestions were coming from a deep well of concern for me. His query triggered a poignant memory: even my in-laws had wondered aloud whether I had some interest in a new man. I had squirmed and replied that my friend Jane and I were thinking about going to a church-sponsored singles mixer.

As if silently confronting my inner issues wasn't enough, the next day, my divorced friend Nancy called to say there was a meeting of singles at the new bookstore.

When I hung up the phone, I wondered what I had just gotten myself into. Just a few days ago, I found myself totally out of whack emotionally, feeling like I might cry at any moment though nothing catastrophic was happening in my life. I looked at the calendar and was aware of the date. I had thought I could handle it. The anniversary of my husband's death was approaching and I felt that I should be over it. After all, it had been three years.

Soon after Jerry died, my daughters and I joined a support group for grieving families. I felt it was important for them to have a place where they could not only express their sorrow, but where they could heal through participation with others. I found that I dealt with his death in a more peaceful manner than some of the others in the group, which I attributed to the metaphysical philosophy my husband and I shared. We believed we had spent past lives together, playing out various roles to help each other learn lessons at this school called Earth. We also felt that all events provide valuable opportunities from which to learn and that things happen for reasons which were perhaps beyond our limited ability to comprehend. My belief system was a great comfort to me. I knew Jer's soul had not died, but rather had gone through a transition. However, this knowledge did not eradicate my need to deal with pain, anger, loss, and all the stages of grieving.

I was stoic until another friend called to let me know the date of Jerry's death had not been forgotten by others. I burst into tears, letting go of stored up pain, disappointment, and frustration. Amazingly, I felt lighter and more relaxed when we hung up.

As Merritt, Lindsay, and I lit a candle in my husband's honor and memory, I realized I had the power to make each day be a new day. When I drove the girls to school, I told them I was ready to meet some men. My daughters expressed mixed feelings, a combination of enthusiasm and hesitancy, but supported me in my adventure out into the world of singles.

Nancy called just before we left.

"I have nothing to wear," I complained. "God, I haven't bought new things since Jer died."

I had spent about an hour figuring out what to wear. I finally chose white jeans and my favorite shirt that sported a bold Aztec design in bright colors.

"Maybe you shouldn't worry," Nancy said. "I'm sure it's very casual; I'm just wearing my white jeans and a navy blue blouse."

"White jeans?! That's what I was planning to wear." Nancy was kind. She knew this was my first time out and immediately offered to put together another outfit for herself.

"Want to forget about going to this thing and just go shopping?"

I almost said yes, but I was on a mission.

While I was getting dressed, I tried on four pairs of shoes, two belts (I ended up not wearing one), and several pairs of earrings. I still wasn't happy with what I saw in the mirror. I was complaining about my hair when I heard from the next room, "Get over it, Mom. Just think positive so that you can project that feeling and be attractive to others." I laughed, knowing that I was being handed the same message I have given both the girls from time to time.

I flashed back to what my husband used to say: "Just smile and you'll look beautiful." With that I was out the door.

On the road, I began to worry about my severe case of SHS (Sweaty Hand Syndrome). I've been known to leave wet fingerprints on bank counters, lawyers' desks, and doctors' tables all over town.

Once I arrived at the bookstore, I ran into one of the principals at my daughters' school who was browsing for leisure reading. I told her I was browsing for leisure men, who hopefully would not be wearing leisure suits! She laughed and wished me luck.

The singles' area centered around a food table loaded with punch, cookies, pita triangles and dip. I decided not to eat. I was too nervous and I wanted to keep my lipstick looking good.

Nancy showed up and I pointed out the people who wore name tags with the word "Solo" on top. I asked Nancy, "Is that what singles are called these days?" I started singing, "I'm a solo, you're a solo, wouldn't you like to be a solo too?" We laughed, relaxed, and moved into the throng separately.

I saw a tall, interesting looking fellow. I imagined him to be a professor. He smiled, put out his hand, and told me his name. *We've made contact, Houston!* I thought to myself playfully, still being in the "mission" mode.

Morty asked where I lived, and in rapid fire progression wanted to know what kind of house it was and whether or not I lived alone. Was he going to ask the location so he could plan a heist? Was the next question going to be about my income? I responded slowly with similar questions and gave the kind of nods that mean "interesting", although the conversation wasn't. I knew in my gut that this was going nowhere, but I didn't know how to move on gracefully: I was out of practice.

Morty racingly jumped into the topic of music. "Do you like Zydeko?" *Did he say Art Deco? What's that got to do with music? No, it started with a "Z" sound.* I had no idea who or what he was talking about. I felt sure my daughters would shake their heads at my ignorance, but I was clueless.

"It's not my favorite," I answered neutrally.

He went on quickly—with the kind of speed that comes from nervousness—about how he won lots of concert tickets by being the ninth caller on radio programs. He said the most recent tickets were for a show by the group he had just mentioned before. He talked incessantly about music and the myriad concerts he'd seen.

I asked what type of work he did. He paused, for once, and said he was currently unemployed. He continued to talk, but because of the noise in the room and the food in his mouth, all I caught was that he was looking for a "pro-fessional" job.

I felt paralyzed. I wanted out, but I couldn't move; I was stuck. Determined to keep the conversation alive, Morty moved us into the topic of high school. He asked me where I'd gone. I told him I doubted that he'd ever heard of it; it was an all girls school.

"Was it Catholic?"

"No."

"Oh, well the reason I asked is that most girls' schools are."

"Yes, I know, but it wasn't. It was a private school, Miss Potter's, very exclusive." I don't as a rule like to sound snobbish, but I thought it might turn him off. It was worth a try.

"I went to Frances Bacon. It was exclusive too."

"Oh?" I said, knowing it hadn't been in the same social category at all.

"Yeah, only boys were allowed."

I could only surmise that we were using different definitions of the word "exclusive". I lifted an eyebrow, and he continued.

"Yeah, but it's not all boys now, you know."

"Oh, you mean they merged with a girls' school?"

He nodded yes as he said Our Lady of something or other. Then he added, "You know what they call it now?"

"No."

"Bacon and L'eggs."

Oh good, a little sexist humor! What am I doing here? I thought, as I gave an outward smile.

"So, what year did you graduate?" Morty asked.

"'66, and you?"

"'74."

"So you're quite a bit younger," I said, thinking eight years was a pretty big age gap and that he might want to move on for a younger woman.

Instead he said, "I like older women."

"Oh?" I said with a knowing smile. I was almost positive about where he was going.

He leaned toward me, whispering, "Do you know why?"

Oh, God, I was right. "Why?"

"Because they have more experience," he said with a sly smile. I'm not sure what look came over my face, but he quickly added that he had meant about life in general.

Yeah, right. I nodded.

I started feeling sorry for this man. Part of me, I guess, felt sorry for all of us there. As I watched him frantically try to think of the next thing to say, I could almost see his mental checklist, a list he'd probably put together over time and used before. He was a nice guy, but not my type.

As our encounter was winding down, he continued to query quickly about different topics. I was removing myself mentally, and then physically, when I suddenly heard him say, "So, do you want to go to the concert with me?"

Oh no, I thought we were past that topic. Do I have to do an official rejection? I don't want to hurt this guy, but NO! "Oh, thanks, but no. I'm not really fond of that style of music." *What kind was it again?*

Maybe because of a desire to let him down gently, or a strong desire to protect myself, I blurted out, "I don't think I'm ready for all this . . . today happens to be the anniversary of my husband's death." *Is that you I hear laughing, Jer? Hey, you got me into this situation; now you can get me out of it!*

I have to give Morty credit. He didn't turn green or run away out of shock or embarrassment. Instead he told me he once "knew" another widow. His ability to switch gears was admirable. I had a momentary, whimsical flash as I wondered how he would have handled some other kind of shocking fact. *"Morty, I have to be honest with you; I just found out today that I have alien ancestors." "Oh, that's okay; I've dated aliens before."* Instead I came up with a brilliant, "Oh?"

"She had white hair. I mean her whole head was white and it was beautiful."

Yeah, well I pay about $60 a month so mine won't look like that. "That's nice."

"I helped her out."

"I know how much it meant to me when my friends helped me."

"I like to help people."

He's a sincere person, but not for me. It was really time to end this. "Well, it's been nice meeting you."

"It's been nice meeting you too," he said as he reached out to shake hands. "You are really pretty," he said.

Oh, sure, lay on the guilt as I leave. "Thank you; I hope you find someone to go to the concert with you."

I headed over to the snack table. I needed nourishment. My interlude with Morty had taken a lot out of me, so I didn't care if I had pale lips or not. I bit into a pita triangle. Thank goodness I hadn't eaten one earlier and then met the man of my dreams. What had the staff been thinking in planning this menu? "Let's see, we have a bunch of single people coming who want to make a good impression upon and be attractive to strangers. Now what would be a good thing to serve? Garlic! Yes! Lots and lots of garlic, and then let's add a blue cheese dip."

I knew olfactory memories of this evening would literally be with me for days.

***

So, that's the story of my first outing as an available woman. In some ways it was awful, but I came away with a good lesson. That night, I had been into a negative type of self absorption: I was concerned that I might not be found attractive. I was worried about myself. I left the bookstore thinking I was okay, and as I drove home I formulated a new strategy for upcoming excursions. Instead of focusing on my perceived flaws or self-doubts, I could shift my energy to helping the person I was meeting to feel more comfortable. Being less self-conscious, we would both have a better chance of enjoying the encounter.

Postscript: As for the title of this piece, I've remembered that line from *Alice in Wonderland* since childhood when I had to memorize it. It popped into my head when I was writing about this experience. My husband was a handsome man and a really good dad. He had a big, thick mustache, and more than once we said he looked like a walrus. From wherever he is now, I know he's encouraging me to move on and enjoy life.

Mourning Turned To Dancing
by Barbara Linde Parks

When a dear family member passes away, we may feel a sense of emptiness. For me, it took the form of not wanting to be downstairs after I had supper, and I would go upstairs, get into bed, and turn on the television. The time was not completely wasted, I did needlework. The time spent in this manner is measured by the fact that I quilted four bedspreads and knit three sweaters in five months. Gradually, I became aware of the fact that I was accepting limitations and letting myself grow old.

For five years I had made caring for my husband my prime concern both when he was at home and in a nursing home. For the first year-and-a-half we spent every minute together. We shared many of his boyhood memories during this time.

An orphan, he lived with various uncles who offered very little affection. He began working early as an errand boy. Later on, he cleaned carpets and worked on a farm. When one uncle insisted that he give up school to work full-time on the farm, he ran away from home at the age of fourteen to continue his education. He got a job helping the owner of a drugstore who allowed him to occupy a room above the store for studying and sleeping.

There was one period when he had a more normal family experience. A friend at school invited him to have supper with his five brothers and sisters and his widowed mother. When the mother learned of his situation, he was invited to live at their home. It was the happiest time of his early years. This boyhood friend remained as close as a brother for the rest of their lives. After my husband and I were married, we spent many delightful vacations with his friend, wife, and two sons at their modest seaside home in a quaint village on Long Island.

Three years after my husband's passing, I had this account of his boyhood memories bound in a hard cover so that I could give each of our children a copy as a Christmas gift.

The caregiving had become more intense and, at the urging of friends, I made arrangements to have my husband live at a nearby nursing home. For almost four years I spent at least three hours with him late in the day after I had finished working at his engraving business. After my husband broke his hip, we used a wheelchair for our daily walks and for taking him to church.

When he was finally released from his anguish and discomfort, I felt a sense of release, but a feeling of emptiness still surrounded me. After forty-five years of marriage to the finest man I had ever known, I was no longer needed. He was recognized for his integrity and humility. His greatest joy was in being of service to others. I still feel a twinge when I remember his words, "I tried so hard to be good."

Months later, as the dark days of winter were approaching, I knew I had to do something to avoid just retreating to the bedroom. I asked myself, "What am I interested in? What do I enjoy doing?" The answer came: dancing. A widowed friend told me about the singles dances down at a nearby church, and I determined that I would attend on the following Friday. It rained that night and I don't like driving at night in the rain, but I had promised myself that I would go. While driving down, I began to wonder just who would be putting his arm around me. I suddenly alerted myself and changed my thought to considering the man of God's creation. Our Bible lesson of the week was on that very subject, and I began to ponder the qualities God's man would be expressing. He would be ageless, intelligent, considerate, and I would not judge him by his appearance.

I entered the dimly lit room where the dance was being held and signed in at the reception desk. Finding my way to the refreshment table, I poured myself a soft drink and looked around to find a place to sit. I spied an empty table up in the corner and sat down. I sat and sat. I was beginning to feel uneasy. Just then a gentleman came over and said, "I notice that this is your first time at our single dances. Let me introduce you to some of our regular members."

He took me back toward the refreshment table and introduced me to two couples who were standing nearby. We chatted for a few moments, but I was still a fifth wheel. When the music started again, two men approached and one of them asked me to dance. I was surprised that he then invited me to sit at his table, and more or less, became my escort for the evening. Toward the end of the evening he asked if I would like to go out for a drink after the dance. I replied, "Thank you, but I don't drink." He then commented, "I was planning to order cranberry juice."

I was grateful that I had gone to the dance alone since that enabled me to accept. We went to a nearby restaurant and spent about an hour getting better acquainted. I learned that he was a judge working full-time, didn't smoke or drink, had been widowed for six years, had a married son living nearby who was an air-traffic controller and a daughter living in Montana. When I asked if he had ever done any camping with his family, he answered, "No. But I did attend camp as a Boy Scout." And then he casually added, "I am an Eagle Scout."

That impressed me. Because I was acquainted with the ten scout laws (trustworthy, loyal, helpful, friendly, kind, obedient, cheerful, thrifty, brave, clean, and reverent), I thought to myself *There are all those qualities I associate with God's man.*

Of course I had not dated anyone other than my husband for forty-five years and I suddenly remembered that my mother always said that I should get home by midnight. So, I hurriedly thanked him, said good night, and drove off.

At the next dance he said, "You didn't give me your phone number," and being new at this business of getting acquainted, I replied, "I don't give out my phone number to strangers!" At this point I realized that I was putting all kinds of stumbling blocks in the way of our becoming friends, and I really did want to spend more time with this gentleman. He had told me his last name and where he lived, but how was I going to solve this problem without being too forward?

Fortunately, Providence had already come up with the solution. Shortly after my husband passed away, a group of friends took me to a jazz concert at a local restaurant and while there I won two complimentary tickets to dinner. I decided to write him a note and invite him to be my guest. Of course, I had to include my telephone number. He phoned the very night he received it and we made arrangements.

I am happy to report that we have become dancing partners and have enjoyed dancing twice a week for the last five-and-a-half years. We have become very good friends and enjoy doing things for each other and with each other. He is a modern thinker with old-fashioned manners. In addition to our dancing, he has established foundations at four law colleges and, as a result, we are invited to a variety of social functions.

This chapter in my life is full of joy. Like the passage in Psalms 30:11, I am so very grateful that my mourning has turned into dancing.

Danny's Gift
by John W. Carlsen

A few months before Danny was born, my wife and I were told that there was something wrong with our son. Ultrasound had shown that he had hydrocephalus or "water on the brain". The doctors gave us a few options, one of which was to end the pregnancy. After many prayers and lots of tears, we decided to let him be born, to love him, and to find the inner strength to deal with his problems.

On June 6, 1983, Danny was born, six weeks premature and weighing in at four-and-a-half pounds. As it turned out, the hydrocephalus was the least of his problems.

Danny was born with a hole in his spine, a condition called *spina bifida*. From his head to his toes, Danny's function was impaired. He was virtually paralyzed below the knees; his bowels and bladder didn't work properly. His hips kept coming out of their sockets; and he developed severe curvature of the spine; still later, we discovered that he had a whole host of learning disabilities.

When he was an hour old, Danny was whisked into surgery where a shunt was implanted into his brain and the hole in his back was repaired by a skilled neurosurgeon. The doctors, however, were not optimistic. We were told that he would fight for his life over the next few days, and if he survived, he would be retarded, never walk, and never say "momma". For all of us, life could not have been more bleak.

But something happened. Danny not only survived, he prospered. Spina bifida seemed to be a mere inconvenience for him, and the dire predictions for his future never materialized. Sure, he was still seriously disabled, but that didn't matter to him or others. People were drawn to Danny. He was bright and friendly and outgoing. Those who expected to pity this poor child found themselves charmed by and loving him. For a young boy who faced challenges every day that would humble most of us, he lived a rich and full life. Without any of us knowing it, he had embarked on a life-long mission of teaching others about the person behind the disability.

Throughout the years, Danny would have nine surgeries, including a complete spinal fusion. Despite all the pain, the anxiety, and knowing that he couldn't do all the things the other kids did, Danny was remarkably happy and upbeat. He attended a regular neighborhood school and had a whole pack of non-disabled friends. His presence and personality taught hundreds of children to look beyond the disability. His measure of success was that, after a while, he became "just plain Danny", a popular fixture in his school, his neighborhood, and his community. Danny's trademark was a smile that spread from ear to ear.

Every year after the age of six, Danny would compete in the New York State Games for the Physically Challenged. He loved the excitement, the festive air, the competition, and, in the six years that he competed, he won more than twenty gold medals. What was more important was that for the last few years his school would send several bus loads of kids to watch Danny compete. They were impressed with the determination and the *abilities* of all the disabled kids. They saw that these kids could compete and could have fun too. In this simple way, Danny's classmates were taught a lesson that will serve them for the rest of their lives.

Somewhere along the way, Danny discovered what policemen were, what they did, and especially, that his dad was one of them. Danny loved the police department. He was so proud of me and beamed when his friends saw me in my uniform. Everywhere he went, every officer he met, he asked the same question: "Do you know my dad?" He felt so special because his dad was a policeman. He played cops and robbers constantly. He had his own uniform and his own police radio. He even took to writing his own crime reports about our neighbors. Most of all, he loved to be with police officers. For most of his life, I was assigned to the elite Emergency Services Bureau, where Danny was a frequent visitor. He loved the attention the men paid to him. He thought that cops were the greatest people on earth.

Danny always dreamed of being a policeman just like his dad. I never had the heart to tell him that the disabilities which made him so special would also keep him from being the cop he always wanted to be. His mom and I had told him many times that he could be or do anything that he wanted, and I just couldn't bring myself to disappoint the little boy who looked up to his dad and the uniform he wore.

One morning in August of 1995, Danny developed what seemed like a bad cold. His mom and I tended to him that morning, but as we sat with him in his bed, Danny suddenly collapsed. He wasn't breathing. I started CPR while my wife called for help. Within minutes, the very cops he admired so much arrived to try to save him. They worked feverishly to resuscitate him. He was brought to a local hospital. The emergency room doctor ushered me in to be with him while they worked. Danny had been without a heartbeat for almost forty minutes. I grabbed his hand and pleaded with him to pull through. At that very moment, the monitors showed a few heartbeats, and then there were none. I believe that was his goodbye, his way of telling me that he knew I was there with him as he left this world.

Despite the best efforts of many dedicated professionals, Danny died, the victim of a fast-moving heart infection called myocarditis. He was twelve years old. Imagine how it feels to be a cop, a hero in your son's eyes, and not be able to save him. *I live with that every day.*

In the darkest moment of our lives, God gave us the strength to offer Danny's eyes for donation. Throughout his life, Danny gave so much to others that we wanted his final act of giving to be to help someone else see the beautiful world he so enjoyed.

Some months later, my wife and I began a search to find the people who received his corneas. We wanted to tell them about this special boy and help them to understand how precious was the gift they had received.

The process wasn't easy. I had to write a letter, which was forwarded by the Eye Bank to the recipient. He could decide to respond or not. For many, it is a difficult issue, since with it comes the realization that another person had to die so they could receive a transplant. Knowing that the donation came from a twelve year old boy could undoubtedly make the decision to respond particularly painful. We prayed for a response.

After some time, we received a letter from a young man who had gotten one of Danny's corneas two days after his death. The man had been almost blind in one eye as a result of an infection and had faced the loss of his job and an uncertain future. But the cornea transplant had given him a new lease on life, a second chance. *That man was a New York City Police Officer.*

All those who knew Danny also knew that he had a special reason for being on this earth. He fulfilled a life-long mission of teaching others. He showed countless people how to love and how to laugh. He taught them to be more tolerant and sensitive to those whose bodies are less than perfect. He let the world know that being disabled is largely a state of mind and that it's the person that counts, not the disability. In his death, Danny was able to save the sight and career of a police officer. And in doing so, he became the cop he always wanted to be.

I've come to believe that there are no coincidences in life, *but there are miracles.*

The story doesn't end here. Danny was our only child. There is no experience like losing your child; the pain is like nothing I had ever felt before. It was constant and unrelenting and I wondered if I'd survive. It was pain that can't be described. It must be lived to be understood, but I did survive, if only minute by minute and hour by hour. Out of that hurt and emptiness, my wife and I realized how much being parents meant to us. Danny had taught us so much about ourselves. He taught us how to love unconditionally and how to give unselfishly. He taught us patience and acceptance and how to smile while struggling uphill every day. He taught us to appreciate what's really important in life. Danny had wisdom beyond his years and he left a legacy that will guide us for the rest of our lives. For his sake, for his memory, for everything we had learned from him, we knew that we needed to be Mom and Dad again.

We looked deep into our hearts and into our souls and with God's help we decided to adopt children, to share our love and our lives again. These children would be the brothers and sisters that Danny always wanted, but never had. It was, perhaps, the last of the significant decisions we made in Danny's life.

A few months after completing all the paperwork and processing to be adoptive parents, we received a phone call from the adoption agency. They had located three children living in an orphanage in southern Russia. Two brothers, ages four and two, and a little two year old girl were among the 600,000 orphans in Russia waiting for a home and a loving family, and the agency wanted to know if we would consider adopting them. *That phone call came on the first anniversary of Danny's death, one year to the day after he had died.* We could see Danny's loving hand in it, telling us that these were the children selected by God to receive our love. There was no doubt that these children were meant for us. *No coincidences—only miracles.*

In September of 1996, my wife and I traveled to Russia and returned with Michael, Gregory, and Anastasia, three beautiful children. So many people have told us that we've done such a wonderful thing, saving these kids from a bleak and dismal orphanage, and giving them a warm and loving family. However, we have a secret: these children are saving us. By the grace of God and Danny's love, we have been blessed with the opportunity and privilege to be Mom and Dad again. Someday, when they're old enough to understand, we'll tell them all about their brother Danny, who we know is with us always and watching over his new family. He is still very much a part of us, living in our hearts, our thoughts, and our memories. For us, there is once again the laughter of children in our house and happiness has returned to our lives. Some people have made a point of telling us how absolutely lucky we are. I know it isn't luck—we have our own guardian angel watching over us, cheering us on, helping us over the rough spots, and showing us how to use the many lessons he taught us.

Better Than I've Ever Been
by Cindy Bullens

The following lyrics are from the CD Somewhere Between Heaven and Earth *(©1999 Blue Lobster Records).*

There's been a lot of things said about me
Since that awful day
I'm not the person that I used to be
And that I'll never be the same
That's true—no doubt
But I know more now what life is about

I laugh louder
Cry harder

Take less time to make up my mind and I
Think smarter
Go slower
I know what I want
And what I don't
I'll be better than I've ever been
Maybe I'll be better than I've ever been

If someone told me twenty years ago
That this would be my life
I'd lose the greatest gift that love can show
I'd have said—No, I won't survive
But don't count me out
Sometimes I'm stronger than I've ever felt

And I laugh louder
Cry harder
Take less time to make up my mind and I
Think smarter
Go slower
I know what I want
And what I don't
I'll be better than I've ever been
Maybe I'll be better than I've ever been

There's a curious freedom
Rising up from the dark
Some kind of strength I've never had

Though I'd trade it in a second
To have you back
I gotta try to make some good out of the bad

So I laugh louder
Cry harder
Take less time to make up my mind and I

Think smarter
Love deeper
I know what I want
And what I don't
And I'll be better than I've ever been
Better than I've ever been

CLOSING STATEMENT

I hesitate to write the following because I fear I might be misunderstood by those people who have not reached the place in their grieving process that I presently have, but I feel that my message is important enough to take the chance.

I've come to the point in my life where I view my husband's death as a gift. Don't get me wrong. I would have never consciously chosen to have him die—believe me. Not only did I love him and share wonderful plans for the future with him, but I was scared "to death" about the idea of being alone. I was totally frightened by the thought of raising my daughters by myself and handling our business affairs. I would have never consciously picked this path.

However, with hindsight, after years of doing the hard work of healing, I realize that I have grown stronger and wiser. I would have never created this book, which I truly believe will help many, many people heal themselves following the loss of people close to them, if my husband had not died. God chose to take Jerry back when he did, and I have come to accept his death as a gift from God . . . a gift which stretched me and has given me another purpose for my life . . . a gift for which I can finally say thank you.

Cynthia

THE COVER STORY

The first step my father, Raymond O. Strom, took on his arduous journey to joy after my mother, Lois Chase Strom, died in 1990 was to commission a work of art in her memory. Though he was consumed with and almost paralyzed by indescribable grief, he managed to contact world-renowned fiber artist and lacemaker Robin Lewis-Wild. He humbly asked her whether she might consider such a project. Without hesitation, she said she would. Regarding the nature of the piece, he suggested that she work with me. When he called me to discuss this project, I was moved that he had chosen me to be involved and was thrilled to be working with an artist of such stature.

In her own right, my mother was a gifted fiber artist who over the years had mastered basketry, beadwork, needlepoint, quilting, miniatures, knitting, crochet, weaving, rugmaking, dollmaking, garment construction, découpage and countless other crafts. Until she discovered lacemaking, however, she considered herself to be a dilettante who left many projects unfinished. Taking her first class with Robin changed that—she had finally found her passion. Though we lived miles from each other, Mom and I talked on the phone several times a week, and in her last years most of our conversations revolved around her work with Robin, who she said reminded her of me. Of course, her saying this made my heart sing.

I learned that Robin was a moving force in keeping the ancient, intricate art of bobbin lacemaking alive in this topsy turvy world. She had been awarded a major architectural commission for the Tennessee Valley Authority (TVA), a Georgia National Endowment for the Arts (NEA) grant for contemporary work, and had completed numerous commissioned works such as the one she was now embarking upon in memory of my mother. The minute I heard about this project from my dad I knew that, wherever she now was in her new life-after-life, my mother was filled with joy, as was I. Knowing that my role in the creation of this magnificent memorial was quite insignificant, it is only fitting that I intersperse this story with Robin's own words. In summer of 1993, she wrote:

"I received the commission in the spring of 1990. Lois had been a lace student, active in the Gainesville lace group for many years, and she and her husband both were supportive of my work . . .

"Ray called with a request for the piece, leaving the size and subject matter up to me. This was not an easy assignment. I needed to choose an appropriate subject, determine the size and style of the lace . . . it was an honor to be selected for this and the opportunity to dedicate time and effort on an experimental project was thrilling. And experimental it was!

" . . . I called and discussed the project with Ray's daughter Kristina. She was very helpful in distilling the concept to its final stages. A floral scene with two birds would best convey the sentiment that I felt the piece needed. Although I do not know what losing a life companion is like, I tried to imagine what might best communicate the joy and sorrow, the unspoken longing, the bond felt between two people. I had married that spring, and our outdoor wedding was graced with a bed of pink and green caladiums that were the inspiration for the leaves in the piece. As Josef and I were beginning our life together, I grew to understand the significance of the joining, and therefore the sweet sorrow and song Ray felt at the loss of his Lois. My aim was to capture this in my piece."

During the gestation of "Enchanted Garden", the mail flew between Robin and me. She sent tissue paper templates for my perusal and we discussed materials and size in depth. While her original vision was to include color in the piece, she felt time constraints would preclude that. Because my mom had always been fond of whitework, I felt that would be more appropriate anyway. During the course of the work, which extended from the estimated one year to two, Robin encountered many technical obstacles which she creatively overcame. To me, her having to do this was emblematic of how my mother had lived her life—Mom always had a precise plan about how things should work, but was forced over and over to adjust and adapt, which she managed with grace and panache. Robin's description of her struggles at that time could have poured from my mother's mouth:

"I found that as soon as I completed an element, I wanted to make it again with modification. I wanted to try it with a different combination or even re-fashion it entirely. At the start of the project, I would frequently do this but eventually, due to time constraints and my own sanity, I decided to just let it flow. I recognized that to a certain degree the piece needed to evolve on its own in the same way a painting would. In retrospect, the 'painterly' look that I achieved came from somewhere inside. By giving up some control, the lace from my bobbins flowed onto the pillow the way colors flow from a brush onto the canvas."

Mystic that I am, I was convinced that during this difficult time the Essence of my mother was hovering around her beloved teacher, encouraging her to trust that the piece would be all that she envisioned and more. Here on the earth plane, I did my best to support Robin and assure her that neither I nor my father were concerned about how long this project was taking.

When, at last, "Enchanted Garden" was completed, Robin wrote the following to my father:

"I am pleased with the results. It has taken much longer than expected . . . I thought of Lois—my work and teaching students such as Lois—a lot as I worked on this piece. The various aspects of bringing this work to fruition reminded me of the dedication and persistence the ongoing upward challenge of my involvement in this art has been. There is the work itself, the creative aspect and the teaching process. There is the love of the work: the spirit in its evolution; the thrill of the challenge; the overcoming obstacles; the constant reappraisal; the need of shaping/capturing that spirit and force/energy as it evolves. It's hard to separate the two—as even the process of the work itself is an attempt to communicate the love, this energy to another, to challenge the mind to see and comprehend a bit of the process, of the joy. I hope this work gives you some joy and peace as you view it. Listen quietly for the music, the conversation, if you will—it's there in the work. What is shaped is ever-present. Thank you for the opportunity for growth this project has given me, and the opportunity to share it with you."

When Cynthia and I began considering covers for *From Eulogy to Joy*, "Enchanted Garden" spoke to us in a way no other concepts had. From countless sources we were told that this cover is fraught with poignant meaning: the delicacy of the lace reflects the fragile nature of the subject matter;

the intricacy reflects the complexity of any significant death; and the art form reflects how truly interwoven our lives and our deaths are.

In the summer of 2000, I connected with Robin once again, to let her know when the book was coming out. During our conversation I wept, realizing once more that surviving and growing through death is a long journey and perhaps always will be . . . a never-ending journey that we all learn from in ways we least expect in the moment. This is what Robin said:

"So much has happened since we last spoke, which has added to the poignancy of 'Enchanted Garden' for me, and the irony of its reappearance in my life at this time. As I reflect upon what I wrote about the piece in 1993, about not knowing what losing a partner was like, I have since lost my Josef to suicide. In contemplating the imagery for the work so many years ago, I said that I had 'tried to imagine what might best communicate the joy and sorrow, the unspoken longing, and the joy felt between two people.'

"I no longer have to imagine, as it has become a part of my life to have this experience brought to me far sooner than I could imagine was possible.

"I finally was beginning to rebound after an extensive depression after his death when I was diagnosed with breast cancer. During the past two years of treatment I have had to contemplate all over again the impact of Joe's death, the significance of living, or not living, and wanting or needing a reason to go on living, which seems paramount in one doing so. The loss is never forgotten.

"On good days the memories are bittersweet treasures that, like sweet perfume, float in and out of your consciousness as you go along your way. On rough days they jar you as you try to regain your sense of balance. I have found time to be the most significant element in healing, and I struggle to return to my work which I know will restore some inner sense of peace and of purpose. 'Enchanted Garden' now captures and accentuates the fragility of life, the significance of the loss of a loved one, and the need to restore tranquil beauty during a time of seemingly insurmountable pain."

My father donated this magnificent piece to the Quinlan Visual Arts Center in Gainesville, Georgia, where it is a part of the permanent collection. Home to local, regional, national and international exhibits of art, my mother considered the Center to be "the best kept secret in North Georgia". The gift shop there is a treasure unto itself; the classes offered run the gamut from watercolor to basketry to photography to childrens' art. To learn more about the Center, or see "En-chanted Garden" in person, call 770-536-2575.

Kristina

BIOGRAPHICAL INFORMATION ABOUT

THE CONTRIBUTORS

Ellen Appleby lives in Columbus, Ohio. She is the mother of four and grandmother of one, and works for the Postal Service as a window clerk, all of which give her plenty of material for her personal essay and humor pieces. She is now at work on a children's book.

George Ayetin was born in Nigeria. He graduated from SUNY New Paltz and Howard University where he received his BSc and MBA respectively. He is a certified Information System Auditor and lives in Washington, DC metropolitan area with his wife and four children.

Stephen Baggs is a funeral director and grief counselor in country Victoria, Australia. He regards his work as an everyday opportunity to make a practical difference in people's lives.

Violeta Balhas is a freelance writer and educator of creative writing. She writes in twelve acres of muss and clutter in country Victoria, Australia. She and Stephen Baggs are also parents to Roma's three clever and lovely siblings.

Born in Monterey, **Sylvia Beddoe** is a twelfth generation Mayflower descendent of a literary family. She attended Mountain View Academy (California), then seventeen years later enrolled in college at Foothill College (Los Altos Hills, California). Mother of four, grandmother of seven, she fills her time writing and dabbling in photography.

Kelly Beischel is the mother of three children and has been married to Joe for almost fifteen years. She lives in Cincinnati, working part-time as a nurse for Children's Hospital Medical Center and Yavneh Day School. She stays active walking and cardio-kickboxing, is an avid reader, and coaches soccer and softball.

Lindsay Piper Beischel is currently a senior in high school. She was in middle school when she wrote the piece included in this book.

Merritt Ann Beischel is a recent graduate of Earlham College where she majored in Women's Studies and minored in Theater Arts.

Judith Jacklin Belushi moved to NYC with her late husband in 1972 where she worked as a writer, designer, and producer for fourteen years. Today she lives happily on Martha's Vineyard with her husband, Victor, three beautiful step-daughters and her nine-year-old son. Life is good.

Chad M. Bice is from Macomb, Illinois. He typically writes poetry and short stories, but plans to write a novel. Being a System Builder, he has a strong interest in computers and does tech support, as well as teach the basics. His hobbies include working with HTML and his Star Trek collection.

Loren Bondurant was a sixth-grader when he wrote his essay for Mrs. Klinge's Humanities class at LOGOS Lab School in Richmond, Indiana. Loren now plays "boogie-woogie" in his high school's jazz band and his bass guitar in a Praise band. Many aspects of Loren's life are a tribute to his grandpa.

Veronica Breen is a legal secretary in New York City and also a part-time college student. Her plan is to attend law school. She was born and continues to live in Brooklyn, New York, close to her family and friends.

Debra Ayres Brown's inspirational stories are found in *Guideposts*, the *Chocolate* series, and *Chicken Soup*. She is Marketing Director for Savannah Technical College and involved with Quixtar, an internet-based company. Debra is a Southeastern Writer's Association board member, a graduate of the University of Georgia, and has a Master's of Business Administration.

Cindy Bullens is a two-time Grammy nominee and acclaimed singer/songwriter who's career has spanned 25 years. Her early work included touring and/or recording with Elton John, Rod Stewart, Bob Dylan, Bryan Adams,

Joe Cocker, and others. Her heartfelt and spirited 1999 CD "Somewhere Between Heaven and Earth" was inspired by the life and death of her eleven year old daughter, Jessie.

John Carlsen, a lifelong resident of Long Island, New York, is a twenty-eight year police veteran. Married to Kathleen for twenty-five years, he's the proud father of four. In his off hours, John serves in various church and civic roles and tries to keep up with his three very active children.

Florence Clowes has had two books, *Polish-Americans in Pittsfield, Massachusetts* and *Polish Legends*, published, and is a book reviewer for *The Polish American*. With grown children scattered across the country, she now has time for painting, writing, and traveling. She is presently retired in Florida and working on a mystery.

Gabriel Constans has writen for numerous journals, newspapers, and magazines in North America and Europe, and has four books published in the U.S. He lives with his partner, Audrey, in Northern California. They are co-parents to five "amazing" children and an assortment of chickens, fish, one cat, and a neurotic bird.

God has blessed **Suzanne S. Craft** with a wonderful husband, who is a Baptist minister, and three beautiful children. She grew up in rural Louisiana and loves life in the country. She also loves children and thanks God for allowing her to work with them.

Joan C. Curtis manages her own freelance writing business. Her writing highlights include two articles published in *Reader's Digest* and a book titled *Strategic Interviewing* which was published in fall 2000 by Greenwood Publishing Group, Inc. She lives and writes in Athens, Georgia.

Frances Davis is a short story writer and public speaker on the loss of a child and its impact on the family. Her studies include receiving a ministerial degree in 1993 and a Vocational Nursing Diploma in February 2000. Her goal is to become a Hospice Nurse. Contact her at: frantasy@a-omega.net

Adele DelSavio was born in New York in 1952 and received a BA in English from Brooklyn College. Her oldest son, Michael, drowned in 1994 in a body-boarding accident in Hawaii. She lives in Central New York with her husband, Bernardo, and three survivng children, Christopher, Katherine, and Valerie.

Writing is **Donna L. DeMagistris**' passion! She studied creative writing at the University of Southern California, earning her BA in 1995. Although she currently works as a Finance Professional in New Jersey and will graduate with her MBA in 2001 from Seton Hall University, she still pursues writing on a freelance basis.

Wanda Denson was sixty-four years old when she passed away. She was an artist, an LPN, and the head bookkeeper for H.R. Gibson. She wrote for the Odessa, Texas, *American* and the Big Springs, Texas, *Hero*. She was a wonderful mother, grandmother, and wife. (Information supplied by B.H. Denson, her husband.)

PC Denver, a Nashville-based Screenwriter/Playwright, is the co-founder of Women of Music and Entertainment Network, an organization dedicated to the education, support, and recognition of women of the arts. Her work in the anthology is a piece close to her heart and spirit.

Desconocido was born in Puerto Rico and came to the United States after graduating from school. He is involved in a variety of non-profit and volunteer organizations. He hopes his piece will help people understand the array of complex emotions that humans experience after the death of a loved one.

Teresa Donley's father committed suicide when Teresa was thirty years old. As part of the grieving process, she read as much as she could find about suicide and joined support groups to meet others sharing a similar grief. She is married and has a twenty-one year old daughter.

Nancy A. Dubuc is mother, grandmother, Master Lead Teacher, Antibias Curriculum Coordinator, youth bus driver, and crone. She works full-time, plus numerous after-hour meetings. Her three dogs, three cats, and she share her home. In her spare time, she gardens, works on the house, crochets, and writes. She is a survivor.

Tim Elliot is a former owner of radio stations and a licensed Broker for Commercial/Industrial real estate. He is now retired and living in West Des Moines, Iowa. He is the author of several novels and short stories. One novel, *Three Brothers*, can be obtained through Xlibris.com.

Linda Bonner Ewing has been a devoted seeker-server all her life. She plays Tai Chi and practices Chi Kung. Linda is President of *Silent Messages from the Source*, in addition to owning and operating two other mainstream service businesses in Cincinnati, Ohio.

Jan R. Faust lives in Kansas; however, her most profound elemental attraction is the ocean. She is a social worker, nurse, and webmaster. She finds life the most challenging adventure ever. Her hobbies include learning, scuba diving, horseback riding, and sailing. She has a son, Christian, of whom she is very proud.

Adrienne Folmar, a thirty year old administrative assistant by day and an aspiring poet/novelist in heart, currently resides in the East. While still testing the theory that time heals all wounds, her confidence is that faith in God will.

Grace Forbes is an Ohio free lance writer. Her fiction has appeared in national magazines. She is the married mother of two sons.

Carolyn Mott Ford enjoys writing essays, poetry, reviews, and children's stories. Her first early-reader, *Nothing In The Mailbox*, was published after her five children were grown. Her work has appeared in numerous newspapers and magazines, including *Highlights for Children, The Journal of New Jersey Poets, Moondance*, and *Ladybug*.

Carol Fortiere has had six poems published and is now working on a collection of short stories. She is studying to become an animal care specialist, and is currently offering in-home care services for the elderly. She lives with one dog and two cats.

Lydia Z. Frescaz lives in Texas. The proud mother of six children and four grandchildren, following the 1992 murder of her daughter, founded "Survivors of Homicide". In 1997, she again dealt with loss when her son died. Very active in community events, she won the Nell Myers Advocacy Award in 1999.

BJ Gardner was born and raised in Cincinnati, Ohio, and married Dan Gardner in 1970. She has three adult children and continues to live in the home where she and her husband raised them.

Sue Gallehugh, PhD, is a marriage and family therapist and a professional speaker. She is also the author of the best selling book *Bedtime Stories for Grown-ups, Fairy-Tale Psychology* which is published by Health Communications, Inc and available in all bookstores.

Georgeanne Gaulden-Falstrom lives in Texas with her husband, Jim, and mother, Laura. She is director of student services and editor of *The Patriot* at Parker College. Her greatest joy is special time spent with granddaughters, Chelsea and Chloe. She feels blessed she and her living son, Scott, have come full circle.

Pat Goehe has spent most of her life teaching communication and drama in high school and university settings. She also has a counseling background. A mother and grandmother, Pat currently lives in Santa Fe, New Mexico, where she is writing a novel about St. Clare of Assisi.

After leaving the marriage and children track, **Mary Goodlander** quickly earned three university degrees. These qualified her, at middle age, to start a sixteen year teaching career. Now, near the finish line, she acknowledges she loves learning and the magic of language, and wishes to embrace all that is human.

Judy Goodman's access to information from the physical and non-physical realms is unparalleled. She is internationally recognized and has been featured on numerous radio and television shows. Judy may be without peer in her experiences of the events and workings of the physical and spiritual realms. Judy's website is: www.judygoodman.com

Rabbi Earl A. Grollman, DHL, DD, is a writer and lecturer whose books on coping with death and bereavement have helped thousands of people. His most recent work, *Living with Loss: Healing with Hope—A Jewish Perspective*, has been heralded by Rabbi Harold Kushner as a "gem of wisdom".

Karen Gurmankin is a social worker/manager in Philadelphia, Pennsylvania, and a Temple University graduate. In addition to writing work-related essays, she enjoys writing children's stories for her nephew Zachary. She is the daughter of Ethel and Joseph Gurmankin of blessed memory who inspired the writing of her essay.

Bonnie Haley, LSW, is the Special Care Center Manager at Brighton Gardens by Marriott, an assisted living community in Dedham, Massachusetts. She also does Alzheimer's training for other Marriott Senior Living Services managers. Bonnie lives with her family in coastal Scituate, Massachusetts.

Paul Handermann was born in 1959 and raised in Cincinnati, Ohio. He is now remarried to a wonderful woman. He has three children (one in heaven) and four step-children. He considers Kayla the greatest gift God has ever allowed him to share in. He currently lives in Mason, Ohio.

Kim Harcarik is a free-lance writer who lives in Littleton, Colorado. She is re-married and has had two more daughters. She is a stay-at-home mom of Steve, age thirteen, Allison, six, and Jessica who is twenty months. On Christmas Eve, 1999, her mother also died.

Marlynne Harrison grew up in Bridge City, Texas, as Lois Marlynne Jackson. She has a Bachelor of Science in Education, and she is also a Licensed Vocational Nurse. She is employed as a teacher and patient advocate. Her hobbies are painting professionally and writing.

Emily Sue Harvey prepared to teach English. Her daughter's death turned her instead to writing. Her upbeat stories have appeared in the *Chocolate* series, *Woman's World, True Story,* and *Chicken Soup*. She is currently working on *God Only Knows*, a fictional novel about the struggles of a preacher's family.

Grant Hasty was born in the middle of a blizzard in Buffalo, NY. Maybe that was a portent of his life being always on the edge. He started writing short poems in high school, then stories, some of which were published. He opened a book and gift shop called "The Shoe String". (Information supplied by Betty Hasty, his mother.)

Corrie Lynn Hausman is a recent graduate of Earlham College. She has been writing "ever since she can remember", most recently turning her pen to editing the diary of an early ninetenth-century Quaker reformer. She currently resides in Columbus, Ohio, but will soon be moving across the country to Portland, Oregon.

Janice Porter Hayes has been a freelance writer for nearly fifteen years. Her writing is influenced in large part by experiences from her own life, as in her story, *Entries From Eternity*. She lives in Highland, Utah, with her husband and their three wonderful children.

Sandra Hein is a mother of twin daughters and a son, living in a small town in Southeast Indiana. She is a healthcare worker with body/energy work training and is an avid life adventurer.

Alfredo J. Herrera, MD, lives in Ellicott City, Maryland, where he is a practicing Pediatrician specializing in Neonatology-Perinatal medicine. Among his credits: over forty published articles, research projects, the "You Are Responsible" seminar which educates teenagers about safe driving, and involvement with organ and tissue donation.

Michael Ortiz Hill is a registered nurse and a traditional healer (Nganga) among Bantu tribespeople in Zimbabwe, Africa. He is the author of *Dreaming The End Of The World* and the forthcoming *Capable*

Of Such Beauty, a study of racial healing and an account of his initiation into African medicine.

Jacqueline M. Honoré's first novel, *Sorrow's Pleasures*, depicting Sorrow's scandlous lifestyle as a Creole adolescent in post-WWII Paris, is curently being considered for publication. She recently completed the sequel, *Nobody Knows My Sorrow*, about the bittersweet events leading up to Sorrow's chance encounter with her black father, Victor Kingdom.

Clinton T. Howard is a freelance writer. Since his wife's illness and death, he frequently authors magazine and newspaper articles on cancer and other diseases to spotlight the need for regular examinations and early detection. Howard volunteers as a spokesperson for hospice organizations.

Wendell G. Hubbard is a graduate of Writer's Digest school of writing. His poetry appears in several anthologies: *Best Poems Of The Nineties, American Poetry Annual, On the Threshold Of A Dream*, and *Days Of Futures Past*. His motto is: never sacrifice self for the sake of belonging.

Cheri Lynn Hunter is a native of Wichita Falls, Texas. Cheri has had several poems published which are about and dedicated to the grandmother she loved so dearly. She volunteers in her local community and is a strong advocate for the rights of abused women, children, and the elderly.

Francesca A. Jackson maintains a practice in chiropractic and classical homeopathy, teaches a workshop— The Art Of Living With HIV— for the Art Of Living Foundation, volunteers as a lay chaplain for hospice and, inspired by Ernestine, is working on a multimedia project to teach lay people about their body temple.

Molly H. Jenkins enjoys the serenity of her home in the Texas hills near New Braunsfels. She is retired from medical secretarial work. She loves classical music, is an avid reader, and enjoys crossword puzzles. She and her husband are very proud of their son, Bruce, and enjoy traveling, especially cruises.

Kathleen Moore Joiner lives and writes in Brandon, Mississippi. She and her husband are the parents of two grown children. She claims to have been "practically born writing" and her poetry has appeared in numerous literary journals and anthologies. A collection of her work, entitled "Skimming the Surface", was published in 1995.

After the death of their son, **Sherwin Kaufman**, MD, and his wife, Claire, began having experiences of communication with the beyond so extraordinary and comforting that he, originally a skeptic, wrote "Messages From Michael". "Perhaps others, too, may find peace in knowing that the bonds of love can be greater than death."

Christina Keenan has been published widely in the United States and Canada. She is the winner of several writing awards including: *The Golden Poet*. Most recently her work has appeared in *Every Woman Has A Story!* and the National Bestseller, *Chicken Soup For The Mother's Soul*. She lives in Frankfort, IL.

William Kern, 51, lives in Gig Harbor, Washington, where he met his wife, Maggie, in 1992. Born and raised in the Netherlands and Arizona, he now calls the Pacific Northwest "home". He enjoys international travel with his daughters, Audrey and Ashley. Away from work, he builds homes with Habitat for Humanity.

Cynthia Keyes is an internationally known and respected spiritual visionary, and co-founder, with her husband Gordon-Michael Scallion, of Matrix Institute. She is a writer and editor of the newsletter, *IntuitiveFlash* (formerly called the *Earth Changes Report*), and her articles on ecospirituality have appeared in magazines and newspapers throughout the world.

Vera Koppler, a widow for twenty-five years, belongs to the Poets Study Club of Terre Haute, Indiana, and is Poet Laureate of the Honey Bee Festival of Paris, Illinois. Credits include *Days Of Blue Weather, Ghosts And Glass Houses, Lilac Is Different*, and humorous cookbook, *Let's Have Elephant Stew*.

Mary E. Kuenzig was born Mary E. Puleo in Oil City, Pennsylvania. She graduated from the University of Dayton, Ohio, in 1980. Mary now resides in Mason, Ohio, with her husband Mark and their two living children, Adam and Nathan. She has actively volunteered with Reach Out To Grieving Parents and Altrusa International, Inc.

Jessica Kuzimier is a fiction writer and poet who currently resides in upstate New York. Her credits include a book of poetry and articles in *Long Island Voice*. She is currently working on a novel dealing with the fallout of racial violence.

Nanette Lang is married to Darrell and is the mother of John, Jason, Jared, Joshua, and Joe. She lives in Shawnee, Oklahoma, and is employed at First National Bank & Trust Company. On September 30, 1995, she became a member of a very elite group of people—she became a Donor Mom.

Though not a pleasant one, **Tim Lanham** is grateful for his childhood. It taught him many things at a very early age and has given him an appreciation for what he has, instead of thinking about what he doesn't. He is thankful he didn't venture down the wrong path in life.

Stanley M. Lefco is a graduate of the University of Virginia and Emory University School of Law. He has had articles published in various newspapers and magazines, and is involved in several community service organizations.

Since the loss of a baby and the subsequent loss of her mother, **Holly Lentz** has found the peace and purpose of a Christ-centered life. The birth of a son, Kurt, in 1996 completed her family. A former Marketing Manager, she is now a Stay-at-home Mom.

Gail Lewis lives with her husband in sunny Florida. She has earned a BA degree from the University of South Florida. She is self-employed, working as a seamstress from her home.

Robin Lewis-Wild, artist and lacemaker, author of *101 Torchon Patterns*, has taught lacework and lectured extensively for over twenty years throughout the US. She has studied lacework in the US, England, and Belgium. She is the proprietor of Robin's Bobbins & Other Things, a lace supply business in Mineral Bluff, Georgia.

Rebecca Lincoln is a Wyoming native, a recent college graduate, mother, grandmother, writer, and survivor. Her college education began as a method of dealing with her grief after her husband's suicide, and it reawakened her life-long love of writing and the power of self-expression through language and words used well.

Eloise Y. Lott was born in DeKalb County, Alabama, the youngest of nine children. At age eleven, osteomyelitis, an infection of the bone, caused her leg to burst on the way to the hospital. Multiple surgeries began: tumors, appendectomy, cancer, bladder, hysterectomy, bi-lateral mastectomy, knee replacement, and ruptured disc. She has a desire to encourage others.

Sara Lyons had a mental breakdown at nineteen, was hospitalized (where Zelda Fitzgerald spent her last days!) and diagnosed (incorrectly) as Schizophrenic. She graduated with honors from college, is happily married, with one child, is a successful business owner, and currently working on a (humorous) book about the KKK meeting hippies.

Sylvie Malaborsa, a bilingual freelance writer who lives in Montreal, has sold articles to magazines such as *Canadian Catholic Review, Canadian Messenger Of The Sacred Heart,* and *Our Family.* She also frequently contributes to *Les Annales de Sainte-Anne-de-Beaupre,* a Francophone publication. She hopes her writing will continue to touch people.

Steven Mayfield is a neonatologist and the author of forty medical publications. His fiction most recently appeared in *Event, The Long Story,* and *cold-drill,* and he previously edited the literary journal, *Cabin Fever.* A past recipient of the Mari Sandoz award for fiction, he lives with his family in Idaho.

Gloria McAndrews has been a critical care nurse for almost twenty years. Other passions are Boston Terriers, gardening, music, and computing. She lives in Northern Kentucky, just outside of Cincinnati, Ohio. She is currently lucky enough to be owned by two Boston Terriers, Brandy and Skipper.

Katherine McDonald was born in 1976 in Toledo, Ohio. She now resides in Columbus, Ohio, with her boyfriend, Bradley. She is currently working on a comic book collective and brings home the bacon as an editor of literary content for an adult web page.

Isabel Meisler lives in Pittsburgh, PA, is a former meditation teacher, a current practitioner of energy healing, a writer, and a storyteller. She has produced tapes on self-healing and relaxation, and is currently co-editing an anthology about finding gifts from crisis. As often as life allows, she heads for the woods.

Sydnea Miles, MEd, a retired middle-school teacher of math and science, is an award-winning author of numerous poems and short stories. Currently, she is working on a novel and a history book. She is the curator of her church which is on the National Register of Historic Places.

Jean McElroy Miller published non-fiction in *Home* and *Portfolio* magazines, mainstream fiction in *Chips Off The Writer's Block* and *Agapae*, plus two horror stories in *After Hours*. She received an Honorable Mention in the 1987 *Writer's Digest* writing competition, article category. Presently, she is working on a horror novel.

Sara Miller lives in the foothills of Colorado with her husband, Kevin. Sara has worked in marketing in the non-profit sector, the performing arts, and landscape architecture. She has traveled extensively throughout the world, and many of these adventures are detailed in her writing.

Bill Millhollon, seventy-two (and holding), is an ex-Air Force pilot, rancher, home builder, writer, poet, mechanical contractor, real estate broker, and investor. He has a Catholic wife who lit candles for him for twenty-five years. He saw the light and became a non-denominational charismatic—still doubting, but full of faith.

Lilamae Mueller was born in Salt Lake City, Utah, in 1932. She attended Westminster College, the University of Utah, Principia College, San Francisco State College, and the University of Cincinnati. She has been a teacher for twenty-nine years. She has two children, Michael Mueller (deceased) and Martha Gerhardt, and two grandchildren.

Barbara Murdock enjoys the diversity of Cincinnati, Ohio, where she was born and raised. The mother of three children and grandmother of four, she has worked for twenty-two years in the nurturing environment of a private school setting. She cherishes travelling and longs to live abroad in the near future.

Jane Lawliss Murphy, singer and songwriter, has five albums of songs for children published by Kimbo Educational. Her poems have won awards and been published in several poetry quarterlies. She is an essayist whose work has appeared in the *New York Times*. She lives on Long Island, New York.

Joyce Murray was widowed in 1989 and is raising her children in Cincinnati, Ohio, surrounded by family and supportive friends. She is strong in her faithwalk, depending on the Lord to provide answers and inspiration. She works in Public Affairs for Proctor and Gamble, and is an avid aerobics participant.

Elysha Nichols originally wrote her piece at the age of thirteen. She now lives in Nashville, Tennessee, with her husband, Dan, and two cats, Miel and Julius. In the evenings, they all enjoy sitting on their back deck to watch the sun set through the trees.

Christiane Northrup, MD, a visionary pioneer in her field, is a board-certified OB/GYN who helps empower women to tune into their inner wisdom and take charge of their health. Among her accomplishments: Assistant

Clinical Professor; the host of public television specials; *Women's Bodies, Women's Wisdom*, and *Health for Women*.

Now living in Mechanicsburg, PA, **Ron Orendi** grew up in the Steel Valley area of Pittsburgh. His works have been published in small market magazines and trade publications. In 1994 Ron began doing freelance writing for the Tonight Show with Jay Leno. He currently works with the Literacy Empowerment Foundation (http://www.literacyempowerment.org).

Bruce Owens, 37, is married with two children and resides in Georgetown, Kentucky. He is a football coach and an adjunct professor at the local college.

Barbara Linde Parks grew up in West Hartford, Connecticut. She and her husband Richard raised their two sons and daughter there until a move to the Formica Corporation home office brought them to the lovely village of Glendale, Ohio, where, for a time, she lived next door to Cynthia Beischel.

Marguerite Hughes Phelps is founder and director of The Writers' Edge, a collective of writers, artists, and performers who meet regularly to share works-in-progress. Marge is a columnist for an on-line publication: www.findri.com, and has written for regional publications. She has facilitated creative writing and journal writing workshops for adults.

William L. Phelps has mined his experiences as a former intelligence analyst and foreign operative during twenty years in the military to create prose and poetry that speaks with sensitivity to aspects unique to veterans of the Viet Nam era. Bill has been a headline performance poet at Brown University Faculty Club.

Susan Ragland is a retired lawyer who has had diverse careers: women's hats buyer, interior decorator, managing director of a laboratory, wife, mother. She enjoys painting and writing. She has recently completed a book of short stories, a stage play, a screenplay, and is at work on two novels.

Maryanne Raphael, author of *Mother Teresa, Called To Love*, was in South Africa with Mother Teresa's Missionaries of Charity when Mother died. Co-author of *Runaways, America's Lost Youth*, her work has appeared in national and international periodicals. With her ex-husband and son, she is writing *Autobiography Of A Marriage*.

Su Ready is a teacher, writer, and photographer in Cincinnati, Ohio. She teaches writing and drama in middle school, and she is working on a collection of her photographs, as well as a play about women, work, and power.

A former full-time mother of six children for twenty-six years, **Jane Remillard** devotes her time to pastoral counseling, spiritual direction, and retreat work. Jane resides in Ft. Thomas, Kentucky, and pursues additional interests in Hospice and post-abortion support groups.

Tracy Rose is a graduate of Eastern Michigan University. She has a Bachelor's degree in Written Communication. She has suffered the loss of many loved ones recently, including her father, and has attended support meetings. She lives in Michigan with her husband Kevin and their son Nicholas.

Bob Ross, a veteran of forty-five years in show business as an Actor/Comedian, has performed throughout the country: stage & musicals; numerous commercials; films & televsion, including "That Girl", "Mary Tyler Moore", "L.A. Law", and "Rich Man, Poor Man". His Master's Thesis Show on "Vaudeville" was a hit at the Pasadena Playhouse.

Mary Ruddis lives in the Pacific Northwest with her eleven-year old son, Matthew. Since writing "Changes", her other son, Michael, passed away after a two-year battle with cancer in 1999. He was twelve years old. Ms. Ruddis is currently pursuing returning to college and normalizing her life after so many upheavals.

Paul Rupright has lived and worked most of his life in the Chicago area. He made his living by working for forty-two years as a boilermaker and welder for the boilermakers union. He also has studied art, sung with the Lyric Opera Chorus, and did musical programs with his wife.

Margaret Ryan, a recently retired English/Theater Arts teacher owns and operates a Bed and Breakfast in northern Vermont. Mother of four grown sons, she enjoys grandchildren, gardening, writing, gourmet cooking, and theater.

M. Darlene Sandrey is married, has three grown children, two grand-children, one dog, and four grand-dogs. After retirement, she took creative writing classes and volunteered at her local hospice. She listened to many people grieve their losses and then she experienced her own grieving which inspired her article.

Al Sandvik is a free-lance writer of essays (newspaper and magazine columns) and short stories. His stories have appeared in *The Tampa Review, Potpourri, The Belletrist Review*, and others. His guest columns have appeared in several newspapers around the country. He writes a regular column for his suburb's newspaper, *The Edina Sun-Current*.

Career woman **Roberta Schlerf** is lavished with the blessings of a loving husband, beautiful children, her dogs, parrots, and a thoroughbred horse. Her lifestyle glows as an example of breaking the curse of death and sorrow. Robbie hopes that "The Mountain Moved" will encourage and empower its readers.

Gail Schroer, mother of seven and grandmother of fourteen, lives by northern Minnesota's Ottertail Lake with her husband Jerry. A freelance writer and poet, she has had several poems published and an article on prostate cancer treatment. She is a retired legal secretary who enjoys golf, travel, music, needlework, and reading.

Julie Seier lives and works in Chicago, Illinois. She graduated from the University of Iowa in 1994. She is working on a novel.

Jo Seier-Doofe is a free-lance writer living in Davenport, Iowa. Married. Ten children with two deaths. Divorced/Former spouse died. Remarried. Five step-children. Fourteen grandchildren. Started writing seriously at age sixty-two. Feature stories and children's fiction are her passion. Dabbles in poetry. Knows more about grief than she wants to know.

Phyliss Shanken is a psychologist in Colmar, Pennsylvania, whose poetry, prose, and short stories have appeared in many magazines. Formerly a weekly columnist for *The Reporter*, she is author of *Silhouettes Of Woman* and *Laughter Is A Stressbuster*, and is presently a columnist for the diversity magazine, *Next Step*.

Patricia Hamaker Shrimpton lives in a log home with two friends, five dogs, and four cats. After fifty-three years of marriage to Thomas E. Shrimpton, Patricia is now a widow. Following three and one-half years getting her grief under control, she enjoys boating, fishing, reading, and spending time alone with the Lord.

Todd Skugain occasionally writes as a freelance art critic and journalist. He has over 150 published articles and short stories ranging from fiction to special needs education, and entertainment to murder.

Ginny Stahlman is a widow who resides in Corsica, Pennsylvania. She has three children and seven grandchildren. Her passion is writing, especially poetry. She uses this gift as a ministry in her church by sending cards and poems to help and encourage those who are hurting.

Linda Stein-Luthke is a metaphysical teacher and healer, medical intuitive, and astrologer. In her healing work, she frequently accesses higher vibrational beings, primarily the Ascended Masters, and often facilitates communication with departed loved ones. Her books contain channeled writing from the Ascended Master St. Germain. For more information visit www.u-r-light.com.

Martha Strom grew up in Ohio, Pennsylvania, and Missouri; she went to college at Boston and Princeton Universities. Her interest in writing poetry began in her youth. She comes from a large family where literature was an essential part of life.

Bonnie Sutton is a semi-retired RN who loves reading, writing, traveling, quilting, and crocheting. She has five children, twenty grandchildren, and two great-grands. Nursing is a rewarding profession, but also emotionally draining. Eventually the draining far outweighs the rewards. The most logical outcome is to leave nursing.

Lois Truffa is retired and lives in Flagstaff, Arizona. She was active in Phoenix business and community affairs. She received the Metropolitan Business and Professional Women's Woman of Achievement in 1994 and Woman of the Year in 1995. Truffa has been published both locally and nationally.

Linda Vissat, a native of Colorado, who was raised in Wyoming and educated in California, has wanted to be an artist since childhood and has expressed herself through writing and sculpture. She is a single parent of two teenage daughters. She has been reunited with her oldest son who was adopted at birth.

Crystal Armes Wagner is the Director/Teacher of a preschool. Her other publications include *Bereavement* magazine, *The Compassionate Friends Newsletter, S.H.A.R.E. Newsletter, Healing Hearts Network,* and *The Silver Quill.* She has served as guest columnist for her local newspaper and is currently under contract with a literary agent for her first novel.

Neale Donald Walsch is the author of the best selling trilogy of *Conversations with God,* and *Friendship with God.* He and his wife Nancy formed *ReCreation*, a non-profit foundation for personal growth and spiritual understanding, with the goal of giving people back to themselves. Walsch lectures and hosts workshops around the world.

Andrea Warren writes for magazines and is the author of several historical nonfiction books for young readers, including *Pioneer Girl: Growing Up on the Prairie; Surviving Hitler: A Boy in the Nazi Death Camps;* and *Orphan Train Rider: One Boy's True Story*, which was awarded the prestigious Boston Globe-Horn Book Award.

Alabama resident **Anne C. Watkins** has been a freelance writer for over fifteen years. Her work has appeared in a wide variety of publications, ranging from *Angels on Earth* to *Bird Talk Magazine*. Her husband Allen is a professional musician and she has one daughter, Laura.

Jacki Webb lives in Oregon, Wisconsin. She currently works in a sports bar while working on her Master's degree in Holistic Therapy.

Rebecca Wright has been a Registered Nurse for over twenty years. The last seven years she has worked in Hospice, caring for terminally ill patients and their families. Ms. Wright resides in Cincinnati, Ohio, with her daughter, Rachel, and cat, Chloe.

Gayle Young was born and has lived most of her life in Birmingham, Alabama, where she worked as a legal secretary and raised four children, much of the time as a single mother. She is now a grandmother and resides happily with her husband, dog, and two cats.

Ruth M. Zellers was born in 1974 in Ephrata, Pennsylvania, to C. Nevin and Marie Hurst. She married Marc B. Zellers with whom she had one child, Avery Thomas. She now lives and works as an Assistant Office Manager in Terre Haute, Pennsylvania. Her message: Let God's grace carry you as you grieve.

While creating one-liners for Catskill comedians, **Alan Zweibel** was discovered by Lorne Michaels and hired as one of the original Saturday Night Live writers. Since then, he has won 5 Emmy, 6 Ace and 2 Writer's Guild awards. Alan lives in Los Angeles with his wife Robin and their children, Adam, Lindsay and Sari.

Cynthia Kuhn Beischel unexpectedly became a widow and single mother on June 7, 1992, when her husband died in a drowning. Eight years later, she has opened herself to new beginnings and the desire to offer support, information, and hope to grieving individuals. Previously published work includes *Discover The Past*, a story book about Cincinnati history that encourages children and their families to enjoy learning about the past through experiencing first-hand those events and places that still exist. Her educational background includes a Bachelor of Science in Design at the University of Cincinnati and a Master's Degree in Montessori Education from Xavier University. Cynthia lives with her two daughters and two dogs in a quiet village near Cincinnati, Ohio, and is deeply involved with dream interpretation, metaphysics, and spirituality.

(Photo taken by Tim Lanham.)

Kristina Chase Strom has worked in the fields of the verbal and visual arts for thirty years, as well as being a metaphysical teacher and consultant. Though she was formally educated at Wells College, the University of Cincinnati, Edgecliff College, and the University of Science and Philosophy, she considers life itself to be the ultimate classroom. While she has lived as far south as New Orleans and as far north as Aiyansh, British Columbia, Canada, the mother of four daughters now divides her time between a small village north of Cincinnati and her land in southeastern Ohio with her companion Michael. Her life is dedicated to loving others and learning.